STUDENT WORKBOOK

Comprehensive Health Insurance
Billing, Coding, and Reimbursement

Third Edition

DEBORAH VINES-ALLEN

ANN BRACELAND

ELIZABETH STAGER ROLLINS

SUSAN MILLER

D1292694

 Pearson   330 Hudson Street, NY, NY 10013

Vice President, Health Science and TED: Julie Levin Alexander

Director of Portfolio Management: Marlene McHugh Pratt

Development Editor: Joan Gill

Portfolio Management Assistant: Emily Edling

Vice President, Content Production and Digital Studio: Paul DeLuca

Managing Producer, Health Science: Melissa Bashe

Content Producer: Faye Gemmellaro

Project Monitor: Meghan DeMaio

Operations Specialist: Mary Ann Gloriande

Creative Director: Blair Brown

Creative Digital Lead: Mary Siener

Managing Producer, Digital Studio, Health Science: Amy Peltier

Digital Studio Producer, REVEL and e-text 2.0: Jeff Henn

Digital Content Team Lead: Brian Prybella

Digital Content Project Lead: Lisa Rinaldi

Vice President, Product Marketing: David Gesell

Field Marketing Manager: Brittany Hammond

Full-Service Project Management and Composition: iEnergizer Aptara®, Ltd.

Full-Service Project Manager: Kailash Jadli

Inventory Manager: Vatche Demirdjian

Interior and Cover Design: iEnergizer Aptara®, Ltd.

Cover Art: Frank Rohde/Shutterstock

Printer/Binder: LSC Communications, Harrisonburg

Cover Printer: LSC Communications, Harrisonburg

Credits: CMS-1500 Health Insurance Claim Form. Published by Centers for Medicare and Medicaid Services. The figure appears on pages 99 (fig. 10-2), 104 (fig. 10-4), 109 (fig. 10-6), 114 (fig. 10-8), 119 (fig. 10-10), 163 (fig. 12-2), 168 (fig. 12-4), 173 (fig. 12-6), 178 (fig. 12-8), 183 (fig. 12-10), 196 (fig. 13-2), 201 (fig. 13-4), 206 (fig. 13-6), 211 (fig. 13-8), 216 (fig. 13-10), 227 (fig. 14-2), 232 (fig. 14-4), 235 (fig. 14-6), 240 (fig. 14-8), 245 (fig. 14-10), 284 (fig. 17-2), 289 (fig. 17-4), 294 (fig. 17-6), 299 (fig. 17-8), 304 (fig. 17-10)], 326 (fig. T-2), 332 (fig. T-4), 337 (fig. T-6), 343 (fig. T-8), 349 (fig. T-10), 355 (fig. T-12)

Uniform Billing (UB-04) Form. Published by Centers for Medicare and Medicaid Services. The figure appears on pages 134 (fig. 11-1), 137 (fig. 11-2), 140 (fig. 11-3), 143 (fig. 11-4), 146 (fig. 11-5), 358 (fig. T-13).

Copyright © 2018, 2013, 2009 by Pearson Education, Inc. All rights reserved. Manufactured in the United States of America. This publication is protected by Copyright and permission should be obtained from the publisher prior to any prohibited reproduction, storage in a retrieval system, or transmission in any form or by any means, electronic, mechanical, photocopying, recording, or likewise. For information regarding permissions, request forms, and the appropriate contacts within the Pearson Education Global Rights and Permissions department, please visit www.pearsoned.com/permissions/.

1 17

ISBN-13: 978-0-13-478729-9

ISBN-10:   0-13-478729-3

Contents

How to Use the Workbook

STUDENT WORKBOOK LEARNING OBJECTIVES

After reading the core student textbook and completing the workbook, the student should be able to do the following:

- Define and spell the key terms and abbreviations from each chapter.

- Understand and utilize all chapter objectives.

- Use critical thinking skills and the knowledge presented in the core student textbook to read case-based scenarios and answer critical thinking questions. The student should be able to do the following:

  - Recognize the importance of obtaining certification and membership status.

  - Understand laws, regulations, and penalties associated with coding compliance.

  - Understand the ethics of a medical coder.

  - Prepare for an internal and an external audit.

  - Understand Medicare insurance.

  - Understand Medicaid insurance.

  - Recognize the difference between primary and secondary insurance.

  - Understand workers' compensation insurance and disability insurance.

  - Understand TRICARE and CHAMPVA insurance.

  - Recognize the different types of insurance reimbursement fraud and abuse.

  - Submit a completed insurance claim.

  - Understand the different reasons that an insurance claim may be denied.

  - Know when and how to rebill an insurance claim.

  - Know when and how to appeal a denied insurance claim.

  - Enter necessary data to a patient's account, using medical practice management software.

  - Enter necessary data to prepare an insurance claim, using medical practice management software.

  - Balance the batch at the end of each day.

- Accurately complete practice exercises on coding and creating claim forms using source documents (patient information forms, encounter forms, SOAP notes) and fee schedules. The student should be able to do the following:

  - Select the correct diagnostic codes, using the ICD-10-CM manual.

  - Select the correct hospital procedure codes, using the ICD-10-PCS manual.

  - Select the correct E/M codes for place of service coding, using the CPT manual.

  - Select the correct procedure codes and HCPCS codes, using the CPT manual.

  - Apply CPT modifiers to procedure codes when applicable.

- o Review and analyze medical records and medical documentation for completeness and accuracy.
- o Correctly complete CMS-1500 claim forms for commercial insurance carriers.
- o Correctly complete UB-04 claim forms for hospital billing.
- o Accurately calculate the Medicare fee.
- o Accurately calculate participating and nonparticipating Medicare providers that accept assignment.
- o Accurately calculate nonparticipating Medicare providers that do not accept assignment.
- o Correctly complete a Medicare claim form.
- o Correctly complete a Medicaid claim form.
- o Correctly complete a TRICARE and CHAMPVA claim form.
- o Correctly complete a secondary claim form.
- o Correctly complete a workers' compensation claim form.
- o Write an appeal letter for a denied claim.
- o Accurately calculate and issue a refund.
- o Correctly read and calculate an explanation of benefits form.
- • Accurately complete chapter review questions in true–false, short answer, multiple choice, and matching formats to measure understanding of the material presented in the core student text.
- • Accurately complete the tests presented at the end of the workbook. These tests can be used by instructors as an outcomes assessment to measure student understanding and mastery of skills. The following tests are offered:
  - o TEST 1: Identify the Correct Diagnostic Code
  - o TEST 2: Coding Hospital Procedures
  - o TEST 3: Coding Outpatient Procedures and Diagnoses
  - o TEST 4: Coding Outpatient Radiology and/or Pathology Procedures and Diagnoses
  - o TEST 5: Coding Procedures and Diagnoses, Using E/M Codes
  - o TEST 6: Explanation of Benefits
  - o TEST 7: Explanation of Benefits
  - o TEST 8: Complete a Medicare Claim
  - o TEST 9: Complete a Medicaid Claim
  - o TEST 10: Complete a Medi–Medi Claim
  - o TEST 11: Complete a TRICARE Claim
  - o TEST 12: Complete a Workers' Compensation Claim
  - o TEST 13: Complete a CMS-1500 Claim Form for Commercial Insurance
  - o TEST 14: Complete a UB-04 Claim Form for Hospital Billing

INSTRUCTIONS TO THE STUDENT

This workbook is designed to be used with your student text, *Comprehensive Health Insurance: Billing, Coding, and Reimbursement, Third Edition.* The workbook will prepare you to complete medical billing and coding procedures, and it will provide opportunities to practice on and further develop your knowledge of the different types of health insurances, medical fees and calculations, proper medical documentation, coding compliance, audits, appeals, and CMS-1500 and UB-04 claim forms. Following are the main features of this workbook:

- **Chapter Objectives**—a bulleted list taken from the beginning of each chapter in your core textbook appears at the beginning of each workbook chapter.

- **Chapter Outlines** of your student text are available for your review at the beginning of each workbook chapter. If any content area is unclear, the student is urged to review that area before beginning the workbook exercises.

- **Key Terms**—medical terminology that correlates with each chapter in the textbook reinforces student spelling and mastery of key vocabulary. Students are directed to use the glossary in their core text to provide definitions of key terminology.

- **Critical Thinking Questions**—individual, group, and scenario-based questions develop and enhance critical thinking skills and problem-solving skills.

- **Practice Exercises**—many chapters contain reinforcement practice exercises similar to those found in the core textbook that provide additional opportunities for coding, creating claim forms, reading and calculating an explanation of benefits form, and writing a letter of appeal for a denied claim. Practice exercises are designed to measure student mastery of these key skills. Patient information forms, SOAP notes, encounter forms, fee schedules, and blank CMS-1500 and UB-04 claim forms are provided within the workbook to complete all insurance claim practice exercises.

- **Chapter Review Questions**—each chapter of the workbook contains a variety of questions in matching, multiple choice, true–false, and short answer format, designed to reinforce student learning and mastery of key concepts presented in the core textbook.

- **Test Your Knowledge** tests, found at the end of the student workbook, can be used at the discretion of the instructor to evaluate student learning and understanding of coding, creating claim forms, and calculating explanation of benefits forms.

CHAPTER 1
Introduction to Professional Billing and Coding Careers

CHAPTER OBJECTIVES

After reading this chapter, the student should be able to:

1. Recognize different types of facilities that would employ allied health personnel.
2. Define job descriptions pertaining to a position.
3. Discuss options available for certification.

CHAPTER OUTLINE

Employment Demand

Facilities
> *Physician's Practice*
> *Multispecialty Clinic*
> *Hospital*
> *Centralized Billing Office*

Job Titles and Responsibilities
> *Medical Office Assistant (MOA)*
> *Medical Biller*
> *Payment Poster*
> *Medical Collector*
> *Refund Specialist*
> *Insurance Verification Representative*
> *Admitting Clerk or Front Desk Representative*

Certifications
> *Medical Coder*
> *Privacy Compliance Officer*

Registered Health Information Administrator (RHIA)
> *Registered Health Information Technician (RHIT)*
> *Health Information Clerk*
> *Medical and Health Services Manager*

Listing of Certifications
> *Medical Office Assistant Certification*
> *Medical Billing Certifications*
> *Medical Coding Certifications*
> *Medical Records Certification*

Professional Memberships

KEY TERMS

Using the highlighted terms and glossary in the textbook, define the following terms.

1. admitting clerk _____
   _____

2. centralized billing office (CBO) _____
   _____

3. certifications _____
   _____

4. health information clerk _____
   _____

5. insurance verification representative _____
   _____

6. managed care _____
   _____

7. medical and health services manager _____
   _____

8. medical biller _____
   _____

9. medical coder _____
   _____

10. patient financial services (PFS) _____
    _____

11. payer (payor) _____
    _____

12. registered health information administrator (RHIA) _____
    _____

13. registered health information technician (RHIT) _____
    _____

CRITICAL THINKING QUESTIONS

Using the knowledge you have gained from reading the textbook, apply critical thinking skills to answer the following questions.

1. In your own words, explain the benefits of belonging to a professional organization.
   _____
   _____
   _____
   _____

© 2018 Pearson Education, Inc.

2. Relate the following questions to your last doctor's appointment:
   a. What type of specialty was/were practiced by the physician(s)? _____
   b. How many physicians worked in this practice? _____
   c. Which one of the following three would this practice qualify as: a solo/private practice, a small-group practice, or a large-group practice? _____

3. Of all the types of medical careers listed in the text, which one would you most like to pursue and why? _____

_____

_____

_____

4. Using an online job search engine, locate all the positions that you will qualify for after completing your schooling. Referring to these open positions, answer the following questions:
   a. How many jobs will you qualify for? _____
   b. Which of these jobs would you be most interested in doing, and why? _____

_____

_____

_____

_____

   c. Describe the position that most interested you, and discuss why.

5. Write down the educational, career, and personal goals that you would like to accomplish within the periods defined here (discuss your answers in class):

   a. One year _____

   _____

   _____

   _____

   b. Five years _____

   _____

   _____

   _____

6. Discuss why it is important to have both career and educational goals _____

   _____

   _____

   _____

PRACTICE EXERCISES

1. Provide a brief description of the following types of healthcare organizations that a medical office specialist may work for:

   a. Solo/private practice _____

   _____

   _____

   b. Small-group practice _____

   _____

   _____

   c. Large-group practice _____

   _____

   _____

   d. Multispecialty clinic _____

   _____

   _____

© 2018 Pearson Education, Inc.

e. Hospital _____

_____

_____

_____

f. Patient financial services (PFS) _____

_____

_____

_____

g. Centralized billing office (CBO) _____

_____

_____

_____

2. Write the job descriptions for the following different types of medical careers:
   a. Medical office assistant _____

_____

_____

_____

   b. Medical biller _____

_____

_____

_____

   c. Medical coder _____

_____

_____

_____

   d. Registered health information technician (RHIT) _____

_____

_____

_____

   e. Payment poster _____

_____

_____

_____

   f. Medical collector _____

_____

_____

_____

g. Refund specialist _____

_____

_____

h. Insurance verification representative _____

_____

_____

i. Admitting clerk/front desk representative _____

_____

_____

_____

_____

j. Privacy compliance officer _____

_____

_____

3. Provide a brief description of each different type of medical certification listed next. Access any related websites provided in the Resources section of this chapter, if necessary.

a. National certified medical office assistant (NCMOA) _____

_____

_____

b. Certified medical administrative assistant (CMAA) _____

_____

_____

c. Certified medical billing specialist (CMBS) _____

_____

_____

d. Certified medical reimbursement specialist (CMRS) _____

_____

_____

e. Certified coding associate (CCA) _____

_____

_____

© 2018 Pearson Education, Inc.

f. Certified professional coder (CPC) _____

_____

_____

_____

g. Certified professional coder-hospital (CPC-H) _____

_____

_____

_____

h. Certified coding specialist (CCS) _____

_____

_____

_____

i. Certified coding specialist-physician (CCS-P) _____

_____

_____

_____

j. Registered health information technician (RHIT) _____

_____

_____

_____

k. Registered health information administrator (RHIA) _____

_____

_____

_____

REVIEW QUESTIONS

MATCHING

Choose the correct answer and write its corresponding letter in the space provided.

a. Certification
b. Allied health employees
c. American Health Information Management Association (AHIMA)
d. National Healthcareer Association (NHA)
e. National Center for Competency Testing (NCCT)

1. _____ Awards the CCA, CCS, and RHIT.
2. _____ Voluntary (optional) credentialing in a professional organization that shows a person's qualifications, involvement, and dedication in a particular field.
3. _____ Awards the CMAA.
4. _____ Awards the NCMOA.
5. _____ Members of the clinical healthcare profession who work together in a healthcare team to make the healthcare system function.

MULTIPLE CHOICE

Circle the letter of the choice that best completes the statement or answers the question.

1. Which of the following has affected physician offices due to managed care?
   a. Additional staff had to be added for daily financial operations to be carried out.
   b. Payments for services were not received up front from the patient.
   c. Money was not readily available for operation costs.
   d. All of the above

2. Which of the following is a benefit of holding a professional membership in your field?
   a. Professional membership provides professional development opportunities.
   b. Professional membership makes available up-to-date information on important issues.
   c. Professional membership provides employment opportunities.
   d. All of the above

3. Which of the following associations is the professional association for coders?
   a. AAPC
   b. AHIMA
   c. AAMT
   d. None of the above

4. A small physician group practice consists of _____ .
   a. 10-plus physicians
   b. three through nine physicians
   c. physicians usually practicing the same specialty
   d. Both b and c

5. A large physician group practice consists of _____ .
   a. 10-plus physicians
   b. three through nine physicians
   c. physicians who usually practice in different specialties
   d. Both a and c

SHORT ANSWER

Provide the correct response to each question that follows.

1. What did physicians have to do to improve reimbursement once managed care was implemented? _____

2. Before managed care, when did most patients pay for physician services? _____

3. What are two other titles for a medical office assistant?
   1. _____
   2. _____

4. What are six other titles for a medical biller?
   1. _____
   2. _____

© 2018 Pearson Education, Inc.

3. _____

4. _____

5. _____

6. _____

5. What are four other titles for a medical coder?

1. _____

2. _____

3. _____

4. _____

TRUE/FALSE

Identify each statement as true (T) or false (F).

1. _____ Physicians and nurses make up 60 percent of all healthcare providers, whereas the other 40 percent are allied health employees.

2. _____ Medical office specialists work only in outpatient settings.

3. _____ After graduating, the medical office specialist must obtain certification.

4. _____ With managed care it is the responsibility of the physician to file the claim and wait for payment.

5. _____ Certification is an important addition to your resume.

CHAPTER 2
Understanding Managed Care: Insurance Plans

CHAPTER OBJECTIVES

After reading this chapter, the student should be able to:

1. Understand the history and impact of managed care.
2. Be able to discuss the organization of managed care and how it affects the provider, employee, and policyholder.
3. Calculate the financial responsibility of the patient.
4. Identify the type of managed care plan in which the patient is enrolled.
5. Recognize various types of insurance coverage.

CHAPTER OUTLINE

Hospital Indemnity Insurance
Medical Insurance
Surgical Insurance
Outpatient Insurance
Major Medical Insurance
Special Risk Insurance
Catastrophic Health Insurance
Short-Term Health Insurance
COBRA Insurance
Long-Term Care Insurance
Supplemental Insurance

Health Savings Accounts

HSA

HRA

FSA

Affordable Care Act

The Provider's View of Managed Care
    Patient Care
    Facility Operations

Verifying Insurance Coverage

Collecting Insurance Payments
    Assignment of Benefits

KEY TERMS

Using the highlighted terms and glossary in the textbook, define the following terms.

1. Affordable Care Act (ACA) _____
_____

2. allowed charge _____
_____

3. assignment of benefits _____
_____

4. carriers _____
_____

5. case manager _____
_____

6. coinsurance _____
_____

7. commercial health insurance _____
_____

8. commercial-driven healthcare (CDHC) _____
_____

© 2018 Pearson Education, Inc.

9. copay _____

10. deductible _____

11. discounted fee _____

12. Employee Retirement Income Security Act (ERISA) _____

13. enrollee _____

14. flexible spending accounts (FSA) _____

15. group insurance _____

16. health maintenance organization (HMO) _____

17. Health Reimbursement Accounts (HRAs) _____

18. health savings accounts (HSA) _____

19. high-deductible health plans (HDHP) _____

20. inpatient _____

21. insured _____

22. managed care _____

23. managed care organization (MCO) _____

24. Obamacare _____

25. outpatient _____

26. Patient Protection and Affordable Care Act (PPACA) _____

27. point-of-service (POS) _____

28. policyholder _____

29. preauthorization _____

_____

30. pre-existing condition _____

_____

31. preferred provider organization (PPO) _____

_____

32. premiums _____

_____

33. primary care physician (PCP) _____

_____

34. providers _____

_____

35. referral _____

_____

36. special risk insurance _____

_____

37. subscriber _____

_____

38. utilization guidelines _____

_____

39. write-off (contractual adjustment) _____

_____

CRITICAL THINKING QUESTIONS

Using the knowledge you have gained from reading the textbook, apply critical thinking skills to answer the following questions.

1. A new patient, Lucy Vrabel, has just given you her insurance information. Answer the following questions related to Lucy's insurance plan:

   a. Why is it important to gather insurance information during the first visit and verify it on subsequent visits?

   _____

   _____

   _____

   _____

   _____

   b. How is insurance verified each time a patient comes in?

   _____

   _____

   _____

© 2018 Pearson Education, Inc.

c. After establishing Lucy's type of insurance plan, what eight questions should be asked of the insurance company about her plan?

1. _____
2. _____
3. _____
4. _____
5. _____
6. _____
7. _____
8. _____

d. What should be documented after receiving Lucy's insurance information in case of a claim denial or collection problems after services have been rendered?

_____
_____
_____
_____
_____

2. Samuel Ridge just learned that he will be laid off from his job at the end of the week. He works for a corporation of 100-plus employees. Answer the following questions related to Samuel's situation:

a. What is the name of the federal law that will allow Samuel, after his termination from the company, to continue the group coverage that he had through his workplace?

_____
_____

b. How long a period is Samuel allowed to keep this coverage?

_____

c. What are the two other reasons, besides termination of employment, that a person may qualify for this coverage?

1. _____
_____
2. _____
_____

3. The physician for whom you work does not contract with and accept assignment for the type of insurance Linda has, which is TRICARE.

a. What process is followed when a physician does not accept assignment?

_____

b. Will Linda have to pay up front for these services? Why or why not?

_____

4. Patient Julia Watson needs a surgical procedure that is not covered by her insurance plan. Answer the following questions related to the medical necessity of this procedure:

a. What must be obtained from Julia's insurance company to allow this procedure?

_____
_____

b. If Julia's insurance company's utilization protocol is different from that of the physician and the procedure is denied, what could be the action brought against the provider if this surgical procedure was, in fact, medically necessary?

_____

_____

_____

_____

5. In your own words, explain how Obamacare/Affordable Care Act has changed healthcare in America.

_____

_____

_____

_____

_____

_____

_____

_____

_____

PRACTICE EXERCISES

1. In each case scenario that follows, calculate the financial responsibility of the patient and/or carrier and the discounted amount that the physician must write off, and put your answers in the spaces provided.

a. Felix Grossman was seen today for an upper respiratory infection. Total charges for today's services are $140. The allowed amount is $90.

_____   _____

Discount amount   Carrier pays provider

b. Emma Mastrangelo had a CT scan of the brain today because of recurrent migraines. Total charges are $720.50. Her benefits pay 90 percent of this procedure. The allowed amount is $462.60.

_____   _____   _____

Patient responsibility   Discount amount   Carrier pays provider

c. Mabel Smith was seen in the office today for a checkup on her rheumatoid arthritis. Total charges are $85. The allowed amount is $52. She has a copay of $10.

_____   _____

Discount amount   Carrier pays provider

d. Rufus Durst had a cholecystectomy performed today. Total charges are $2995.70. His benefits pay 60 percent of this procedure. The allowed amount is $1745.32.

_____   _____   _____

Patient responsibility   Discount amount   Carrier pays provider

What amount will the physician write off? _____

© 2018 Pearson Education, Inc.

2. Answer the following questions in detail:

    a. Phyllis Gould is being seen today for her annual gynecological examination by a physician who is not in her HMO network. Who will be financially responsible for her medical bill?

        _____

        1. Why?

           _____

           _____

    b. Rodger McMurray has an HMO insurance plan. He did not obtain permission from his PCP for today's visit to the orthopedic specialist. Who will be financially responsible for his medical bill?

        _____

        1. Why?

           _____

           _____

3. Discuss usual, reasonable, and customary fees, and describe all three terms in detail.

_____

_____

_____

_____

4. How do MCOs provide high-quality care while managing and controlling costs?

_____

_____

_____

_____

5. What are the five different types of government plans under the Affordable Care Act (ACA)?

_____

_____

_____

6. Provide answers to the following questions:

    a. What are the six advantages of managed care as presented in the textbook?

        1. _____

        2. _____

        3. _____

        4. _____

        5. _____

        6. _____

    b. What are the six disadvantages of managed care as listed in the textbook?

        1. _____

        2. _____

        3. _____

4. _____

5. _____

6. _____

c. List the different characteristics of each type of MCO:

HMO

1. _____

2. _____

3. _____

4. _____

5. _____

6. _____

PPO

1. _____

2. _____

3. _____

4. _____

EPO

1. _____

2. _____

3. _____

4. _____

POS

1. _____

2. _____

3. _____

4. _____

5. _____

6. _____

IPA Model HMO

1. _____

2. _____

Staff Model HMO

1. _____

2. _____

3. _____

Group Model HMO

1. _____

2. _____

© 2018 Pearson Education, Inc.

Network Model HMO

1. _____

2. _____

d. In what way does an MCO withholding program encourage or discourage physician incentives?

_____

_____

_____

_____

_____

_____

e. Describe the following different types of insurance coverage:

1. Hospital _____

_____

_____

2. Hospital indemnity _____

_____

_____

3. Medical _____

_____

_____

4. Surgical _____

_____

_____

5. Outpatient _____

_____

_____

6. Major medical _____

_____

_____

7. Special risk _____

_____

_____

8. Catastrophic _____

_____

_____

9. Short-term _____

_____

_____

© 2018 Pearson Education, Inc.

10. COBRA insurance _____

_____

_____

11. Long-term _____

_____

_____

12. Supplemental _____

_____

_____

f.   List three ways in which MCOs can create administrative burdens on physicians.

1. _____

2. _____

3. _____

REVIEW QUESTIONS

MATCHING

Choose the correct answer and write its corresponding letter in the space provided.

a. utilization
b. capitation
c. PCP
d. outpatient
e. copay

1. _____ Fixed amount that is paid for each office visit or hospital encounter.

2. _____ Fixed fees paid monthly by health insurance plans, calculated on the basis of the number of enrollees seen by the physician

3. _____ Gatekeeper

4. _____ Person who receives medical care at a medical facility, but does not require admittance for more than 24 hours

5. _____ The process of a health insurance company reviewing patient data to establish medically necessary healthcare

MULTIPLE CHOICE

Circle the letter of the choice that best completes the statement or answers the question.

1. A fee agreed on by a physician and that is reimbursed by an insurance carrier for services rendered is the _____

a. contracted fee
b. controlled fee

c. discounted fee
d. Both a and c

© 2018 Pearson Education, Inc.

2. Which of the following helps an MCO determine whether a medical service is medically necessary?
   a. Premium
   b. Utilization
   c. Special risk insurance
   d. All of the above

3. A person who is covered under an insurance policy is known as the
   a. subscriber
   b. insured
   c. policyholder
   d. All of the above

4. What is a written authorization obtained by the provider before a hospital admission or certain procedures?
   a. Special risk insurance
   b. Preauthorization
   c. Referral
   d. Premium

5. What law establishes guidelines to ensure patient privacy compliance and health plan portability provisions?
   a. OSHA
   b. HMO
   c. HIPAA
   d. POS

6. What Act requires that all individuals have health insurance beginning in 2014?
   a. Patient Protection and Affordable Care Act
   b. Health Insurance Portability and Accountability Act
   c. Employee Retirement Income Security Act
   d. Consolidated Omnibus Budget Reconciliation Act

SHORT ANSWER

Provide the correct response to each question that follows.

1. Discuss the terms *coinsurance* and *copayments*. What is the difference between the two?

   _____
   _____
   _____
   _____
   _____
   _____

2. What are three terms (other than *subscriber*) that can be used interchangeably to refer to a subscriber of an insurance plan?
   1. _____
   2. _____
   3. _____

3. Provide three examples of preventative medical procedures covered by HMOs.
   1. _____
   2. _____
   3. _____

4. List three types of healthcare providers with which a PPO or an HMO may enter into a contract.

   1. _____

   2. _____

   3. _____

5. In the spaces that follow, describe a group insurance plan, an individual insurance plan, and a self-insured employers plan, highlighting the differences between the three plans.

   1. Group insurance _____

   _____

   _____

   2. Individual insurance _____

   _____

   _____

   3. Self-insured employers plan _____

   _____

   _____

6. Explain the goal and requirements of the Affordable Care Act that Congress passed in 2010? _____

_____

_____

_____

TRUE/FALSE

Identify each statement as true (T) or false (F).

1. _____ Subscribers to HMOs and PPOs will not have out-of-pocket expenses when they see physicians who are out of the network.

2. _____ It is the physician's responsibility to make sure that he or she is compensated for services rendered to patients.

3. _____ Defensive medicine is aiding in curbing the rising costs of healthcare delivery.

4. _____ The medical office specialist should collect insurance information up front and verify on each subsequent visit.

5. _____ Many physicians are joining larger groups of physicians to aid in financial burdens and create a greater patient load opportunity.

6. _____ In 2011, 16% of all U.S. citizens of working age experienced a gap in medical health insurance coverage, many due to unemployment or job changing.

© 2018 Pearson Education, Inc.

CHAPTER 3
Understanding Managed Care: Medical Contracts and Ethics

CHAPTER OBJECTIVES

After reading this chapter, the student should be able to:

1. Understand the key elements of a managed care contract that dictates the provider's compensation for services.
2. Identify covered services for patients, which can include preventive medical services and types of office visits.
3. Recognize the obligation of a medical office specialist to uphold a standard of ethics.
4. Understand a concierge contract and an ACO contract.
5. Know definitions that are used in a managed care contract in order to understand the contract and discuss claims issues with the patient and carrier.
6. Discuss the Patient's Bill of Rights and the protection it reflects under the Affordable Care Act.
7. Conduct discussions with patients regarding their accounts, copays, coinsurance, and deductibles.

CHAPTER OUTLINE

Purpose of a Contract

A Legal Agreement

Compensation and Billing Guidelines
   Covered Medical Expenses
   Payment

Ethics in Managed Care
   Changes in Healthcare Delivery
   MCO and Provider Credentialing
   Ethics of the Medical Office Specialist

Contract Definitions

Compensation for Services

Patient's Bill of Rights

Concierge Contract

KEY TERMS

Using the highlighted terms and glossary in the textbook, define the following terms.

1. accountable care organization (ACO) _____

_____

2. concierge medicine _____

_____

3. manage care organization (MCO) _____

_____

4. National Committee for Quality Assurance (NCQA) _____

_____

5. network _____

_____

6. nonparticipating provider (non-PAR) _____

_____

7. participating provider (PAR) _____

_____

8. schedule of benefits _____

_____

CRITICAL THINKING QUESTIONS

Using the knowledge you have gained from reading the textbook, apply critical thinking skills to answer the following questions.

1. As the medical office specialist (MOS), you are asked by the physician to review a managed care contract. List the compensation and billing guidelines information that should be reviewed for each of the following processes:

   a. Submitting claims _____

   _____

   _____

   b. Coordination of benefits _____

   _____

   _____

   c. Capitated plan payment _____

   _____

   _____

   d. Fee schedule _____

   _____

   _____

2. In your own words, explain how managed care organizations (MCOs) are reducing costs in relationship to the patient and the provider.

_____

_____

_____

_____

© 2018 Pearson Education, Inc.

3. What are some of the corporate business values that are making their way into the healthcare sector now that managed care has been implemented? Are these positive or negative changes? _____

_____

_____

_____

_____

4. Read the following scenario, and determine whether the medical billing specialist is acting ethically concerning the physician's office billing procedures:

   a. Randi Collins, the medical billing specialist, is coding an office wart removal procedure. She bills this procedure as complicated, but the patient's chart does not specify that it was a complicated wart removal. She knows that part of her job is to code all procedures to the highest level of specificity for proper reimbursement. Is this an ethical billing practice? _____

   If she is unsure of the clarity of the diagnosis, what should she do before billing this procedure as complicated? _____

5. The physician you work for demands that you code a patient's diagnosis falsely. You explain to him that you are not comfortable doing this, and you refuse. He threatens your job. What should you do? _____

   _____

   a. What could happen to you and the physician for falsifying this document?

   _____

PRACTICE EXERCISES

1. In layperson's terms, define the following managed care organization (MCO) contract terms for patient Fredrick Call:

   a. Benefit plan

   _____

   _____

   b. Contracted services

   _____

   _____

   c. Coordination of Benefits (COB)

   _____

   _____

   d. Copayment

   _____

   _____

   e. Covered person

   _____

   _____

f. Covered services

_____

_____

g. Emergency services

_____

_____

h. Fee maximum

_____

_____

i. Medical director

_____

_____

j. Medically necessary

_____

_____

k. Participating hospital

_____

_____

l. Participating provider

_____

_____

m. Nonparticipating provider

_____

_____

2. Using the sample contents of a managed care contact in your text (Figure 3.1), define in your own words the following MCO contract terms for compensation for services rendered by the provider.

a. Billing

_____

_____

b. Coordination of benefits (COB) recoveries

_____

_____

c. Third-party liability recoveries and subrogation

_____

_____

d. Payment

_____

_____

© 2018 Pearson Education, Inc.

e. No balance bill

_____

_____

f. Limitations regarding payment

_____

_____

g. Hold harmless provision for utilization review decision

_____

_____

3. What is the Patient's Bill of Rights, and how is it used by MCOs and providers? How has the Affordable Care Act changed the Patient's Bill of Rights? Who has this helped to support, insurance companies or consumers? Why?

_____

_____

_____

_____

_____

_____

_____

_____

_____

_____

_____

_____

_____

_____

_____

4. Explain what a managed care organization's (MCO's) credentialing process for a provider consists of.

_____

_____

_____

_____

5. Why does credentialing need to be done for providers within the MCO?

_____

_____

_____

_____

REVIEW QUESTIONS

MATCHING

Choose the correct answer and write its corresponding letter in the space provided.

a. coordination of benefits
b. fee-for-service
c. rebundle
d. per case
e. capitation

1. _____ Type of managed care contract payment where the payer compensates the provider on a predetermined rate for each episode of care provided

2. _____ Type of managed care contract payment where covered services are compensated at a discount of the provider's usual and customary charges

3. _____ Determining which payer should be billed first when a patient has two payers

4. _____ When an MCO adds to the covered services included to a single fee or amends any terms of the compensation arrangement without prior review by the provider

5. _____ Type of managed care contract payment where a provider is compensated for covered services at a fixed monthly payment (per-member-per-month amount)

MULTIPLE CHOICE

Circle the letter of the choice that best completes the statement or answers the question.

1. Which of the following are standards for licensed personnel and other employees of medical practices?
   a. Courtesy
   b. Ethics
   c. Respect
   d. All the above are standards for providers

2. Which of the following is *not* another name for a policyholder?
   a. Owner
   b. Enrollee
   c. Member
   d. All the above are names for a policyholder.

3. Which of the following is *not* a type of preventative medicine service?
   a. Physical examination
   b. Pap smear
   c. Both a and b
   d. None of the above

4. The usual time limit for submitting claims to an MCO is _____.
   a. 6 to 12 months
   b. 4 to 12 months
   c. 3 to 6 months
   d. 4 to 6 months

© 2018 Pearson Education, Inc.

5. On which day(s) of the month do most capitation plans pay a provider?
   a. 1st
   b. 15th
   c. 30th
   d. Both b and c

6. These organizations were formed to provide comprehensive, coordinated, and seamless, high-quality medical care to patients.
   a. MCOs
   b. HMOs
   c. ACOs
   d. CBOs

SHORT ANSWER

Provide the correct response to each question that follows.

1. What is the medical office specialist's role when it comes to managed care contracts? _____
   _____

2. List the four most common types of managed care contract payment arrangements.
   1. _____
   2. _____
   3. _____
   4. _____

3. When should an MCO contract agreement be modified or amended regarding the best interest of the provider? _____
   _____
   _____

4. What are laws called that set forth principles of protection for all patients concerning healthcare delivery?
   _____
   _____

5. What organization requires that an MCO plan being reviewed for accreditation demonstrate that it conducts a thorough credentialing process of providers? _____
   _____

6. What are some advantages that physicians gain by becoming part of an ACO? What are some disadvantages?
   _____

7. What are some advantages that physicians gain by becoming involved with concierge medicine?
   _____

TRUE/FALSE

Identify each statement as true (T) or false (F).

1. _____ An MCO should not contract with a physician who has a questionable background.
2. _____ A participating provider is a provider that is under contract with the MCO.

3. _____ A provider does not have to sign a contract with an MCO to be in its network.

4. _____ MCO contracts do not network with laboratories.

5. _____ A medical office specialist must document, sign, and date all conversations regarding a patient's account, whether the conversation is with the provider, insurance carrier, or even the patient.

6. _____ Concierge physicians do not participate in any plans, including Medicare and Medicaid.

7. _____ ACOs are a part of the Medicare Advantage plan.

© 2018 Pearson Education, Inc.

CHAPTER 4

Introduction to the Health Insurance Portability and Accountability Act (HIPAA)

CHAPTER OBJECTIVES

After reading this chapter, the student should be able to:

1. Describe the responsibility of the medical office specialist to protect all protected health information (PHI).
2. Discuss what is required to disclose patient information to family members, friends, and when ordered by courts or government entities.
3. Understand the patient's right to request access or correction to his or her medical records.
4. Explain HIPAA security standards that require a healthcare provider to have security policies and procedures.
5. Discuss the penalties and fines involved for not being in compliance with HIPAA regulations.
6. Understand HITECH's mandatory requirements for healthcare providers to implement "meaningful use" by managing patient information and treatment through electronic health records (EHR).

CHAPTER OUTLINE

HIPAA Privacy Rule
> *Omnibus Rule*
> *Legal Request*

Pharmacies and Durable Medical Equipment
> *Language Barrier*
> *Patient Access and Corrections*

Transactions and Code Set Rule

Uniform Code Sets

Security Rule
> *Electronic Medical Record*
> *Electronic Health Record*

Unique Identifiers Rule
> *National Provider Identifier*

HIPAA Enforcement Rule
> *Civil Penalties*
> *Federal Criminal Penalties*

HITECH Act
> *Meaningful Use*

Privacy and Security Protection

Healthcare Reform

© 2018 Pearson Education, Inc.

KEY TERMS

Using the highlighted terms and glossary in the textbook, define the following terms.

1. business associates (BA) _____

    _____

2. civil money penalty (CMP) _____

    _____

3. computerized patient order entry (CPOE) _____

    _____

4. covered entities (CE) _____

    _____

5. durable medical equipment (DME) _____

    _____

6. electronic data interchange (EDI) _____

    _____

7. electronic health record (EHR) _____

    _____

8. electronic medical record (EMR) _____

    _____

9. electronic protected health information (EPHI) _____

    _____

10. encrypted _____

    _____

11. enforcement rule _____

12. Food and Drug Administration (FDA) _____

    _____

13. Health and Human Services (HHS) _____

    _____

14. Health Information Technology for Economic and Clinical Health (HITECH) Act _____

    _____

15. meaningful use _____

    _____

16. National Provider Identifier (NPI) _____

    _____

17. Office of Civil Rights (OCR) _____

    _____

18. Office of the National Coordinator (ONC) for Health Information _____

    _____

© 2018 Pearson Education, Inc.

19. Privacy Compliance Officer _____

_____

20. Privacy rule _____

21. protected health information (PHI) _____

22. Security Rule _____

23. transactions and code set rule _____

24. unique identifier rule_____

_____

CRITICAL THINKING QUESTIONS

Using the knowledge you have gained from reading the textbook, apply critical thinking skills to answer the following questions.

1. If a patient comes into the office and wants to access their medical records, what should be done before they are given access, and why? _____

_____

_____

2. Discuss the differences between an EHR and EMR. _____

_____

_____

3. You are working as an office manager and are asked to outline the purpose of the HIPAA Security Rules to share with new employees. Discuss the following areas of the HIPAA Security Rule:
   a. Administrative safeguards _____

   _____

   b. Physical safeguards _____

   _____

   c. Technical safeguards _____

   _____

4. Discuss the three unique identifiers and what they are used for. _____

_____

_____

5. What is the HITECH Act, and how does it relate to meaningful use? _____

_____

_____

PRACTICE EXERCISES

1. Discuss the three rules that are part of the Health Insurance Portability and Accountability Act.

   a. Privacy Rule _____
   _____
   _____

   b. Security Rule _____
   _____
   _____

   c. Transactions and Code Set Rule _____
   _____
   _____

2. Write a job description for the following position: privacy compliance officer. _____
   _____
   _____
   _____

3. Give the five reasons for most of the HIPAA privacy complaints.

   1. _____
   _____
   _____

   2. _____
   _____
   _____

   3. _____
   _____
   _____

   4. _____
   _____
   _____

   5. _____
   _____
   _____

4. Refer to Figure 4.1 in your book. What information is required on the legal request for information?
   _____
   _____
   _____
   _____

© 2018 Pearson Education, Inc.

5. What are the four examples of when patient information may be released without a patient consent?

_____

_____

_____

_____

REVIEW QUESTIONS

MATCHING

Choose the correct answer and write its corresponding letter in the space provided.

a. Privacy Compliance Officer
b. Office of Civil Rights
c. encryption
d. Uniform Code Sets
e. computerized provider order entry (CPOE)

1. ____ Method for the provider to enter orders via the electronic record
2. ____ Person who is responsible for receiving and responding to records requests
3. ____ When the information is scrambled during transmission
4. ____ Agency responsible for overseeing HIPAA regulations
5. ____ Uniform set of medical codes to simplify the process of submitting claims

MULTIPLE CHOICE

Circle the letter of the choice that best completes the statement or answers the question.

1. What are the civil penalties that will be imposed for violating HIPAA regulations?
   a. $100 per person up to $50,000 per person
   b. $100 per person up to $25,000 per person
   c. $100 per person up to $75,000 per person
   d. $100 per person up to $150,000 per person

2. What are the criminal penalties that will be imposed for violating HIPAA regulations?
   a. $25,000 to $250,000 and 1–10 years in prison
   b. $50,000 to $250,000 and 5–10 years in prison
   c. $50,000 to $250,000 and 1–10 years in prison
   d. $50,000 to $250,000 and 1–20 years in prison

3. What organization would you contact to file a HIPAA complaint?
   a. ONC
   b. OIG
   c. HHS
   d. All of the above

4. Who is responsible for training all employees on HIPAA?

   a. Security officer   c. Compliance officer

   b. Privacy compliance officer   d. All of the above

5. Which of the following safeguards includes encryption?

   a. Physical safeguards   c. Technical safeguards

   b. Administrative safeguards   d. All of the above

SHORT ANSWER

Provide the correct response to each question that follows.

1. What are the criminal penalties for violating HIPAA?

   a. _____

   b. _____

   c. _____

2. What must a CPOE allow a provider to be able to do?

   a. _____

   b. _____

   c. _____

   d. _____

   e. _____

   f. _____

   g. _____

3. What types of criteria will be included in Stage II of meaningful use? _____

_____

4. What types of healthcare professionals are eligible for Medicare incentives under meaningful use? _____

_____

5. Who has the authority to grant authorization for uses and disclosures of PHI? _____

_____

TRUE/FALSE

Identify each statement as true (T) or false (F).

1. _____ Incentives for meaningful use will begin in 2015.

2. _____ EMRs and EHRs are basically the same.

3. _____ The privacy rule protects each patient's PHI.

4. _____ The National Provider Identifier is considered a unique patient identifier.

5. _____ Several covered entities have developed their own proprietary EDI systems.

© 2018 Pearson Education, Inc.

CHAPTER 5
ICD-10-CM Medical Coding

CHAPTER OBJECTIVES

After reading this chapter, the student should be able to:

1. State the purpose of the ICD-10-CM and ICD-10-PCS.
2. Define abbreviations, symbols, typefaces, punctuation, and formatting conventions.
3. Use the correct Alphabetic Index and the Tabular List of ICD-10-CM to find the appropriate code.
4. Code to the highest level of certainty and specificity.
5. Assign the correct code in the proper order.
6. List the ten steps of accurate ICD-10-CM coding.
7. Understand the code structure for ICD-10-PCS.

CHAPTER OUTLINE

Definition of Diagnosis Coding

ICD-10-CM Guidelines

The Alphabetic Index

Neoplasm Table

Table of Drugs and Chemicals

External Causes Index

Structure of ICD-10-CM

Hyphen Usage (-)

✓ Checkmark

The Tabular List

Placeholder

Laterality
    Coding Convention
    BMI
    Correct Coding Steps
    Abbreviations
    Surgical Coding
    Coding Late Effects
    Acute and Chronic Conditions
    Combination Codes: Multiple Coding

KEY TERMS

Using the highlighted terms and glossary in the textbook, define the following terms:

1. adverse effect _____

2. Alphabetic Index _____

3. body mass index (BMI) _____

4. combination code _____

5. complication code _____

6. conventions _____

7. default code _____

8. diagnosis _____

9. diagnostic statement _____

10. eponym _____

11. etiology _____

12. ICD-10-CM _____

13. ICD-10-PCS _____

14. late effect _____

15. main term _____

16. manifestation _____

17. morbidity _____

18. morphology _____

© 2018 Pearson Education, Inc.

19. NEC (not elsewhere classified) _____

_____

20. NOS (not otherwise specified) _____

_____

21. primary diagnosis _____

_____

22. principal diagnosis _____

_____

23. residual effect _____

_____

24. rule out _____

_____

25. secondary _____

_____

26. sequela _____

_____

27. sign _____

_____

28. subterms _____

_____

29. supplementary terms _____

_____

30. symptom _____

_____

31. syndrome _____

_____

32. tabular list _____

_____

CRITICAL THINKING QUESTIONS

Using the knowledge you have gained from reading the textbook, apply critical thinking skills to answer the following questions:

1. Discuss the various ways that ICD-10-CM coding is used throughout the United States. Why is accuracy in coding so important?

_____

_____

_____

_____

_____

_____

2. In your own words, answer the following questions related to the ICD-10-CM:
   a. What impact does the ICM-10-CM manual have on healthcare and medicine in today's world?

   _____

   _____

   _____

   _____

   b. Your office just received the new annual edition of the ICM-10-CM. What updates will be included?

   _____

   _____

   _____

3. Answer the following questions related to the three volumes of the ICD-10-CM, and if applicable, supply an example, using the manual:
   a. Give an example of a chapter heading in the Classification of Diseases and Injuries.

   _____

   b. Give an example of a category and supply the code.

   _____

   c. Give an example of a subcategory and supply the code.

   _____

   d. Give an example of a subheading in the Classification of Diseases and Injuries.

   _____

   e. Find a sixth-digit subcategory code. What additional information does the sixth digit supply to the code?

   _____

   _____

   _____

   f. In your own words, what is the difference between a V, W, X, or Y code and a Z code?

   _____

   _____

   _____

   g. When would a coder need to use a code from the Table of Drugs and Chemicals?

   _____

   _____

   _____

   h. Using the ICD-10-CM, where would you find a code for thyroid cancer, primary?

   _____

   _____

   _____

4. a. What code book does Crawford Hospital need to use to code procedures?

   _____

   b. Can Crawford Outpatient Radiology use this volume to code procedures?

   _____

© 2018 Pearson Education, Inc.

5. Define the following conventions and symbols found in the ICD-10-CM, and if applicable, provide an example, using the manual:

a. main term _____
_____

b. subterm _____
_____

c. supplementary terms _____
_____

d. carryover lines/turnover lines _____
_____

e. see _____
_____

f. see also _____
_____

g. see category _____
_____

h. see also category _____
_____

i. eponym _____
_____

j. NEC _____
_____

k. : _____
_____

l. NOS _____
_____

m. [ ] _____
_____

n. ( ) _____
_____

o. instructional notes _____
_____

p. use additional code _____
_____

q. code first underlying disease _____
_____

r. includes _____
_____

s. excludes1 _____
_____

t. excludes2 _____

_____

u. placeholder _____

_____

v. Bilateral condition _____

_____

_____

w. Uncertain behavior of a neoplasm _____

_____

x. Unspecified behavior of a neoplasm _____

_____

PRACTICE EXERCISES

1. Place a double underline below the main terms and a single underline below any subterms in each of the following medical conditions:
   a. rheumatoid arthritis
   b. first-degree burn
   c. myocardial infarction
   d. dog bite
   e. Parkinson's dementia
   f. paroxysmal atrial fibrillation
   g. acute pharyngitis
   h. hand pain
   i. heart palpitations
   j. squamous cell melanoma
   k. kidney stones
   l. chronic alcoholism
   m. malignant hypertension
   n. chronic kidney failure
   o. polycystic ovarian disease
   p. atopic dermatitis
   q. cerebrovascular accident

2. Using the ICD-10-CM manual, code the following medical conditions:
   a. Signs and symptoms
      1. headache _____
      2. facial pain _____
      3. weight loss _____
      4. epistaxis _____
      5. abnormal liver function test _____

© 2018 Pearson Education, Inc.

6. hyperglycemia _____

7. inconclusive HIV test _____

b. Illnesses/Diseases/Disorders

1. hypothyroidism _____

2. bell's palsy _____

3. diaper rash _____

4. cocaine abuse _____

5. cystic acne _____

6. gastroesophageal reflux disease _____

7. tubal pregnancy _____

8. premature birth at 30 weeks, birthweight: 2200 g _____

9. moderate retardation _____

10. congestive heart failure _____

11. DM I, with hyperglycemia _____

12. gestational diabetes, during childbirth, diet controlled _____

13. acute MI, anterolateral wall, initial _____

14. erectile dysfunction _____

15. strep throat _____

16. Kaposi's sarcoma of skin M code _____

17. left hip fracture _____

c. Combination codes (Note: Some conditions will have one code; others will have two.)

1. acute bronchitis with COPD _____

2. acute and chronic pancreatitis _____

3. hypertension with chronic kidney disease, stage 3 _____

4. hypertension with congestive heart failure _____

5. DM II with cataract _____

6. DM I with coma and ketoacidosis _____

7. comminuted L index finger and L thumb fracture _____

8. concussion, loss of consciousness 40 min _____

9. urinary infection due to *E. coli* _____

10. acute and chronic blood loss anemia _____

d. Neoplasm/Drug and Chemical Tables

1. benign hypertension _____

2. HTN, unspecified _____

3. cancer of bladder _____

4. bone cancer, coccyx, secondary _____

5. cervical cancer _____

6. carcinoma of brain metastasized from LUL of lung _____

7. intentional underdosing of Lasix due to financial hardship _____

8. ingested Clorox, accidental _____

9. OD barbiturate, suicide attempt _____

10. anaphylaxis due to prescription cephalosporin _____

e. Late effects

1. ataxia due to CVA

Cause _____ Residual _____

Code(s) _____

2. Arthritis due to past right ankle fracture

Cause _____ Residual _____

Code(s) _____

3. Dysphasia due to CVA

Cause _____ Residual _____

Code(s) _____

f. Burns

1. First-degree burns of nose, second-degree burns of cheek and chin, and third-degree burns of forehead due to bleach. 9% of total body burned _____

g. Z codes

1. HIV positive _____

2. Hearing exam _____

3. Sickle-cell trait screen _____

4. Denture fitting _____

5. Physical, child for school _____

6. Contact with rabies _____

7. Blood alcohol testing _____

8. Chemotherapy visit for pancreatic cancer _____

9. Encounter for oral birth control, initial visit _____

10. Removal of surgical dressing of wound _____

11. Hospice care _____

12. DTP vaccination _____

13. Allergy desensitization _____

14. History of pulmonary embolism. Pt. on anticoagulants _____

15. Family history of ovarian cancer _____

16. History of colon polyps _____

h. Y codes

1. Heel injury (wound) due to broken glass _____

2. Concussion due to MVA that hit a tree. Pt was driver of car _____

3. Read the following diagnostic statements, determine the primary and secondary diagnoses, and write the appropriate codes:

a. Patient presents with an elevated white blood cell count. Patient has staph infection due to infection of surgical wound.

Primary diagnosis _____ Code(s) _____

Secondary diagnosis _____ Code(s) _____

© 2018 Pearson Education, Inc.

b. Patient's mammogram shows evidence of left breast mass. There is a family history of breast cancer.

Primary diagnosis _____ Code(s) _____

Secondary diagnosis _____ Code(s) _____

c. Patient experiencing syncope and epistaxis. Patient also has essential HTN, malignant.

Primary diagnosis _____ Code(s) _____

Secondary diagnosis _____ Code(s) _____

d. Patient is seen today for acute and chronic sinusitis.

Primary diagnosis _____ Code(s) _____

Secondary diagnosis _____ Code(s) _____

e. Patient has unstable angina with CAD. He has an old MI from 5 years ago.

Primary diagnosis _____ Code(s) _____

Secondary diagnosis _____ Code(s) _____

f. Patient with right toe ulceration due to DM II.

Primary diagnosis _____ Code(s) _____

Secondary diagnosis _____ Code(s) _____

4. What are the ten steps for accurate ICD-10-CM coding?

1. _____

2. _____

3. _____

4. _____

5. _____

6. _____

7. _____

8. _____

9. _____

10. _____

5. What are the three coding guidelines that will help medical office specialists as they code claims?

1. _____

2. _____

3. _____

6. Using ICD-10-PCS manual, code the following hospital procedures:

1. Hemorrhoidectomy, excision _____

2. Laparoscopic holecystectomy _____

3. Dilation and curettage via hysteroscopy _____

4. Right knee arthroscopy _____

5. RBC transfusion via CVC _____

6. Chemotherapy infusion via PICC _____

7. Biopsy, needle aspiration of right breast _____

8. Aorto-coronary artery bypass graft, one vessel using saphenous vein graft _____

9. Cast application of left finger _____

10. Atrial cardioversion _____

11. Gastric lavage via EGD _____

12. Laparoscopic bilateral tubal ligation done using fulguration _____

13. Bladder catheter replacement via cystoscopy _____

14. Spinal tap for decompression of thoracic spinal cord _____

15. Chest x-ray _____

REVIEW QUESTIONS

MATCHING

Choose the correct answer and place its corresponding letter in the space provided.

a. primary diagnosis
b. principal diagnosis
c. benign
d. malignant
e. carcinoma in situ

1. _____ Slow progression; not cancerous
2. _____ Represents the patient's most serious condition, regardless of the reason for encounter
3. _____ Tumor cells that have cancerous changes, but do not extend beyond the point of origin or invade surrounding normal tissue
4. _____ The final diagnosis after tests and examination have been performed
5. _____ Rapid progression; cancerous

MULTIPLE CHOICE

Circle the letter of the choice that best completes the statement or answers the question.

1. Which of the following determines the percentage of body surface area that has been burned?
   a. Burn Mass index
   b. Rule of Nines
   c. Neither a nor b
   d. Both a and b

2. When did ICD-10-CM and ICD-10-PCS replace ICD-9-CM?
   a. October 1, 2015
   b. October 1, 1999
   c. October 1, 2014
   d. October 1, 2016

3. Which of the following terms alerts a coder to a combination code?
   a. Due to
   b. Without
   c. Following
   d. All of the above

4. Which of the following terms alerts a coder that a code may be an V, W, X, or Y code?
   a. Illness
   b. Injury
   c. Caused by
   d. Both b and c

© 2018 Pearson Education, Inc.

5. Which is *not* a reason for agencies or organizations to use the ICD-10-CM?
   a. To forecast healthcare needs and evaluate facilities and services
   b. To conduct studies of trends in diseases over the years
   c. To review costs
   d. All of the above are reasons that the ICD-10-CM is used by agencies and organizations.

SHORT ANSWER

Provide the correct response to each question that follows.

1. When are ICD-10-CM and ICD-10-PCS updated?
   _____
   _____

2. What are the three main steps to coding accurately?
   1. _____
      _____
   2. _____
      _____
   3. _____
      _____

3. What is a subclassification in the ICD-10-CM?
   _____
   _____

4. What is an adverse reaction?
   _____
   _____
   _____

5. Discuss Z codes and how they are used for coding encounters.
   _____
   _____
   _____

TRUE/FALSE

Identify each statement as true (T) or false (F).

1. _____ A diagnosis does not need to match a procedure to prove medical necessity.
2. _____ Only Y codes can be used as the primary diagnosis.
3. _____ The alphabetic index of the ICD-10-CM is needed only to find an accurate code.
4. _____ Medicaid and most private insurance carriers adopt rules and regulations for healthcare reimbursement that are based on Medicare.
5. _____ Conventions can vary per the ICD-10-CM publishing company.

CHAPTER 6
Introduction to CPT® and Place of Service Coding

CHAPTER OBJECTIVES

After reading this chapter, the student should be able to:

1. Understand the history of CPT.
2. Understand evaluation and management (E/M) services.
3. Explain the three types of CPT categories.
4. Distinguish the need for modifiers.
5. Distinguish between a new and established patient.
6. Know the three key elements in choosing an E/M code.
7. Determine the correct E/M code.

CHAPTER OUTLINE

CPT is a registered trademark of the American Medical Association.

Level of E/M Service
Extent of Patient's History
Extent of Examination
Complexity of Medical Decision Making
Additional Components
Assigning the Code

KEY TERMS

Using the highlighted terms and glossary in the textbook, define the following terms.

1. American Medical Association (AMA) _____

_____

2. Centers for Medicare and Medicaid Services (CMS) _____

_____

3. chief complaint (CC) _____

_____

4. consultation _____

_____

5. counseling _____

_____

6. Current Procedural Terminology (CPT) _____

_____

7. E/M codes _____

_____

8. established patient _____

_____

9. examination _____

_____

10. history _____

_____

11. history of present illness (HPI) _____

_____

12. medical decision making (MDM) _____

_____

13. modifiers _____

_____

14. nature of the presenting problem _____

_____

15. new patient _____

_____

© 2018 Pearson Education, Inc.

16. nomenclature _____

_____

17. past, family, and social history (PFSH) _____

_____

18. review of systems (ROS) _____

_____

CRITICAL THINKING QUESTIONS

Using the knowledge you have gained from reading the textbook, apply critical thinking skills to answer the following questions:

1. What is the history of CPT coding? Write a summary describing how coding has changed throughout the years.

_____

_____

_____

_____

_____

_____

2. Samuel Lewis, MD, is coding an E/M service for patient Marge Mahoney. What are three important components for Dr. Lewis to use when selecting the appropriate code for Mrs. Mahoney's visit?

1. _____

2. _____

3. _____

3. Read the following scenarios, and determine what part of the medical history it identifies:

   a. The patient's mother had diabetes.

   _____

   b. The patient smokes cigarettes, 1 pack per day.

   _____

   c. The patient has a history of herpes simplex virus.

   _____

   d. The patient currently takes Prednisone t.i.d.

   _____

   e. The patient had a cholecystectomy in 1998.

   _____

4. Determine whether the following is/are considered a body area or an organ system, as recognized by the CPT manual:

   a. The patient's neurologic exam reveals orientation X3.

   _____

   b. The abdomen is soft, nontender.

   _____

c. The head presents as normocephalic, atraumatic.

_____

d. Skin shows no lesions, bruises, or rashes.

_____

e. Eyes: Pupils are equal, round, and reactive to light. Sclera is white.

_____

f. Ears, nose, mouth, and throat are unremarkable.

_____

g. Psychiatric: Patient's mood is pleasant and upbeat.

_____

h. Chest: No wheezes, rubs, or rhonci.

_____

5. A patient's E/M code is 99214. The physician spent over 25 minutes of counseling and coordination of care time with this patient. What code(s), if any, should be reported to ensure the maximum reimbursement level for this service?

_____

PRACTICE EXERCISES

1. Using the CPT manual, choose the correct E/M code for each scenario that follows:

   a. A new patient is seen today for an infection on the right index finger. The nail is examined and has evidence of a fungal infection. Patient is started on antibiotics.

   E/M code _____

   b. A patient is seen for a checkup on arthritis of the knees and for hypertension. The patient has no new complaints. His blood pressure is stable with medication therapy, and his arthritis has presented only mild symptoms since the last visit.

   E/M code _____

   c. A patient being seen for an initial hospital visit presents with unstable angina and elevated cardiac enzymes. The patient has a history of hypertension, DM II, and smoking two packs of cigarettes per day for 12 years.

   E/M code _____

   d. A patient is being seen for the second day of admission for an emergency appendectomy. Patient is healthy otherwise and presents stable.

   E/M code _____

   e. A patient is being discharged after an episode of shingles. The physician completes the discharge within 20 minutes.

   E/M code _____

   f. A patient is seeing the endocrinologist for his rheumatoid arthritis follow-up. The progression has slowly advanced since the last visit. Labs are unremarkable.

   E/M code _____

© 2018 Pearson Education, Inc.

g. A patient's internal medicine doctor orders a neurologist consult for the patient regarding seizure disorder. The patient was admitted for cellulitis and has begun to seize.

E/M code _____

h. A patient presents to the ER with complaints of an asthma attack. The patient also has COPD. After administration of medications, CXR, and lab, the patient is stable and is discharged.

E/M code _____

i. The physician spends 1 hour and 40 minutes providing critical care to a CCU patient.

E/M code _____

j. The physician visits a newborn for day three in the neonatal ICU. The child should be able to be released in a couple more days.

E/M code _____

k. A newborn weighing 1600 g is admitted to the neonatal ICU.

E/M code _____

l. A patient is being examined for the first time in a long-term care facility. The patient's health consists of glaucoma due to DM I, old MI, and recent CVA. The patient has hemiplegia of her dominant side. A full ROS is completed.

E/M code _____

m. A patient who was admitted yesterday to skilled nursing is being seen today for postop surgery of left hip replacement. The patient shows no signs of infection and is eating and eliminating well.

E/M code _____

n. A physician spends 40 minutes redeveloping a care plan for a patient in a nursing home.

E/M code _____

o. A physician spends an extra 35 minutes with a new patient discussing fertility options.

E/M code _____

p. A physician reassesses the anticoagulant management of a patient.

E/M code _____

q. A new patient, age 15, is seen for a physical examination. Exam is unremarkable.

Patient was given the first series of hepatitis B vaccination.

E/M code _____

r. An established patient, age 25, is seen for an annual gynecological exam.

E/M code _____

s. A 2-year-old is seen today for a well-child exam. Patient is developing normally.

E/M code _____

t. The physician spends 30 minutes counseling a patient on a weight-loss program.

E/M code _____

u. A patient is seen today for a disability evaluation. The patient has congestive heart failure and renal failure.

E/M code _____

v. A patient is seen in the hospital on the first hospital day. Patient is an inpatient. Patient has been admitted for chest pain. The physician sees the patient for 30 minutes.

E/M code _____

2. Using the CPT manual, code the following scenarios and apply the appropriate E/M modifier:

   a. A patient is seen by his family doctor for chronic bronchitis. A chest x-ray was performed. The patient also complains of numbness and tingling in his right hand and wrist. An x-ray of the right hand and wrist was also performed.

     E/M code and modifier _____

   b. The Social Security Administration required a 40-year-old disabled patient to be seen today for an annual physical exam.

     E/M code and modifier _____

   c. The otorhinolaryngologist sees a referred patient for chronic sinusitis. The physician explains to the patient that the sinusitis is not getting better and determines that surgery is the best option.

     E/M code and modifier _____

   d. A patient presents for postop care due to a hysterectomy. The patient has a new complaint of four lesions that have appeared on her perineal area. She has a history of herpes simplex virus.

     Modifier _____

   e. A patient is prepped and going in to have a colonoscopy. The procedure is discontinued due to problems with the patient's heart.

     Modifier _____

3. Think of your last doctor's visit. Without identifying any personal information, select the appropriate E/M code that would have been used for the visit. Use the CPT manual to complete this exercise.

   E/M code _____

REVIEW QUESTIONS

MATCHING

Choose the correct answer and write its corresponding letter in the space provided.

a. inpatient
b. outpatient
c. new patient
d. established patient
e. observation status

1. _____ Person who has *not* been seen by a physician or practice for 3 years

2. _____ Medical care provided at a doctor's office or outside health facility

3. _____ Patients who are being observed to see if they should be admitted to the hospital

4. _____ Admittance to the hospital, a skilled nursing facility, or a nursing home for 24+ hours

5. _____ Person who *has* been seen by a physician or practice within 3 years

© 2018 Pearson Education, Inc.

MULTIPLE CHOICE

Circle the letter of the choice that best completes the statement or answers the question.

1. Which of the following CPT symbols alerts the coder to new or revised text enclosed?
   a. ▲
   b. ●
   c. ▶◀
   d. +

2. Which of the following CPT symbols alerts the coder to a revised code that has been changed?
   a. ▲
   b. ●
   c. ▶◀
   d. +

3. Which of the following CPT symbols alerts the coder that the code is new to the edition?
   a. ▲
   b. ●
   c. ▶◀
   d. +

4. Which of the following describes the purpose of CPT modifiers?
   a. Describe the procedure
   b. Describe issues with the procedure
   c. Describe an alteration to the procedure
   d. None of the above

5. Which association/organization publishes the CPT manual?
   a. HIPAA
   b. AMA
   c. WHO
   d. CMS

SHORT ANSWER

Provide the correct response to each question that follows.

1. What are the eight sections of the CPT manual and their respective code ranges?
   1. _____
   2. _____
   3. _____
   4. _____
   5. _____
   6. _____
   7. _____
   8. _____

2. Out of the eight sections just listed, in which sections are Category I codes found? _____

3. Where are the CPT guidelines found in the manual, and what is their purpose? _____

4. Why is the use of modifiers that are added to a code so important? _____

_____

_____

_____

5. The E/M section is divided into broad services. What are some examples of these services?

_____

_____

_____

TRUE/FALSE

Identify each statement as true (T) or false (F).

1. _____ Category II codes contain performance management tracking codes.

2. _____ The CPT may have some procedures that appear in certain sections other than those sections where these procedures may seem to ordinarily be classified.

3. _____ You must first determine the place of service when coding from the E/M section.

4. _____ Most services for established patients and subsequent care require all three key components when the appropriate E/M code is being chosen.

5. _____ A referred patient and a consultation mean the same thing.

© 2018 Pearson Education, Inc.

CHAPTER 7
Coding Procedures and Services

CHAPTER OBJECTIVES

After reading this chapter, the student should be able to:

1. Correctly use the CPT® current procedural terminology index.
2. Understand the four primary classes of main entries in the CPT index.
3. Understand code ranges and conventions.
4. Discuss the purpose of each section and the guidelines.
5. Know how to use modifiers correctly.
6. Use add-on codes properly.
7. Review codes for accuracy.
8. Given procedural statements, apply coding guidelines to determine the correct CPT codes.

CHAPTER OUTLINE

Organization of the CPT Index
Instructions for Using the CPT Code Range

Formatting and Cross-References
Formatting
Cross-references

Section Guidelines

Modifiers

Add-on Codes (+)

Coding Steps
Coding for Anesthesia

Surgical Coding

Separate Procedure

Surgical Package or Global Surgery Concept

Supplies and Services

Radiology Codes

Pathology and Laboratory Codes

Medicine Codes

CPT is a registered trademark of the American Medical Association.

© 2018 Pearson Education, Inc.

KEY TERMS

Using the highlighted terms and glossary in the textbook, define the following terms:

1. add-on codes _____

2. bundled code _____
   _____

3. Clinical Laboratory Improvement Amendment (CLIA) _____
   _____

4. cross-references _____
   _____

5. descriptor _____
   _____

6. fragmented billing _____

7. global period _____
   _____

8. global surgical concept _____
   _____

9. panel _____
   _____

10. physical status modifier _____
    _____

11. primary procedure _____
    _____

12. professional component _____
    _____

13. secondary procedure _____
    _____

14. separate procedure _____
    _____

15. special report _____
    _____

16. surgical package _____
    _____

17. technical component _____
    _____

18. unbundling _____
    _____

© 2018 Pearson Education, Inc.

CRITICAL THINKING QUESTIONS

Using the knowledge you have gained from reading the textbook, apply critical thinking skills to answer the following questions:

1. Answer each of the following as it relates to the CPT index:
    a. What are the four primary classes of entries in the main index? Give an example for each.
        1. _____
        2. _____
        3. _____
        4. _____
    b. When codes are sequential, what are they separated by? When codes are not sequential, what are they separated by? _____
    _____

2. Answer each of the following as it relates to the CPT format:
    a. Using the CPT, locate the following descriptors for code 15780, and answer the given three questions related to this code:
        1. What is the full descriptor for this parent code?
        _____

        2. What is the full descriptor for the indented code 15781?
        _____

        3. What is the full descriptor for the indented code 15782?
        _____

    b. Code 15786 is for abrasion of a single lesion. What code(s) would be used to bill for abrasion of five lesions?

    _____

    c. Where in the CPT manual would you find vital supplemental information that is used to correctly code from each section?

    _____

3. Answer the following questions related to anesthesia coding:
    a. To bill anesthesia services correctly, what guide would you use?

    _____
    _____

    b. Maryann Grull is having a partial hysterectomy. What services are included in the anesthesia code?

    _____
    _____

    c. When does Maryann's anesthesia period begin and end during her surgery?

    _____
    _____

4. Answer the following questions related to CPT coding:

   a. When a patient has a major procedure, what services and/or care would be part of the surgical package?

     _____

     _____

   b. What services and/or care would not be part of the patient's surgical package?

     _____

     _____

   c. Read each procedure that follows. Identify whether each procedure is normally bundled in a surgical package by writing **YES** in the space provided. If the procedure is *not* normally bundled in a surgical package, write **NO** in the space provided.

     1. _____ Administration of sedative, local or regional anesthesia by the performing physician

     2. _____ Complicated debridement of traumatized tissue and lysis of adhesions

     3. _____ Application of a cast, sling, or splint

     4. _____ Removal of polyps or other benign lesions during a colonoscopy

     5. _____ Surgical supplies

     6. _____ Administration of general anesthesia by the anesthesiologist

   d. In your own words, what would be some examples of situations where a modifier would be used?

     _____

     _____

     _____

5. What are the three steps to perform procedural coding? Give a brief explanation for each.

   1. _____

     _____

     _____

   2. _____

     _____

     _____

   3. _____

     _____

     _____

PRACTICE EXERCISES

1. Using the CPT manual, choose the correct codes for each procedure that follows:

Anesthesia

   Liver transplantation on a patient who will not live unless the surgery is performed:

   Code(s) _____

   Surgical wrist arthroscopy on a healthy patient:

   Code(s) _____

 © 2018 Pearson Education, Inc.

Burr hole on a 72-year-old patient in severe distress:

Code(s) _____

Skin

Destruction of seven lesions by laser:

Code(s) _____

I&D of cyst, simple:

Code(s) _____

Simple repair of wounds of the scalp 0.5 cm, neck 1.2 cm, and shoulder 3.6 cm:

Code(s) _____

Biopsy of right breast by needle core with ultrasound guidance, percutaneous:

Code(s) _____

Local treatment of first-degree burn, initial:

Code(s) _____

Moh's surgery of arm, first stage, four tissue blocks:

Code(s) _____

Musculoskeletal

Closed treatment of acetabular fracture, skeletal traction:

Code(s) _____

Application of short cast:

Code(s) _____

Bone biopsy of greater trochanter:

Code(s) _____

Amputation of ankle:

Code(s) _____

Local arthrodesis of elbow joint:

Code(s) _____

Fracture, two ribs, open treatment:

Code(s) _____

Closed treatment, acetabulum with manipulation:

Code(s) _____

Reinsertion of spinal fixation device:

Code(s) _____

Respiratory

Direct laryngoscopy with biopsy:

Code(s) _____

Removal of a rock lodged in the nose:

Code(s) _____

Thoracotomy; with exploration

Code(s) _____

Open lung lobectomy, two lobes:

Code(s) _____

© 2018 Pearson Education, Inc.

Sinusotomy of the frontal sinuses:

Code(s) _____

Bronchoscopy with bronchial alveolar lavage:

Code(s) _____

Cardiovascular

Pulmendartectomy with embolectomy:

Code(s) _____

CABG, three coronary vessels:

Code(s) _____

Insertion of ventricular pacemaker:

Code(s) _____

Ruptured aneurysm repair of the abdominal aorta, hypogastric, direct:

Code(s) _____

Closure of atrial septal and ventricular septal defect, direct:

Code(s) _____

Coronary endarterectomy; open:

Code(s) _____

TAVR via transaortic approach:

Code(s) _____

Hemic and Lymphatic

Partial splenectomy:

Code(s) _____

Resection of the diaphragm, complex:

Code(s) _____

Lymph biopsy of left axillea, deep:

Code(s) _____

Digestive

Upper GI endoscopy with biopsy:

Code(s) _____

Destruction of herpetic lesion of the anus by cryosurgery:

Code(s) _____

Repair of strangulated umbilical hernia:

Code(s) _____

Hemorrhoidopexy:

Code(s) _____

Cleft palate repair, hard and soft:

Code(s) _____

Esophagogastroduodenoscopy; with biopsy:

Code(s) _____

© 2018 Pearson Education, Inc.

Urinary

Closure of pyelocutaneous fistula:

Code(s) _____

Urodynamic uroflowmetry, complex:

Code(s) _____

Ureterectomy, abdominal approach:

Code(s) _____

Cystourethroscopy with internal urethrotomy, female patient:

Code(s) _____

Nephrotomy for renal calculi:

Code(s) _____

Male

Circumcision with clamp on newborn:

Code(s) _____

Urethroplasty of 2.7 cm hypospadias:

Code(s) _____

Circumcision, adult:

Code(s) _____

Destruction of penis lesion, laser technique:

Code(s) _____

Punch biopsy of the prostate:

Code(s) _____

Female

Hysteroscopy of the endometrium with biopsy and D&C:

Code(s) _____

Total hysterectomy:

Code(s) _____

Colpopexy, vaginal; extraperitoneal approach:

Code(s) _____

Perineal biopsy of one lesion:

Code(s) _____

Partial oophorectomy, one ovary:

Code(s) _____

Tubal ligation, vaginal approach:

Code(s) _____

Maternity Care and Delivery

Induced abortion by evacuation with D&C:

Code(s) _____

Fetal contraction stress test:

Code(s) _____

Antepartum, delivery, and postpartum care after previous C-section:

Code(s) _____

Surgical treatment of ectopic pregnancy, with salpingectomy, vaginal:

Code(s) _____

Cesarean delivery only:

Code(s) _____

Endocrine

Removal of carotid bay tumor:

Code(s) _____

Thyroidectomy, subtotal for malignancy with radical neck dissection:

Code(s) _____

Nervous

Stereotactic stimulation of spinal cord, percutaneous:

Code(s) _____

Subdural hematoma drainage by burr hole technique:

Code(s) _____

Implant of intrathecal catheter with laminectomy:

Code(s) _____

5.1 cm meningocele repair:

Code(s) _____

Cervical laminoplasty with decompression, two vertebral segments:

Code(s) _____

Sciatic neuroplasty:

Code(s) _____

Eye and Ocular Adnexa

Nonperforated cornea laceration repair:

Code(s) _____

Removal of embedded glass from right eyelid with simple skin repair, 1.0 cm:

Code(s) _____

Removal of cataract of right eye, secondary:

Code(s) _____

Auditory

Removal of foreign body from external auditory canal, without anesthesia:

Code(s) _____

Radiology

Cholecystogram

Code(s) _____

Saline infused sonohysterography with Doppler color flow:

Code(s) _____

CT, soft tissue of neck without contrast, followed by contrast:

Code(s) _____

© 2018 Pearson Education, Inc.

DXA scan, axial skeleton:

Code(s) _____

Retrograde intravenous urography with KUB:

Code(s) _____

CXR, complete, 4 views:

Code(s) _____

Bilateral mammogram, diagnostic:

Code(s) _____

Swallowing function test with cineradiography:

Code(s) _____

Radiation treatment delivery, single area with simple blocking, 8 MeV:

Code(s) _____

Radiation treatment, five treatments:

Code(s) _____

Single thyroid uptake study:

Code(s) _____

Pathology

Total creatine kinase:

Code(s) _____

ANA titer:

Code(s) _____

Hepatitis panel:

Code(s) _____

Aerobic stool culture for salmonella:

Code(s) _____

Quantitative HCG:

Code(s) _____

Semen analysis:

Code(s) _____

Western Blot with interpretation and report:

Code(s) _____

ABO blood typing:

Code(s) _____

Surgical pathology, needle biopsy of the prostate:

Code(s) _____

Bone marrow smear with interpretation:

Code(s) _____

CBC with differential:

Code(s) _____

ESR, automated:

Code(s) _____

Quantitative Quinidine assay:

Code(s) _____

Pap smear screen, thin layer, automated:

Code(s) _____

Cocaine screen and confirmation:

Code(s) _____

Surgical pathology, uterus and tubes after prolapse:

Code(s) _____

Medicine

Family psychotherapy:

Code(s) _____

MMR vaccination for 2-year-old boy:

Code(s) _____

Hemodialysis for ESRD, full month for 69-year-old female with one face-to face visit:

Code(s) _____

Intranasal influenza immunization:

Code(s) _____

IV hydration infusion, four hours:

Code(s) _____

Telemedicine psychiatric diagnostic interview examination:

Code(s) _____

Hepatitis A vaccination, adult:

Code(s) _____

Ophthalmology examination, new patient, intermediate:

Code(s) _____

Fitting for spectacles, monofocal:

Code(s) _____

Visual field exam:

Code(s) _____

Hearing aid check, left ear:

Code(s) _____

Pure tone audiometry, air only:

Code(s) _____

Echocardiography with realtime 2-D imaging, M-mode with Doppler, complete:

Code(s) _____

Elective atrial cardioversion:

Code(s) _____

Telephonic pace analysis for dual chamber pacemaker:

Code(s) _____

Arterial and venous duplex, bilateral:

Code(s) _____

© 2018 Pearson Education, Inc.

Pulse oximetry on exercise:

Code(s) _____

Laser treatment for psoriasis, 190 sq. cm:

Code(s) _____

Allergy injection, two:

Code(s) _____

Physical therapy evaluation, moderate complexity:

Code(s) _____

Needle EMG of the arm, bilateral:

Code(s) _____

Central nervous system chemotherapy administration with spinal puncture:

Code(s) _____

Chiropractic spinal manipulation treatment:

Code(s) _____

Home health visit for stoma care:

Code(s) _____

2. Using the CPT manual, apply the appropriate modifier for the following procedures:

Liver transplantation with surgical team:

Code(s) _____

Radical mastectomy, bilateral:

Code(s) _____

TURP, second stage:

Code(s) _____

Arthroscopy, knee, infected from surgery, with medial meniscus repair performed by two surgeons:

Code(s) _____

Stopped, treadmill exercise stress test, myocardial perfusion imaging, multiple studies:

Code(s) _____

Repeat bleeding time:

Code(s) _____

Lead testing performed by outside lab:

Code(s) _____

Avulsion, vagus nerve, abdominal, surgical care only:

Code(s) _____

Laparoscopic hysterectomy of uterus weighing 24 lb; was to be total, but was determined to be partial removal at the time of surgery:

Code(s) _____

Emergency endotracheal intubation on infant weighing 3.5 kg:

Code(s) _____

Discontinued outpatient breast biopsy by fine needle due to patient reaction to regional anesthetic:

Code(s) _____

3. Using the CPT and the ICD-10-CM manuals, code the following scenarios:

   a. A patient is seen for a follow-up after cholecystomy 2 weeks ago. Patient is not having diarrhea. Review of the abdomen is unremarkable.

      Code(s) _____

   b. A patient is seen for the first time by the allergist for asthma and allergic rhinitis. A prick allergy test is administered for 15 allergens. Reaction is present for grass pollen, dust mites, and dog dander. The patient was started on Allegra-D and Singulair, and Claritin was administered after the testing. The patient is to return in 1 month to assess the advisability of allergy injections.

      Code(s) _____

   c. A new patient sees a family physician for missed menses of approximately 2 weeks. A urine pregnancy test is performed in the office, which is negative. The patient is referred to her gynecologist for further evaluation.

      Code(s) _____

REVIEW QUESTIONS

MATCHING

Choose the correct answer and write its corresponding letter in the space provided.

a. modifier TC
b. professional component (S&I)
c. See, or Use
d. See Also
e. Ø

1. Direction in the CPT to look under another main term to reference a code
2. Denotes that a code cannot be used with a particular modifier, such as −51
3. Technical component; used when a test is performed, but the physician does not interpret
4. Points to another code and also denotes synonyms, eponyms, and abbreviations
5. A cardiologist interprets and reports a Holter monitor report for a family physician

MULTIPLE CHOICE

Circle the letter of the choice that best completes the statement or answers the question.

1. Procedures and services for laboratory are listed in the index under which of the following terms?
   a. Panels
   b. Name of the test
   c. Panel, blood test, or hormone assay
   d. All of the above

2. Which of the following procedures and services are found in the medicine section?
   a. Audiology
   b. Otorhinolaryngology
   c. Physical therapy, speech therapy, and rehabilitation
   d. All of the above

© 2018 Pearson Education, Inc.

3. How many codes are needed to code an immunization?
   a. 1
   b. 2
   c. 3
   d. None of the above

4. What do anesthesia codes usually cover?
   a. Postoperative follow-up visits
   b. Preop and postop care
   c. Administration of fluids
   d. All of the above
   e. Both b and c are correct

5. Which of the following is true regarding bundled codes?
   a. Related procedures are covered by a single code.
   b. Separate procedures cannot be coded under bundled codes.
   c. Bundled codes include usual procedures that are performed together.
   d. Both a and c are correct.

SHORT ANSWER

Provide the correct response to each question that follows:

1. What code do physicians use to keep track of the number of postop visits?
   _____

2. What code is used to report supplies not covered under a procedure?
   _____

3. What symbol is used when the codes given in the index are a range of codes? What if the codes are two codes, whether sequential or not? _____
   _____
   _____

4. What are the two routes of contrast administration that should be coded as "without contrast"?
   1. _____
   2. _____

5. To code tests from the pathology 8000 series, you will need a code for the _____ and another code to report the _____ of the specimen.

TRUE/FALSE

Identify each statement as true (T) or false (F):

1. _____ The medical office specialist should always check the main text to verify accuracy of the code given.

2. _____ A panel blood test can be coded if most of the tests in it are performed.

3. _____ A patient's diagnosis may determine the need for modifiers.

4. _____ Besides physicians, other healthcare professionals can code from the medicine section of the CPT.

5. _____ An unlisted or a new procedure does not usually require a special report from the reporting physician.

CHAPTER 8
HCPCS and Coding Compliance

CHAPTER OBJECTIVES

After reading this chapter, the student should be able to:

1. Understand the two levels of HCPCS.
2. Recognize the need for HCPCS coding and when to report HCPCS codes.
3. Learn how to use HCPCS modifiers.
4. Interpret and identify correct code linkages.
5. Review the coding for accuracy.
6. Understand federal laws, regulations, and penalties that pertain to coding compliance.
7. Understand the responsibilities of coding and coding compliance.
8. Explain the National Correct Coding Initiative.
9. Understand medical ethics for the medical coder.

CHAPTER OUTLINE

History of HCPCS

HCPCS Level of Codes
    Level I: CPT® Codes
    Level II: HCPCS National Codes

HCPCS Modifiers
    Use of the GA Modifier

HCPCS Index

Coding Compliance

Code Linkage

Billing CPT Codes
    Fraudulent Claims
    Physician Self-Referral (Stark Law)
    Government Investigations and Advice
    Errors Relating to Code Linkage and Medical Necessity
    Errors Relating to the Coding Process
    Errors Relating to the Billing Process

National Correct Coding Initiative

Fraudulent Actions

Federal Compliance
    How to Be Compliant
    Benefits of a Compliance Program
    Ethics for the Medical Coder

KEY TERMS

Using the highlighted terms and glossary in the textbook, define the following terms:

1. abuse _____

2. advanced beneficiary notice (ABN) _____

3. advisory opinion _____

4. assumption coding _____

5. code linkage _____

6. durable medical equipment (DME) _____

7. fraud _____

8. HCPCS _____

9. Level I HCPCS _____

10. Level II HCPCS _____

11. National Correct Coding Initiative (NCCI) _____

12. OIG fraud alerts _____

13. OIG Work Plan _____

CRITICAL THINKING QUESTIONS

Using the knowledge you have gained from reading the textbook, apply critical thinking skills to answer the following questions.

1. What are the five reasons that the CMS has maintained HCPCS?

   1. _____
   2. _____
   3. _____
   4. _____
   5. _____

© 2018 Pearson Education, Inc.

2. Answer the following questions related to the two levels of HCPCS:

  a. In your own words, briefly describe Level I codes.

  _____

  _____

  _____

  _____

  b. In your own words, briefly describe Level II codes.

  _____

  _____

  _____

  _____

  _____

  _____

  c. How do you look up the HCPCS codes, and how does this compare to locating CPT codes?

  _____

  _____

  _____

  _____

  _____

3. Answer the following questions related to HCPCS modifiers:

  a. Discuss HCPCS modifiers and how they are used.

  _____

  _____

  _____

  _____

  _____

  b. Identify the correct HCPCS modifier for each scenario that follows:

  1. A patient has trigger finger release on right 2nd finger.

  _____

  2. A patient is seen by a locum tenens physician in the clinic.

  _____

  3. A patient has a blepharoplasty on the right upper eyelid.

  _____

  4. A patient had a surgical procedure for her left, 4th-digit hammer toe.

  _____

  c. A patient has a tummy tuck following a gastric bypass. The tummy tuck may not be covered under his insurance policy. What form needs to be signed by this patient and filed in his chart?

  _____

  _____

d. Why would this form need to be signed and filed?

_____

_____

e. How would you notify the insurance carrier that this form was obtained?

_____

_____

4. Answer the following questions related to compliance:

a. In your own words, what is the Federal Register and what is its purpose?

_____

_____

_____

_____

_____

b. You are assigned the duty of creating a compliance plan for your office. What important information can be obtained from the Compliance Program Guidance that will help you to implement a compliance plan?

_____

_____

_____

_____

PRACTICE EXERCISES

1. Referring to Chapter 8 in your text, read each of the given scenarios and identify what type of billing and/or coding error has occurred. Write **CL** for an error in code linkage, **CP** for an error in the coding process, and **BP** for an error in the billing process.

a. _____ The medical office specialist submits a claim before the physician documents the visit.

b. _____ The physician asks the coder to code for a procedure that is not performed, and the coder does this for him.

c. _____ The coder changes a diagnosis for a procedure that does not meet medical necessity.

d. _____ The physician orders a head CT for a patient with COPD.

2. Using HCPCS codes, code the following:

1. Ambulance emergency service with BLS

   Code _____

2. Replacement of tubing for breast pump

   Code _____

3. Blood glucose reagent strips for home monitoring, 50 strips

   Code _____

4. Above-the-knee surgical stockings (2)

   Code _____

5. Dome and mouthpiece for small-volume ultrasonic nebulizer

   Code _____

© 2018 Pearson Education, Inc.

6. Enteral nutrition infusion pump with alarm

Code _____

7. Pair of wooden underarm crutches

Code _____

8. Raised toilet seat

Code _____

9. Hospital bed with mattress, semi-electric

Code _____

10. Standard adult manual wheelchair

Code _____

11. 40 mg of methylprednisolone acetate, injection

Code _____

12. Chemotherapy administration by push

Code _____

13. Surgical boot, left foot

Code _____

3. In your own words, how can you help to code medical services and procedures ethically?

_____

_____

_____

_____

_____

REVIEW QUESTIONS

MATCHING

Choose the correct answer and write its corresponding letter in the space provided.

a. progress note
b. clean claim
c. fraud
d. Federal Civil False Claims Act
e. abuse

1. _____ Intentional deception when submitting or coding claims

2. _____ Updates the patient's clinical course of treatment and summarizes the assessment and plan of care

3. _____ An action that misuses the money that the government has allocated, such as Medicare funds

4. _____ A claim without errors that displays proper code linkage

5. _____ Prohibits making fraudulent statements or representation in connection with a claim and outlines liability of these fraudulent acts

MULTIPLE CHOICE

Circle the letter of each choice that best completes the statement or answers the question.

1. Which of the following is a type of law that can prohibit a physician from practicing as a provider to government health programs?
   a. Civil
   b. Criminal
   c. Administrative
   d. None of the above

2. Which of the following is a type of law that requires that an individual found guilty be subject to serving a jail sentence?
   a. Civil
   b. Criminal
   c. Administrative
   d. None of the above

3. Which of the following is a type of law that requires that monies be awarded and fines ordered if an individual is found guilty?
   a. Civil
   b. Criminal
   c. Administrative
   d. None of the above

4. Which of the following does the Stark law govern?
   a. Compliance plans
   b. Fraud and abuse
   c. Physician self-referral
   d. All of the above

5. Which of the following is *not* a benefit of having a voluntary compliance program?
   a. Reducing the chances of an external audit
   b. Avoiding conflicts with the self-referral and antikickbacks statutes
   c. Speeding and optimizing proper payment of claims
   d. All of the above are benefits of having a voluntary compliance program.

SHORT ANSWER

Provide the correct response to each question that follows.

1. What are seven consequences of inaccurate coding and incorrect billing?
   1. _____
   2. _____
   3. _____
   4. _____
   5. _____
   6. _____
   7. _____

© 2018 Pearson Education, Inc.

2. What five questions can you ask yourself to ensure that a claim is "clean" for submittal?

    1. _____

    2. _____

    3. _____

    4. _____

    5. _____

3. What are HCPCS codes that begin with J usually used for?

    _____

    _____

4. What program was created by HIPAA to uncover fraud and abuse in Medicare and Medicaid programs?

    _____

    _____

5. What are the four parts of government that investigate and prosecute suspected medical fraud and abuse under the HIPAA program described in question #4?

    1. _____

    2. _____

    3. _____

    4. _____

TRUE/FALSE

Identify each statement as true (T) or false (F).

1. _____ If a physician has poor documentation, this opens up the clinic to issues with fraud and abuse.

2. _____ It doesn't matter in what order procedure codes are listed on the CMS-1500 claim form, as long as the claim includes every procedure rendered.

3. _____ To encourage whistleblowing of suspected fraud and abuse against the government, the reporting persons involved can be offered protection and rewards.

4. _____ Occasional billing and coding errors can be interpreted as possible fraud.

5. _____ If a physician claims that he/she didn't know about billing and coding guidelines, then he/she will not be held liable for errors.

CHAPTER 9

Auditing

CHAPTER OBJECTIVES

After reading this chapter, the student should be able to:

1. Understand and know how to implement a coding audit.
2. Be able to review and analyze medical records.
3. Know how to use an audit tool.
4. Recognize the content and documentation requirements.
5. Demonstrate the ability to review for coding accuracy.

CHAPTER OUTLINE

Purpose of an Audit

Types of Audits
  External Audit
  Internal Audit
  Accreditation Audits

Private Payer Regulations

Medical Necessity for E/M Services

Audit Tool

Key Elements of Service
  History
  Examination
  Medical Decision Making

Tips for Preventing Coding Errors with Specific E/M Codes

KEY TERMS

Using the highlighted terms and glossary in the textbook, define the following terms:

1. audit _____

   _____

2. code edits _____

   _____

3. downcode _____

   _____

© 2018 Pearson Education, Inc.

4. external audit _____

_____

5. internal audit _____

_____

6. Patient Protection and Affordable Care Act (PPACA) _____

_____

7. prospective audit _____

_____

8. retrospective audit _____

_____

9. upcode _____

_____

CRITICAL THINKING QUESTIONS

Using the knowledge you have gained from reading the textbook, apply critical thinking skills to answer the following questions:

1. Answer the following questions related to medical audits:

   a. In your own words, what is the main purpose of an audit?

   _____

   _____

   _____

   _____

   _____

   b. Why should a medical office perform an internal audit?

   _____

   _____

   _____

   _____

   c. Medicare has scheduled an audit with your medical practice. What will the auditor check during the audit?

   _____

   _____

   _____

   _____

© 2018 Pearson Education, Inc.

2. What is the medical necessity for the E/M codes based on?

_____

_____

_____

_____

3. a. Read the following scenarios, and determine which type of HPI is being conducted in each one:

   1. A patient is seen for asthma, chronic bronchitis, and chronic sinusitis. The patient complains of facial pain for three days now. He has been coughing up greenish-brown mucus. He denies any chest tightness or wheezing.

   _____

   2. A patient presents in the office with complaints of watering, redness, and pain in her left eye that started this morning.

   _____

b. Read the following scenarios and determine which type of ROS is being conducted in each one:

   1. A patient is seen for asthma, chronic bronchitis, and chronic sinusitis. The patient complains of facial pain for three days now. He has been coughing up greenish-brown mucus. He denies any chest tightness or wheezing. The Physician examines the ears, nose, and throat. TMs are clear. The nose is red and swollen. The throat shows postnasal drip. On A&P, the chest presents with congestion. No wheezing or rub is heard. Bowels sounds are normal. Skin shows no clubbing, cyanosis, or breaks.

   _____

   2. A patient is seen for a follow-up on congestive heart failure (CHF), hypertension (HTN), and hypothyroidism. She has no complaints at this time. Vitals are stable. BP: 132/70, P: 82, R: 14. HEENT: Normocephalic, atraumatic. Eyes are clear. Pupils are equal, round, and reactive to light. TMs are clear. Oropharynx is clear. Back exam is negative. Chest is negative for wheezes, rubs, or rhonchi. CARDIOVASCULAR: S1, S2 present with normal rhythm and rate. GI: Bowel sounds normal. No visceromegaly, nausea, vomiting, diarrhea, or constipation. Abdomen is soft, nontender. GU: No urinary retention is noted. HEMIC/LYMPHATIC: No lymphadenopathy. MS: No pain or injuries. EXTREMITIES: No bruising or clubbing. Pedal pulses normal. No pitting edema present. SKIN: No lesions or rashes. NEUROLOGIC: Patient is oriented × 3. PSYCHIATRIC: Mood and affect is upbeat and pleasant.

   _____

c. Read the following scenario and determine which type of PFSH is being conducted:

   1. Patient has no known drug allergies (KNDA). He is a nonsmoker. He drinks two to three glasses of wine a month. Patient lives with his wife. He has no children. His mother is alive and well. She has DM II. Father's health is unknown. He has one sibling that also has DM II. He has had no operations. He was hospitalized at age 21 with cellulitis as a result of an infected tattoo on his right calf.

   _____

d. Refer back to question #3 in b 2. What type of exam is being performed on this patient?

   _____

4. Answer the following questions related to proper documentation for the selection of a correct E/M code under auditing compliance:

   a. You are reviewing the physician's documentation for a patient's ROS. The physician has written that the patient's blood count is abnormal. There is no other specific data entered concerning the abnormal blood count. Is this acceptable documentation? Why or why not?

   _____

   _____

   _____

   _____

   b. A physician does not examine the patient's abdomen, but documents that the exam is normal. Is this acceptable documentation? Why or why not?

   _____

   _____

   _____

   _____

   c. A physician documents EENT as negative, but did not review the eyes. Is this acceptable? Why or why not?

   _____

   _____

   _____

   _____

   d. A physician has documented that a patient's cardiovascular system is "unremarkable." Is this acceptable documentation? Why or why not?

   _____

   _____

   _____

   _____

5. Answer the following questions related to medical decision making (MDM) in selection of a proper E/M code:

   a. How can the number and type of diagnosed tests performed help the coder to select the proper MDM?

   _____

   _____

   b. What information must be included for a physician to properly document the number of diagnoses and/or treatment options for a patient?

   1. _____

   2. _____

   3. _____

   4. _____

© 2018 Pearson Education, Inc.

c. What information needs to be included for a physician to properly document the amount and/or complexity of data reviewed?

1. _____
2. _____
3. _____
4. _____
5. _____
6. _____

d. What types of health risks to a patient are taken into consideration by physicians when selecting the correct E/M code?

1. _____
2. _____
3. _____

PRACTICE EXERCISES

1. From Chapter 9 in your text, read the scenarios described next and identify what type of coding error has occurred. Write your answer in the space provided.

   a. A physician sees a patient in the ER for an ear infection. The E/M code used is 99285.

   _____

   b. A physician bills for reviewing x-rays with the patient, but does not document this in the chart.

   _____

   c. A new patient is seen for abdominal pain; only one key component is documented.

   _____

   d. An established patient is seen for chest pain and has several issues; all five key components are documented.

   _____

   e. The attending physician sees a patient for an initial inpatient visit. The RN has already documented the HPI. The physician documents only the diagnoses and treatment plans.

   _____

   f. A physician codes for critical care for a patient. The chart does not indicate any direct personal management or frequent personal assessment and manipulation.

   _____

   g. A neurologist submits a code for an inpatient consultation. There is no clear order in this patient's chart. The coding specialist codes for the consultation.

   _____

2. What two steps should be taken to prepare for an internal audit?

   1. _____
   2. _____

3. Using the audit tools and tables provided in Chapter 9 of your text, read the following scenarios and identify the correct E/M code for each:

a. A patient is seen for the first time by her family physician, complaining of a shooting left-leg pain that starts in her lumbar spine and travels down to her toes. This started about a month ago and occurs every couple of days. She says that it lasts for almost the whole day. She has a family history of heart disease. She denies smoking, taking drugs, and alcohol use. She does work as a relay operator for BU&U. Her job requires her to sit for long periods of time. ROS reveals associated pain with palpation on her left lumbar region. The rest of the musculoskeletal system is negative for pain, edema, or ROM limitations. The cardiovascular system shows no signs of bruit, heart murmur, or circulatory problems. Pedal pulses X 3. BP: 118/72, P: 80. She denies headaches. No blurred vision. Skin intact without clubbing, cyanosis, or rash. GI: No distention, heartburn, or diarrhea. Abdomen is soft to palpation and nontender. Patient is pleasant, alert, and oriented X 3. The severity and location of the pain can lead to impairment if not treated immediately. Diagnosis of sciatica. Patient to start Medrol Dose Pak, have x-ray of lumbar spine and left leg, upper. Patient to return in 1 week to assess the nature of physical therapy versus surgery. If the x-rays are negative, she will be sent for an MRI of the lumbar spine.

   1. Is this patient being seen as an inpatient or outpatient?

   _____

   2. Is this patient new or established?

   _____

   3. What is the proper E/M code?

   _____

b. A patient is seeing his PCP for a cough and scratchy throat that started 3 days ago. He also admits to sneezing more often than usual. The patient is a smoker: Two packs a day × 6 years. He has no past history of allergies. On review, HEENT shows watery, red eyes, inflammation in the nasal mucosa, and a reddened throat. Head and ears are unremarkable to exam. There is noted postnasal drainage. Chest is clear to auscultation and percussion. Diagnosis is acute sinusitis with allergic rhinitis. He is prescribed amoxicillin and Nasonex. Patient is to use Claritin OTC. He is to return to the office if his seasonal allergies persist.

   1. Is this patient being seen as an inpatient or outpatient?

   _____

   2. Is this patient new or established?

   _____

   3. What is the proper E/M code?

   _____

c. A patient is being seen for the second day of her hospital course for CHF. She has a history of malignant hypertension that has affected her kidney function in the past. She has never smoked and doesn't drink. She denies any increased salt intake before this episode. ROS is consistent with HPI and past history. Kidneys show worsened state than yesterday, and the thoracentesis will have to be postponed until the patient's kidney function is stable.

   1. Is this patient being seen as an inpatient or outpatient?

   _____

   2. Is this initial or subsequent care?

   _____

   3. What is the proper E/M code?

   _____

    © 2018 Pearson Education, Inc.

d. A patient is being seen today by the dermatologist, per her PCP. This patient presents with complaints of adult cystic acne that keeps getting worse as he ages. It started when he was 19 years old. He has tried OTC products and prescription medication, without relief. He is here to discuss his options. He denies any family members with cystic acne. On exam, there is cystic acne noted on the face, shoulders, and back. He was here last month and started on oral and topical antibiotics. Since then, there has been no improvement. His face appears dry and cracked. The option of using Accutane for the treatment of his acne was discussed. He is given the information and is told to read it thoroughly. He will need to obtain fasting labs before and during treatment to assess any liver, sugar, or circulatory problems. He is to call the office with any questions before his next appointment in a week. He will need to sign all consenting papers and return them at this appointment. He understands the treatment, side effects, and possible adverse reactions, including suicidal tendencies. If the labs present as normal and he consents to this treatment, we will proceed with the prescription and regimen.

1. Is this patient being seen as an inpatient or outpatient?

_____

2. What type of encounter is this?

_____

3. What is the proper E/M code?

_____

REVIEW QUESTIONS

MATCHING

Choose the correct answer and write its corresponding letter in the space provided.

a. HPI
b. PFSH
c. ROS
d. organ systems
e. chief complaint

1. _____ Elements that include operations, hospitalizations, and personal health
2. _____ Elements that include eyes, ears, nose, throat, skin, and psychiatric
3. _____ An inventory of body systems obtained by a series of questions
4. _____ Elements that include the patient's current health problem in the patient's own words
5. _____ Elements that include timing, duration, location, severity, and context

MULTIPLE CHOICE

Circle the letter of the choice that best completes the statement or answers the question.

1. Who would normally perform an internal audit?
   a. Outside agency
   b. Consultant
   c. Employee
   d. Both b and c

2. Which types of CPT codes are audited the most?
   a. Surgery
   b. Radiology
   c. E/M
   d. Medicine

3. The first step in determining an E/M code is to
   a. count all diagnoses.
   b. determine whether the patient is new or established.
   c. determine whether the encounter involves a complete ROS.
   d. Both a and c

4. Which of the following questions alerts the coder *not* to code as a consultation?
   a. Has the provider provided a written report of opinion/advice to the referring physician?
   b. Was a request for an opinion from another physician received?
   c. Will the provider's opinion be used by and affect the requesting physician's own management of the patient?
   d. All of the above.

5. Which of the following qualifies for coding critical care services?
   a. There is a lack of documented work.
   b. The physician consulted the surrogate decision-making family member.
   c. The specific time spent is not recorded.
   d. Time spent performing procedures is included.

SHORT ANSWER

Provide the correct response to each question that follows.

1. What are two ways an audit can be performed? _____
   1. _____
   2. _____

2. What are the two main ways that medical necessity of E/M services is generally expressed?
   1. _____
   2. _____

3. If the OIG finds an auditing problem in a certain area, what will be the result?
   _____

4. When is time considered the key factor to assigning a proper E/M code?
   _____

5. What are the 15 top coding and documentation errors?
   1. _____
   2. _____
   3. _____
   4. _____
   5. _____
   6. _____
   7. _____
   8. _____

© 2018 Pearson Education, Inc.

9. _____

10. _____

11. _____

12. _____

13. _____

14. _____

15. _____

TRUE/FALSE

Identify each statement as true (T) or false (F).

1. _____ The auditor should check to see that the physician properly documents and compare with code assignment.

2. _____ Even though most third-party payers may have their own rules for submitting a clean claim, most states do not require third-party payers to give a reason for a denied claim.

3. _____ A physician can perform both a multi-system and a single-organ exam during one encounter.

4. _____ An audit tool can be used for internal audits, as well as external audits.

5. _____ Auditing software will always match all third-party payers' policies for a clean claim.

© 2018 Pearson Education, Inc.

CHAPTER 10
Physician Medical Billing

CHAPTER OBJECTIVES

After reading this chapter, the student should be able to:

1. Differentiate and complete medical claim forms accurately, both manually and electronically.
2. Define claim form parts, sections, and required information.
3. Exhibit the ability to complete claim forms without omitting information.
4. Understand the common reasons why claim forms are delayed or rejected, and submit a claim without payer rejection.
5. File a secondary claim.

CHAPTER OUTLINE

Conversion to Electronic Health Records

Patient Information

Superbills

Types of Insurance Claims: Paper vs. Electronic

Optical Character Recognition

CMS-1500 Provider Billing Claim Form

Completing the CMS-1500 Claim Form

Form Locators for the CMS-1500 Form

Physicians' Identification Numbers
  Practice Exercises

Common Reasons for Delayed or Rejected CMS-1500 Claim Forms

HIPAA Compliance Alert

Filing Secondary Claims
  Determining Primary Coverage
  Practice Exercises

KEY TERMS

Using the highlighted terms and glossary in the textbook, define the following terms:

1. assignment of benefits form _____

_____

2. audit/edit report _____

_____

3. billing services _____

_____

4. birthday rule _____

_____

5. claim attachment _____

_____

6. clean claims _____

_____

7. clearinghouse _____

_____

8. CMS-1500 claim form _____

_____

9. coordination of benefits (COB) _____

_____

10. dirty claim _____

_____

11. electronic claims, electronic media claims (EMCs) _____

_____

12. employer identification number (EIN) _____

_____

13. encryption _____

_____

14. facility provider number (FPN) _____

_____

15. form locators _____

_____

16. group provider number (GPN) _____

_____

17. guarantor _____

_____

18. optical character recognition (OCR) _____

_____

19. patient information form _____

_____

20. provider identification number (PIN) _____

_____

© 2018 Pearson Education, Inc.

21. release of information form _____

22. secondary insurance _____

23. state license number _____

24. superbills _____

25. supplemental insurance _____

26. tax identification number (TIN) _____

27. UB-04 claim form _____

28. verification of benefits (VOB) form _____

CRITICAL THINKING QUESTIONS

Using the knowledge you have gained from reading the textbook, apply critical thinking skills to answer the following questions.

1. Answer the following questions related to verification of a patient's insurance benefits:

   a. By what three steps can verifying insurance benefits for a patient be accomplished?

      1. _____
      2. _____
      3. _____

   b. Charles Bingham, Jr., is a new patient with your office. What nine pertinent pieces of information do you need when verifying his insurance benefits?

      1. _____
      2. _____
      3. _____
      4. _____
      5. _____
      6. _____
      7. _____
      8. _____
      9. _____

© 2018 Pearson Education, Inc.

c. Now that you have gathered all nine pieces of pertinent information to verify Mr. Bingham's insurance benefits, what are the standard questions that you ask his insurance carrier for this verification?

    1. _____

    2. _____

    3. _____

    4. _____

    5. _____

    6. _____

    7. _____

    8. _____

2. What is the superbill, and how is it used for billing?

    1. _____

    2. _____

    3. _____

3. Answer the following questions related to medical claim forms:

a. What claim form does the following type of provider use for reimbursement?

    1. Physicians _____

    2. Hospitals _____

b. List the three advantages of electronic claim forms.

    1. _____

    2. _____

    3. _____

    _____

    _____

    _____

c. What do you do if an insurance carrier requires additional information for an electronic claim?

    _____

    _____

    _____

d. What are the three advantages of an electronic claim?

    1. _____

    2. _____

    3. _____

e. What are the four disadvantages of an electronic claim?

    1. _____

    2. _____

    3. _____

    4. _____

f. What are two advantages of OCR devices?

    1. _____

    2. _____

© 2018 Pearson Education, Inc.

4. a. What is the purpose of the HIPAA security standard rules?

_____

_____

_____

_____

b. Work together in a small group to list the six ways that your office complies with the HIPAA security standard rules. Discuss your answers with the class.

1. _____

2. _____

3. _____

4. _____

5. _____

6. _____

c. What could be the result of breaching a patient's confidentiality?

_____

_____

_____

_____

5. a. Read the following scenarios and determine which insurance policy is the primary insurance:

1. Sara Lind has both Medicare and Blue Cross/Blue Shield insurance. She is retired, but is covered under her husband's Blue Cross/Blue Shield plan. Mr. Lind works for the postal service. Which insurance will be her primary insurance?

_____

2. Miranda Lee has two insurance policies under which she is the primary policyholder for both. Which insurance will be her primary insurance?

_____

3. Benjamin Nadzam has two insurance policies. He is the policyholder of his Aetna plan, but he is also covered as a dependent under his father's Health America plan. Which insurance will be his primary insurance?

_____

4. Nolan Espinosa has health insurance coverage through his employer's Blue Cross/Blue Shield plan. He is also covered through Medicare. Which insurance will be his primary insurance?

_____

5. Cheyenne Yanul has insurance through both of her parents. Her parents are still married. Which insurance will be her primary insurance?

_____

6. If Cheyenne's parents are divorced and do not share joint custody of Cheyenne, how can her primary insurance plan be determined?

_____

_____

_____

b. How would you submit a secondary claim?

_____

_____

_____

PRACTICE EXERCISES

1. Using the form locator information supplied in your textbook, write each form locator's directions for the CMS-1500 on an index card. Flag each form locator for easy referencing.

2. Define the following CMS-1500 abbreviations:

   1. CCYY _____

   2. CLIA _____

   3. CMS _____

   4. CPT _____

   5. DD _____

   6. EIN _____

   7. EMG _____

   8. ICD-10-CM _____

   9. ID _____

   10. INFO _____

   11. M _____

   12. MM _____

   13. TRICARE/CHAMPUS _____

3. The case studies that follow are provided for additional practice in completing the CMS-1500 claim form for physician outpatient billing. By applying what you have learned in your student text, you are to accurately code and complete each case study. Patient demographics and a brief case history are provided. Complete the cases on the basis of the following criteria:

   - All patients have release of information and assignment of benefit signatures on file.

   - All providers are participating and accept assignment by contractual agreement. Item 27 is not marked.

   - The group practice is the billing entity.

   - The national transition to NPI numbers is complete, and legacy PINs of individual payers are no longer used. If legacy PINs are still being used by selected payers in your region, your instructor may provide legacy PINS in addition to the NPI.

   - 2017 ICD-10-CM and CPT codes are used.

   - Use eight-digit dates for birthdates. Use six-digit dates for all other dates.

   - All street names should be entered with standard postal abbreviations, even if they are spelled out on the source documents.

   - Enter ICD-10 codes in the order in which they appear on the encounter form.

   - When entering CPT codes, enter the E/M code first. Enter remaining codes in descending price order.

To determine the correct fees, refer to the Capital City Medical Fee Schedule, a copy of which is located after each case's source documents. Use the blank CMS-1500 form provided after each case.

   a. Using the given source documents, the Capital City Medical Fee Schedule (Figure 10-1), and the blank CMS-1500 form provided (Figure 10-2), complete the following case study for patient Hayden Montana (Case 10-1):

© 2018 Pearson Education, Inc.

CASE 10-1

Capital City Medical—123 Unknown Boulevard, Capital City, NY 12345-2222 (555) 555-1234

Phil Wells, MD, Mannie Mends, MD, Bette R. Soone, MD

Patient Information Form

Tax ID: 75-0246810

Group NPI: 1513171216

Patient Information:

Name: (Last, First) Montana, Hayden ☐ Male ☒ Female Birth Date: 06/26/2010

Address: 60 Grove St. Capital City, NY 12345 Phone: (555) 555-1253

Social Security Number: 346-82-3077 Full-Time Student: ☐ Yes ☒ No

Marital Status: ☒ Single ☐ Married ☐ Divorced ☐ Other

- -

Employment:

Employer: N/A Phone: ( )

Address:

Condition Related to: ☐ Auto Accident ☐ Employment ☐ Other Accident

Date of Accident: State:

Emergency Contact: Phone: ( )

- -

Primary Insurance: Blue Cross Blue Shield Phone: ( )

Address: 379 Blue Plaza, Capital City, NY 12345

Insurance Policyholder's Name: Jordan Montana ☒ M ☐ F DOB: 05/12/1979

Address: Same

Phone: ( ) Relationship to Insured: ☐ Self ☐ Spouse ☒ Child ☐ Other

Employer: Capital City Police Department Phone: (555) 555-0911

Employer's Address: 3055 Samaritan Blvd, Capital City, NY 12345

Policy/ID No: YYZ401333213 Group No: 064835 Percent Covered: ___% Copay Amt: $25.00

- -

Secondary Insurance: Aetna Phone: ( )

Address: 1625 Healthcare Bldg, Capital City, NY 12345

Insurance Policyholder's Name: Riley Montana ☐ M ☒ F DOB: 08/19/1979

Address: Same

Phone: ( ) Relationship to Insured: ☐ Self ☐ Spouse ☒ Child ☐ Other

Employer: The Daily Globe Co. Phone: (555) 555-5757

Employer's Address: 19 W. Eastern Rd, Capital City, NY 12345

Policy/ID No: 32059138 Group No: 3132 Percent Covered: 80 % Copay Amt: $

Reason for Visit: Rash and fever

Known Allergies:

Referred by:

CASE 10-1
SOAP

02/11/20XX
Assignment of Benefits: Y
Signature on File: Y
Referring Physician: N

S: Hayden Montana presents in the office with her mother today for complaints of a fever and a rash.

O: The rash appeared two days ago and seems to be getting worse. She does have a temperature of 101.8°F. There is no vomiting at this time.

A: 1. Measles–B05.9

P: 1. Liquid diet and plenty of rest.
2. Children's Tylenol.
3. Go to ER if temperature elevates.
4. Home from school until next appointment.
5. Return in 7 days.

_____

Phil Wells, MD
Family Practice
NPI: 1234567890

© 2018 Pearson Education, Inc.

CASE 10-1

Patient Name Hayden Montana

Capital City Medical
123 Unknown Boulevard, Capital City, NY 12345-2222

Date of Service 02-11-20XX

New Patient			Arthrocentesis/Aspiration/Injection			Laboratory	
Problem Focused	99201		Small Joint		20600	Amylase	82150
Expanded Problem, Focused	99202		Interm Joint		20605	B12	82607
Detailed	99203		Major Joint		20610	CBC & Diff	85025
Comprehensive	99204		**Other Invasive/Noninvasive**			Comp Metabolic Panel	80053
Comprehensive/High Complex	99205		Audiometry		92552	Chlamydia Screen	87110
Well Exam Infant (up to 12 mos.)	99381		Cast Application			Cholesterol	82465
Well Exam 1–4 yrs.	99382		Location Long Short			Digoxin	80162
Well Exam 5–11 yrs.	99383		Catheterization		51701	Electrolytes	80051
Well Exam 12–17 yrs.	99384		Circumcision		54150	Ferritin	82728
Well Exam 18–39 yrs.	99385		Colposcopy		57452	Folate	82746
Well Exam 40–64 yrs.	99386		Colposcopy w/Biopsy		57454	GC Screen	87070
			Cryosurgery Premalignant Lesion			Glucose	82947
			Location (s):			Glucose 1 HR	82950
						Glycosylated HGB A1C	83036
Established Patient			Cryosurgery Warts			HCT	85014
Post-Op Follow Up Visit	99024		Location (s):			HDL	83718
Minimum	99211		Curettement Lesion			Hep BSAG	87340
Problem Focused	99212	X	Single		11055	Hepatitis panel, acute	80074
Expanded Problem Focused	99213		2–4		11056	HGB	85018
Detailed	99214		>4		11057	HIV	86703
Comprehensive/High Complex	99215		Diaphragm Fitting		57170	Iron & TIBC	83550
Well Exam Infant (up to 12 mos.)	99391		Ear Irrigation		69210	Kidney Profile	80069
Well exam 1–4 yrs.	99392		ECG		93000	Lead	83655
Well Exam 5–11 yrs.	99393		Endometrial Biopsy		58100	Liver Profile	80076
Well Exam 12–17 yrs.	99394		Exc. Lesion Malignant			Mono Test	86308
Well Exam 18–39 yrs.	99395		Benign			Pap Smear	88155
Well Exam 40–64 yrs.	99396		Location			Pregnancy Test	84703
Obstetrics			Exc. Skin Tags (1–15)		11200	Obstetric Panel	80055
Total OB Care	59400		Each Additional 10		11201	Pro Time	85610
Injections			Fracture Treatment			PSA	84153
Administration Sub. / IM	90772		Loc			RPR	86592
Drug			w/Reduc w/o Reduc			Sed. Rate	85651
Dosage			I & D Abscess Single/Simple		10060	Stool Culture	87045
Allergy	95115		Multiple or Comp		10061	Stool O & P	87177
Cocci Skin Test	86490		I & D Pilonidal Cyst Simple		10080	Strep Screen	87880
DPT	90701		Pilonidal Cyst Complex		10081	Theophylline	80198
Hemophilus	90646		IV Therapy—To One Hour		90760	Thyroid Uptake	84479
Influenza	90658		Each Additional Hour		90761	TSH	84443
MMR	90707		Laceration Repair			Urinalysis	81000
OPV	90712		Location Size Simp/Comp			Urine Culture	87088
Pneumovax	90732		Laryngoscopy		31505	Drawing Fee	36415
TB Skin Test	86580		Oximetry		94760	Specimen Collection	99000
TD	90718		Punch Biopsy			**Other:**	
Unlisted Immun	90749		Rhythm Strip		93040		
Tetanus Toxoid	90703		Treadmill		93015		
Vaccine/Toxoid Admin <8 Yr Old w/ Counseling	90465		Trigger Point or Tendon Sheath Inj.		20550		
Vaccine/Toxoid Administration for Adult	90471		Tympanometry		92567		

Diagnosis/ICD-10: **B05.9**

I acknowledge receipt of medical services and authorize the release of any medical information necessary to process this claim for healthcare payment only. I do authorize payment to the provider.

Patient Signature _Jordan Montana_

Total Estimated Charges: _____

Payment Amount: _____

Next Appointment: _____

Figure 10-1

Capital City Medical
Fee Schedule

New Patient OV		Punch Biopsy various codes	$80
Problem Focused 99201	$45	Nebulizer various codes	$45
Expanded Problem Focused 99202	$65	Cast Application various codes	$85
Detailed 99203	$85	Laryngoscopy 31505	$255
Comprehensive 99204	$105	Audiometry 92552	$85
Comprehensive/High Complex 99205	$115	Tympanometry 92567	$85
Well Exam infant (less than 1 year) 99381	$45	Ear Irrigation 69210	$25
Well Exam 1–4 yrs. 99382	$50	Diaphragm Fitting 57170	$30
Well Exam 5–11 yrs. 99383	$55	IV Therapy (up to one hour) 90760	$65
Well Exam 12–17 yrs. 99384	$65	Each additional hour 90761	$50
Well Exam 18–39 yrs. 99385	$85	Oximetry 94760	$10
Well Exam 40–64 yrs. 99386	$105	ECG 93000	$75
Established Patient OV		Holter Monitor various codes	$170
Post Op Follow Up Visit 99024	$0	Rhythm Strip 93040	$60
Minimum 99211	$35	Treadmill 93015	$375
Problem Focused 99212	$45	Cocci Skin Test 86490	$20
Expanded Problem Focused 99213	$55	X-ray, spine, chest, bone—any area various codes	$275
Detailed 99214	$65	Avulsion Nail 11730	$200
Comprehensive/High Complex 99215	$75	**Laboratory**	
Well exam infant (less than 1 year) 99391	$35	Amylase 82150	$40
Well Exam 1–4 yrs. 99392	$40	B12 82607	$30
Well Exam 5–11 yrs. 99393	$45	CBC & Diff 85025	$95
Well Exam 12–17 yrs. 99394	$55	Comp Metabolic Panel 80053	$75
Well Exam 18–39 yrs. 99395	$65	Chlamydia Screen 87110	$70
Well Exam 40–64 yrs. 99396	$75	Cholestrerol 82465	$75
Obstetrics		Digoxin 80162	$40
Total OB Care 59400	$1700	Electrolytes 80051	$70
Injections		Estrogen, Total 82672	$50
Administration 90772	$10	Ferritin 82728	$40
Allergy 95115	$35	Folate 82746	$30
DPT 90701	$50	GC Screen 87070	$60
Drug various codes	$35	Glucose 82947	$35
Influenza 90658	$25	Glycosylated HGB A1C 83036	$45
MMR 90707	$50	HCT 85014	$30
OPV 90712	$40	HDL 83718	$35
Pneumovax 90732	$35	HGB 85018	$30
TB Skin Test 86580	$15	Hep BSAG 83740	$40
TD 90718	$40	Hepatitis panel, acute 80074	$95
Tetanus Toxoid 90703	$40	HIV 86703	$100
Vaccine/Toxoid Administration for Younger Than 8 Years Old w/ counseling 90465	$10	Iron & TIBC 83550	$45
		Kidney Profile 80069	$95
Vaccine/Toxoid Administration for Adult 90471	$10	Lead 83665	$55
Arthrocentesis/Aspiration/Injection		Lipase 83690	$40
Small Joint 20600	$50	Lipid Panel 80061	$95
Interm Joint 20605	$60	Liver Profile 80076	$95
Major Joint 20610	$70	Mono Test 86308	$30
Trigger Point/Tendon Sheath Inj. 20550	$90	Pap Smear 88155	$90
Other Invasive/Noninvasive Procedures		Pap Collection/Supervision 88142	$95
Catheterization 51701	$55	Pregnancy Test 84703	$90
Circumcision 54150	$150	Obstetric Panel 80055	$85
Colposcopy 57452	$225	Pro Time 85610	$50
Colposcopy w/Biopsy 57454	$250	PSA 84153	$50
Cryosurgery Premalignant Lesion various codes	$160	RPR 86592	$55
Endometrial Biopsy 58100	$190	Sed. Rate 85651	$50
Excision Lesion Malignant various codes	$145	Stool Culture 87045	$80
Excision Lesion Benign various codes	$125	Stool O & P 87177	$105
Curettement Lesion		Strep Screen 87880	$35
Single 11055	$70	Theophylline 80198	$40
2–4 11056	$80	Thyroid Uptake 84479	$75
>4 11057	$90	TSH 84443	$50
Excision Skin Tags (1–15) 11200	$55	Urinalysis 81000	$35
Each Additional 10 11201	$30	Urine Culture 87088	$80
I & D Abscess Single/Simple 10060	$75	Drawing Fee 36415	$15
Multiple/Complex 10061	$95	Specimen Collection 99000	$10
I & D Pilonidal Cyst Simple 10080	$105		
I & D Pilonidal Cyst Complex 10081	$130		
Laceration Repair various codes	$60		

HEALTH INSURANCE CLAIM FORM

APPROVED BY NATIONAL UNIFORM CLAIM COMMITTEE (NUCC) 02/12

CARRIER

| | | | | PICA | | | | | | PICA | |

| 1. MEDICARE | MEDICAID | TRICARE | CHAMPVA | GROUP HEALTH PLAN | FECA BLK LUNG | OTHER | 1a. INSURED'S I.D. NUMBER | | (For Program in Item 1) |
| [X] (Medicare#) | [ ] (Medicaid#) | [ ] (ID#/DoD#) | [ ] (Member ID#) | [ ] (ID#) | [ ] (ID#) | [ ] (ID#) | | | |

| 2. PATIENT'S NAME (Last Name, First Name, Middle Initial) | 3. PATIENT'S BIRTH DATE | SEX | 4. INSURED'S NAME (Last Name, First Name, Middle Initial) |
| | MM DD YY | M [ ] F [ ] | |

5. PATIENT'S ADDRESS (No., Street)

6. PATIENT RELATIONSHIP TO INSURED Self [ ] Spouse [ ] Child [ ] Other [ ]

7. INSURED'S ADDRESS (No., Street)

CITY ____ STATE ____ 8. RESERVED FOR NUCC USE CITY ____ STATE ____

ZIP CODE ____ TELEPHONE (Include Area Code) ( ) ZIP CODE ____ TELEPHONE (Include Area Code) ( )

9. OTHER INSURED'S NAME (Last Name, First Name, Middle Initial)

10. IS PATIENT'S CONDITION RELATED TO:

11. INSURED'S POLICY GROUP OR FECA NUMBER

a. OTHER INSURED'S POLICY OR GROUP NUMBER

a. EMPLOYMENT? (Current or Previous) YES [ ] NO [ ]

a. INSURED'S DATE OF BIRTH MM DD YY SEX M [ ] F [ ]

b. RESERVED FOR NUCC USE

b. AUTO ACCIDENT? PLACE (State) YES [ ] NO [ ]

b. OTHER CLAIM ID (Designated by NUCC)

c. RESERVED FOR NUCC USE

c. OTHER ACCIDENT? YES [ ] NO [ ]

c. INSURANCE PLAN NAME OR PROGRAM NAME

d. INSURANCE PLAN NAME OR PROGRAM NAME

10d. CLAIM CODES (Designated by NUCC)

d. IS THERE ANOTHER HEALTH BENEFIT PLAN? YES [ ] NO [ ] If yes, complete items 9, 9a, and 9d.

READ BACK OF FORM BEFORE COMPLETING & SIGNING THIS FORM.

12. PATIENT'S OR AUTHORIZED PERSON'S SIGNATURE I authorize the release of any medical or other information necessary to process this claim. I also request payment of government benefits either to myself or to the party who accepts assignment below.

SIGNED _____ DATE _____

13. INSURED'S OR AUTHORIZED PERSON'S SIGNATURE I authorize payment of medical benefits to the undersigned physician or supplier for services described below.

SIGNED _____

PATIENT AND INSURED INFORMATION

14. DATE OF CURRENT ILLNESS, INJURY, or PREGNANCY (LMP) MM DD YY QUAL.

15. OTHER DATE QUAL. MM DD YY

16. DATES PATIENT UNABLE TO WORK IN CURRENT OCCUPATION MM DD YY FROM ____ TO ____ MM DD YY

17. NAME OF REFERRING PROVIDER OR OTHER SOURCE 17a. ____ 17b. NPI ____

18. HOSPITALIZATION DATES RELATED TO CURRENT SERVICES MM DD YY FROM ____ TO ____ MM DD YY

19. ADDITIONAL CLAIM INFORMATION (Designated by NUCC)

20. OUTSIDE LAB? YES [ ] NO [ ] $ CHARGES

21. DIAGNOSIS OR NATURE OF ILLNESS OR INJURY Relate A-L to service line below (24E) ICD Ind. ____

A. ____ B. ____ C. ____ D. ____
E. ____ F. ____ G. ____ H. ____
I. ____ J. ____ K. ____ L. ____

22. RESUBMISSION CODE ____ ORIGINAL REF. NO. ____

23. PRIOR AUTHORIZATION NUMBER

24. A. DATE(S) OF SERVICE					B. PLACE OF SERVICE	C. EMG	D. PROCEDURES, SERVICES, OR SUPPLIES (Explain Unusual Circumstances)		E. DIAGNOSIS POINTER	F. $ CHARGES	G. DAYS OR UNITS	H. EPSDT Family Plan	I. ID. QUAL	J. RENDERING PROVIDER ID. #
From			To					CPT/HCPCS	MODIFIER						
MM	DD	YY	MM	DD	YY										
1															NPI
2															NPI
3															NPI
4															NPI
5															NPI
6															NPI

| 25. FEDERAL TAX I.D. NUMBER SSN [ ] EIN [ ] | 26. PATIENT'S ACCOUNT NO. | 27. ACCEPT ASSIGNMENT? (For govt. claims, see back) YES [ ] NO [ ] | 28. TOTAL CHARGE $ | 29. AMOUNT PAID $ | 30. Rsvd. for NUCC Use |

31. SIGNATURE OF PHYSICIAN OR SUPPLIER INCLUDING DEGREES OR CREDENTIALS (I certify that the statements on the reverse apply to this bill and are made a part thereof.)

SIGNED _____ DATE _____

32. SERVICE FACILITY LOCATION INFORMATION a. NPI b.

33. BILLING PROVIDER INFO & PH # ( ) a. NPI b.

PHYSICIAN OR SUPPLIER INFORMATION

NUCC Instruction Manual available at: www.nucc.org

PLEASE PRINT OR TYPE

APPROVED OMB-0938-1197 FORM 1500 (02-12)

Clear Form

Figure 10-2

© 2018 Pearson Education, Inc.

b. Using the given source documents, the Capital City Medical Fee Schedule (Figure 10-3), and the blank CMS-1500 form provided (Figure 10-4), complete the following case study for patient Eric Avery (Case 10-2):

CASE 10-2

Capital City Medical—123 Unknown Boulevard, Capital City, NY 12345-2222 (555) 555-1234 Phil Wells, MD, Mannie Mends, MD, Bette R. Soone, MD	Patient Information Form Tax ID: 75-0246810 Group NPI: 1513171216

Patient Information:

Name: (Last, First) Avery, Eric ☒ Male ☐ Female   Birth Date: 09/21/1997

Address: 803 Highland Ave, Capital, NY 12345   Phone: (555) 555-1759

Social Security Number: 298-22-3647   Full-Time Student: ☐ Yes ☒ No

Marital Status: ☒ Single ☐ Married ☐ Divorced ☐ Other

Employment:

Employer: N/A   Phone: ( )

Address:

Condition Related to: ☐ Auto Accident ☐ Employment ☐ Other Accident

Date of Accident: _____ State: _____

Emergency Contact: _____ **Phone: ( )** _____

Primary Insurance: Blue Cross Blue Shield   Phone: ( )

Address: 379 Blue Plaza, Capital City, NY 12345

Insurance Policyholder's Name: Lex Avery ☒ M ☐ F DOB: 07/14/1980

Address: Same

Phone: ( ) _____ Relationship to Insured: ☐ Self ☐ Spouse ☒ Child ☐ Other

Employer: Avery and Associates   Phone: (555) 555-0911

Employer's Address: 4587 Plaza South, Capital City, NY 12345

Policy/ID No: YYZ236548722   Group No: 789654 Percent Covered: ____% Copay Amt: $15.00

Secondary Insurance: _____ Phone: ( ) _____

Address:

Insurance Policyholder's Name: _____ ☐ M ☐ F DOB: _____

Address:

Phone: ( ) _____ Relationship to Insured: ☐ Self ☐ Spouse ☐ Child ☐ Other

Employer: _____ Phone: ( ) _____

Employer's Address:

Policy/ID No: _____ Group No: _____ Percent Covered: ____% Copay Amt: $_____

Reason for Visit: Rash and fever

Known Allergies: _____

Referred by: _____

CASE 10-2
SOAP

05/18/20XX
Assignment of Benefits: Y
Signature on File: Y
Referring Physician: N

S: Eric Avery is being seen today for a rash on his lower abdomen. He noticed it yesterday. It is itchy and painful.

O: On review, this rash is found to be infected and appears tender. The infection looks localized at this time. The Pt. denies vomiting, diarrhea, and tiredness. Presently, a student at his school does have a case of MRSA.

A: 1. Methicillin-resistant staphylococcus aureus (MRSA)—B95.62, L03.311

P: 1. Will treat with oral antibiotics and hydrocortisone cream.
2. Home from school until next appointment.
3. Pt. to stay indoors.
4. Keep linens and clothing clean.
5. Mother and father aware of progressive symptoms, and to call if infection and/or symptoms worsen.
6. Return in 5 days.

Phil Wells, MD
Family Practice
NPI: 1234567890

© 2018 Pearson Education, Inc.

CASE 10-2

Patient Name Eric Avery

Capital City Medical
123 Unknown Boulevard, Capital City, NY 12345-2222

Date of Service
05-18-20XX

New Patient			Arthrocentesis/Aspiration/Injection		Laboratory	
Problem Focused	99201		Small Joint	20600	Amylase	82150
Expanded Problem, Focused	99202		Interm Joint	20605	B12	82607
Detailed	99203		Major Joint	20610	CBC & Diff	85025
Comprehensive	99204		**Other Invasive/Noninvasive**		Comp Metabolic Panel	80053
Comprehensive/High Complex	99205		Audiometry	92552	Chlamydia Screen	87110
Well Exam Infant (up to 12 mos.)	99381		Cast Application		Cholesterol	82465
Well Exam 1–4 yrs.	99382		Location Long Short		Digoxin	80162
Well Exam 5–11 yrs.	99383		Catheterization	51701	Electrolytes	80051
Well Exam 12–17 yrs.	99384		Circumcision	54150	Ferritin	82728
Well Exam 18–39 yrs.	99385		Colposcopy	57452	Folate	82746
Well Exam 40–64 yrs.	99386		Colposcopy w/Biopsy	57454	GC Screen	87070
			Cryosurgery Premalignant Lesion		Glucose	82947
			Location (s):		Glucose 1 HR	82950
			Cryosurgery Warts		Glycosylated HGB A1C	83036
Established Patient			Location (s):		HCT	85014
Post-Op Follow Up Visit	99024		Curettement Lesion		HDL	83718
Minimum	99211		Single	11055	Hep BSAG	87340
Problem Focused	99212		2–4	11056	Hepatitis panel, acute	80074
Expanded Problem Focused	99213	X	>4	11057	HGB	85018
Detailed	99214		Diaphragm Fitting	57170	HIV	86703
Comprehensive/High Complex	99215		Ear Irrigation	69210	Iron & TIBC	83550
Well Exam Infant (up to 12 mos.)	99391		ECG	93000	Kidney Profile	80069
Well exam 1–4 yrs.	99392		Endometrial Biopsy	58100	Lead	83655
Well Exam 5–11 yrs.	99393		Exc. Lesion Malignant		Liver Profile	80076
Well Exam 12–17 yrs.	99394		Benign		Mono Test	86308
Well Exam 18–39 yrs.	99395		Location		Pap Smear	88155
Well Exam 40–64 yrs.	99396		Exc. Skin Tags (1–15)	11200	Pregnancy Test	84703
Obstetrics			Each Additional 10	11201	Obstetric Panel	80055
Total OB Care	59400		Fracture Treatment		Pro Time	85610
Injections			Loc		PSA	84153
Administration Sub. / IM	90772		w/Reduc w/o Reduc		RPR	86592
Drug			I & D Abscess Single/Simple	10060	Sed. Rate	85651
Dosage			Multiple or Comp	10061	Stool Culture	87045
Allergy	95115		I & D Pilonidal Cyst Simple	10080	Stool O & P	87177
Cocci Skin Test	86490		Pilonidal Cyst Complex	10081	Strep Screen	87880
DPT	90701		IV Therapy—To One Hour	90760	Theophylline	80198
Hemophilus	90646		Each Additional Hour	90761	Thyroid Uptake	84479
Influenza	90658		Laceration Repair		TSH	84443
MMR	90707		Location Size Simp/Comp		Urinalysis	81000
OPV	90712		Laryngoscopy	31505	Urine Culture	87088
Pneumovax	90732		Oximetry	94760	Drawing Fee	36415
TB Skin Test	86580		Punch Biopsy		Specimen Collection	99000
TD	90718		Rhythm Strip	93040	**Other:**	
Unlisted Immun	90749		Treadmill	93015		
Tetanus Toxoid	90703		Trigger Point or Tendon Sheath Inj.	20550		
Vaccine/Toxoid Admin <8 Yr Old w/ Counseling	90465		Tympanometry	92567		
Vaccine/Toxoid Administration for Adult	90471					

Diagnosis/ICD-10: **B95.62, L03.311**

I acknowledge receipt of medical services and authorize the release of any medical information necessary to process this claim for healthcare payment only. I do authorize payment to the provider.

Patient Signature Lex Avery

Total Estimated Charges: _____

Payment Amount: _____

Next Appointment: _____

Figure 10-3

Capital City Medical
Fee Schedule

New Patient OV		Punch Biopsy various codes	$80
Problem Focused 99201	$45	Nebulizer various codes	$45
Expanded Problem Focused 99202	$65	Cast Application various codes	$85
Detailed 99203	$85	Laryngoscopy 31505	$255
Comprehensive 99204	$105	Audiometry 92552	$85
Comprehensive/High Complex 99205	$115	Tympanometry 92567	$85
Well Exam infant (less than 1 year) 99381	$45	Ear Irrigation 69210	$25
Well Exam 1–4 yrs. 99382	$50	Diaphragm Fitting 57170	$30
Well Exam 5–11 yrs. 99383	$55	IV Therapy (up to one hour) 90760	$65
Well Exam 12–17 yrs. 99384	$65	Each additional hour 90761	$50
Well Exam 18–39 yrs. 99385	$85	Oximetry 94760	$10
Well Exam 40–64 yrs. 99386	$105	ECG 93000	$75
Established Patient OV		Holter Monitor various codes	$170
Post Op Follow Up Visit 99024	$0	Rhythm Strip 93040	$60
Minimum 99211	$35	Treadmill 93015	$375
Problem Focused 99212	$45	Cocci Skin Test 86490	$20
Expanded Problem Focused 99213	$55	X-ray, spine, chest, bone—any area various codes	$275
Detailed 99214	$65	Avulsion Nail 11730	$200
Comprehensive/High Complex 99215	$75	**Laboratory**	
Well exam infant (less than 1 year) 99391	$35	Amylase 82150	$40
Well Exam 1–4 yrs. 99392	$40	B12 82607	$30
Well Exam 5–11 yrs. 99393	$45	CBC & Diff 85025	$95
Well Exam 12–17 yrs. 99394	$55	Comp Metabolic Panel 80053	$75
Well Exam 18–39 yrs. 99395	$65	Chlamydia Screen 87110	$70
Well Exam 40–64 yrs. 99396	$75	Cholestrerol 82465	$75
Obstetrics		Digoxin 80162	$40
Total OB Care 59400	$1700	Electrolytes 80051	$70
Injections		Estrogen, Total 82672	$50
Administration 90772	$10	Ferritin 82728	$40
Allergy 95115	$35	Folate 82746	$30
DPT 90701	$50	GC Screen 87070	$60
Drug various codes	$35	Glucose 82947	$35
Influenza 90658	$25	Glycosylated HGB A1C 83036	$45
MMR 90707	$50	HCT 85014	$30
OPV 90712	$40	HDL 83718	$35
Pneumovax 90732	$35	HGB 85018	$30
TB Skin Test 86580	$15	Hep BSAG 83740	$40
TD 90718	$40	Hepatitis panel, acute 80074	$95
Tetanus Toxoid 90703	$40	HIV 86703	$100
Vaccine/Toxoid Administration for Younger Than 8 Years Old w/ counseling 90465	$10	Iron & TIBC 83550	$45
		Kidney Profile 80069	$95
Vaccine/Toxoid Administration for Adult 90471	$10	Lead 83665	$55
Arthrocentesis/Aspiration/Injection		Lipase 83690	$40
Small Joint 20600	$50	Lipid Panel 80061	$95
Interm Joint 20605	$60	Liver Profile 80076	$95
Major Joint 20610	$70	Mono Test 86308	$30
Trigger Point/Tendon Sheath Inj. 20550	$90	Pap Smear 88155	$90
Other Invasive/Noninvasive Procedures		Pap Collection/Supervision 88142	$95
Catheterization 51701	$55	Pregnancy Test 84703	$90
Circumcision 54150	$150	Obstetric Panel 80055	$85
Colposcopy 57452	$225	Pro Time 85610	$50
Colposcopy w/Biopsy 57454	$250	PSA 84153	$50
Cryosurgery Premalignant Lesion various codes	$160	RPR 86592	$55
Endometrial Biopsy 58100	$190	Sed. Rate 85651	$50
Excision Lesion Malignant various codes	$145	Stool Culture 87045	$80
Excision Lesion Benign various codes	$125	Stool O & P 87177	$105
Curettement Lesion		Strep Screen 87880	$35
Single 11055	$70	Theophylline 80198	$40
2–4 11056	$80	Thyroid Uptake 84479	$75
>4 11057	$90	TSH 84443	$50
Excision Skin Tags (1–15) 11200	$55	Urinalysis 81000	$35
Each Additional 10 11201	$30	Urine Culture 87088	$80
I & D Abscess Single/Simple 10060	$75	Drawing Fee 36415	$15
Multiple/Complex 10061	$95	Specimen Collection 99000	$10
I & D Pilonidal Cyst Simple 10080	$105		
I & D Pilonidal Cyst Complex 10081	$130		
Laceration Repair various codes	$60		

HEALTH INSURANCE CLAIM FORM

APPROVED BY NATIONAL UNIFORM CLAIM COMMITTEE (NUCC) 02/12

PICA ┌┬┐

1. MEDICARE ☒ (Medicare#) MEDICAID ☐ (Medicaid#) TRICARE ☐ (ID#/DoD#) CHAMPVA ☐ (Member ID#) GROUP HEALTH PLAN ☐ (ID#) FECA BLK LUNG ☐ (ID#) OTHER ☐ (ID#) **1a. INSURED'S I.D. NUMBER** (For Program in Item 1)

2. PATIENT'S NAME (Last Name, First Name, Middle Initial)

3. PATIENT'S BIRTH DATE MM DD YY **SEX** M ☐ F ☐

4. INSURED'S NAME (Last Name, First Name, Middle Initial)

5. PATIENT'S ADDRESS (No., Street)

6. PATIENT RELATIONSHIP TO INSURED Self ☐ Spouse ☐ Child ☐ Other ☐

7. INSURED'S ADDRESS (No., Street)

CITY | STATE | **8. RESERVED FOR NUCC USE**

CITY | STATE

ZIP CODE | TELEPHONE (Include Area Code) ( )

ZIP CODE | TELEPHONE (Include Area Code) ( )

9. OTHER INSURED'S NAME (Last Name, First Name, Middle Initial)

10. IS PATIENT'S CONDITION RELATED TO:

11. INSURED'S POLICY GROUP OR FECA NUMBER

a. OTHER INSURED'S POLICY OR GROUP NUMBER

a. EMPLOYMENT? (Current or Previous) ☐ YES ☐ NO

a. INSURED'S DATE OF BIRTH MM DD YY **SEX** M ☐ F ☐

b. RESERVED FOR NUCC USE

b. AUTO ACCIDENT? ☐ YES ☐ NO PLACE (State)

b. OTHER CLAIM ID (Designated by NUCC)

c. RESERVED FOR NUCC USE

c. OTHER ACCIDENT? ☐ YES ☐ NO

c. INSURANCE PLAN NAME OR PROGRAM NAME

d. INSURANCE PLAN NAME OR PROGRAM NAME

10d. CLAIM CODES (Designated by NUCC)

d. IS THERE ANOTHER HEALTH BENEFIT PLAN? ☐ YES ☐ NO *If yes*, complete items 9, 9a, and 9d.

READ BACK OF FORM BEFORE COMPLETING & SIGNING THIS FORM.
12. PATIENT'S OR AUTHORIZED PERSON'S SIGNATURE I authorize the release of any medical or other information necessary to process this claim. I also request payment of government benefits either to myself or to the party who accepts assignment below.

SIGNED _____ DATE _____

13. INSURED'S OR AUTHORIZED PERSON'S SIGNATURE I authorize payment of medical benefits to the undersigned physician or supplier for services described below.

SIGNED _____

14. DATE OF CURRENT ILLNESS, INJURY, or PREGNANCY (LMP) MM DD YY QUAL.

15. OTHER DATE QUAL. MM DD YY

16. DATES PATIENT UNABLE TO WORK IN CURRENT OCCUPATION FROM MM DD YY TO MM DD YY

17. NAME OF REFERRING PROVIDER OR OTHER SOURCE 17a. 17b. NPI

18. HOSPITALIZATION DATES RELATED TO CURRENT SERVICES FROM MM DD YY TO MM DD YY

19. ADDITIONAL CLAIM INFORMATION (Designated by NUCC)

20. OUTSIDE LAB? ☐ YES ☐ NO $ CHARGES

21. DIAGNOSIS OR NATURE OF ILLNESS OR INJURY Relate A-L to service line below (24E) ICD Ind. ___

A. ___ B. ___ C. ___ D. ___
E. ___ F. ___ G. ___ H. ___
I. ___ J. ___ K. ___ L. ___

22. RESUBMISSION CODE ORIGINAL REF. NO

23. PRIOR AUTHORIZATION NUMBER

24. A. DATE(S) OF SERVICE From MM DD YY To MM DD YY	B. PLACE OF SERVICE	C. EMG	D. PROCEDURES, SERVICES, OR SUPPLIES (Explain Unusual Circumstances) CPT/HCPCS MODIFIER	E. DIAGNOSIS POINTER	F. $ CHARGES	G. DAYS OR UNITS	H. EPSDT Family Plan	I. ID QUAL	J. RENDERING PROVIDER ID. #
1									NPI
2									NPI
3									NPI
4									NPI
5									NPI
6									NPI

25. FEDERAL TAX I.D. NUMBER SSN ☐ EIN ☐

26. PATIENT'S ACCOUNT NO.

27. ACCEPT ASSIGNMENT? (For govt. claims, see back) ☐ YES ☐ NO

28. TOTAL CHARGE $

29. AMOUNT PAID $

30. Rsvd. for NUCC Use

31. SIGNATURE OF PHYSICIAN OR SUPPLIER INCLUDING DEGREES OR CREDENTIALS (I certify that the statements on the reverse apply to this bill and are made a part thereof.)

SIGNED _____ DATE _____

32. SERVICE FACILITY LOCATION INFORMATION

a. NPI b.

33. BILLING PROVIDER INFO & PH # ( )

a. NPI b.

NUCC Instruction Manual available at: www.nucc.org   **PLEASE PRINT OR TYPE**   APPROVED OMB-0938-1197 FORM 1500 (02-12)

Clear Form

CARRIER | PATIENT AND INSURED INFORMATION | PHYSICIAN OR SUPPLIER INFORMATION

Figure 10-4

© 2018 Pearson Education, Inc.

c. Using the given source documents, the Capital City Medical Fee Schedule (Figure 10-5), and the blank CMS-1500 form provided (Figure 10-6), complete the following case study for patient Darpin Ramin (Case 10-3):

CASE 10-3

Capital City Medical—123 Unknown Boulevard, Capital City, NY 12345-2222 (555) 555-1234 Phil Wells, MD, Mannie Mends, MD, Bette R. Soone, MD	Patient Information Form Tax ID: 75-0246810 Group NPI: 1513171216

Patient Information:

Name: (Last, First) Ramin, Darpin ❑ Male ☒ Female Birth Date: 03/28/1989

Address: 51 Garfield Ave, Capital City, NY 12345 Phone: (555) 555-8881

Social Security Number: 950-60-8027 Full-Time Student: ❑ Yes ☒ No

Marital Status: ☒ Single ❑ Married ❑ Divorced ❑ Other

Employment:

Employer: Satellite Broadcasting Phone: (555) 555-2330

Address: 1232 Columbus Highway, Capital City, Ny 12345

Condition Related to: ❑ Auto Accident ❑ Employment ❑ Other Accident

Date of Accident: _____ State _____

Emergency Contact: _____ **Phone: ( )** _____

Primary Insurance: Aetna Phone: ( ) _____

Address: 1625 Healthcare Bldg, Capital City, NY 12345

Insurance Policyholder's Name: Same ❑ M ❑ F DOB: _____

Address: _____

Phone: ( ) _____ Relationship to Insured: ☒ Self ❑ Spouse ❑ Child ❑ Other

Employer: _____ Phone: ( ) _____

Employer's Address: _____

Policy/ID No: 2565799 Group No: 6235 Percent Covered: ___% Copay Amt: $20.00

Secondary Insurance: _____ Phone: ( ) _____

Address: _____

Insurance Policyholder's Name: _____ ❑ M ❑ F DOB: _____

Address: _____

Phone: ( ) _____ Relationship to Insured: ❑ Self ❑ Spouse ❑ Child ❑ Other

Employer: _____ Phone: ( ) _____

Employer's Address: _____

Policy/ID No: _____ Group No: _____ Percent Covered: ___% Copay Amt: $_____

Reason for Visit: I am here for a check on anemia.

Known Allergies: _____

Referred by: _____

CASE 10-3
SOAP

11/08/20XX
Assignment of Benefits: Y
Signature on File: Y
Referring Physician: N

S: Darpin Ramin is here to have a check on her anemia.
O: Pt. still complains of tiredness. Her blood values have not shown improvement. Vitals are normal.
A: 1. Iron deficiency anemia—D50.9
P: 1. Continue iron supplement.
    2. Refer to the hospital dietician for diet counseling.
    3. Return in 3 months.

_____

Phil Wells, MD
Family Practice
NPI: 1234567890

© 2018 Pearson Education, Inc.

CASE 10-3

Patient Name Darpin Ramin

Capital City Medical
123 Unknown Boulevard, Capital City, NY 12345-2222

Date of Service _____

New Patient			Arthrocentesis/Aspiration/Injection		Laboratory		
Problem Focused	99201		Arthrocentesis/Aspiration/Injection		Amylase	82150	
Expanded Problem, Focused	99202		Small Joint	20600	B12	82607	
Detailed	99203		Interm Joint	20605	CBC & Diff	85025	
Comprehensive	99204		Major Joint	20610	Comp Metabolic Panel	80053	
Comprehensive/High Complex	99205		**Other Invasive/Noninvasive**		Chlamydia Screen	87110	
Well Exam Infant (up to 12 mos.)	99381		Audiometry	92552	Cholesterol	82465	
Well Exam 1–4 yrs.	99382		Cast Application		Digoxin	80162	
Well Exam 5–11 yrs.	99383		Location Long Short		Electrolytes	80051	
Well Exam 12–17 yrs.	99384		Catheterization	51701	Ferritin	82728	
Well Exam 18–39 yrs.	99385		Circumcision	54150	Folate	82746	
Well Exam 40–64 yrs.	99386		Colposcopy	57452	GC Screen	87070	
			Colposcopy w/Biopsy	57454	Glucose	82947	
			Cryosurgery Premalignant Lesion		Glucose 1 HR	82950	
			Location (s):		Glycosylated HGB A1C	83036	
Established Patient			Cryosurgery Warts		HCT	85014	X
Post-Op Follow Up Visit	99024		Location (s):		HDL	83718	
Minimum	99211		Curettement Lesion		Hep BSAG	87340	
Problem Focused	99212	X	Single	11055	Hepatitis panel, acute	80074	
Expanded Problem Focused	99213		2–4	11056	HGB	85018	X
Detailed	99214		>4	11057	HIV	86703	
Comprehensive/High Complex	99215		Diaphragm Fitting	57170	Iron & TIBC	83550	
Well Exam Infant (up to 12 mos.)	99391		Ear Irrigation	69210	Kidney Profile	80069	
Well exam 1–4 yrs.	99392		ECG	93000	Lead	83655	
Well Exam 5–11 yrs.	99393		Endometrial Biopsy	58100	Liver Profile	80076	
Well Exam 12–17 yrs.	99394		Exc. Lesion Malignant		Mono Test	86308	
Well Exam 18–39 yrs.	99395		Benign		Pap Smear	88155	
Well Exam 40–64 yrs.	99396		Location		Pregnancy Test	84703	
Obstetrics			Exc. Skin Tags (1–15)	11200	Obstetric Panel	80055	
Total OB Care	59400		Each Additional 10	11201	Pro Time	85610	
Injections			Fracture Treatment		PSA	84153	
Administration Sub. / IM	90772		Loc		RPR	86592	
Drug			w/Reduc w/o Reduc		Sed. Rate	85651	
Dosage			I & D Abscess Single/Simple	10060	Stool Culture	87045	
Allergy	95115		Multiple or Comp	10061	Stool O & P	87177	
Cocci Skin Test	86490		I & D Pilonidal Cyst Simple	10080	Strep Screen	87880	
DPT	90701		Pilonidal Cyst Complex	10081	Theophylline	80198	
Hemophilus	90646		IV Therapy—To One Hour	90760	Thyroid Uptake	84479	
Influenza	90658		Each Additional Hour	90761	TSH	84443	
MMR	90707		Laceration Repair		Urinalysis	81000	
OPV	90712		Location Size Simp/Comp		Urine Culture	87088	
Pneumovax	90732		Laryngoscopy	31505	Drawing Fee	36415	X
TB Skin Test	86580		Oximetry	94760	Specimen Collection	99000	
TD	90718		Punch Biopsy		**Other:**		
Unlisted Immun	90749		Rhythm Strip	93040			
Tetanus Toxoid	90703		Treadmill	93015			
Vaccine/Toxoid Admin <8 Yr Old w/ Counseling	90465		Trigger Point or Tendon Sheath Inj.	20550			
Vaccine/Toxoid Administration for Adult	90471		Tympanometry	92567			

Diagnosis/ICD-10: **D50.9**

I acknowledge receipt of medical services and authorize the release of any medical information necessary to process this claim for healthcare payment only. I do authorize payment to the provider.

Total Estimated Charges: _____

Payment Amount: _____

Patient Signature Darpin Ramin _____

Next Appointment: _____

Figure 10-5

Capital City Medical
Fee Schedule

New Patient OV			Punch Biopsy various codes	$80
Problem Focused 99201	$45		Nebulizer various codes	$45
Expanded Problem Focused 99202	$65		Cast Application various codes	$85
Detailed 99203	$85		Laryngoscopy 31505	$255
Comprehensive 99204	$105		Audiometry 92552	$85
Comprehensive/High Complex 99205	$115		Tympanometry 92567	$85
Well Exam infant (less than 1 year) 99381	$45		Ear Irrigation 69210	$25
Well Exam 1–4 yrs. 99382	$50		Diaphragm Fitting 57170	$30
Well Exam 5–11 yrs. 99383	$55		IV Therapy (up to one hour) 90760	$65
Well Exam 12–17 yrs. 99384	$65		Each additional hour 90761	$50
Well Exam 18–39 yrs. 99385	$85		Oximetry 94760	$10
Well Exam 40–64 yrs. 99386	$105		ECG 93000	$75
Established Patient OV			Holter Monitor various codes	$170
Post Op Follow Up Visit 99024	$0		Rhythm Strip 93040	$60
Minimum 99211	$35		Treadmill 93015	$375
Problem Focused 99212	$45		Cocci Skin Test 86490	$20
Expanded Problem Focused 99213	$55		X-ray, spine, chest, bone—any area various codes	$275
Detailed 99214	$65		Avulsion Nail 11730	$200
Comprehensive/High Complex 99215	$75		**Laboratory**	
Well exam infant (less than 1 year) 99391	$35		Amylase 82150	$40
Well Exam 1–4 yrs. 99392	$40		B12 82607	$30
Well Exam 5–11 yrs. 99393	$45		CBC & Diff 85025	$95
Well Exam 12–17 yrs. 99394	$55		Comp Metabolic Panel 80053	$75
Well Exam 18–39 yrs. 99395	$65		Chlamydia Screen 87110	$70
Well Exam 40–64 yrs. 99396	$75		Cholestrerol 82465	$75
Obstetrics			Digoxin 80162	$40
Total OB Care 59400	$1700		Electrolytes 80051	$70
Injections			Estrogen, Total 82672	$50
Administration 90772	$10		Ferritin 82728	$40
Allergy 95115	$35		Folate 82746	$30
DPT 90701	$50		GC Screen 87070	$60
Drug various codes	$35		Glucose 82947	$35
Influenza 90658	$25		Glycosylated HGB A1C 83036	$45
MMR 90707	$50		HCT 85014	$30
OPV 90712	$40		HDL 83718	$35
Pneumovax 90732	$35		HGB 85018	$30
TB Skin Test 86580	$15		Hep BSAG 83740	$40
TD 90718	$40		Hepatitis panel, acute 80074	$95
Tetanus Toxoid 90703	$40		HIV 86703	$100
Vaccine/Toxoid Administration for Younger			Iron & TIBC 83550	$45
Than 8 Years Old w/ counseling 90465	$10		Kidney Profile 80069	$95
Vaccine/Toxoid Administration for Adult 90471 $10			Lead 83665	$55
Arthrocentesis/Aspiration/Injection			Lipase 83690	$40
Small Joint 20600	$50		Lipid Panel 80061	$95
Interm Joint 20605	$60		Liver Profile 80076	$95
Major Joint 20610	$70		Mono Test 86308	$30
Trigger Point/Tendon Sheath Inj. 20550	$90		Pap Smear 88155	$90
Other Invasive/Noninvasive Procedures			Pap Collection/Supervision 88142	$95
Catheterization 51701	$55		Pregnancy Test 84703	$90
Circumcision 54150	$150		Obstetric Panel 80055	$85
Colposcopy 57452	$225		Pro Time 85610	$50
Colposcopy w/Biopsy 57454	$250		PSA 84153	$50
Cryosurgery Premalignant Lesion various codes$160			RPR 86592	$55
Endometrial Biopsy 58100	$190		Sed. Rate 85651	$50
Excision Lesion Malignant various codes	$145		Stool Culture 87045	$80
Excision Lesion Benign various codes	$125		Stool O & P 87177	$105
Curettement Lesion			Strep Screen 87880	$35
Single 11055	$70		Theophylline 80198	$40
2–4 11056	$80		Thyroid Uptake 84479	$75
>4 11057	$90		TSH 84443	$50
Excision Skin Tags (1–15) 11200	$55		Urinalysis 81000	$35
Each Additional 10 11201	$30		Urine Culture 87088	$80
I & D Abscess Single/Simple 10060	$75		Drawing Fee 36415	$15
Multiple/Complex 10061	$95		Specimen Collection 99000	$10
I & D Pilonidal Cyst Simple 10080	$105			
I & D Pilonidal Cyst Complex 10081	$130			
Laceration Repair various codes	$60			

HEALTH INSURANCE CLAIM FORM

APPROVED BY NATIONAL UNIFORM CLAIM COMMITTEE (NUCC) 02/12

CARRIER

| | PICA | | | | | | | PICA | |

1. MEDICARE MEDICAID TRICARE CHAMPVA GROUP HEALTH PLAN FECA BLK LUNG OTHER
[X] (Medicare#) (Medicaid#) (ID#/DoD#) (Member ID#) (ID#) (ID#) (ID#)

1a. INSURED'S I.D. NUMBER (For Program in Item 1)

2. PATIENT'S NAME (Last Name, First Name, Middle Initial)

3. PATIENT'S BIRTH DATE MM | DD | YY **SEX** M F

4. INSURED'S NAME (Last Name, First Name, Middle Initial)

5. PATIENT'S ADDRESS (No., Street)

6. PATIENT RELATIONSHIP TO INSURED Self Spouse Child Other

7. INSURED'S ADDRESS (No., Street)

CITY STATE

8. RESERVED FOR NUCC USE

CITY STATE

ZIP CODE TELEPHONE (Include Area Code) ( )

ZIP CODE TELEPHONE (Include Area Code) ( )

9. OTHER INSURED'S NAME (Last Name, First Name, Middle Initial)

10. IS PATIENT'S CONDITION RELATED TO:

11. INSURED'S POLICY GROUP OR FECA NUMBER

a. OTHER INSURED'S POLICY OR GROUP NUMBER

a. EMPLOYMENT? (Current or Previous) YES NO

a. INSURED'S DATE OF BIRTH MM | DD | YY **SEX** M F

b. RESERVED FOR NUCC USE

b. AUTO ACCIDENT? PLACE (State) YES NO

b. OTHER CLAIM ID (Designated by NUCC)

c. RESERVED FOR NUCC USE

c. OTHER ACCIDENT? YES NO

c. INSURANCE PLAN NAME OR PROGRAM NAME

d. INSURANCE PLAN NAME OR PROGRAM NAME

10d. CLAIM CODES (Designated by NUCC)

d. IS THERE ANOTHER HEALTH BENEFIT PLAN? YES NO *If yes*, complete items 9, 9a, and 9d.

READ BACK OF FORM BEFORE COMPLETING & SIGNING THIS FORM.

12. PATIENT'S OR AUTHORIZED PERSON'S SIGNATURE I authorize the release of any medical or other information necessary to process this claim. I also request payment of government benefits either to myself or to the party who accepts assignment below.

SIGNED _____ DATE _____

13. INSURED'S OR AUTHORIZED PERSON'S SIGNATURE I authorize payment of medical benefits to the undersigned physician or supplier for services described below.

SIGNED _____

PATIENT AND INSURED INFORMATION

14. DATE OF CURRENT ILLNESS, INJURY, or PREGNANCY (LMP) MM | DD | YY QUAL.

15. OTHER DATE QUAL. MM | DD | YY

16. DATES PATIENT UNABLE TO WORK IN CURRENT OCCUPATION FROM MM | DD | YY TO MM | DD | YY

17. NAME OF REFERRING PROVIDER OR OTHER SOURCE 17a. 17b. NPI

18. HOSPITALIZATION DATES RELATED TO CURRENT SERVICES FROM MM | DD | YY TO MM | DD | YY

19. ADDITIONAL CLAIM INFORMATION (Designated by NUCC)

20. OUTSIDE LAB? YES NO $ CHARGES

21. DIAGNOSIS OR NATURE OF ILLNESS OR INJURY Relate A-L to service line below (24E) ICD Ind.
A. ___ B. ___ C. ___ D. ___
E. ___ F. ___ G. ___ H. ___
I. ___ J. ___ K. ___ L. ___

22. RESUBMISSION CODE ORIGINAL REF. NO.

23. PRIOR AUTHORIZATION NUMBER

24. A. DATE(S) OF SERVICE						B. PLACE OF SERVICE	C. EMG	D. PROCEDURES, SERVICES, OR SUPPLIES (Explain Unusual Circumstances) CPT/HCPCS	MODIFIER	E. DIAGNOSIS POINTER	F. $ CHARGES	G. DAYS OR UNITS	H. EPSDT Family Plan	I. ID. QUAL	J. RENDERING PROVIDER ID. #
From MM	DD	YY	To MM	DD	YY										
1														NPI	
2														NPI	
3														NPI	
4														NPI	
5														NPI	
6														NPI	

25. FEDERAL TAX I.D. NUMBER SSN EIN

26. PATIENT'S ACCOUNT NO.

27. ACCEPT ASSIGNMENT? (For govt. claims, see back) YES NO

28. TOTAL CHARGE $

29. AMOUNT PAID $

30. Rsvd. for NUCC Use

31. SIGNATURE OF PHYSICIAN OR SUPPLIER INCLUDING DEGREES OR CREDENTIALS (I certify that the statements on the reverse apply to this bill and are made a part thereof.)

SIGNED _____ DATE _____

32. SERVICE FACILITY LOCATION INFORMATION
a. NPI b.

33. BILLING PROVIDER INFO & PH # ( )
a. NPI b.

PHYSICIAN OR SUPPLIER INFORMATION

NUCC Instruction Manual available at: www.nucc.org **PLEASE PRINT OR TYPE** APPROVED OMB-0938-1197 FORM 1500 (02-12)

Clear Form

Figure 10-6

d. Using the given source documents, the Capital City Medical Fee Schedule (Figure 10-7), and the blank CMS-1500 form provided (Figure 10-8), complete the following case study for patient Rhianna Burley (Case 10-4):

CASE 10-4

Capital City Medical—123 Unknown Boulevard, Capital City, NY 12345-2222 (555) 555-1234 Phil Wells, MD, Mannie Mends, MD, Bette R. Soone, MD	Patient Information Form Tax ID: 75-0246810 Group NPI: 1513171216

Patient Information:

Name: (Last, First) Burley, Rhianna ☐ Male ☒ Female Birth Date: 10/15/1982

Address: 91 Harper Ln, Capital City, NY 12345 Phone: (555) 555-8881

Social Security Number: 642-89-8999 Full-Time Student: ☐ Yes ☒ No

Marital Status: ☐ Single ☒ Married ☐ Divorced ☐ Other

Employment:

Employer: _____ Phone: ( ) _____

Address: _____

Condition Related to: ☐ Auto Accident ☐ Employment ☐ Other Accident

Date of Accident: _____ State: _____

Emergency Contact: _____ **Phone: ( )** _____

Primary Insurance: Health America Phone: ( ) _____

Address: 2031 Healthica Center, Capital City, NY 12345

Insurance Policyholder's Name: Pat Burley ☒ M ☐ F DOB: 01/18/1982

Address: Same

Phone: ( ) _____ Relationship to Insured: ☐ Self ☒ Spouse ☐ Child ☐ Other

Employer: Capital Engineering Phone: (555) 555-7949

Employer's Address: 3605 Graph Rd, Capital City, NY 12345

Policy/ID No: 45753331 Group No: 594615 Percent Covered: ____% Copay Amt: $25.00

Secondary Insurance: _____ Phone: ( ) _____

Address: _____

Insurance Policyholder's Name: _____ ☐ M ☐ F DOB: _____

Address: _____

Phone: ( ) _____ Relationship to Insured: ☐ Self ☐ Spouse ☐ Child ☐ Other

Employer: _____ Phone: ( ) _____

Employer's Address: _____

Policy/ID No: _____ Group No: _____ Percent Covered: ____% Copay Amt: $_____

Reason for Visit: I feel nauseated, and I think I have a fever.

Known Allergies: _____

Referred by: _____

CASE 10-4
SOAP

09/22/20XX
Assignment of Benefits: Y
Signature on File: Y
Referring Physician: N

S: Rhianna Burley is complaining of nausea and headache. She started feeling ill yesterday evening. During the day, she played paintball with her husband and a few friends in the woods behind her house.

O: On exam, pt. has a fever of 101.8°F. She denies vomiting or diarrhea. She does have a mosquito bite on her right calf. The area around the bite is red, swollen, and 2 in. in diameter. CBC and diff is negative. Sed rate presents as normal.

A: 1. West Nile Virus—A92.30

P: 1. Take meds as directed.
2. If symptoms worsen, go to the ER immediately.
3. Return in 3 days.

_____

Phil Wells, MD
Family Practice
NPI: 1234567890

CASE 10-4

Patient Name Rhianna Burley

Capital City Medical
123 Unknown Boulevard, Capital City, NY 12345-2222

Date of Service
09-22-20XX

New Patient			Arthrocentesis/Aspiration/Injection		Laboratory		
Problem Focused	99201		Arthrocentesis/Aspiration/Injection		Amylase	82150	
Expanded Problem, Focused	99202		Small Joint	20600	B12	82607	
Detailed	99203		Interm Joint	20605	CBC & Diff	85025	X
Comprehensive	99204		Major Joint	20610	Comp Metabolic Panel	80053	
Comprehensive/High Complex	99205		**Other Invasive/Noninvasive**		Chlamydia Screen	87110	
Well Exam Infant (up to 12 mos.)	99381		Audiometry	92552	Cholesterol	82465	
Well Exam 1–4 yrs.	99382		Cast Application		Digoxin	80162	
Well Exam 5–11 yrs.	99383		Location Long Short		Electrolytes	80051	
Well Exam 12–17 yrs.	99384		Catheterization	51701	Ferritin	82728	
Well Exam 18–39 yrs.	99385		Circumcision	54150	Folate	82746	
Well Exam 40–64 yrs.	99386		Colposcopy	57452	GC Screen	87070	
			Colposcopy w/Biopsy	57454	Glucose	82947	
			Cryosurgery Premalignant Lesion		Glucose 1 HR	82950	
			Location (s):		Glycosylated HGB A1C	83036	
Established Patient			Cryosurgery Warts		HCT	85014	
Post-Op Follow Up Visit	99024		Location (s):		HDL	83718	
Minimum	99211		Curettement Lesion		Hep BSAG	87340	
Problem Focused	99212		Single	11055	Hepatitis panel, acute	80074	
Expanded Problem Focused	99213	X	2–4	11056	HGB	85018	
Detailed	99214		>4	11057	HIV	86703	
Comprehensive/High Complex	99215		Diaphragm Fitting	57170	Iron & TIBC	83550	
Well Exam Infant (up to 12 mos.)	99391		Ear Irrigation	69210	Kidney Profile	80069	
Well exam 1–4 yrs.	99392		ECG	93000	Lead	83655	
Well Exam 5–11 yrs.	99393		Endometrial Biopsy	58100	Liver Profile	80076	
Well Exam 12–17 yrs.	99394		Exc. Lesion Malignant		Mono Test	86308	
Well Exam 18–39 yrs.	99395		Benign		Pap Smear	88155	
Well Exam 40–64 yrs.	99396		Location		Pregnancy Test	84703	
Obstetrics			Exc. Skin Tags (1–15)	11200	Obstetric Panel	80055	
Total OB Care	59400		Each Additional 10	11201	Pro Time	85610	
Injections			Fracture Treatment		PSA	84153	
Administration Sub. / IM	90772		Loc		RPR	86592	
Drug			w/Reduc w/o Reduc		Sed. Rate	85651	X
Dosage			I & D Abscess Single/Simple	10060	Stool Culture	87045	
Allergy	95115		Multiple or Comp	10061	Stool O & P	87177	
Cocci Skin Test	86490		I & D Pilonidal Cyst Simple	10080	Strep Screen	87880	
DPT	90701		Pilonidal Cyst Complex	10081	Theophylline	80198	
Hemophilus	90646		IV Therapy—To One Hour	90760	Thyroid Uptake	84479	
Influenza	90658		Each Additional Hour	90761	TSH	84443	
MMR	90707		Laceration Repair		Urinalysis	81000	
OPV	90712		Location Size Simp/Comp		Urine Culture	87088	
Pneumovax	90732		Laryngoscopy	31505	Drawing Fee	36415	X
TB Skin Test	86580		Oximetry	94760	Specimen Collection	99000	
TD	90718		Punch Biopsy		**Other:**		
Unlisted Immun	90749		Rhythm Strip	93040			
Tetanus Toxoid	90703		Treadmill	93015			
Vaccine/Toxoid Admin <8 Yr Old w/ Counseling	90465		Trigger Point or Tendon Sheath Inj.	20550			
Vaccine/Toxoid Administration for Adult	90471		Tympanometry	92567			

Diagnosis/ICD-10: **A92.30**

I acknowledge receipt of medical services and authorize the release of any medical information necessary to process this claim for healthcare payment only. I do authorize payment to the provider.

Total Estimated Charges: _____

Payment Amount: _____

Patient Signature Rhianna Burley

Next Appointment: _____

Figure 10-7

Capital City Medical
Fee Schedule

New Patient OV				Punch Biopsy various codes	$80
Problem Focused 99201	$45			Nebulizer various codes	$45
Expanded Problem Focused 99202	$65			Cast Application various codes	$85
Detailed 99203	$85			Laryngoscopy 31505	$255
Comprehensive 99204	$105			Audiometry 92552	$85
Comprehensive/High Complex 99205	$115			Tympanometry 92567	$85
Well Exam infant (less than 1 year) 99381	$45			Ear Irrigation 69210	$25
Well Exam 1–4 yrs. 99382	$50			Diaphragm Fitting 57170	$30
Well Exam 5–11 yrs. 99383	$55			IV Therapy (up to one hour) 90760	$65
Well Exam 12–17 yrs. 99384	$65			Each additional hour 90761	$50
Well Exam 18–39 yrs. 99385	$85			Oximetry 94760	$10
Well Exam 40–64 yrs. 99386	$105			ECG 93000	$75
Established Patient OV				Holter Monitor various codes	$170
Post Op Follow Up Visit 99024	$0			Rhythm Strip 93040	$60
Minimum 99211	$35			Treadmill 93015	$375
Problem Focused 99212	$45			Cocci Skin Test 86490	$20
Expanded Problem Focused 99213	$55			X-ray, spine, chest, bone—any area various codes	$275
Detailed 99214	$65			Avulsion Nail 11730	$200
Comprehensive/High Complex 99215	$75			**Laboratory**	
Well exam infant (less than 1 year) 99391	$35			Amylase 82150	$40
Well Exam 1–4 yrs. 99392	$40			B12 82607	$30
Well Exam 5–11 yrs. 99393	$45			CBC & Diff 85025	$95
Well Exam 12–17 yrs. 99394	$55			Comp Metabolic Panel 80053	$75
Well Exam 18–39 yrs. 99395	$65			Chlamydia Screen 87110	$70
Well Exam 40–64 yrs. 99396	$75			Cholestrerol 82465	$75
Obstetrics				Digoxin 80162	$40
Total OB Care 59400	$1700			Electrolytes 80051	$70
Injections				Estrogen, Total 82672	$50
Administration 90772	$10			Ferritin 82728	$40
Allergy 95115	$35			Folate 82746	$30
DPT 90701	$50			GC Screen 87070	$60
Drug various codes	$35			Glucose 82947	$35
Influenza 90658	$25			Glycosylated HGB A1C 83036	$45
MMR 90707	$50			HCT 85014	$30
OPV 90712	$40			HDL 83718	$35
Pneumovax 90732	$35			HGB 85018	$30
TB Skin Test 86580	$15			Hep BSAG 83740	$40
TD 90718	$40			Hepatitis panel, acute 80074	$95
Tetanus Toxoid 90703	$40			HIV 86703	$100
Vaccine/Toxoid Administration for Younger Than 8 Years Old w/ counseling 90465	$10			Iron & TIBC 83550	$45
				Kidney Profile 80069	$95
Vaccine/Toxoid Administration for Adult 90471	$10			Lead 83665	$55
Arthrocentesis/Aspiration/Injection				Lipase 83690	$40
Small Joint 20600	$50			Lipid Panel 80061	$95
Interm Joint 20605	$60			Liver Profile 80076	$95
Major Joint 20610	$70			Mono Test 86308	$30
Trigger Point/Tendon Sheath Inj. 20550	$90			Pap Smear 88155	$90
Other Invasive/Noninvasive Procedures				Pap Collection/Supervision 88142	$95
Catheterization 51701	$55			Pregnancy Test 84703	$90
Circumcision 54150	$150			Obstetric Panel 80055	$85
Colposcopy 57452	$225			Pro Time 85610	$50
Colposcopy w/Biopsy 57454	$250			PSA 84153	$50
Cryosurgery Premalignant Lesion various codes	$160			RPR 86592	$55
Endometrial Biopsy 58100	$190			Sed. Rate 85651	$50
Excision Lesion Malignant various codes	$145			Stool Culture 87045	$80
Excision Lesion Benign various codes	$125			Stool O & P 87177	$105
Curettement Lesion				Strep Screen 87880	$35
Single 11055	$70			Theophylline 80198	$40
2–4 11056	$80			Thyroid Uptake 84479	$75
>4 11057	$90			TSH 84443	$50
Excision Skin Tags (1–15) 11200	$55			Urinalysis 81000	$35
Each Additional 10 11201	$30			Urine Culture 87088	$80
I & D Abscess Single/Simple 10060	$75			Drawing Fee 36415	$15
Multiple/Complex 10061	$95			Specimen Collection 99000	$10
I & D Pilonidal Cyst Simple 10080	$105				
I & D Pilonidal Cyst Complex 10081	$130				
Laceration Repair various codes	$60				

HEALTH INSURANCE CLAIM FORM

APPROVED BY NATIONAL UNIFORM CLAIM COMMITTEE (NUCC) 02/12

PICA | | |

1. MEDICARE	MEDICAID	TRICARE	CHAMPVA	GROUP HEALTH PLAN	FECA BLK LUNG	OTHER	1a. INSURED'S I.D. NUMBER	(For Program in Item 1)
[X] (Medicare#)	[ ] (Medicaid#)	[ ] (ID#/DoD#)	[ ] (Member ID#)	[ ] (ID#)	[ ] (ID#)	[ ] (ID#)		

2. PATIENT'S NAME (Last Name, First Name, Middle Initial)

3. PATIENT'S BIRTH DATE MM DD YY **SEX** M [ ] F [ ]

4. INSURED'S NAME (Last Name, First Name, Middle Initial)

5. PATIENT'S ADDRESS (No., Street)

6. PATIENT RELATIONSHIP TO INSURED Self [ ] Spouse [ ] Child [ ] Other [ ]

7. INSURED'S ADDRESS (No., Street)

CITY | STATE

8. RESERVED FOR NUCC USE

CITY | STATE

ZIP CODE | TELEPHONE (Include Area Code) ( )

ZIP CODE | TELEPHONE (Include Area Code) ( )

9. OTHER INSURED'S NAME (Last Name, First Name, Middle Initial)

10. IS PATIENT'S CONDITION RELATED TO:

11. INSURED'S POLICY GROUP OR FECA NUMBER

a. OTHER INSURED'S POLICY OR GROUP NUMBER

a. EMPLOYMENT? (Current or Previous) YES [ ] NO [ ]

a. INSURED'S DATE OF BIRTH MM DD YY **SEX** M [ ] F [ ]

b. RESERVED FOR NUCC USE

b. AUTO ACCIDENT? PLACE (State) YES [ ] NO [ ]

b. OTHER CLAIM ID (Designated by NUCC)

c. RESERVED FOR NUCC USE

c. OTHER ACCIDENT? YES [ ] NO [ ]

c. INSURANCE PLAN NAME OR PROGRAM NAME

d. INSURANCE PLAN NAME OR PROGRAM NAME

10d. CLAIM CODES (Designated by NUCC)

d. IS THERE ANOTHER HEALTH BENEFIT PLAN? YES [ ] NO [ ] *If yes, complete items 9, 9a, and 9d.*

READ BACK OF FORM BEFORE COMPLETING & SIGNING THIS FORM.

12. PATIENT'S OR AUTHORIZED PERSON'S SIGNATURE I authorize the release of any medical or other information necessary to process this claim. I also request payment of government benefits either to myself or to the party who accepts assignment below.

SIGNED _____ DATE _____

13. INSURED'S OR AUTHORIZED PERSON'S SIGNATURE I authorize payment of medical benefits to the undersigned physician or supplier for services described below.

SIGNED _____

14. DATE OF CURRENT ILLNESS, INJURY, or PREGNANCY (LMP) MM DD YY QUAL

15. OTHER DATE QUAL MM DD YY

16. DATES PATIENT UNABLE TO WORK IN CURRENT OCCUPATION MM DD YY FROM TO MM DD YY

17. NAME OF REFERRING PROVIDER OR OTHER SOURCE

17a. 17b. NPI

18. HOSPITALIZATION DATES RELATED TO CURRENT SERVICES MM DD YY FROM TO MM DD YY

19. ADDITIONAL CLAIM INFORMATION (Designated by NUCC)

20. OUTSIDE LAB? YES [ ] NO [ ] $ CHARGES

21. DIAGNOSIS OR NATURE OF ILLNESS OR INJURY Relate A-L to service line below (24E) ICD Ind.

A. | B. | C. | D.
E. | F. | G. | H.
I. | J. | K. | L.

22. RESUBMISSION CODE ORIGINAL REF. NO.

23. PRIOR AUTHORIZATION NUMBER

24. A. DATE(S) OF SERVICE From MM DD YY To MM DD YY	B. PLACE OF SERVICE	C. EMG	D. PROCEDURES, SERVICES, OR SUPPLIES (Explain Unusual Circumstances) CPT/HCPCS MODIFIER	E. DIAGNOSIS POINTER	F. $ CHARGES	G. DAYS OR UNITS	H. EPSDT Family Plan	I. ID. QUAL	J. RENDERING PROVIDER ID. #
1									NPI
2									NPI
3									NPI
4									NPI
5									NPI
6									NPI

25. FEDERAL TAX I.D. NUMBER SSN EIN [ ]

26. PATIENT'S ACCOUNT NO.

27. ACCEPT ASSIGNMENT? (For govt claims, see back) YES [ ] NO [ ]

28. TOTAL CHARGE $

29. AMOUNT PAID $

30. Rsvd for NUCC Use

31. SIGNATURE OF PHYSICIAN OR SUPPLIER INCLUDING DEGREES OR CREDENTIALS (I certify that the statements on the reverse apply to this bill and are made a part thereof.)

SIGNED _____ DATE _____

32. SERVICE FACILITY LOCATION INFORMATION

a. NPI b.

33. BILLING PROVIDER INFO & PH # ( )

a. NPI b.

NUCC Instruction Manual available at: www.nucc.org **PLEASE PRINT OR TYPE** APPROVED OMB-0938-1197 FORM 1500 (02-12)

Clear Form

Figure 10-8

© 2018 Pearson Education, Inc.

e. Using the given source documents, the Capital City Medical Fee Schedule (Figure 10-9), and the blank CMS-1500 form provided (Figure 10-10), complete the following case study for patient Linda Freed (Case 10-5):

CASE 10-5

Capital City Medical—123 Unknown Boulevard, Capital City, NY 12345-2222 (555) 555-1234 Phil Wells, MD, Mannie Mends, MD, Bette R. Soone, MD	Patient Information Form Tax ID: 75-0246810 Group NPI: 1513171216

Patient Information:

Name: (Last, First) Freed, Linda ☐ Male ☒ Female Birth Date: 04/06/1969

Address: 23 Penn Ave, Capital City, NY 12345 Phone: (555) 555-6622

Social Security Number: 402-31-1775 Full-Time Student: ☐ Yes ☒ No

Marital Status: ☐ Single ☐ Married ☒ Divorced ☐ Other

Employment:

Employer: Extreme Hair, Ltd. Phone: (555) 555-8220

Address: 333 Long Ave., Capital City, NY 12345

Condition Related to: ☐ Auto Accident ☐ Employment ☐ Other Accident

Date of Accident: _____ State: _____

Emergency Contact: _____ Phone: ( ) _____

Primary Insurance: Blue Cross Blue Shield Phone: ( ) _____

Address: 379 Blue Plaza, Capital City, NY 12345

Insurance Policyholder's Name: Same ☐ M ☐ F DOB: _____

Address: _____

Phone: ( ) _____ Relationship to Insured: ☒ Self ☐ Spouse ☐ Child ☐ Other

Employer: _____ Phone: ( ) _____

Employer's Address: _____

Policy/ID No: YYJ288236692 Group No: 023443 Percent Covered: ___% Copay Amt: $10.00

Secondary Insurance: _____ Phone: ( ) _____

Address: _____

Insurance Policyholder's Name: _____ ☐ M ☐ F DOB: _____

Address: _____

Phone: ( ) _____ Relationship to Insured: ☐ Self ☐ Spouse ☐ Child ☐ Other

Employer: _____ Phone: ( ) _____

Employer's Address: _____

Policy/ID No: _____ Group No: _____ Percent Covered: ___% Copay Amt: $_____

Reason for Visit: Check up on my diabetes, Type I

Known Allergies: _____

Referred by: _____

CASE 10-5
SOAP

02/16/20XX
Assignment of Benefits: Y
Signature on File: Y
Referring Physician: N

S: Linda Freed is in the office today for a checkup on her DMI. She says her sugar has been stable.

O: Pt. has lost a few pounds since her last visit. EENT: Clear. No edema of the lower extremities. Her glucose in the office today is 124.

A: 1. DMI, controlled—E10.8

P: 1. Refill insulin and test strips.
    2. Return in 3 months.
    3. Continue testing 3 times a day.

_____

Phil Wells, MD
Family Practice
NPI: 1234567890

© 2018 Pearson Education, Inc.

CASE 10-5

Capital City Medical
123 Unknown Boulevard, Capital City, NY 12345-2222

Date of Service
02-16-200X

New Patient			Arthrocentesis/Aspiration/Injection			Laboratory		
Problem Focused	99201		Arthrocentesis/Aspiration/Injection			Amylase	82150	
Expanded Problem, Focused	99202		Small Joint		20600	B12	82607	
Detailed	99203		Interm Joint		20605	CBC & Diff	85025	X
Comprehensive	99204		Major Joint		20610	Comp Metabolic Panel	80053	
Comprehensive/High Complex	99205		**Other Invasive/Noninvasive**			Chlamydia Screen	87110	
Well Exam Infant (up to 12 mos.)	99381		Audiometry		92552	Cholesterol	82465	
Well Exam 1–4 yrs.	99382		Cast Application			Digoxin	80162	
Well Exam 5–11 yrs.	99383		Location Long Short			Electrolytes	80051	
Well Exam 12–17 yrs.	99384		Catheterization		51701	Ferritin	82728	
Well Exam 18–39 yrs.	99385		Circumcision		54150	Folate	82746	
Well Exam 40–64 yrs.	99386		Colposcopy		57452	GC Screen	87070	
			Colposcopy w/Biopsy		57454	Glucose	82947	
			Cryosurgery Premalignant Lesion			Glucose 1 HR	82950	
			Location(s):			Glycosylated HGB A1C	83036	
Established Patient			Cryosurgery Warts			HCT	85014	
Post-Op Follow Up Visit	99024		Location(s):			HDL	83718	
Minimum	99211		Curettement Lesion			Hep BSAG	87340	
Problem Focused	99212		Single		11055	Hepatitis panel, acute	80074	
Expanded Problem Focused	99213	X	2–4		11056	HGB	85018	
Detailed	99214		>4		11057	HIV	86703	
Comprehensive/High Complex	99215		Diaphragm Fitting		57170	Iron & TIBC	83550	
Well Exam Infant (up to 12 mos.)	99391		Ear Irrigation		69210	Kidney Profile	80069	
Well exam 1–4 yrs.	99392		ECG		93000	Lead	83655	
Well Exam 5–11 yrs.	99393		Endometrial Biopsy		58100	Liver Profile	80076	
Well Exam 12–17 yrs.	99394		Exc. Lesion Malignant			Mono Test	86308	
Well Exam 18–39 yrs.	99395		Benign			Pap Smear	88155	
Well Exam 40–64 yrs.	99396		Location			Pregnancy Test	84703	
Obstetrics			Exc. Skin Tags (1–15)		11200	Obstetric Panel	80055	
Total OB Care	59400		Each Additional 10		11201	Pro Time	85610	
Injections			Fracture Treatment			PSA	84153	
Administration Sub. / IM	90772		Loc			RPR	86592	
Drug			w/Reduc		w/o Reduc	Sed. Rate	85651	
Dosage			I & D Abscess Single/Simple		10060	Stool Culture	87045	
Allergy	95115		Multiple or Comp		10061	Stool O & P	87177	
Cocci Skin Test	86490		I & D Pilonidal Cyst Simple		10080	Strep Screen	87880	
DPT	90701		Pilonidal Cyst Complex		10081	Theophylline	80198	
Hemophilus	90646		IV Therapy—To One Hour		90760	Thyroid Uptake	84479	
Influenza	90658		Each Additional Hour		90761	TSH	84443	
MMR	90707		Laceration Repair			Urinalysis	81000	
OPV	90712		Location Size Simp/Comp			Urine Culture	87088	
Pneumovax	90732		Laryngoscopy		31505	Drawing Fee	36415	X
TB Skin Test	86580		Oximetry		94760	Specimen Collection	99000	
TD	90718		Punch Biopsy			**Other:**		
Unlisted Immun	90749		Rhythm Strip		93040			
Tetanus Toxoid	90703		Treadmill		93015			
Vaccine/Toxoid Admin <8 Yr Old w/ Counseling	90465		Trigger Point or Tendon Sheath Inj.		20550			
Vaccine/Toxoid Administration for Adult	90471		Tympanometry		92567			

Diagnosis/ICD-10: **250.01**

I acknowledge receipt of medical services and authorize the release of any medical information necessary to process this claim for healthcare payment only. I do authorize payment to the provider.

Patient Signature Linda Freed

Total Estimated Charges: _____

Payment Amount: _____

Next Appointment: _____

Figure 10-9

Capital City Medical
Fee Schedule

New Patient OV		Punch Biopsy various codes	$80
Problem Focused 99201	$45	Nebulizer various codes	$45
Expanded Problem Focused 99202	$65	Cast Application various codes	$85
Detailed 99203	$85	Laryngoscopy 31505	$255
Comprehensive 99204	$105	Audiometry 92552	$85
Comprehensive/High Complex 99205	$115	Tympanometry 92567	$85
Well Exam infant (less than 1 year) 99381	$45	Ear Irrigation 69210	$25
Well Exam 1–4 yrs. 99382	$50	Diaphragm Fitting 57170	$30
Well Exam 5–11 yrs. 99383	$55	IV Therapy (up to one hour) 90760	$65
Well Exam 12–17 yrs. 99384	$65	Each additional hour 90761	$50
Well Exam 18–39 yrs. 99385	$85	Oximetry 94760	$10
Well Exam 40–64 yrs. 99386	$105	ECG 93000	$75
Established Patient OV		Holter Monitor various codes	$170
Post Op Follow Up Visit 99024	$0	Rhythm Strip 93040	$60
Minimum 99211	$35	Treadmill 93015	$375
Problem Focused 99212	$45	Cocci Skin Test 86490	$20
Expanded Problem Focused 99213	$55	X-ray, spine, chest, bone—any area various codes	$275
Detailed 99214	$65	Avulsion Nail 11730	$200
Comprehensive/High Complex 99215	$75	**Laboratory**	
Well exam infant (less than 1 year) 99391	$35	Amylase 82150	$40
Well Exam 1–4 yrs. 99392	$40	B12 82607	$30
Well Exam 5–11 yrs. 99393	$45	CBC & Diff 85025	$95
Well Exam 12–17 yrs. 99394	$55	Comp Metabolic Panel 80053	$75
Well Exam 18–39 yrs. 99395	$65	Chlamydia Screen 87110	$70
Well Exam 40–64 yrs. 99396	$75	Cholestrerol 82465	$75
Obstetrics		Digoxin 80162	$40
Total OB Care 59400	$1700	Electrolytes 80051	$70
Injections		Estrogen, Total 82672	$50
Administration 90772	$10	Ferritin 82728	$40
Allergy 95115	$35	Folate 82746	$30
DPT 90701	$50	GC Screen 87070	$60
Drug various codes	$35	Glucose 82947	$35
Influenza 90658	$25	Glycosylated HGB A1C 83036	$45
MMR 90707	$50	HCT 85014	$30
OPV 90712	$40	HDL 83718	$35
Pneumovax 90732	$35	HGB 85018	$30
TB Skin Test 86580	$15	Hep BSAG 83740	$40
TD 90718	$40	Hepatitis panel, acute 80074	$95
Tetanus Toxoid 90703	$40	HIV 86703	$100
Vaccine/Toxoid Administration for Younger Than 8 Years Old w/ counseling 90465	$10	Iron & TIBC 83550	$45
		Kidney Profile 80069	$95
Vaccine/Toxoid Administration for Adult 90471	$10	Lead 83665	$55
Arthrocentesis/Aspiration/Injection		Lipase 83690	$40
Small Joint 20600	$50	Lipid Panel 80061	$95
Interm Joint 20605	$60	Liver Profile 80076	$95
Major Joint 20610	$70	Mono Test 86308	$30
Trigger Point/Tendon Sheath Inj. 20550	$90	Pap Smear 88155	$90
Other Invasive/Noninvasive Procedures		Pap Collection/Supervision 88142	$95
Catheterization 51701	$55	Pregnancy Test 84703	$90
Circumcision 54150	$150	Obstetric Panel 80055	$85
Colposcopy 57452	$225	Pro Time 85610	$50
Colposcopy w/Biopsy 57454	$250	PSA 84153	$50
Cryosurgery Premalignant Lesion various codes	$160	RPR 86592	$55
Endometrial Biopsy 58100	$190	Sed. Rate 85651	$50
Excision Lesion Malignant various codes	$145	Stool Culture 87045	$80
Excision Lesion Benign various codes	$125	Stool O & P 87177	$105
Curettement Lesion		Strep Screen 87880	$35
Single 11055	$70	Theophylline 80198	$40
2–4 11056	$80	Thyroid Uptake 84479	$75
>4 11057	$90	TSH 84443	$50
Excision Skin Tags (1–15) 11200	$55	Urinalysis 81000	$35
Each Additional 10 11201	$30	Urine Culture 87088	$80
I & D Abscess Single/Simple 10060	$75	Drawing Fee 36415	$15
Multiple/Complex 10061	$95	Specimen Collection 99000	$10
I & D Pilonidal Cyst Simple 10080	$105		
I & D Pilonidal Cyst Complex 10081	$130		
Laceration Repair various codes	$60		

HEALTH INSURANCE CLAIM FORM

APPROVED BY NATIONAL UNIFORM CLAIM COMMITTEE (NUCC) 02/12

[CARRIER]

| PICA | | | | | | | PICA | | |

1. MEDICARE ☐ (Medicare#) MEDICAID ☐ (Medicaid#) TRICARE ☐ (ID#/DoD#) CHAMPVA ☐ (Member ID#) GROUP HEALTH PLAN ☐ (ID#) FECA BLK LUNG ☐ (ID#) OTHER ☐ (ID#)
MEDICARE: ☒ (Medicare#)

1a. INSURED'S I.D. NUMBER (For Program in Item 1)

2. PATIENT'S NAME (Last Name, First Name, Middle Initial)

3. PATIENT'S BIRTH DATE MM | DD | YY   SEX M ☐ F ☐

4. INSURED'S NAME (Last Name, First Name, Middle Initial)

5. PATIENT'S ADDRESS (No., Street)

6. PATIENT RELATIONSHIP TO INSURED Self ☐ Spouse ☐ Child ☐ Other ☐

7. INSURED'S ADDRESS (No., Street)

CITY | STATE

8. RESERVED FOR NUCC USE

CITY | STATE

ZIP CODE | TELEPHONE (Include Area Code) ( )

ZIP CODE | TELEPHONE (Include Area Code) ( )

9. OTHER INSURED'S NAME (Last Name, First Name, Middle Initial)

10. IS PATIENT'S CONDITION RELATED TO:

11. INSURED'S POLICY GROUP OR FECA NUMBER

a. OTHER INSURED'S POLICY OR GROUP NUMBER

a. EMPLOYMENT? (Current or Previous) YES ☐ NO ☐

a. INSURED'S DATE OF BIRTH MM | DD | YY   SEX M ☐ F ☐

b. RESERVED FOR NUCC USE

b. AUTO ACCIDENT? YES ☐ NO ☐   PLACE (State)

b. OTHER CLAIM ID (Designated by NUCC)

c. RESERVED FOR NUCC USE

c. OTHER ACCIDENT? YES ☐ NO ☐

c. INSURANCE PLAN NAME OR PROGRAM NAME

d. INSURANCE PLAN NAME OR PROGRAM NAME

10d. CLAIM CODES (Designated by NUCC)

d. IS THERE ANOTHER HEALTH BENEFIT PLAN? YES ☐ NO ☐ If yes, complete items 9, 9a, and 9d.

READ BACK OF FORM BEFORE COMPLETING & SIGNING THIS FORM.

12. PATIENT'S OR AUTHORIZED PERSON'S SIGNATURE I authorize the release of any medical or other information necessary to process this claim. I also request payment of government benefits either to myself or to the party who accepts assignment below.

SIGNED _____ DATE _____

13. INSURED'S OR AUTHORIZED PERSON'S SIGNATURE I authorize payment of medical benefits to the undersigned physician or supplier for services described below.

SIGNED _____

[PATIENT AND INSURED INFORMATION]

14. DATE OF CURRENT ILLNESS, INJURY, or PREGNANCY (LMP) MM | DD | YY   QUAL.

15. OTHER DATE QUAL. MM | DD | YY

16. DATES PATIENT UNABLE TO WORK IN CURRENT OCCUPATION FROM MM | DD | YY TO MM | DD | YY

17. NAME OF REFERRING PROVIDER OR OTHER SOURCE 17a. 17b. NPI

18. HOSPITALIZATION DATES RELATED TO CURRENT SERVICES FROM MM | DD | YY TO MM | DD | YY

19. ADDITIONAL CLAIM INFORMATION (Designated by NUCC)

20. OUTSIDE LAB? YES ☐ NO ☐ $ CHARGES

21. DIAGNOSIS OR NATURE OF ILLNESS OR INJURY Relate A-L to service line below (24E) ICD Ind.

A. |____ B. |____ C. |____ D. |____
E. |____ F. |____ G. |____ H. |____
I. |____ J. |____ K. |____ L. |____

22. RESUBMISSION CODE ORIGINAL REF. NO.

23. PRIOR AUTHORIZATION NUMBER

24. A. DATE(S) OF SERVICE From MM DD YY To MM DD YY	B. PLACE OF SERVICE	C. EMG	D. PROCEDURES, SERVICES, OR SUPPLIES (Explain Unusual Circumstances) CPT/HCPCS	MODIFIER	E. DIAGNOSIS POINTER	F. $ CHARGES	G. DAYS OR UNITS	H. EPSDT Family Plan	I. ID. QUAL	J. RENDERING PROVIDER ID. #
1										NPI
2										NPI
3										NPI
4										NPI
5										NPI
6										NPI

25. FEDERAL TAX I.D. NUMBER SSN ☐ EIN ☐

26. PATIENT'S ACCOUNT NO.

27. ACCEPT ASSIGNMENT? (For govt. claims, see back) YES ☐ NO ☐

28. TOTAL CHARGE $

29. AMOUNT PAID $

30. Rsvd. for NUCC Use

31. SIGNATURE OF PHYSICIAN OR SUPPLIER INCLUDING DEGREES OR CREDENTIALS (I certify that the statements on the reverse apply to this bill and are made a part thereof.)

SIGNED _____ DATE _____

32. SERVICE FACILITY LOCATION INFORMATION

a. NPI b.

33. BILLING PROVIDER INFO & PH # ( )

a. NPI b.

[PHYSICIAN OR SUPPLIER INFORMATION]

NUCC Instruction Manual available at: www.nucc.org   **PLEASE PRINT OR TYPE**   APPROVED OMB-0938-1197 FORM 1500 (02-12)

Clear Form

Figure 10-10

REVIEW QUESTIONS

MATCHING

Choose the correct answer and write its corresponding letter in the space provided.

a. encryption
b. guarantor
c. release of information form
d. clearinghouse
e. EMCs

1. _____ The person financially responsible for medical services
2. _____ Electronic medical claims
3. _____ Written authorization by a patient to disclose personal information to a specifically named entity
4. _____ Scrambling of information during transmission so that the information cannot be intercepted and read by anyone other than the intended recipient
5. _____ A company that receives claims from medical facilities, audits the claims for errors, and then forwards clean claims to the insurance company for the purpose of reimbursement

MULTIPLE CHOICE

Circle the letter of the choice that best completes each statement or answers the question.

1. Which of the following is a disadvantage of electronic medical claims?
   a. They are more efficient.
   b. Claims can sometimes be slowed down.
   c. There are issues with claims attachments.
   d. None of the above

2. Which of the following is another name for a superbill?
   a. Encounter form
   b. Routing slip
   c. Charge slip
   d. All of the above

3. When is the amount paid filled in for FL 29?
   a. When submitting the primary claim
   b. After the primary insurance EOB has been received and the secondary claim is to be submitted
   c. Never
   d. When submitting both the primary and secondary claims

4. How much of the physician's income can be generated by insurance claims?
   a. 60 percent
   b. 70 percent
   c. 80 percent
   d. 75 percent

© 2018 Pearson Education, Inc.

5. Which of the following is the definition of the birthday rule?

   a. If a dependent child is covered by both parents' insurance plans, and the parents are not separated or divorced, the primary insurance plan is determined by the parent whose birthday is earlier in the calendar year.

   b. If two or more plans cover a dependent child of separated or divorced parents who do not have joint custody, the primary insurance plan is determined by the parent whose birthday is earlier in the calendar year.

   c. Both a and b

   d. None of the above

SHORT ANSWER

Provide the correct response to each question that follows.

1. a. What is the result of not acquiring a patient's signature on the assignment of benefits form?

   _____

   _____

   _____

   b. What is a signed assignment of benefits form called in most medical offices?

   _____

   c. If a signed assignment of benefits form is not on file, should you still submit a claim to the insurance carrier? Why or why not?

   _____

   _____

   _____

2. a. What patient information is needed for a billing service to process claims?

   _____

   _____

   _____

   b. If a medical office uses a billing service, where will the insurance payment be sent, and how will this payment be handled?

   _____

   _____

   _____

3. What items does the patient information form include?

   1. _____

   2. _____

4. When an assignment of benefits form is signed, indicating "signature on file," can this form be used to release a patient's healthcare information to other entities other than the insurance carrier? Why or why not?

   _____

   _____

   _____

5. HIPAA implemented the 10 Transaction Standards, which eliminated confusion when medical information is exchanged between the provider and the insurance carrier. What are the 10 Transaction Standards?

1. _____

2. _____

3. _____

4. _____

5. _____

6. _____

7. _____

8. _____

9. _____

10. _____

TRUE/FALSE

Identify each statement as true (T) or false (F).

1. _____ An incorrect claim must be corrected, but does not cost any additional fees each time it is returned for errors.

2. _____ Original CMS-1500 claim forms must be used for submittal; thus, copied claims cannot be submitted.

3. _____ Guidelines for completing the CMS-1500 form do not vary at state and local levels.

4. _____ When entering the amount of charges in FL 24, you must use a dollar sign and a decimal point.

5. _____ The term "signature on file" can be used in box 12.

© 2018 Pearson Education, Inc.

CHAPTER 11
Hospital Medical Billing

CHAPTER OBJECTIVES

After reading this chapter, the student should be able to:

1. Understand the inpatient billing process used by hospitals.
2. Submit accurate and timely hospital claims and practice good follow-up and collection techniques.
3. Identify the different types of facilities and differentiate between inpatient and outpatient services.
4. Understand that hospital billing and coding are based on revenue.
5. Recognize that hospital reimbursement is not a fee for service, but a fixed fee payment based on the diagnosis rather than on time or services rendered.
6. Complete the UB-04 hospital billing claim form.

CHAPTER OUTLINE

Inpatient Billing Process

Charge Description Master

Types of Payers

Coding and Reimbursement Methods

Diagnosis Related Group System
    Cost Outliers

UB-04 Hospital Billing Claim Form

Instructions for Completing the UB-04 Claim Form

Codes for Use on the UB-04 Claim Form
    Type of Bill Codes (Form Locator 4)
    Sex Codes (Form Locator 11)
    Admission/Discharge Hour Codes (Form Locators 13 and 16)
    Admission Type Codes (Form Locator 14)
    Source of Admission (Form Locator 15)
    Discharge Status Codes (Form Locator 17)
    Condition Codes (Form Locators 18–28)
    Occurrence Code Examples (Form Locators 31–34)
    Value Codes (Form Locators 39–41)
    Revenue Codes (Form Locator 42)
    Patient Relationship (Form Locator 59)
    Practice Exercises

© 2018 Pearson Education, Inc.

KEY TERMS

Using the highlighted terms and glossary in the textbook, define the following terms:

1. admitting physician _____

   _____

2. Ambulatory Payment Classification (APC) system _____

   _____

3. ambulatory surgical center (ASC) _____

   _____

4. ambulatory surgical unit (ASU) _____

   _____

5. attending physician _____

   _____

6. charge description master (CDM) _____

   _____

7. comorbidity _____

   _____

8. cost outlier _____

   _____

9. Diagnosis Related Group (DRG) _____

   _____

10. emergency care _____

    _____

11. grouper _____

    _____

12. health information system (HIS) _____

    _____

13. hospice _____

    _____

14. inpatient care _____

    _____

15. master patient index _____

    _____

16. Medicare DRG (CMS-DRG & MS-DRG) _____

    _____

17. occurrence span codes _____

    _____

18. operating physician _____

    _____

© 2018 Pearson Education, Inc.

19. outpatient care _____

_____

20. Outpatient Prospective Payment System (OPPS) _____

_____

21. patient control number (PCN) _____

_____

22. present on admission (POA) _____

_____

23. principal diagnosis _____

_____

24. prospective payment system _____

_____

25. registration _____

_____

26. rendering physician _____

_____

27. skilled nursing facility (SNF) _____

_____

28. urgent care _____

_____

CRITICAL THINKING QUESTIONS

Using the knowledge you have gained from reading the textbook, apply critical thinking skills to answer the following questions.

1. Answer the following questions related to the Ambulatory Payment Classification (APC) system:

   a. In your own words, briefly describe the purpose of the APC.

   _____

   _____

   _____

   _____

   _____

   b. During billing, who assigns an APC?

   _____

   _____

   _____

   c. What 13 types of services are APCs applied to?

   1. _____

   2. _____

3. _____

4. _____

5. _____

6. _____

7. _____

8. _____

9. _____

10. _____

11. _____

12. _____

13. _____

2. Answer the following questions related to Diagnosis Related Groups (DRGs) and case mixes:

a. In your own words, briefly describe the purpose of a DRG.

_____

_____

_____

_____

_____

b. During billing, who assigns a DRG?

_____

_____

c. In what seven ways is a DRG classified?

1. _____

2. _____

3. _____

4. _____

5. _____

6. _____

7. _____

d. How can a hospital determine reimbursement for a DRG?

_____

_____

_____

e. How does a hospital determine its charges for a DRG?

_____

_____

_____

_____

_____

© 2018 Pearson Education, Inc.

f. What are the five factors that contribute to a facility's case mix?

1. _____
2. _____
3. _____
4. _____
5. _____

g. In your own words, how has DRG reimbursement changed hospital reimbursement?

_____
_____
_____
_____
_____

h. What are the eight situations that could cause a DRG cost outlier?

1. _____
2. _____
3. _____
4. _____
5. _____
6. _____
7. _____
8. _____

i. If a cost outlier occurs, how is it reimbursed by the insurance carrier?

_____
_____
_____

3. Answer the following questions related to ICD-10-PCS:
   a. What type of medical facility uses ICD-10-PCS?

   _____

   b. Under what four circumstances should ICD-10-PCS be used?

   1. _____
   2. _____
   3. _____
   4. _____

4. Answer the following questions related to hospital billing and the UB-04 form:
   a. What claim form is used for billing hospital services?

   b. Why is the UB-04 printed in red ink on white paper?

   _____
   _____
   _____

c. What are revenue codes used for?

_____

_____

_____

d. What are value codes used for?

_____

_____

_____

e. What are type of bill codes used for?

_____

_____

_____

f. What are sex codes used for?

_____

_____

_____

g. What are source of admission codes used for?

_____

_____

_____

h. What are discharge codes used for?

_____

_____

_____

i. What are condition codes used for?

_____

_____

_____

j. What are occurrence codes used for?

_____

_____

_____

k. What are patient relationship codes used for?

_____

_____

_____

5. a. How would you show where the patient was discharged to?

_____

_____

_____

   © 2018 Pearson Education, Inc.

b. What are some examples of discharge status codes with their descriptions?

_____

_____

_____

c. What is discharge status, and why is accuracy important when entering the discharge status code?

_____

_____

_____

PRACTICE EXERCISES

1. Using the form locator information supplied in the textbook, write each form locator for the UB-04 along with the description for each. Add any notes you think will be helpful when filling out cases.

2. Using the ICD-10-PCS, code the following procedures:

Partial open epiglottidectomy

Code _____

Secondary insertion of intraocular lens prosthesis

Code _____

Percutaneous implantation of chemotherapy wafer into brain

Code _____

Laparoscopically assisted vaginal hysterectomy

Code _____

Dilation of urethra via cystoscopy

Code _____

Open repair of right diaphragmatic hernia with mesh, abdominal approach

Code _____

Iliac bone marrow aspiration from donor for transplant

Code _____

Arthroscopic bursotomy of left hand for aspiration of fluid

Code _____

Insertion of indwelling urethral catheterization

Code _____

Classical Cesarean section

Code _____

Control of epistaxis by cauterization and packing

Code _____

Bronchoscopic destruction of lesion, LUL lung

Code _____

Paracentesis with biopsy

Code _____

Retinal electrolysis for tear repair, right eye

Code _____

Renal function study, nonimaging using iodine 123

Code _____

Autologous skin graft for bilateral breast augmentation

Code _____

Percutaneous insertion for drainage tube, right kidney

Code _____

Fusion for hammer toe, left foot, 2nd digit, with internal fixation

Code _____

Lengthening of right femoral shaft with external fixation device

Code _____

Laparoscopic lysis of mesenteric adhesions

Code _____

Systemic arterial blood gas measurement, external

Code _____

Right kidney transplant from living donor

Code _____

Bilateral retrograde pyelogram

Code _____

Reattachment of amputated left thumb

Code _____

Whole body PET scan

Code _____

Suture of laceration of external right ear

Code _____

Open Denver shunt (VP shunt)

Code _____

Total open sigmoidectomy with transverse colon colostomy

Code _____

3. The case studies that follow are provided for additional practice in completing the UB-04 claim form for hospital billing. By applying what you have learned in your student text, accurately complete each case study. All the information you need is provided, including patient demographics, diagnostic and procedure codes, and a brief case history of each patient's health problem. Complete the cases based on the following criteria:

- All patients have release of information and assignment of benefit signatures on file.
- All physicians and hospitals participate in all the healthcare plans listed, and all physicians and hospitals accept assignment for these plans.
- The hospital is the billing entity.
- The national transition to NPI numbers is complete, and legacy PINs of individual payers are no longer used. If legacy PINs are still being used by selected payers in your region, your instructor may provide legacy PINs in addition to the NPI.

© 2018 Pearson Education, Inc.

- 2017 ICD-10-CM and CPT codes are used.
- Use six-digit dates for *all* dates.
- All street names should be entered with standard postal abbreviations, even if they are spelled out on the source documents.
- Room charges reflect the daily rate and should be multiplied times the number of days to get the total room charge for the stay.
- All other services reflect the total charges for all units provided.
- Revenue codes should be entered in ascending order.

To complete each case study, use the blank UB-04 form provided after each case.

a. Using the given source documents and the blank UB-04 form provided (Figure 11-1), complete the following case study for patient Cristal McLean (Case 11-1):

CASE 11-1

Capital City General Hospital
1000 Cherry Street
Capital City, NY 12345-2222
(555) 555-1000

Patient Information:	Cristal McLean
	921 Sweet Street, Capital City, NY 12345
	555-555-6644
DOB:	10-17-1982
Sex:	Female
SSN:	186-03-1982
Status:	Single **Student:** No
Employer:	Shopaholic's
	3829 Clearview Mall, Capital City, NY 12345
	555-555-7467
Responsible Party:	Cristal McLean
Responsible Party Address:	Same
Insurance Information:	Blue Cross Blue Shield
	379 Blue Plaza Capital City, NY 12345
ID #:	YYJ674976211 **Group #:** 10203
Insured's Name:	Same **Relationship to Patient:** Self
Insured's DOB:	
❑ **Male** ❑ **Female**	
Insured's Address:	
Insured's Employer:	
Authorization:	565688221 **Approved # of Days:** 2
Attending Physician:	Bette R. Soone, MD
Federal Tax ID #:	75-7654321
NPI:	0987654321

Reason for visit: I am having a lot of ankle swelling and headaches.

© 2018 Pearson Education, Inc.

CASE 11-1

HPI: This is a white female admitted on August 2, 20XX, at 7:15 am for elevated BP: 140/88, B/L edema of lower extremities, and albuminuria. Pt. has pre-eclampsia. Pt. has no history of complications with previous pregnancy. She is 29 weeks pregnant. LMP12/03/XX Pt. has healthy two-year-old boy at home. No effects to baby's health at this time. Her BP and albumin have stayed mildly elevated at this time. If no improvement within 1 week, we may have to induce labor. Pt. was discharged on August 5, 20XX, at 11:00 a.m.

Patient Control #:	658423	Type of Admission:	1
MR #:	0123573356	Source of Admission:	1
Hospital NPI:	1212121212	Discharge Status:	01
Hospital Tax ID:	75-7575757	Type of Bill Code:	111

Fees:

Revenue Codes	Units	Total Charges	Dates of Service
110 Room/Board/Semi	3	$ 400.00/day	08/02/20XX–08/04/20XX
250 Pharmacy	3	$ 300.00	08/02/20XX–08/04/20XX
260 IV Therapy	2	$ 550.00	08/02/20XX–08/03/20XX
270 Med/Surg Supplies	3	$ 450.00	08/02/20XX–08/04/20XX
320 Radiology	1	$ 250.00	08/02/20XX
001 TOTAL		$2350.00	

Principal DX:	O14.93
Admitting DX:	O14.93
Principal Procedure Code:	These ICD-10-PCS codes are not typically picked up

Figure 11-1

© 2018 Pearson Education, Inc.

b. Using the given source documents and the blank UB-04 form provided (Figure 11-2), complete the following case study for patient Raquel Freeman (Case 11-2):

CASE 11-2

Capital City General Hospital
1000 Cherry Street
Capital City, NY 12345-2222
(555) 555-1000

Patient Information:	Raquel Freeman
	22 Lock Drive, Capital City, NY 12345
	555-555-9924
DOB:	09-20-1995
Sex:	Female
SSN:	810-10-2240
Status:	Single **Student:** Yes
Employer:	

Responsible Party:	Seth Freeman
Responsible Party Address:	Same
Insurance Information:	Blue Cross Blue Shield
	379 Blue Plaza Capital City, NY 12345
ID #:	YYZ546676122 **Group #:** 9001
Insured's Name:	Seth Freeman **Relationship to Patient:** Father
Insured's DOB:	10/03/1972
☒ Male ☐ Female	
Insured's Address:	Same

Insured's Employer:	Private Investivations, Inc.
	62 Catch Way
	Capital City, NY 12345
Authorization:	565688221 **Approved # of Days:** 4
Attending Physician:	Phil Wells, MD
Federal Tax ID #:	75-0246810
NPI:	1234567890

Reason for visit: My daughter is running a high fever and her head hurts.

CASE 11-2

HPI: This is an African American female admitted on September 4, 20XX, at 8:00 am for bacterial meningitis. The patient has a severe headache that is accompanied by a fever of 102.4°F. Over the course of treatment, the pt. improved remarkably with current treatment. Pt. was discharged on September 8, 20XX, at 9:30 a.m.

Patient Control #:	135535	Type of Admission:	1
MR #:	85735681	Source of Admission:	1
Hospital NPI:	1212121212	Discharge Status:	01
Hospital Tax ID:	75-7575757	Type of Bill Code:	111

Fees:

Revenue Codes	Units	Total Charges	Dates of Service
110 Room/Board/Semi	4	$ 400.00/day	09/04/20XX–09/08/20XX
250 Pharmacy	5	$ 450.00	09/04/20XX–09/08/20XX
260 IV Therapy	4	$ 400.00	09/04/20XX–09/07/20XX
270 Med/Surg Supplies	4	$ 480.00	09/04/20XX–09/07/20XX
300 Pathology	1	$ 450.00	09/04/20XX
001 TOTAL		$3380.00	

Principal DX:	G00.9
Admitting DX:	G00.9
Principal Procedure Code:	009U3ZX

© 2018 Pearson Education, Inc.

Figure 11-2

c. Using the given source documents and the blank UB-04 form provided (Figure 11-3), complete the following case study for patient Jamal Clinton (Case 11-3):

CASE 11-3

Capital City General Hospital
1000 Cherry Street
Capital City, NY 12345-2222
(555) 555-1000

Patient Information:	Jamal Clinton
	189 Maryland Avenue, Capital City, NY 12345
	555-555-1456
DOB:	05-19-1962
Sex:	Male
SSN:	727-22-1581
Status:	Divorced **Student:** No
Employer:	Capital City College
	400 College Road, Capital City, NY 12345
	555-555-4001
Responsible Party:	Jamal Clinton
Responsible Party Address:	Same
Insurance Information:	Aetna
	1625 Healthcare Bldg., Capital City, NY 12345
ID #:	300265 **Group #:** 7224
Insured's Name:	Same **Relationship to Patient:** Self
Insured's DOB:	
❏ Male ❏ Female	
Insured's Address:	
Insured's Employer:	
Authorization:	8630656131 **Approved # of Days:** 2
Attending Physician:	Phil Wells, MD
Federal Tax ID #:	75-0246810
NPI:	1234567890

Reason for visit: Kidney infection.

© 2018 Pearson Education, Inc.

CASE 11-3

HPI: This is an African American male admitted on December 12, 20XX, at 10:15 a.m. for a kidney infection. Pt. has a history of kidney infections. There is no evidence of damage to the kidneys. Pt. was discharged on December 14, 20XX, at 10:00 a.m.

Patient Control #:	523523	Type of Admission:	1
MR #:	2563216841	Source of Admission:	1
Hospital NPI:	1212121212	Discharge Status:	01
Hospital Tax ID:	75-7575757	Type of Bill Code:	111

Fees:

Revenue Codes	Units	Total Charges	Dates of Service
110 Room/Board/Semi	2	$ 400.00/day	12/12/20XX–12/14/20XX
250 Pharmacy	3	$ 300.00	12/12/20XX–12/14/20XX
260 IV Therapy	2	$ 500.00	12/12/20XX–12/13/20XX
270 Med/Surg Supplies	2	$ 200.00	12/12/20XX–12/13/20XX
320 Radiology	2	$ 500.00	12/13/20XX
001 TOTAL		$2300.00	

Principal DX:	N15.9, B96.20
Admitting DX:	N15.9
Principal Procedure Code:	These ICD-10-PCS codes are not typically picked up

Figure 11-3

© 2018 Pearson Education, Inc.

d. Using the given source documents and the blank UB-04 form provided (Figure 11-4), complete the following case study for patient Dalton Sizer (Case 11-4):

CASE 11-4

Capital City General Hospital
1000 Cherry Street
Capital City, NY 12345-2222
(555) 555-1000

Patient Information:	Dalton Sizer
	16 Marigold Lane, Capital City, NY 12345
	555-555-3007
DOB:	01-20-1970
Sex:	Male
SSN:	301-19-0431
Status:	Married **Student:** No
Employer:	Woodlands Excavating Co.
	2112 Sycamore Drive, Capital City, NY 12345
	555-555-1887
Responsible Party:	Dalton Sizer
Responsible Party Address:	Same
Insurance Information:	Aetna
	1625 Healthcare Bldg., Capital City NY 12345
ID #:	6543684 **Group #:** 5493
Insured's Name:	Same **Relationship to Patient:** Self
Insured's DOB:	
❏ Male ❏ Female	
Insured's Address:	
Insured's Employer:	
Authorization:	**Approved # of Days:** 2
Attending Physician:	Elby Alright, MD
Federal Tax ID #:	75-7654321
NPI:	9876543210

Reason for visit: I hit the back of my head on the corner of the bathroom sink counter while standing up from bending over in the bathroom.

CASE 11-4

Capital City General Hospital Outpatient Radiology

Patient's Name: Dalton Sizer   **DOB:** 01/20/1970

Date of Procedure: 11/08/20XX   **PCP:** Elby Alright, MD

Ordering Physician: Elby Alright, MD   **MR #:** DS163540

Report #: DS-01907

Diagnosis: Wound, posterior scalp, open due to striking head against bathroom counter

Procedure: MRI OF BRAIN

Exam is performed with the administration of IV contrast. Study reveals a wound on the posterior portion of the scalp that is consistent with recent trauma. This wound measures 2 × 0.2 in.

The brain presents normal in size without any hematoma, hemorrhage, laceration, or lesion. There is no evidence of disease at this time.

DX Code: S01.01XA, W22.8XXA   **Source of Admission:**   1

CPT Procedure Code: 70552   **Discharge Status:**   01

Hospital NPI:	6767676767		**Type of Bill Code:**	131
Hospital Tax ID:	75-7575757		**Patient Control #:**	006314

Fees:

Revenue Codes	Units	Total Charges	Dates of Service
250 Pharmacy	1	$ 90.00	11/08/20XX
260 IV Therapy	1	$ 375.00	11/08/20XX
320 Radiology	1	$ 920.00	11/08/20XX
001 TOTAL		$1385.00	

© 2018 Pearson Education, Inc.

Figure 11-4

e. Using the given source documents and the blank UB-04 form provided (Figure 11-5), complete the following case study for patient Marvin Hall (Case 11-5):

CASE 11-5

Capital City General Hospital
1000 Cherry Street
Capital City, NY 12345-2222
(555) 555-1000

Patient Information: Marvin Hall
510 County Line Road, Capital City, NY 12345
555-555-2505

DOB: 05-29-1943

Sex: Male

SSN: 625-44-0827

Status: Married   **Student:** No

Employer: Retired

Responsible Party: Marvin Hall

Responsible Party Address: Same

Insurance Information: Medicare
P.O. Box 9834, Capital City, NY 12345

ID #:   564695238A   **Group #:**

Insured's Name: Same   **Relationship to Patient:** Self

Insured's DOB:

❑ Male   ❑ Female

Insured's Address:

Insured's Employer:

Authorization: **Approved # of Days:**

Attending Physician: Elby Alright, MD

Federal Tax ID #:   75-7654321

NPI: 9876543210

Reason for visit: My doctor sent me to get a chest X-ray to see whether I have pleurisy.

© 2018 Pearson Education, Inc.

CASE 11-5

Capital City General Hospital Outpatient Radiology

Patient's Name: Marvin Hall

Date of Procedure: 01/07/20XX

Ordering Physician: Elby Alright, MD

Report #: MH-624702

Diagnosis: Pleurisy

Procedure: X-ray of chest

DOB: 05/29/1943

PCP: Elby Alright, MD

MR #: 22668874

Study compared with previous CXR. The pleural membrane shows evidence of inflammation and infection. Films are consistent with diagnosis.

DX Code: R09.1

CPT Procedure Code: 71030

Source of Admission: 1

Discharge Status: 01

Hospital NPI:		6767676767	Type of Bill Code:	132
Hospital Tax ID:		75-7575757	Patient Control #:	883070

Fees:

Revenue Codes	Units	Total Charges	Dates of Service
972 Radiologist	1	$250.00	01/07/20XX
320 Radiology	1	$280.00	01/07/20XX
001 TOTAL		$530.00	

Figure 11-5

© 2018 Pearson Education, Inc.

REVIEW QUESTIONS

MATCHING

Choose the correct answer and write its corresponding letter in the space provided.

a. Master Patient Index
b. discharge Analyst
c. chargemaster
d. inlier
e. outlier

1. _____ The main database for all of a hospital's patients
2. _____ A hospital case that exceeds a specific DRG length of stay
3. _____ A hospital case that falls below the mean average or expected length of stay for a specific DRG
4. _____ Organizes revenue codes, procedure codes, descriptions, and charges
5. _____ Used to check the completeness of a patient's medical record for dictated reports and signatures

MULTIPLE CHOICE

Circle the letter of the choice that best completes each statement or answers the question.

1. When does a hospital submit a bill for its services for an inpatient case?
   a. Every day of the hospital stay
   b. After the admission sheet is completed and signed by the physician
   c. After the discharge summary is completed and signed by the physician
   d. At the end of the month

2. What is the term for the process of a grouper searching all listed diagnoses, comorbidities, complications, and procedures to assign and calculate a DRG for a patient's case?
   a. Analyzing
   b. Grouping
   c. Looping
   d. All of the above

3. What is a cost outlier?
   a. When the hospital has to cut costs
   b. Upcoding a patient's case
   c. A DRG cannot be assigned due to an atypical situation
   d. None of the above

4. Which of the following is *not* considered inpatient care?
   a. Ambulatory Surgical Unit in the hospital
   b. Skilled nursing facility
   c. Hospice
   d. Rehabilitation Center

5. Which of the following medical facilities does *not* utilize the UB-04 for billing purposes?
   a. A physician's office
   b. Hospital outpatient departments and rural health clinics
   c. Hospital inpatient departments
   d. Both a and b

SHORT ANSWER

Provide the correct response to each question that follows.

1. What are the discharge analyst's duties?

   _____

2. What are the three sex codes? List and define each.

   1. _____
      _____
      _____

   2. _____
      _____
      _____

   3. _____
      _____
      _____

3. Where is a hospital's Patient Account Service Department (PAS) usually located?

   _____

4. What is the purpose of the PAS?

   _____
   _____
   _____

5. What five pieces of information are included in the charge master that is printed out on the UB-04 for reimbursement? Briefly explain each.

   1. _____
      _____
      _____

   2. _____
      _____
      _____

   3. _____
      _____
      _____

   4. _____
      _____
      _____

   5. _____
      _____
      _____

© 2018 Pearson Education, Inc.

TRUE/FALSE

Identify each statement as true (T) or false (F).

1. _____ With APCs, services often rendered with a procedure are often unbundled.

2. _____ A grouper cannot determine the difference between an acute and a chronic condition.

3. _____ When referring to DRGs, the abbreviation CC is used to identify complications or comorbidities.

4. _____ More than one APC can be assigned to one specific patient per outpatient encounter.

5. _____ Admission and discharge hour codes are listed in military time.

6. _____ More than one DRG can be assigned to one specific patient per inpatient encounter.

CHAPTER 12

Medicare Medical Billing

CHAPTER OBJECTIVES

After reading this chapter, the student should be able to:

1. Discuss government billing guidelines.
2. Determine the amount due from the patient for a participating provider.
3. Understand the different Medicare fee schedules.
4. Examine and complete accurate Medicare claims forms.
5. Identify the types of Medicare fraud and abuse that can occur.

CHAPTER OUTLINE

Medicare History
  Medicare Administration

Medicare Part A Coverage and Eligibility Requirements
  Inpatient Hospital Care
  Skilled Nursing Facility
  Home Healthcare
  Hospice Care
  Blood
  Organ Transplants
  Inpatient Benefit Days

Medicare Part B Coverage and Eligibility Requirements

Medicare Part C

Medicare Part D

Services Not Covered by Medicare Parts A and B

Medigap, Medicaid, and Supplemental Insurance

Requirements for Medical Necessity

Medicare Coverage Plans
  Fee-for-Service: The Original Medicare Plan
  Medicare Advantage Plans or Medicare Part C

Value-Based Payment Modifier Program

Medicare Providers
  Part A Providers
  Part B Providers
  Participating versus Nonparticipating Medicare Part B Providers

© 2018 Pearson Education, Inc.

KEY TERMS

Using the highlighted terms and glossary in the textbook, define the following terms.

1. benefit period _____

_____

2. Consolidated Omnibus Budget Reconciliation Act of 1985 (COBRA) _____

_____

3. crossover _____

_____

4. Electronic Remittance Advice (ERA) _____

_____

5. end-stage renal disease (ESRD) _____

_____

6. Healthcare Common Procedure Coding System (HCPCS) _____

_____

© 2018 Pearson Education, Inc.

7. intermediaries _____

8. limiting charge _____

9. Local coverage determination (LCD) _____

10. Medicare abuse _____

11. Medicare Advantage (MA) _____

12. Medicare Administrative Contractor (MAC) _____

13. Medicare Development Letter _____

14. Medicare fraud _____

15. Medicare Part A _____

16. Medicare Part B _____

17. Medicare Part C _____

18. Medicare Part D _____

19. Medicare Remittance Notice (MRN) _____

20. Medicare secondary payer (MSP) _____

21. Medicare Summary Notice (MSN) _____

22. Medigap _____

23. non-par MFS _____

24. Office of Inspector General (OIG) _____

25. Program of All-Inclusive Care for the Elderly (PACE) _____

26. Recovery Audit Contractor (RAC) _____

27. scrubbing _____

_____

28. Tax Relief and Healthcare Act (TRHCA) _____

_____

29. telemedicine (telehealth) _____

_____

CRITICAL THINKING QUESTIONS

Using the knowledge you have gained from reading the textbook, apply critical thinking skills to answer the following questions.

1. a. In your own words, briefly explain the history of Medicare.

_____

_____

_____

_____

_____

b. How has Medicare changed the business of healthcare and health insurance?

_____

_____

_____

_____

c. What will the future of Medicare likely be in 10 years?

_____

_____

_____

_____

_____

2. Answer the following questions related to the administration of Medicare:
    a. Who directs Medicare?

_____

_____

_____

b. What U.S. department is CMS a division of?

_____

_____

c. In your own words, what are the three roles of CMS?

    1. _____

_____

© 2018 Pearson Education, Inc.

2. _____

_____

3. _____

_____

d. What is the primary function of CMS?

_____

_____

_____

e. In your own words, what is a Medicare contractor, and what is its function?

_____

_____

_____

_____

3. Answer the following questions related to the different parts of Medicare:

a. What are seven roles and responsibilities of Medicare Part A: Intermediaries?

1. _____
2. _____
3. _____
4. _____
5. _____
6. _____
7. _____

b. What six groups of people qualify for Medicare Part A benefits?

1. _____
2. _____
3. _____
4. _____
5. _____
6. _____

c. What are the five roles and responsibilities of Medicare Part B: Carriers?

1. _____
2. _____
3. _____
4. _____
5. _____

d. In your own words, what is the primary function of Medicare intermediaries and carriers?

_____

_____

_____

_____

_____

4. Answer the following questions related to Medicare coverage and claim processing:

a. Patient Jon Yates would like to know what his Medicare Part B will cover.

   1. _____
   2. _____
   3. _____
   4. _____

b. Briefly explain to your patient what eligibility requirements must be met to enroll in Medicare Part B.

   _____
   _____
   _____

c. What is the contingency margin for?

   1. _____
   2. _____
   3. _____
   4. _____

d. How is the Medicare Part B premium determined?

   _____
   _____

e. What are the two types of plans that a Medicare Advantage Plan beneficiary can choose from?

   1. _____
   2. _____

f. What seven benefits are covered under patient Perry Austin's Medicare Part C benefits?

   1. _____
   2. _____
   3. _____
   4. _____
   5. _____
   6. _____
   7. _____

g. What is Medicare Part D used for?

   _____

h. Who is eligible for Medicare Part D?

   _____
   _____

5. Answer the following questions related to Medicare fraud and abuse:

a. What are four sanctions that the DHHS will impose on individuals who consistently fail to comply with Medicare law or are deemed abusive to the Medicare program?

   1. _____
   2. _____
   3. _____
   4. _____

© 2018 Pearson Education, Inc.

b. What are the penalties that can be imposed on those convicted of Medicare fraud and/or abuse?

_____

_____

_____

_____

c. As a healthcare professional, how can you avoid committing Medicare fraud and/or abuse?

_____

_____

_____

_____

_____

PRACTICE EXERCISES

1. Using the form locator information written out on your index cards from a prior chapter complete the following activity. Flag those FLs that would be filled out differently for Medicare patients.

2. Determine the amount owed by the patient.

   A. Participating physician's standard fee: $300.00

       Allowed amount $200.00

       Medicare pays 80%:   _____

       Patient or supplemental plan pays 20%:   _____

       Provider adjustment (write-off):   _____

   B. Non-par physician's standard fee (accepts assignment): $250.00

       Medicare non-par fee: _____

       Medicare pays 80%:   _____

       Patient or supplemental plan pays 20%:   _____

       Provider adjustment (write-off):   _____

   C. Non-par physician's standard fee (does not accept assignment): $250.00

       Medicare non-par fee: _____

       Limiting charge: _____

       Patient billed: _____

       Medicare pays patient: _____

       Total provider can collect: _____

       Patient out-of-pocket expense: _____

       Provider adjustment (write-off):   _____

3. The following case studies are provided for additional practice in completing the CMS-1500 claim form for Medicare physician outpatient billing. By applying what you have learned in your student text, accurately code and complete each case study. Patient demographics and a brief case history are provided. Complete the cases based on the following criteria:

   - All patients have release of information and assignment of benefit signatures on file.
   - All providers are participating and accept assignment.
   - The group practice is the billing entity.
   - The national transition to NPI numbers is complete, and legacy PINs and UPINs are no longer used.
   - 2017 ICD-10-CM and CPT codes are used.
   - Use eight-digit dates for birthdates. Use six-digit dates for all other dates.
   - All street names should be entered with standard postal abbreviations, even if they are spelled out on the source documents.
   - Enter ICD-10 codes in the order they are listed on the encounter form.
   - When entering CPT codes, enter the E/M code first. Enter remaining codes in descending price order.

To determine the correct fees, refer to the Capital City Medical Fee Schedule, which is located after each case's source documents. Use the blank CMS-1500 form provided after each case.

   a. Using the source documents, the Capital City Medical Fee Schedule (Figure 12-1), and the blank CMS-1500 form provided (Figure 12-1), complete the following case study for patient Bernard Ward (Case 12-1):

© 2018 Pearson Education, Inc.

CASE 12-1

Capital City Medical—123 Unknown Boulevard, Capital City, NY 12345-2222 (555) 555-1234	**Patient Information Form**
	Tax ID: 75-0246810
Phil Wells, MD, Mannie Mends, MD, Bette R. Soone, MD	**Group NPI: 1513171216**

Patient Information:

Name: (Last, First) <u>Ward, Bernard</u>　　　☒ Male　❏ Female　Birth Date: <u>03/20/1957</u>

Address: <u>420 Cardinal Ct, Township, NY 12345</u>　　　　　Phone: (555) <u>555-2534</u>

Social Security Number: <u>896-80-2944</u>　　　　Full-Time Student:　❏ Yes　☒ No

Marital Status:　❏ Single　☒ Married　❏ Divorced　❏ Other

Employment:

Employer: <u>Retired</u>　　　　　　　　　　Phone: ( ) _____

Address: _____

Condition Related to:　❏ Auto Accident　❏ Employment　❏ Other Accident

Date of Accident: _____　State: _____

Emergency Contact: _____　**Phone: ( )** _____

Primary Insurance: <u>Medicaid</u>　　　　　Phone: ( ) _____

Address: <u>P O. Box , 9834, Capital City, NY 12345</u>

Insurance Policyholder's Name: <u>Same</u>　　　　❏ M　❏ F DOB: _____

Address: _____

Phone: _____　Relationship to Insured: ☒ Self　❏ Spouse　❏ Child　❏ Other

Employer: _____　Phone: ( ) _____

Employer's Address: _____

Policy/ID No: <u>366736530A</u>　Group No: _____　Percent Covered: <u>80</u>__% Copay Amt: $_____

Secondary Insurance: _____　Phone: ( ) _____

Address: _____

Insurance Policyholder's Name: _____　❏ M　❏ F DOB: _____

Address: _____

Phone: _____　Relationship to Insured: ❏ Self　❏ Spouse　❏ Child　❏ Other

Employer: _____　Phone: ( ) _____

Employer's Address: _____

Policy/ID No: _____　Group No: _____　Percent Covered: ___% Copay Amt: $_____

Reason for Visit: <u>I am here for a checkup on my MS.</u>

Known Allergies: _____

Referred by: _____

© 2018 Pearson Education, Inc.

CASE 12-1
SOAP

01/06/20XX
Assignment of Benefits: Y
Signature on File: Y
Referring Physician: N

S: Bernard Ward is here for a checkup on his multiple sclerosis. He has no recent complaints.
O: He denies any numbness, weakness, or stiffness. ROM is full.
A: 1. Multiple sclerosis in remission—G35
P: 1. Continue medications.
    2. Keep appointment with neurologist.
    3. Return in 3 months, unless relapse occurs.

_____

Phil Wells, MD
Family Practice
NPI: 1234567890

© 2018 Pearson Education, Inc.

CASE 12-1

Patient Name Bernard Ward

Capital City Medical
123 Unknown Boulevard, Capital City, NY 12345-2222

Date of Service
01-06-20XX

New Patient			Other Invasive/Noninvasive			Laboratory	
Problem Focused	99201	Arthrocentesis/Aspiration/Injection			Amylase	82150
Expanded Problem, Focused	99202	Small Joint		20600	B12	82607
Detailed	99203	Interm Joint		20605	CBC & Diff	85025
Comprehensive	99204	Major Joint		20610	Comp Metabolic Panel	80053
Comprehensive/High Complex	99205	**Other Invasive/Noninvasive**			Chlamydia Screen	87110
Well Exam Infant (up to 12 mos.)	99381	Audiometry		92552	Cholesterol	82465
Well Exam 1–4 yrs.	99382	Cast Application			Digoxin	80162
Well Exam 5–11 yrs.	99383	Location Long Short			Electrolytes	80051
Well Exam 12–17 yrs.	99384	Catheterization		51701	Ferritin	82728
Well Exam 18–39 yrs.	99385	Circumcision		54150	Folate	82746
Well Exam 40–64 yrs.	99386	Colposcopy		57452	GC Screen	87070
		Colposcopy w/Biopsy		57454	Glucose	82947
		Cryosurgery Premalignant Lesion			Glucose 1 HR	82950
		Location (s):			Glycosylated HGB A1C	83036
Established Patient		Cryosurgery Warts			HCT	85014
Post-Op Follow Up Visit	99024	Location (s):			HDL	83718
Minimum	99211	Curettement Lesion			Hep BSAG	87340
Problem Focused	99212	Single		11055	Hepatitis panel, acute	80074
Expanded Problem Focused	99213 ☒	2–4		11056	HGB	85018
Detailed	99214	>4		11057	HIV	86703
Comprehensive/High Complex	99215	Diaphragm Fitting		57170	Iron & TIBC	83550
Well Exam Infant (up to 12 mos.)	99391	Ear Irrigation		69210	Kidney Profile	80069
Well exam 1–4 yrs.	99392	ECG		93000	Lead	83655
Well Exam 5–11 yrs.	99393	Endometrial Biopsy		58100	Liver Profile	80076
Well Exam 12–17 yrs.	99394	Exc. Lesion Malignant			Mono Test	86308
Well Exam 18–39 yrs.	99395	Benign			Pap Smear	88155
Well Exam 40–64 yrs.	99396	Location			Pregnancy Test	84703
Obstetrics		Exc. Skin Tags (1–15)		11200	Obstetric Panel	80055
Total OB Care	59400	Each Additional 10		11201	Pro Time	85610
Injections		Fracture Treatment			PSA	84153
Administration Sub. / IM	90772	Loc			RPR	86592
Drug		w/Reduc w/o Reduc			Sed. Rate	85651
Dosage		I & D Abscess Single/Simple		10060	Stool Culture	87045
Allergy	95115	Multiple or Comp		10061	Stool O & P	87177
Cocci Skin Test	86490	I & D Pilonidal Cyst Simple		10080	Strep Screen	87880
DPT	90701	Pilonidal Cyst Complex		10081	Theophylline	80198
Hemophilus	90646	IV Therapy—To One Hour		90760	Thyroid Uptake	84479
Influenza	90658	Each Additional Hour		90761	TSH	84443
MMR	90707	Laceration Repair			Urinalysis	81000
OPV	90712	Location Size Simp/Comp			Urine Culture	87088
Pneumovax	90732	Laryngoscopy		31505	Drawing Fee	36415
TB Skin Test	86580	Oximetry		94760	Specimen Collection	99000
TD	90718	Punch Biopsy			**Other:**	
Unlisted Immun	90749	Rhythm Strip		93040		
Tetanus Toxoid	90703	Treadmill		93015		
Vaccine/Toxoid Admin <8 Yr Old w/ Counseling	90465	Trigger Point or Tendon Sheath Inj.		20550		
Vaccine/Toxoid Administration for Adult	90471	Tympanometry		92567		

Diagnosis/ICD-10: G35

I acknowledge receipt of medical services and authorize the release of any
medical information necessary to process this claim for healthcare payment only. I do authorize payment to the provider.

Total Estimated Charges: _____

Payment Amount: _____

Patient Signature Bernard Ward

Next Appointment:

Figure 12-1

Capital City Medical
Fee Schedule

New Patient OV		Punch Biopsy various codes	$80
Problem Focused 99201	$45	Nebulizer various codes	$45
Expanded Problem Focused 99202	$65	Cast Application various codes	$85
Detailed 99203	$85	Laryngoscopy 31505	$255
Comprehensive 99204	$105	Audiometry 92552	$85
Comprehensive/High Complex 99205	$115	Tympanometry 92567	$85
Well Exam infant (less than 1 year) 99381	$45	Ear Irrigation 69210	$25
Well Exam 1–4 yrs. 99382	$50	Diaphragm Fitting 57170	$30
Well Exam 5–11 yrs. 99383	$55	IV Therapy (up to one hour) 90760	$65
Well Exam 12–17 yrs. 99384	$65	Each additional hour 90761	$50
Well Exam 18–39 yrs. 99385	$85	Oximetry 94760	$10
Well Exam 40–64 yrs. 99386	$105	ECG 93000	$75
Established Patient OV		Holter Monitor various codes	$170
Post Op Follow Up Visit 99024	$0	Rhythm Strip 93040	$60
Minimum 99211	$35	Treadmill 93015	$375
Problem Focused 99212	$45	Cocci Skin Test 86490	$20
Expanded Problem Focused 99213	$55	X-ray, spine, chest, bone—any area various codes	$275
Detailed 99214	$65	Avulsion Nail 11730	$200
Comprehensive/High Complex 99215	$75	**Laboratory**	
Well exam infant (less than 1 year) 99391	$35	Amylase 82150	$40
Well Exam 1–4 yrs. 99392	$40	B12 82607	$30
Well Exam 5–11 yrs. 99393	$45	CBC & Diff 85025	$95
Well Exam 12–17 yrs. 99394	$55	Comp Metabolic Panel 80053	$75
Well Exam 18–39 yrs. 99395	$65	Chlamydia Screen 87110	$70
Well Exam 40–64 yrs. 99396	$75	Cholestrerol 82465	$75
Obstetrics		Digoxin 80162	$40
Total OB Care 59400	$1700	Electrolytes 80051	$70
Injections		Estrogen, Total 82672	$50
Administration 90772	$10	Ferritin 82728	$40
Allergy 95115	$35	Folate 82746	$30
DPT 90701	$50	GC Screen 87070	$60
Drug various codes	$35	Glucose 82947	$35
Influenza 90658	$25	Glycosylated HGB A1C 83036	$45
MMR 90707	$50	HCT 85014	$30
OPV 90712	$40	HDL 83718	$35
Pneumovax 90732	$35	HGB 85018	$30
TB Skin Test 86580	$15	Hep BSAG 83740	$40
TD 90718	$40	Hepatitis panel, acute 80074	$95
Tetanus Toxoid 90703	$40	HIV 86703	$100
Vaccine/Toxoid Administration for Younger		Iron & TIBC 83550	$45
Than 8 Years Old w/ counseling 90465	$10	Kidney Profile 80069	$95
Vaccine/Toxoid Administration for Adult 90471	$10	Lead 83665	$55
Arthrocentesis/Aspiration/Injection		Lipase 83690	$40
Small Joint 20600	$50	Lipid Panel 80061	$95
Interm Joint 20605	$60	Liver Profile 80076	$95
Major Joint 20610	$70	Mono Test 86308	$30
Trigger Point/Tendon Sheath Inj. 20550	$90	Pap Smear 88155	$90
Other Invasive/Noninvasive Procedures		Pap Collection/Supervision 88142	$95
Catheterization 51701	$55	Pregnancy Test 84703	$90
Circumcision 54150	$150	Obstetric Panel 80055	$85
Colposcopy 57452	$225	Pro Time 85610	$50
Colposcopy w/Biopsy 57454	$250	PSA 84153	$50
Cryosurgery Premalignant Lesion various codes	$160	RPR 86592	$55
Endometrial Biopsy 58100	$190	Sed. Rate 85651	$50
Excision Lesion Malignant various codes	$145	Stool Culture 87045	$80
Excision Lesion Benign various codes	$125	Stool O & P 87177	$105
Curettement Lesion		Strep Screen 87880	$35
Single 11055	$70	Theophylline 80198	$40
2–4 11056	$80	Thyroid Uptake 84479	$75
>4 11057	$90	TSH 84443	$50
Excision Skin Tags (1–15) 11200	$55	Urinalysis 81000	$35
Each Additional 10 11201	$30	Urine Culture 87088	$80
I & D Abscess Single/Simple 10060	$75	Drawing Fee 36415	$15
Multiple/Complex 10061	$95	Specimen Collection 99000	$10
I & D Pilonidal Cyst Simple 10080	$105		
I & D Pilonidal Cyst Complex 10081	$130		
Laceration Repair various codes	$60		

HEALTH INSURANCE CLAIM FORM

APPROVED BY NATIONAL UNIFORM CLAIM COMMITTEE (NUCC) 02/12

		PICA										PICA		

1. MEDICARE	MEDICAID	TRICARE	CHAMPVA	GROUP HEALTH PLAN	FECA BLK LUNG	OTHER	1a. INSURED'S I.D. NUMBER (For Program in Item 1)
[X] (Medicare#)	[ ] (Medicaid#)	[ ] (ID#/DoD#)	[ ] (Member ID#)	[ ] (ID#)	[ ] (ID#)	[ ] (ID#)	

2. PATIENT'S NAME (Last Name, First Name, Middle Initial)

3. PATIENT'S BIRTH DATE MM | DD | YY   SEX   M [ ]   F [ ]

4. INSURED'S NAME (Last Name, First Name, Middle Initial)

5. PATIENT'S ADDRESS (No., Street)

6. PATIENT RELATIONSHIP TO INSURED
Self [ ]   Spouse [ ]   Child [ ]   Other [ ]

7. INSURED'S ADDRESS (No., Street)

CITY ___ STATE ___

8. RESERVED FOR NUCC USE

CITY ___ STATE ___

ZIP CODE ___ TELEPHONE (Include Area Code) ( )

ZIP CODE ___ TELEPHONE (Include Area Code) ( )

9. OTHER INSURED'S NAME (Last Name, First Name, Middle Initial)

10. IS PATIENT'S CONDITION RELATED TO:

11. INSURED'S POLICY GROUP OR FECA NUMBER

a. OTHER INSURED'S POLICY OR GROUP NUMBER

a. EMPLOYMENT? (Current or Previous) [ ] YES [ ] NO

a. INSURED'S DATE OF BIRTH MM | DD | YY   SEX   M [ ]   F [ ]

b. RESERVED FOR NUCC USE

b. AUTO ACCIDENT? [ ] YES [ ] NO   PLACE (State)

b. OTHER CLAIM ID (Designated by NUCC)

c. RESERVED FOR NUCC USE

c. OTHER ACCIDENT? [ ] YES [ ] NO

c. INSURANCE PLAN NAME OR PROGRAM NAME

d. INSURANCE PLAN NAME OR PROGRAM NAME

10d. CLAIM CODES (Designated by NUCC)

d. IS THERE ANOTHER HEALTH BENEFIT PLAN?
[ ] YES [ ] NO   *If yes,* complete items 9, 9a, and 9d.

READ BACK OF FORM BEFORE COMPLETING & SIGNING THIS FORM.

12. PATIENT'S OR AUTHORIZED PERSON'S SIGNATURE I authorize the release of any medical or other information necessary to process this claim. I also request payment of government benefits either to myself or to the party who accepts assignment below.

SIGNED ___ DATE ___

13. INSURED'S OR AUTHORIZED PERSON'S SIGNATURE I authorize payment of medical benefits to the undersigned physician or supplier for services described below.

SIGNED ___

14. DATE OF CURRENT ILLNESS, INJURY, or PREGNANCY (LMP) MM | DD | YY   QUAL.

15. OTHER DATE QUAL. | MM | DD | YY

16. DATES PATIENT UNABLE TO WORK IN CURRENT OCCUPATION FROM MM | DD | YY   TO MM | DD | YY

17. NAME OF REFERRING PROVIDER OR OTHER SOURCE
17a. ___
17b. NPI ___

18. HOSPITALIZATION DATES RELATED TO CURRENT SERVICES FROM MM | DD | YY   TO MM | DD | YY

19. ADDITIONAL CLAIM INFORMATION (Designated by NUCC)

20. OUTSIDE LAB? [ ] YES [ ] NO $ CHARGES

21. DIAGNOSIS OR NATURE OF ILLNESS OR INJURY Relate A-L to service line below (24E)   ICD Ind. ___

A. ___ B. ___ C. ___ D. ___
E. ___ F. ___ G. ___ H. ___
I. ___ J. ___ K. ___ L. ___

22. RESUBMISSION CODE ___ ORIGINAL REF. NO. ___

23. PRIOR AUTHORIZATION NUMBER

24. A. DATE(S) OF SERVICE						B. PLACE OF SERVICE	C. EMG	D. PROCEDURES, SERVICES, OR SUPPLIES (Explain Unusual Circumstances)		E. DIAGNOSIS POINTER	F. $ CHARGES	G. DAYS OR UNITS	H. EPSDT Family Plan	I. ID QUAL	J. RENDERING PROVIDER ID. #
From MM	DD	YY	To MM	DD	YY			CPT/HCPCS	MODIFIER						
1														NPI	
2														NPI	
3														NPI	
4														NPI	
5														NPI	
6														NPI	

25. FEDERAL TAX I.D. NUMBER   SSN EIN [ ]

26. PATIENT'S ACCOUNT NO.

27. ACCEPT ASSIGNMENT? (For govt. claims, see back) [ ] YES [ ] NO

28. TOTAL CHARGE $

29. AMOUNT PAID $

30. Rsvd. for NUCC Use

31. SIGNATURE OF PHYSICIAN OR SUPPLIER INCLUDING DEGREES OR CREDENTIALS (I certify that the statements on the reverse apply to this bill and are made a part thereof.)

SIGNED ___ DATE ___

32. SERVICE FACILITY LOCATION INFORMATION
a. NPI   b.

33. BILLING PROVIDER INFO & PH # ( )
a. NPI   b.

NUCC Instruction Manual available at: www.nucc.org   **PLEASE PRINT OR TYPE**   APPROVED OMB-0938-1197 FORM 1500 (02-12)

Clear Form

Figure 12-2

b. Using the source documents, the Capital City Medical Fee Schedule (Figure 12-3), and the blank CMS-1500 form provided (Figure 12-4), complete the following case study for patient Bradley Hasson (Case 12-2):

CASE 12-2

| Capital City Medical—123 Unknown Boulevard, Capital City, NY 12345-2222 (555) 555-1234 Phil Wells, MD, Mannie Mends, MD, Bette R. Soone, MD | Patient Information Form Tax ID: 75-0246810 Group NPI: 1513171216 |

Patient Information:

Name: (Last, First) Hasson, Bradley   ☒ Male ☐ Female Birth Date: 08/11/1940

Address: 37 Mallow Ave, Capital City, NY 12345   Phone: (555) 555-6187

Social Security Number: 624-90-3754   Full-Time Student: ☐ Yes ☒ No

Marital Status: ☐ Single ☒ Married ☐ Divorced ☐ Other

Employment:

Employer: Retired   Phone: ( )

Address:

Condition Related to: ☐ Auto Accident ☐ Employment ☐ Other Accident

Date of Accident: State:

Emergency Contact: Phone: ( )

Primary Insurance: Medicare   Phone: ( )

Address: P O. Box, 9834, Capital City, NY 12345

Insurance Policyholder's Name: Same   ☐ M ☐ F DOB:

Address:

Phone: Relationship to Insured: ☒ Self ☐ Spouse ☐ Child ☐ Other

Employer: Phone: ( )

Employer's Address:

Policy/ID No: 653524444A   Group No: Percent Covered: 80 % Copay Amt: $

Secondary Insurance: Blue Cross Blue Shield, Medigap   Phone: ( )

Address: 379 Blue Plaza, Capital City, NY 12345

Insurance Policyholder's Name: Same   ☐ M ☐ F DOB:

Address:

Phone: Relationship to Insured: ☒ Self ☐ Spouse ☐ Child ☐ Other

Employer: Phone: ( )

Employer's Address:

Policy/ID No: YYZ6981399   Group No: Percent Covered: % Copay Amt: $20.00

Reason for Visit: Follow-up on my Leukemia

Known Allergies:

Referred by:

CASE 12-2
SOAP

04/17/20XX
Assignment of Benefits: Y
Signature on File: Y
Referring Physician: N

S: Bradley Hasson is here today for a regular checkup on his leukemia. He presents with no complaints.
O: Pt. is responding well to recent therapy regimen. He denies weakness and tiredness.
A: 1. Chronic leukemia in remission—C95.11
P: 1. Continue current therapy.
   2. Keep appointment with oncologist.
   3. Return in 2 months unless relapse or other illness occurs.

_____

Phil Wells, MD
Family Practice
NPI: 1234567890

CASE 12-2

Patient Name <u>Bradley Hasson</u>

Capital City Medical
123 Unknown Boulevard, Capital City, NY 12345-2222

Date of Service
04-17-20XX

New Patient			Arthrocentesis/Aspiration/Injection		Laboratory		
Problem Focused	99201		Small Joint	20600	Amylase	82150
Expanded Problem, Focused	99202		Interm Joint	20605	B12	82607
Detailed	99203		Major Joint	20610	CBC & Diff	85025
Comprehensive	99204		**Other Invasive/Noninvasive**		Comp Metabolic Panel	80053
Comprehensive/High Complex	99205		Audiometry	92552	Chlamydia Screen	87110
Well Exam Infant (up to 12 mos.)	99381		Cast Application		Cholesterol	82465
Well Exam 1–4 yrs.	99382		Location Long Short		Digoxin	80162
Well Exam 5–11 yrs.	99383		Catheterization	51701	Electrolytes	80051
Well Exam 12–17 yrs.	99384		Circumcision	54150	Ferritin	82728
Well Exam 18–39 yrs.	99385		Colposcopy	57452	Folate	82746
Well Exam 40–64 yrs.	99386		Colposcopy w/Biopsy	57454	GC Screen	87070
			Cryosurgery Premalignant Lesion		Glucose	82947
			Location (s):		Glucose 1 HR	82950
			Cryosurgery Warts		Glycosylated HGB A1C	83036
Established Patient			Location (s):		HCT	85014
Post-Op Follow Up Visit	99024		Curettement Lesion		HDL	83718
Minimum	99211		Single	11055	Hep BSAG	87340
Problem Focused	99212		2–4	11056	Hepatitis panel, acute	80074
Expanded Problem Focused	99213	X	>4	11057	HGB	85018
Detailed	99214		Diaphragm Fitting	57170	HIV	86703
Comprehensive/High Complex	99215		Ear Irrigation	69210	Iron & TIBC	83550
Well Exam Infant (up to 12 mos.)	99391		ECG	93000	Kidney Profile	80069
Well exam 1–4 yrs.	99392		Endometrial Biopsy	58100	Lead	83655
Well Exam 5–11 yrs.	99393		Exc. Lesion Malignant		Liver Profile	80076
Well Exam 12–17 yrs.	99394		Benign		Mono Test	86308
Well Exam 18–39 yrs.	99395		Location		Pap Smear	88155
Well Exam 40–64 yrs.	99396		Exc. Skin Tags (1–15)	11200	Pregnancy Test	84703
Obstetrics			Each Additional 10	11201	Obstetric Panel	80055
Total OB Care	59400		Fracture Treatment		Pro Time	85610
Injections			Loc		PSA	84153
Administration Sub. / IM	90772		w/Reduc w/o Reduc		RPR	86592
Drug			I & D Abscess Single/Simple	10060	Sed. Rate	85651
Dosage			Multiple or Comp	10061	Stool Culture	87045
Allergy	95115		I & D Pilonidal Cyst Simple	10080	Stool O & P	87177
Cocci Skin Test	86490		Pilonidal Cyst Complex	10081	Strep Screen	87880
DPT	90701		IV Therapy—To One Hour	90760	Theophylline	80198
Hemophilus	90646		Each Additional Hour	90761	Thyroid Uptake	84479
Influenza	90658		Laceration Repair		TSH	84443
MMR	90707		Location Size Simp/Comp		Urinalysis	81000
OPV	90712		Laryngoscopy	31505	Urine Culture	87088
Pneumovax	90732		Oximetry	94760	Drawing Fee	36415
TB Skin Test	86580		Punch Biopsy		Specimen Collection	99000
TD	90718		Rhythm Strip	93040	**Other:**	
Unlisted Immun	90749		Treadmill	93015		
Tetanus Toxoid	90703		Trigger Point or Tendon Sheath Inj.	20550		
Vaccine/Toxoid Admin <8 Yr Old w/ Counseling	90465					
Vaccine/Toxoid Administration for Adult	90471		Tympanometry	92567		

Diagnosis/ICD-10: C95.11

I acknowledge receipt of medical services and authorize the release of any medical information necessary to process this claim for healthcare payment only. I do authorize payment to the provider.

Patient Signature <u>Bradley Hasson</u>

Total Estimated Charges: _____

Payment Amount: _____

Next Appointment: _____

Figure 12-3

Patient Name <u>Bradley Hasson</u>

Capital City Medical
123 Unknown Boulevard, Capital City, NY 12345-2222

Date of Service
<u>04-17-20XX</u>

New Patient			Other Invasive/Noninvasive			Laboratory	
Problem Focused	99201		Arthrocentesis/Aspiration/Injection			Amylase	82150
Expanded Problem, Focused	99202		Small Joint		20600	B12	82607
Detailed	99203		Interm Joint		20605	CBC & Diff	85025
Comprehensive	99204		Major Joint		20610	Comp Metabolic Panel	80053
Comprehensive/High Complex	99205		**Other Invasive/Noninvasive**			Chlamydia Screen	87110
Well Exam Infant (up to 12 mos.)	99381		Audiometry		92552	Cholesterol	82465
Well Exam 1–4 yrs.	99382		Cast Application			Digoxin	80162
Well Exam 5–11 yrs.	99383		Location Long Short			Electrolytes	80051
Well Exam 12–17 yrs.	99384		Catheterization		51701	Ferritin	82728
Well Exam 18–39 yrs.	99385		Circumcision		54150	Folate	82746
Well Exam 40–64 yrs.	99386		Colposcopy		57452	GC Screen	87070
			Colposcopy w/Biopsy		57454	Glucose	82947
			Cryosurgery Premalignant Lesion			Glucose 1 HR	82950
			Location (s):			Glycosylated HGB A1C	83036
Established Patient			Cryosurgery Warts			HCT	85014
Post-Op Follow Up Visit	99024		Location (s):			HDL	83718
Minimum	99211		Curettement Lesion			Hep BSAG	87340
Problem Focused	99212		Single		11055	Hepatitis panel, acute	80074
Expanded Problem Focused	99213	X	2–4		11056	HGB	85018
Detailed	99214		>4		11057	HIV	86703
Comprehensive/High Complex	99215		Diaphragm Fitting		57170	Iron & TIBC	83550
Well Exam Infant (up to 12 mos.)	99391		Ear Irrigation		69210	Kidney Profile	80069
Well exam 1–4 yrs.	99392		ECG		93000	Lead	83655
Well Exam 5–11 yrs.	99393		Endometrial Biopsy		58100	Liver Profile	80076
Well Exam 12–17 yrs.	99394		Exc. Lesion Malignant			Mono Test	86308
Well Exam 18–39 yrs.	99395		Benign			Pap Smear	88155
Well Exam 40–64 yrs.	99396		Location			Pregnancy Test	84703
Obstetrics			Exc. Skin Tags (1–15)		11200	Obstetric Panel	80055
Total OB Care	59400		Each Additional 10		11201	Pro Time	85610
Injections			Fracture Treatment			PSA	84153
Administration Sub. / IM	90772		Loc			RPR	86592
Drug			w/Reduc	w/o Reduc		Sed. Rate	85651
Dosage			I & D Abscess Single/Simple		10060	Stool Culture	87045
Allergy	95115		Multiple or Comp		10061	Stool O & P	87177
Cocci Skin Test	86490		I & D Pilonidal Cyst Simple		10080	Strep Screen	87880
DPT	90701		Pilonidal Cyst Complex		10081	Theophylline	80198
Hemophilus	90646		IV Therapy—To One Hour		90760	Thyroid Uptake	84479
Influenza	90658		Each Additional Hour		90761	TSH	84443
MMR	90707		Laceration Repair			Urinalysis	81000
OPV	90712		Location Size Simp/Comp			Urine Culture	87088
Pneumovax	90732		Laryngoscopy		31505	Drawing Fee	36415
TB Skin Test	86580		Oximetry		94760	Specimen Collection	99000
TD	90718		Punch Biopsy			**Other:**	
Unlisted Immun	90749		Rhythm Strip		93040		
Tetanus Toxoid	90703		Treadmill		93015		
Vaccine/Toxoid Admin <8 Yr Old w/ Counseling	90465		Trigger Point or Tendon Sheath Inj.		20550		
Vaccine/Toxoid Administration for Adult	90471		Tympanometry		92567		

Diagnosis/ICD-10: **208.11**

I acknowledge receipt of medical services and authorize the release of any medical information necessary to process this claim for healthcare payment only. I do authorize payment to the provider.

Total Estimated Charges: _____

Payment Amount: _____

Patient Signature <u>Bradley Hasson</u>

Next Appointment: _____

HEALTH INSURANCE CLAIM FORM

APPROVED BY NATIONAL UNIFORM CLAIM COMMITTEE (NUCC) 02/12

| | PICA | | | | | | | | | PICA | |

1. MEDICARE ☒(Medicare#) MEDICAID (Medicaid#) TRICARE (ID#/DoD#) CHAMPVA (Member ID#) GROUP HEALTH PLAN (ID#) FECA BLK LUNG (ID#) OTHER (ID#) | **1a. INSURED'S I.D. NUMBER** (For Program in Item 1)

2. PATIENT'S NAME (Last Name, First Name, Middle Initial) | **3. PATIENT'S BIRTH DATE** MM DD YY SEX M F | **4. INSURED'S NAME** (Last Name, First Name, Middle Initial)

5. PATIENT'S ADDRESS (No., Street) | **6. PATIENT RELATIONSHIP TO INSURED** Self Spouse Child Other | **7. INSURED'S ADDRESS** (No., Street)

CITY STATE | **8. RESERVED FOR NUCC USE** | CITY STATE

ZIP CODE TELEPHONE (Include Area Code) ( ) | | ZIP CODE TELEPHONE (Include Area Code) ( )

9. OTHER INSURED'S NAME (Last Name, First Name, Middle Initial) | **10. IS PATIENT'S CONDITION RELATED TO:** | **11. INSURED'S POLICY GROUP OR FECA NUMBER**

a. OTHER INSURED'S POLICY OR GROUP NUMBER | **a.** EMPLOYMENT? (Current or Previous) YES NO | **a.** INSURED'S DATE OF BIRTH MM DD YY SEX M F

b. RESERVED FOR NUCC USE | **b.** AUTO ACCIDENT? PLACE (State) YES NO | **b.** OTHER CLAIM ID (Designated by NUCC)

c. RESERVED FOR NUCC USE | **c.** OTHER ACCIDENT? YES NO | **c.** INSURANCE PLAN NAME OR PROGRAM NAME

d. INSURANCE PLAN NAME OR PROGRAM NAME | **10d. CLAIM CODES** (Designated by NUCC) | **d.** IS THERE ANOTHER HEALTH BENEFIT PLAN? YES NO *If yes*, complete items 9, 9a, and 9d.

READ BACK OF FORM BEFORE COMPLETING & SIGNING THIS FORM.
12. PATIENT'S OR AUTHORIZED PERSON'S SIGNATURE I authorize the release of any medical or other information necessary to process this claim. I also request payment of government benefits either to myself or to the party who accepts assignment below. | **13. INSURED'S OR AUTHORIZED PERSON'S SIGNATURE** I authorize payment of medical benefits to the undersigned physician or supplier for services described below.

SIGNED _____ DATE _____ | SIGNED _____

14. DATE OF CURRENT ILLNESS, INJURY, or PREGNANCY (LMP) MM DD YY QUAL | **15. OTHER DATE** QUAL MM DD YY | **16. DATES PATIENT UNABLE TO WORK IN CURRENT OCCUPATION** FROM MM DD YY TO MM DD YY

17. NAME OF REFERRING PROVIDER OR OTHER SOURCE | 17a. 17b. NPI | **18. HOSPITALIZATION DATES RELATED TO CURRENT SERVICES** FROM MM DD YY TO MM DD YY

19. ADDITIONAL CLAIM INFORMATION (Designated by NUCC) | **20. OUTSIDE LAB?** YES NO $ CHARGES

21. DIAGNOSIS OR NATURE OF ILLNESS OR INJURY Relate A-L to service line below (24E) ICD Ind. | **22. RESUBMISSION CODE** ORIGINAL REF. NO.
A. B. C. D. E. F. G. H. I. J. K. L. | **23. PRIOR AUTHORIZATION NUMBER**

24. A. DATE(S) OF SERVICE			B. PLACE OF SERVICE	C. EMG	D. PROCEDURES, SERVICES, OR SUPPLIES (Explain Unusual Circumstances) CPT/HCPCS MODIFIER	E. DIAGNOSIS POINTER	F. $ CHARGES	G. DAYS OR UNITS	H. EPSDT Family Plan	I. ID. QUAL	J. RENDERING PROVIDER ID. #
From MM DD YY	To MM DD YY										
1										NPI	
2										NPI	
3										NPI	
4										NPI	
5										NPI	
6										NPI	

25. FEDERAL TAX I.D. NUMBER SSN EIN | **26. PATIENT'S ACCOUNT NO.** | **27. ACCEPT ASSIGNMENT?** (For govt. claims, see back) YES NO | **28. TOTAL CHARGE** $ | **29. AMOUNT PAID** $ | **30. Rsvd. for NUCC Use**

31. SIGNATURE OF PHYSICIAN OR SUPPLIER INCLUDING DEGREES OR CREDENTIALS (I certify that the statements on the reverse apply to this bill and are made a part thereof.) SIGNED ___ DATE ___ | **32. SERVICE FACILITY LOCATION INFORMATION** a. NPI b. | **33. BILLING PROVIDER INFO & PH #** ( ) a. NPI b.

Clear Form

Figure 12-4

© 2018 Pearson Education, Inc.

c. Using the source documents, the Capital City Medical Fee Schedule (Figure 12-5), and the blank CMS-1500 form provided (Figure 12-6), complete the following case study for patient Reba Jones (Case 12-3):

CASE 12-3

Capital City Medical—123 Unknown Boulevard, Capital City, NY 12345-2222 (555) 555-1234	Patient Information Form
Phil Wells, MD, Mannie Mends, MD, Bette R. Soone, MD	Tax ID: 75-0246810
	Group NPI: 1513171216

Patient Information:

Name: (Last, First) Jones, Reba   ☐ Male ☒ Female Birth Date: 06/04/1953

Address: 414 Scotland Ln, Capital City, NY 12345   Phone: (555) 555-3777

Social Security Number: 741-10-3685   Full-Time Student: ☐ Yes ☒ No

Marital Status: ☐ Single ☒ Married ☐ Divorced ☐ Other

Employment:

Employer: _____   Phone: ( ) _____

Address: _____

Condition Related to: ☐ Auto Accident ☐ Employment ☐ Other Accident

Date of Accident: _____ State: _____

Emergency Contact: _____ **Phone: ( )** _____

Primary Insurance: Medicare   Phone: ( ) _____

Address: P O. Box , 9834, Capital City, NY 12345

Insurance Policyholder's Name: Warren Jones   ☒ M ☐ F DOB: 11/21/1953

Address: _____

Phone: _____ Relationship to Insured: ☐ Self ☒ Spouse ☐ Child ☐ Other

Employer: _____   Phone: ( ) _____

Employer's Address: _____

Policy/ID No: 658303300A   Group No: _____ Percent Covered: 80 % Copay Amt: $_____

Secondary Insurance: Aetna   Phone: ( ) _____

Address: 1625 Healthcare Bldg, Capital City, NY 12345

Insurance Policyholder's Name: Warren Jones   ☒ M ☐ F DOB: 11/21/1953

Address: Same

Phone: _____ Relationship to Insured: ☐ Self ☒ Spouse ☐ Child ☐ Other

Employer: Capital Hardware   Phone: ( ) _____

Employer's Address: _____

Policy/ID No: 6758562   Group No: 5832 Percent Covered: ___% Copay Amt: $30.00

Reason for Visit: I am here to have my sarcoidosis checked.

Known Allergies: _____

Referred by: _____

CASE 12-3
SOAP

04/24/20XX
Assignment of Benefits: Y
Signature on File: Y
Referring Physician: N

S: Reba Jones is here for a follow-up on her sarcoidosis. Pt. has no complaints at this time. She states that she is feeling "wonderful."

O: On exam, vitals are good. She denies any SOB, hemoptysis, or cough. Heart is regular rate and rhythm, with no gallop or murmur.

A: 1. Sarcoidosis—D86.0

P: 1. Continue current therapy.
2. Keep appointment with pulmonologist.
3. Return in 6 months.

_____
Phil Wells, MD
Family Practice
NPI: 1234567890

© 2018 Pearson Education, Inc.

CASE 12-3

Patient Name Reba Jones

Capital City Medical
123 Unknown Boulevard, Capital City, NY 12345-2222

Date of Service
04-24-20XX

New Patient			Arthrocentesis/Aspiration/Injection			Laboratory	
Problem Focused	99201		Small Joint		20600	Amylase	82150
Expanded Problem, Focused	99202		Interm Joint		20605	B12	82607
Detailed	99203		Major Joint		20610	CBC & Diff	85025
Comprehensive	99204		**Other Invasive/Noninvasive**			Comp Metabolic Panel	80053
Comprehensive/High Complex	99205		Audiometry		92552	Chlamydia Screen	87110
Well Exam Infant (up to 12 mos.)	99381		Cast Application			Cholesterol	82465
Well Exam 1–4 yrs.	99382		Location Long Short			Digoxin	80162
Well Exam 5–11 yrs.	99383		Catheterization		51701	Electrolytes	80051
Well Exam 12–17 yrs.	99384		Circumcision		54150	Ferritin	82728
Well Exam 18–39 yrs.	99385		Colposcopy		57452	Folate	82746
Well Exam 40–64 yrs.	99386		Colposcopy w/Biopsy		57454	GC Screen	87070
			Cryosurgery Premalignant Lesion			Glucose	82947
			Location (s):			Glucose 1 HR	82950
			Cryosurgery Warts			Glycosylated HGB A1C	83036
Established Patient			Location (s):			HCT	85014
Post-Op Follow Up Visit	99024		Curettement Lesion			HDL	83718
Minimum	99211		Single		11055	Hep BSAG	87340
Problem Focused	99212	X	2–4		11056	Hepatitis panel, acute	80074
Expanded Problem Focused	99213		>4		11057	HGB	85018
Detailed	99214		Diaphragm Fitting		57170	HIV	86703
Comprehensive/High Complex	99215		Ear Irrigation		69210	Iron & TIBC	83550
Well Exam Infant (up to 12 mos.)	99391		ECG		93000	Kidney Profile	80069
Well exam 1–4 yrs.	99392		Endometrial Biopsy		58100	Lead	83655
Well Exam 5–11 yrs.	99393		Exc. Lesion Malignant			Liver Profile	80076
Well Exam 12–17 yrs.	99394		Benign			Mono Test	86308
Well Exam 18–39 yrs.	99395		Location			Pap Smear	88155
Well Exam 40–64 yrs.	99396		Exc. Skin Tags (1–15)		11200	Pregnancy Test	84703
Obstetrics			Each Additional 10		11201	Obstetric Panel	80055
Total OB Care	59400		Fracture Treatment			Pro Time	85610
Injections			Loc			PSA	84153
Administration Sub. / IM	90772		w/Reduc w/o Reduc			RPR	86592
Drug			I & D Abscess Single/Simple		10060	Sed. Rate	85651
Dosage			Multiple or Comp		10061	Stool Culture	87045
Allergy	95115		I & D Pilonidal Cyst Simple		10080	Stool O & P	87177
Cocci Skin Test	86490		Pilonidal Cyst Complex		10081	Strep Screen	87880
DPT	90701		IV Therapy—To One Hour		90760	Theophylline	80198
Hemophilus	90646		Each Additional Hour		90761	Thyroid Uptake	84479
Influenza	90658		Laceration Repair			TSH	84443
MMR	90707		Location Size Simp/Comp			Urinalysis	81000
OPV	90712		Laryngoscopy		31505	Urine Culture	87088
Pneumovax	90732		Oximetry		94760	Drawing Fee	36415
TB Skin Test	86580		Punch Biopsy			Specimen Collection	99000
TD	90718		Rhythm Strip		93040	**Other:**	
Unlisted Immun	90749		Treadmill		93015		
Tetanus Toxoid	90703		Trigger Point or Tendon Sheath Inj.		20550		
Vaccine/Toxoid Admin <8 Yr Old w/ Counseling	90465		Tympanometry		92567		
Vaccine/Toxoid Administration for Adult	90471						

Diagnosis/ICD-10: D86.0

I acknowledge receipt of medical services and authorize the release of any medical information necessary to process this claim for healthcare payment only. I do authorize payment to the provider.

Patient Signature Reba Jones

Total Estimated Charges: _____

Payment Amount: _____

Next Appointment: _____

Figure 12-5

Capital City Medical
Fee Schedule

New Patient OV			Punch Biopsy various codes	$80
Problem Focused 99201	$45		Nebulizer various codes	$45
Expanded Problem Focused 99202	$65		Cast Application various codes	$85
Detailed 99203	$85		Laryngoscopy 31505	$255
Comprehensive 99204	$105		Audiometry 92552	$85
Comprehensive/High Complex 99205	$115		Tympanometry 92567	$85
Well Exam infant (less than 1 year) 99381	$45		Ear Irrigation 69210	$25
Well Exam 1–4 yrs. 99382	$50		Diaphragm Fitting 57170	$30
Well Exam 5–11 yrs. 99383	$55		IV Therapy (up to one hour) 90760	$65
Well Exam 12–17 yrs. 99384	$65		Each additional hour 90761	$50
Well Exam 18–39 yrs. 99385	$85		Oximetry 94760	$10
Well Exam 40–64 yrs. 99386	$105		ECG 93000	$75
Established Patient OV			Holter Monitor various codes	$170
Post Op Follow Up Visit 99024	$0		Rhythm Strip 93040	$60
Minimum 99211	$35		Treadmill 93015	$375
Problem Focused 99212	$45		Cocci Skin Test 86490	$20
Expanded Problem Focused 99213	$55		X-ray, spine, chest, bone—any area various codes	$275
Detailed 99214	$65		Avulsion Nail 11730	$200
Comprehensive/High Complex 99215	$75		**Laboratory**	
Well exam infant (less than 1 year) 99391	$35		Amylase 82150	$40
Well Exam 1–4 yrs. 99392	$40		B12 82607	$30
Well Exam 5–11 yrs. 99393	$45		CBC & Diff 85025	$95
Well Exam 12–17 yrs. 99394	$55		Comp Metabolic Panel 80053	$75
Well Exam 18–39 yrs. 99395	$65		Chlamydia Screen 87110	$70
Well Exam 40–64 yrs. 99396	$75		Cholestrerol 82465	$75
Obstetrics			Digoxin 80162	$40
Total OB Care 59400	$1700		Electrolytes 80051	$70
Injections			Estrogen, Total 82672	$50
Administration 90772	$10		Ferritin 82728	$40
Allergy 95115	$35		Folate 82746	$30
DPT 90701	$50		GC Screen 87070	$60
Drug various codes	$35		Glucose 82947	$35
Influenza 90658	$25		Glycosylated HGB A1C 83036	$45
MMR 90707	$50		HCT 85014	$30
OPV 90712	$40		HDL 83718	$35
Pneumovax 90732	$35		HGB 85018	$30
TB Skin Test 86580	$15		Hep BSAG 83740	$40
TD 90718	$40		Hepatitis panel, acute 80074	$95
Tetanus Toxoid 90703	$40		HIV 86703	$100
Vaccine/Toxoid Administration for Younger			Iron & TIBC 83550	$45
Than 8 Years Old w/ counseling 90465	$10		Kidney Profile 80069	$95
Vaccine/Toxoid Administration for Adult 90471	$10		Lead 83665	$55
Arthrocentesis/Aspiration/Injection			Lipase 83690	$40
Small Joint 20600	$50		Lipid Panel 80061	$95
Interm Joint 20605	$60		Liver Profile 80076	$95
Major Joint 20610	$70		Mono Test 86308	$30
Trigger Point/Tendon Sheath Inj. 20550	$90		Pap Smear 88155	$90
Other Invasive/Noninvasive Procedures			Pap Collection/Supervision 88142	$95
Catheterization 51701	$55		Pregnancy Test 84703	$90
Circumcision 54150	$150		Obstetric Panel 80055	$85
Colposcopy 57452	$225		Pro Time 85610	$50
Colposcopy w/Biopsy 57454	$250		PSA 84153	$50
Cryosurgery Premalignant Lesion various codes	$160		RPR 86592	$55
Endometrial Biopsy 58100	$190		Sed. Rate 85651	$50
Excision Lesion Malignant various codes	$145		Stool Culture 87045	$80
Excision Lesion Benign various codes	$125		Stool O & P 87177	$105
Curettement Lesion			Strep Screen 87880	$35
Single 11055	$70		Theophylline 80198	$40
2–4 11056	$80		Thyroid Uptake 84479	$75
>4 11057	$90		TSH 84443	$50
Excision Skin Tags (1–15) 11200	$55		Urinalysis 81000	$35
Each Additional 10 11201	$30		Urine Culture 87088	$80
I & D Abscess Single/Simple 10060	$75		Drawing Fee 36415	$15
Multiple/Complex 10061	$95		Specimen Collection 99000	$10
I & D Pilonidal Cyst Simple 10080	$105			
I & D Pilonidal Cyst Complex 10081	$130			
Laceration Repair various codes	$60			

HEALTH INSURANCE CLAIM FORM

APPROVED BY NATIONAL UNIFORM CLAIM COMMITTEE (NUCC) 02/12

	PICA								PICA	

1 MEDICARE ☒ (Medicare#)   MEDICAID ☐ (Medicaid#)   TRICARE ☐ (ID#/DoD#)   CHAMPVA ☐ (Member ID#)   GROUP HEALTH PLAN ☐ (ID#)   FECA BLK LUNG ☐ (ID#)   OTHER ☐ (ID#)   **1a.** INSURED'S I.D. NUMBER   (For Program in Item 1)

2. PATIENT'S NAME (Last Name, First Name, Middle Initial)

3. PATIENT'S BIRTH DATE   MM ☐ DD ☐ YY   SEX   M ☐ F ☐

4. INSURED'S NAME (Last Name, First Name, Middle Initial)

5. PATIENT'S ADDRESS (No., Street)

6. PATIENT RELATIONSHIP TO INSURED   Self ☐ Spouse ☐ Child ☐ Other ☐

7. INSURED'S ADDRESS (No., Street)

CITY   STATE

8. RESERVED FOR NUCC USE

CITY   STATE

ZIP CODE   TELEPHONE (Include Area Code)   ( )

ZIP CODE   TELEPHONE (Include Area Code)   ( )

9. OTHER INSURED'S NAME (Last Name, First Name, Middle Initial)

10. IS PATIENT'S CONDITION RELATED TO:

11. INSURED'S POLICY GROUP OR FECA NUMBER

a. OTHER INSURED'S POLICY OR GROUP NUMBER

a. EMPLOYMENT? (Current or Previous)   ☐ YES   ☐ NO

a. INSURED'S DATE OF BIRTH   MM ☐ DD ☐ YY   SEX   M ☐ F ☐

b. RESERVED FOR NUCC USE

b. AUTO ACCIDENT?   PLACE (State)   ☐ YES   ☐ NO

b. OTHER CLAIM ID (Designated by NUCC)

c. RESERVED FOR NUCC USE

c. OTHER ACCIDENT?   ☐ YES   ☐ NO

c. INSURANCE PLAN NAME OR PROGRAM NAME

d. INSURANCE PLAN NAME OR PROGRAM NAME

10d. CLAIM CODES (Designated by NUCC)

d. IS THERE ANOTHER HEALTH BENEFIT PLAN?   ☐ YES   ☐ NO   *If yes*, complete items 9, 9a, and 9d.

READ BACK OF FORM BEFORE COMPLETING & SIGNING THIS FORM.
12. PATIENT'S OR AUTHORIZED PERSON'S SIGNATURE I authorize the release of any medical or other information necessary to process this claim. I also request payment of government benefits either to myself or to the party who accepts assignment below.

SIGNED _____ DATE _____

13. INSURED'S OR AUTHORIZED PERSON'S SIGNATURE I authorize payment of medical benefits to the undersigned physician or supplier for services described below.

SIGNED _____

14. DATE OF CURRENT ILLNESS, INJURY, or PREGNANCY (LMP)   MM ☐ DD ☐ YY   QUAL

15. OTHER DATE   QUAL   MM ☐ DD ☐ YY

16. DATES PATIENT UNABLE TO WORK IN CURRENT OCCUPATION   MM ☐ DD ☐ YY   FROM   TO   MM ☐ DD ☐ YY

17. NAME OF REFERRING PROVIDER OR OTHER SOURCE   17a.   17b. NPI

18. HOSPITALIZATION DATES RELATED TO CURRENT SERVICES   MM ☐ DD ☐ YY   FROM   TO   MM ☐ DD ☐ YY

19. ADDITIONAL CLAIM INFORMATION (Designated by NUCC)

20. OUTSIDE LAB?   ☐ YES   ☐ NO $ CHARGES

21. DIAGNOSIS OR NATURE OF ILLNESS OR INJURY Relate A-L to service line below (24E)   ICD Ind.

A. |___ B. |___ C. |___ D. |___
E. |___ F. |___ G. |___ H. |___
I. |___ J. |___ K. |___ L. |___

22. RESUBMISSION CODE   ORIGINAL REF. NO.

23. PRIOR AUTHORIZATION NUMBER

24. A. DATE(S) OF SERVICE			B. PLACE OF SERVICE	C. EMG	D. PROCEDURES, SERVICES, OR SUPPLIES (Explain Unusual Circumstances)		E. DIAGNOSIS POINTER	F. $ CHARGES	G. DAYS OR UNITS	H. EPSDT Family Plan	I. ID. QUAL	J. RENDERING PROVIDER ID. #
From MM DD YY	To MM DD YY				CPT/HCPCS	MODIFIER						
1												NPI
2												NPI
3												NPI
4												NPI
5												NPI
6												NPI

25. FEDERAL TAX I.D. NUMBER   SSN ☐ EIN ☐

26. PATIENT'S ACCOUNT NO.

27. ACCEPT ASSIGNMENT? (For govt. claims, see back)   ☐ YES   ☐ NO

28. TOTAL CHARGE $

29. AMOUNT PAID $

30. Rsvd for NUCC Use

31. SIGNATURE OF PHYSICIAN OR SUPPLIER INCLUDING DEGREES OR CREDENTIALS (I certify that the statements on the reverse apply to this bill and are made a part thereof.)

SIGNED _____ DATE _____

32. SERVICE FACILITY LOCATION INFORMATION   a. NPI   b.

33. BILLING PROVIDER INFO & PH # ( )   a. NPI   b.

NUCC Instruction Manual available at: www.nucc.org   **PLEASE PRINT OR TYPE**   APPROVED OMB-0938-1197 FORM 1500 (02-12)

Clear Form

Figure 12-6

d. Using the source documents, the Capital City Medical Fee Schedule (Figure 12-7), and the blank CMS-1500 form provided (Figure 12-8), complete the following case study for patient Scott Reeves (Case 12-4):

CASE 12-4

Capital City Medical—123 Unknown Boulevard, Capital City, NY 12345-2222 (555)555-1234 Phil Wells, MD, Mannie Mends, MD, Bette R. Soone, MD	Patient Information Form Tax ID: 75-0246810 Group NPI: 1513171216

Patient Information:

Name: (Last, First) Reeves, Scott   ☒ Male   ☐ Female   Birth Date: 08/13/1955

Address: 35 Park Ave, Township, NY 12345   Phone: (555) 555-1700

Social Security Number: 393-55-9020   Full-Time Student: ☐ Yes ☒ No

Marital Status: ☐ Single ☒ Married ☐ Divorced ☐ Other

Employment:

Employer: Retired   Phone: ( )

Address:

Condition Related to: ☐ Auto Accident ☐ Employment ☐ Other Accident

Date of Accident: State:

Emergency Contact: **Phone: ( )**

Primary Insurance: Medicare   Phone: ( )

Address: P O. Box , 9834, Capital City, NY 12345

Insurance Policyholder's Name: Same   ☐ M ☐ F DOB: 11/21/1953

Address:

Phone: Relationship to Insured: ☒ Self ☐ Spouse ☐ Child ☐ Other

Employer: Phone: ( )

Employer's Address:

Policy/ID No: 201048952A   Group No: Percent Covered: 80 % Copay Amt: $

Secondary Insurance: Phone: ( )

Address:

Insurance Policyholder's Name: ☐ M ☐ F DOB:

Address:

Phone: Relationship to Insured: ☐ Self ☐ Spouse ☐ Child ☐ Other

Employer: Phone: ( )

Employer's Address:

Policy/ID No: 6758562   Group No: 5832 Percent Covered: ___% Copay Amt: $

Reason for Visit: I am having an episode of gout.

Known Allergies:

Referred by:

CASE 12-4
SOAP

07/10/20XX
Assignment of Benefits: Y
Signature on File: Y
Referring Physician: N

S: Scott Reeves complains of gout in his left big toe. He says that it is very painful.

O: His left great toe presents as swollen. There is pain with and without movement. His BP in office is 152/78. He denies increased salt intake.

A: 1. Gout, great toe—M10.9
   2. HTN—I10

P: 1. Start cholchicine.
   2. Watch salt intake.
   3. Drink plenty of clear fluids.

_____

Phil Wells, MD
Family Practice
NPI: 1234567890

CASE 12-4

Patient Name <u>Scott Reeves</u>

Capital City Medical
123 Unknown Boulevard, Capital City, NY 12345-2222

Date of Service
<u>07-10-20XX</u>

New Patient			Arthrocentesis/Aspiration/Injection			Laboratory	
Problem Focused	99201		Arthrocentesis/Aspiration/Injection			Amylase	82150
Expanded Problem, Focused	99202		Small Joint		20600	B12	82607
Detailed	99203		Interm Joint		20605	CBC & Diff	85025
Comprehensive	99204		Major Joint		20610	Comp Metabolic Panel	80053
Comprehensive/High Complex	99205		**Other Invasive/Noninvasive**			Chlamydia Screen	87110
Well Exam Infant (up to 12 mos.)	99381		Audiometry		92552	Cholesterol	82465
Well Exam 1–4 yrs.	99382		Cast Application			Digoxin	80162
Well Exam 5–11 yrs.	99383		Location Long Short			Electrolytes	80051
Well Exam 12–17 yrs.	99384		Catheterization		51701	Ferritin	82728
Well Exam 18–39 yrs.	99385		Circumcision		54150	Folate	82746
Well Exam 40–64 yrs.	99386		Colposcopy		57452	GC Screen	87070
			Colposcopy w/Biopsy		57454	Glucose	82947
			Cryosurgery Premalignant Lesion			Glucose 1 HR	82950
			Location (s):			Glycosylated HGB A1C	83036
Established Patient			Cryosurgery Warts			HCT	85014
Post-Op Follow Up Visit	99024		Location (s):			HDL	83718
Minimum	99211		Curettement Lesion			Hep BSAG	87340
Problem Focused	99212		Single		11055	Hepatitis panel, acute	80074
Expanded Problem Focused	99213	X	2–4		11056	HGB	85018
Detailed	99214		>4		11057	HIV	86703
Comprehensive/High Complex	99215		Diaphragm Fitting		57170	Iron & TIBC	83550
Well Exam Infant (up to 12 mos.)	99391		Ear Irrigation		69210	Kidney Profile	80069
Well exam 1–4 yrs.	99392		ECG		93000	Lead	83655
Well Exam 5–11 yrs.	99393		Endometrial Biopsy		58100	Liver Profile	80076
Well Exam 12–17 yrs.	99394		Exc. Lesion Malignant			Mono Test	86308
Well Exam 18–39 yrs.	99395		Benign			Pap Smear	88155
Well Exam 40–64 yrs.	99396		Location			Pregnancy Test	84703
Obstetrics			Exc. Skin Tags (1–15)		11200	Obstetric Panel	80055
Total OB Care	59400		Each Additional 10		11201	Pro Time	85610
Injections			Fracture Treatment			PSA	84153
Administration Sub. / IM	90772		Loc			RPR	86592
Drug			w/Reduc		w/o Reduc	Sed. Rate	85651
Dosage			I & D Abscess Single/Simple		10060	Stool Culture	87045
Allergy	95115		Multiple or Comp		10061	Stool O & P	87177
Cocci Skin Test	86490		I & D Pilonidal Cyst Simple		10080	Strep Screen	87880
DPT	90701		Pilonidal Cyst Complex		10081	Theophylline	80198
Hemophilus	90646		IV Therapy—To One Hour		90760	Thyroid Uptake	84479
Influenza	90658		Each Additional Hour		90761	TSH	84443
MMR	90707		Laceration Repair			Urinalysis	81000
OPV	90712		Location Size Simp/Comp			Urine Culture	87088
Pneumovax	90732		Laryngoscopy		31505	Drawing Fee	36415
TB Skin Test	86580		Oximetry		94760	Specimen Collection	99000
TD	90718		Punch Biopsy			**Other:**	
Unlisted Immun	90749		Rhythm Strip		93040		
Tetanus Toxoid	90703		Treadmill		93015		
Vaccine/Toxoid Admin <8 Yr Old w/ Counseling	90465		Trigger Point or Tendon Sheath Inj.		20550		
Vaccine/Toxoid Administration for Adult	90471		Tympanometry		92567		

Diagnosis/ICD-10: M10.9, I10

I acknowledge receipt of medical services and authorize the release of any medical information necessary to process this claim for healthcare payment only. I do authorize payment to the provider.

Patient Signature <u>Scott Reeves</u>

Total Estimated Charges: _____

Payment Amount: _____

Next Appointment: _____

Figure 12-7

Capital City Medical
Fee Schedule

New Patient OV		Punch Biopsy various codes	$80
Problem Focused 99201	$45	Nebulizer various codes	$45
Expanded Problem Focused 99202	$65	Cast Application various codes	$85
Detailed 99203	$85	Laryngoscopy 31505	$255
Comprehensive 99204	$105	Audiometry 92552	$85
Comprehensive/High Complex 99205	$115	Tympanometry 92567	$85
Well Exam infant (less than 1 year) 99381	$45	Ear Irrigation 69210	$25
Well Exam 1–4 yrs. 99382	$50	Diaphragm Fitting 57170	$30
Well Exam 5–11 yrs. 99383	$55	IV Therapy (up to one hour) 90760	$65
Well Exam 12–17 yrs. 99384	$65	Each additional hour 90761	$50
Well Exam 18–39 yrs. 99385	$85	Oximetry 94760	$10
Well Exam 40–64 yrs. 99386	$105	ECG 93000	$75
Established Patient OV		Holter Monitor various codes	$170
Post Op Follow Up Visit 99024	$0	Rhythm Strip 93040	$60
Minimum 99211	$35	Treadmill 93015	$375
Problem Focused 99212	$45	Cocci Skin Test 86490	$20
Expanded Problem Focused 99213	$55	X-ray, spine, chest, bone—any area various codes	$275
Detailed 99214	$65	Avulsion Nail 11730	$200
Comprehensive/High Complex 99215	$75	**Laboratory**	
Well exam infant (less than 1 year) 99391	$35	Amylase 82150	$40
Well Exam 1–4 yrs. 99392	$40	B12 82607	$30
Well Exam 5–11 yrs. 99393	$45	CBC & Diff 85025	$95
Well Exam 12–17 yrs. 99394	$55	Comp Metabolic Panel 80053	$75
Well Exam 18–39 yrs. 99395	$65	Chlamydia Screen 87110	$70
Well Exam 40–64 yrs. 99396	$75	Cholestrerol 82465	$75
Obstetrics		Digoxin 80162	$40
Total OB Care 59400	$1700	Electrolytes 80051	$70
Injections		Estrogen, Total 82672	$50
Administration 90772	$10	Ferritin 82728	$40
Allergy 95115	$35	Folate 82746	$30
DPT 90701	$50	GC Screen 87070	$60
Drug various codes	$35	Glucose 82947	$35
Influenza 90658	$25	Glycosylated HGB A1C 83036	$45
MMR 90707	$50	HCT 85014	$30
OPV 90712	$40	HDL 83718	$35
Pneumovax 90732	$35	HGB 85018	$30
TB Skin Test 86580	$15	Hep BSAG 83740	$40
TD 90718	$40	Hepatitis panel, acute 80074	$95
Tetanus Toxoid 90703	$40	HIV 86703	$100
Vaccine/Toxoid Administration for Younger		Iron & TIBC 83550	$45
Than 8 Years Old w/ counseling 90465	$10	Kidney Profile 80069	$95
Vaccine/Toxoid Administration for Adult 90471	$10	Lead 83665	$55
Arthrocentesis/Aspiration/Injection		Lipase 83690	$40
Small Joint 20600	$50	Lipid Panel 80061	$95
Interm Joint 20605	$60	Liver Profile 80076	$95
Major Joint 20610	$70	Mono Test 86308	$30
Trigger Point/Tendon Sheath Inj. 20550	$90	Pap Smear 88155	$90
Other Invasive/Noninvasive Procedures		Pap Collection/Supervision 88142	$95
Catheterization 51701	$55	Pregnancy Test 84703	$90
Circumcision 54150	$150	Obstetric Panel 80055	$85
Colposcopy 57452	$225	Pro Time 85610	$50
Colposcopy w/Biopsy 57454	$250	PSA 84153	$50
Cryosurgery Premalignant Lesion various codes	$160	RPR 86592	$55
Endometrial Biopsy 58100	$190	Sed. Rate 85651	$50
Excision Lesion Malignant various codes	$145	Stool Culture 87045	$80
Excision Lesion Benign various codes	$125	Stool O & P 87177	$105
Curettement Lesion		Strep Screen 87880	$35
Single 11055	$70	Theophylline 80198	$40
2–4 11056	$80	Thyroid Uptake 84479	$75
>4 11057	$90	TSH 84443	$50
Excision Skin Tags (1–15) 11200	$55	Urinalysis 81000	$35
Each Additional 10 11201	$30	Urine Culture 87088	$80
I & D Abscess Single/Simple 10060	$75	Drawing Fee 36415	$15
Multiple/Complex 10061	$95	Specimen Collection 99000	$10
I & D Pilonidal Cyst Simple 10080	$105		
I & D Pilonidal Cyst Complex 10081	$130		
Laceration Repair various codes	$60		

HEALTH INSURANCE CLAIM FORM

APPROVED BY NATIONAL UNIFORM CLAIM COMMITTEE (NUCC) 02/12

◀— CARRIER —▶

| PICA | | | | | | | | PICA | |

1.	MEDICARE	MEDICAID	TRICARE	CHAMPVA	GROUP HEALTH PLAN	FECA BLK LUNG	OTHER	1a. INSURED'S I.D. NUMBER	(For Program in Item 1)
	[X] (Medicare#)	[ ] (Medicaid#)	[ ] (ID#/DoD#)	[ ] (Member ID#)	[ ] (ID#)	[ ] (ID#)	[ ] (ID#)		

2. PATIENT'S NAME (Last Name, First Name, Middle Initial)	3. PATIENT'S BIRTH DATE MM DD YY SEX M [ ] F [ ]	4. INSURED'S NAME (Last Name, First Name, Middle Initial)

5. PATIENT'S ADDRESS (No., Street)	6. PATIENT RELATIONSHIP TO INSURED Self [ ] Spouse [ ] Child [ ] Other [ ]	7. INSURED'S ADDRESS (No., Street)

CITY	STATE	8. RESERVED FOR NUCC USE	CITY	STATE

ZIP CODE	TELEPHONE (Include Area Code) ( )		ZIP CODE	TELEPHONE (Include Area Code) ( )

9. OTHER INSURED'S NAME (Last Name, First Name, Middle Initial)	10. IS PATIENT'S CONDITION RELATED TO:	11. INSURED'S POLICY GROUP OR FECA NUMBER
a. OTHER INSURED'S POLICY OR GROUP NUMBER	a. EMPLOYMENT? (Current or Previous) YES [ ] NO [ ]	a. INSURED'S DATE OF BIRTH MM DD YY SEX M [ ] F [ ]
b. RESERVED FOR NUCC USE	b. AUTO ACCIDENT? PLACE (State) YES [ ] NO [ ]	b. OTHER CLAIM ID (Designated by NUCC)
c. RESERVED FOR NUCC USE	c. OTHER ACCIDENT? YES [ ] NO [ ]	c. INSURANCE PLAN NAME OR PROGRAM NAME
d. INSURANCE PLAN NAME OR PROGRAM NAME	10d. CLAIM CODES (Designated by NUCC)	d. IS THERE ANOTHER HEALTH BENEFIT PLAN? YES [ ] NO [ ] If yes, complete items 9, 9a, and 9d.

READ BACK OF FORM BEFORE COMPLETING & SIGNING THIS FORM.

12. PATIENT'S OR AUTHORIZED PERSON'S SIGNATURE I authorize the release of any medical or other information necessary to process this claim. I also request payment of government benefits either to myself or to the party who accepts assignment below.

SIGNED _____ DATE _____

13. INSURED'S OR AUTHORIZED PERSON'S SIGNATURE I authorize payment of medical benefits to the undersigned physician or supplier for services described below.

SIGNED _____

◀— PATIENT AND INSURED INFORMATION —▶

14. DATE OF CURRENT ILLNESS, INJURY, or PREGNANCY (LMP) MM DD YY QUAL.	15. OTHER DATE QUAL. MM DD YY	16. DATES PATIENT UNABLE TO WORK IN CURRENT OCCUPATION MM DD YY MM DD YY FROM TO
17. NAME OF REFERRING PROVIDER OR OTHER SOURCE	17a. 17b NPI	18. HOSPITALIZATION DATES RELATED TO CURRENT SERVICES MM DD YY MM DD YY FROM TO
19. ADDITIONAL CLAIM INFORMATION (Designated by NUCC)		20. OUTSIDE LAB? YES [ ] NO [ ] $ CHARGES

21. DIAGNOSIS OR NATURE OF ILLNESS OR INJURY Relate A-L to service line below (24E) ICD Ind.	22. RESUBMISSION CODE ORIGINAL REF. NO.
A. ____ B. ____ C. ____ D. ____ E. ____ F. ____ G. ____ H. ____ I. ____ J. ____ K. ____ L. ____	23. PRIOR AUTHORIZATION NUMBER

24. A. DATE(S) OF SERVICE		B. PLACE OF SERVICE	C. EMG	D. PROCEDURES, SERVICES, OR SUPPLIES (Explain Unusual Circumstances)		E. DIAGNOSIS POINTER	F. $ CHARGES	G. DAYS OR UNITS	H. EPSDT Family Plan	I. ID. QUAL	J. RENDERING PROVIDER ID #
From MM DD YY	To MM DD YY			CPT/HCPCS	MODIFIER						
1											NPI
2											NPI
3											NPI
4											NPI
5											NPI
6											NPI

25. FEDERAL TAX I.D. NUMBER SSN EIN [ ][ ]	26. PATIENT'S ACCOUNT NO.	27. ACCEPT ASSIGNMENT? (For govt. claims, see back) YES [ ] NO [ ]	28. TOTAL CHARGE $	29. AMOUNT PAID $	30. Rsvd. for NUCC Use

31. SIGNATURE OF PHYSICIAN OR SUPPLIER INCLUDING DEGREES OR CREDENTIALS (I certify that the statements on the reverse apply to this bill and are made a part thereof.) SIGNED _____ DATE _____	32. SERVICE FACILITY LOCATION INFORMATION a. NPI b.	33. BILLING PROVIDER INFO & PH # ( ) a. NPI b.

◀— PHYSICIAN OR SUPPLIER INFORMATION —▶

NUCC Instruction Manual available at: www.nucc.org   **PLEASE PRINT OR TYPE**   APPROVED OMB-0938-1197 FORM 1500 (02-12)

Clear Form

Figure 12-8

© 2018 Pearson Education, Inc.

e. Using the source documents, the Capital City Medical Fee Schedule (Figure 12-9), and the blank CMS-1500 form provided (Figure 12-10), complete the following case study for patient Von Vandusen (Case 12-5):

CASE 12-5

Capital City Medical—123 Unknown Boulevard, Capital City, NY 12345-2222 (555) 555-1234	Patient Information Form
Phil Wells, MD, Mannie Mends, MD, Bette R. Soone, MD	Tax ID: 75-0246810
	Group NPI: 1513171216

Patient Information:

Name: (Last, First) Vandusen, Von ☒ Male ☐ Female Birth Date: 07/11/1947

Address: 67 Field Dr., Township, NY 12345 Phone: (555) 555-8204

Social Security Number: 172-43-1817 Full-Time Student: ☐ Yes ☒ No

Marital Status: ☐ Single ☒ Married ☐ Divorced ☐ Other

Employment:

Employer: Retired Phone: ( )

Address:

Condition Related to: ☐ Auto Accident ☐ Employment ☐ Other Accident

Date of Accident: State:

Emergency Contact: Phone: ( )

Primary Insurance: Medicare Phone: ( )

Address: P O. Box , 9834, Capital City, NY 12345

Insurance Policyholder's Name: Same ☐ M ☐ F DOB: 11/21/1953

Address:

Phone: Relationship to Insured: ☒ Self ☐ Spouse ☐ Child ☐ Other

Employer: Phone: ( )

Employer's Address:

Policy/ID No: 476881270A Group No: Percent Covered: 80 % Copay Amt: $

Secondary Insurance: Phone: ( )

Address:

Insurance Policyholder's Name: ☐ M ☐ F DOB:

Address: Same

Phone: Relationship to Insured: ☐ Self ☐ Spouse ☐ Child ☐ Other

Employer: Phone: ( )

Employer's Address:

Policy/ID No: 6758562 Group No: 5832 Percent Covered: % Copay Amt: $

Reason for Visit: Checkup on my heart condition and blood pressure

Known Allergies:

Referred by:

CASE 12-5
SOAP

10/27/20XX
Assignment of Benefits: Y
Signature on File: Y
Referring Physician: N

S: Von Vandusen is being seen today for HTN. He says that his BP is always running high, but otherwise, he feels fine.

O: BP on exam is 178/88. P: 86 and regular. Wt. 252 lbs. EKG shows old MI. Chest is clear to A&P. Pt. has mild ankle edema bilaterally.

A: 1. Essential HTN benign Lytes are normal values—I10
     2. Old MI—I25.2

P: 1. Add Norvasc q. a.m.
     2. Pt. advised to lose weight.
     3. Return in 1 week to evaluate the addition of new BP med.

_____

Phil Wells, MD
Family Practice
NPI: 1234567890

© 2018 Pearson Education, Inc.

CASE 12-5

Patient Name Von Vandusen

Capital City Medical
123 Unknown Boulevard, Capital City, NY 12345-2222

Date of Service
10-27-20XX

New Patient			Arthrocentesis/Aspiration/Injection			Laboratory		
Problem Focused	99201		Arthrocentesis/Aspiration/Injection			Amylase	82150	
Expanded Problem, Focused	99202		Small Joint	20600		B12	82607	
Detailed	99203		Interm Joint	20605		CBC & Diff	85025	
Comprehensive	99204		Major Joint	20610		Comp Metabolic Panel	80053	
Comprehensive/High Complex	99205		**Other Invasive/Noninvasive**			Chlamydia Screen	87110	
Well Exam Infant (up to 12 mos.)	99381		Audiometry	92552		Cholesterol	82465	
Well Exam 1–4 yrs.	99382		Cast Application			Digoxin	80162	
Well Exam 5–11 yrs.	99383		Location Long Short			Electrolytes	80051	X
Well Exam 12–17 yrs.	99384		Catheterization	51701		Ferritin	82728	
Well Exam 18–39 yrs.	99385		Circumcision	54150		Folate	82746	
Well Exam 40–64 yrs.	99386		Colposcopy	57452		GC Screen	87070	
			Colposcopy w/Biopsy	57454		Glucose	82947	
			Cryosurgery Premalignant Lesion			Glucose 1 HR	82950	
			Location (s):			Glycosylated HGB A1C	83036	
Established Patient			Cryosurgery Warts			HCT	85014	
Post-Op Follow Up Visit	99024		Location (s):			HDL	83718	
Minimum	99211		Curettement Lesion			Hep BSAG	87340	
Problem Focused	99212		Single	11055		Hepatitis panel, acute	80074	
Expanded Problem Focused	99213	X	2–4	11056		HGB	85018	
Detailed	99214		>4	11057		HIV	86703	
Comprehensive/High Complex	99215		Diaphragm Fitting	57170		Iron & TIBC	83550	
Well Exam Infant (up to 12 mos.)	99391		Ear Irrigation	69210		Kidney Profile	80069	
Well exam 1–4 yrs.	99392		ECG	93000	X	Lead	83655	
Well Exam 5–11 yrs.	99393		Endometrial Biopsy	58100		Liver Profile	80076	
Well Exam 12–17 yrs.	99394		Exc. Lesion Malignant			Mono Test	86308	
Well Exam 18–39 yrs.	99395		Benign			Pap Smear	88155	
Well Exam 40–64 yrs.	99396		Location			Pregnancy Test	84703	
Obstetrics			Exc. Skin Tags (1–15)	11200		Obstetric Panel	80055	
Total OB Care	59400		Each Additional 10	11201		Pro Time	85610	
Injections			Fracture Treatment			PSA	84153	
Administration Sub. / IM	90772		Loc			RPR	86592	
Drug			w/Reduc w/o Reduc			Sed. Rate	85651	
Dosage			I & D Abscess Single/Simple	10060		Stool Culture	87045	
Allergy	95115		Multiple or Comp	10061		Stool O & P	87177	
Cocci Skin Test	86490		I & D Pilonidal Cyst Simple	10080		Strep Screen	87880	
DPT	90701		Pilonidal Cyst Complex	10081		Theophylline	80198	
Hemophilus	90646		IV Therapy—To One Hour	90760		Thyroid Uptake	84479	
Influenza	90658		Each Additional Hour	90761		TSH	84443	
MMR	90707		Laceration Repair			Urinalysis	81000	
OPV	90712		Location Size Simp/Comp			Urine Culture	87088	
Pneumovax	90732		Laryngoscopy	31505		Drawing Fee	36415	X
TB Skin Test	86580		Oximetry	94760		Specimen Collection	99000	
TD	90718		Punch Biopsy			**Other:**		
Unlisted Immun	90749		Rhythm Strip	93040				
Tetanus Toxoid	90703		Treadmill	93015				
Vaccine/Toxoid Admin <8 Yr Old w/ Counseling	90465		Trigger Point or Tendon Sheath Inj.	20550				
Vaccine/Toxoid Administration for Adult	90471		Tympanometry	92567				

Diagnosis/ICD-10: I10, I25.2

I acknowledge receipt of medical services and authorize the release of any medical information necessary to process this claim for healthcare payment only. I do authorize payment to the provider.

Total Estimated Charges: _____

Payment Amount: _____

Patient Signature _Von Vandusen_____

Next Appointment: _____

Figure 12-9

Capital City Medical
Fee Schedule

New Patient OV		Punch Biopsy various codes	$80
Problem Focused 99201	$45	Nebulizer various codes	$45
Expanded Problem Focused 99202	$65	Cast Application various codes	$85
Detailed 99203	$85	Laryngoscopy 31505	$255
Comprehensive 99204	$105	Audiometry 92552	$85
Comprehensive/High Complex 99205	$115	Tympanometry 92567	$85
Well Exam infant (less than 1 year) 99381	$45	Ear Irrigation 69210	$25
Well Exam 1–4 yrs. 99382	$50	Diaphragm Fitting 57170	$30
Well Exam 5–11 yrs. 99383	$55	IV Therapy (up to one hour) 90760	$65
Well Exam 12–17 yrs. 99384	$65	Each additional hour 90761	$50
Well Exam 18–39 yrs. 99385	$85	Oximetry 94760	$10
Well Exam 40–64 yrs. 99386	$105	ECG 93000	$75
Established Patient OV		Holter Monitor various codes	$170
Post Op Follow Up Visit 99024	$0	Rhythm Strip 93040	$60
Minimum 99211	$35	Treadmill 93015	$375
Problem Focused 99212	$45	Cocci Skin Test 86490	$20
Expanded Problem Focused 99213	$55	X-ray, spine, chest, bone—any area various codes	$275
Detailed 99214	$65	Avulsion Nail 11730	$200
Comprehensive/High Complex 99215	$75	**Laboratory**	
Well exam infant (less than 1 year) 99391	$35	Amylase 82150	$40
Well Exam 1–4 yrs. 99392	$40	B12 82607	$30
Well Exam 5–11 yrs. 99393	$45	CBC & Diff 85025	$95
Well Exam 12–17 yrs. 99394	$55	Comp Metabolic Panel 80053	$75
Well Exam 18–39 yrs. 99395	$65	Chlamydia Screen 87110	$70
Well Exam 40–64 yrs. 99396	$75	Cholestrerol 82465	$75
Obstetrics		Digoxin 80162	$40
Total OB Care 59400	$1700	Electrolytes 80051	$70
Injections		Estrogen, Total 82672	$50
Administration 90772	$10	Ferritin 82728	$40
Allergy 95115	$35	Folate 82746	$30
DPT 90701	$50	GC Screen 87070	$60
Drug various codes	$35	Glucose 82947	$35
Influenza 90658	$25	Glycosylated HGB A1C 83036	$45
MMR 90707	$50	HCT 85014	$30
OPV 90712	$40	HDL 83718	$35
Pneumovax 90732	$35	HGB 85018	$30
TB Skin Test 86580	$15	Hep BSAG 83740	$40
TD 90718	$40	Hepatitis panel, acute 80074	$95
Tetanus Toxoid 90703	$40	HIV 86703	$100
Vaccine/Toxoid Administration for Younger		Iron & TIBC 83550	$45
Than 8 Years Old w/ counseling 90465	$10	Kidney Profile 80069	$95
Vaccine/Toxoid Administration for Adult 90471	$10	Lead 83665	$55
Arthrocentesis/Aspiration/Injection		Lipase 83690	$40
Small Joint 20600	$50	Lipid Panel 80061	$95
Interm Joint 20605	$60	Liver Profile 80076	$95
Major Joint 20610	$70	Mono Test 86308	$30
Trigger Point/Tendon Sheath Inj. 20550	$90	Pap Smear 88155	$90
Other Invasive/Noninvasive Procedures		Pap Collection/Supervision 88142	$95
Catheterization 51701	$55	Pregnancy Test 84703	$90
Circumcision 54150	$150	Obstetric Panel 80055	$85
Colposcopy 57452	$225	Pro Time 85610	$50
Colposcopy w/Biopsy 57454	$250	PSA 84153	$50
Cryosurgery Premalignant Lesion various codes	$160	RPR 86592	$55
Endometrial Biopsy 58100	$190	Sed. Rate 85651	$50
Excision Lesion Malignant various codes	$145	Stool Culture 87045	$80
Excision Lesion Benign various codes	$125	Stool O & P 87177	$105
Curettement Lesion		Strep Screen 87880	$35
Single 11055	$70	Theophylline 80198	$40
2–4 11056	$80	Thyroid Uptake 84479	$75
>4 11057	$90	TSH 84443	$50
Excision Skin Tags (1–15) 11200	$55	Urinalysis 81000	$35
Each Additional 10 11201	$30	Urine Culture 87088	$80
I & D Abscess Single/Simple 10060	$75	Drawing Fee 36415	$15
Multiple/Complex 10061	$95	Specimen Collection 99000	$10
I & D Pilonidal Cyst Simple 10080	$105		
I & D Pilonidal Cyst Complex 10081	$130		
Laceration Repair various codes	$60		

HEALTH INSURANCE CLAIM FORM

APPROVED BY NATIONAL UNIFORM CLAIM COMMITTEE (NUCC) 02/12

☐☐ PICA   PICA ☐☐

1. MEDICARE	MEDICAID	TRICARE	CHAMPVA	GROUP HEALTH PLAN	FECA BLK LUNG	OTHER	1a. INSURED'S I.D. NUMBER	(For Program in Item 1)
☒ (Medicare#)	☐ (Medicaid#)	☐ (ID#/DoD#)	☐ (Member ID#)	☐ (ID#)	☐ (ID#)	☐ (ID#)		

2. PATIENT'S NAME (Last Name, First Name, Middle Initial)

3. PATIENT'S BIRTH DATE MM | DD | YY   **SEX** M ☐ F ☐

4. INSURED'S NAME (Last Name, First Name, Middle Initial)

5. PATIENT'S ADDRESS (No., Street)

6. PATIENT RELATIONSHIP TO INSURED Self ☐ Spouse ☐ Child ☐ Other ☐

7. INSURED'S ADDRESS (No., Street)

CITY ___ STATE ___ **8. RESERVED FOR NUCC USE**   CITY ___ STATE ___

ZIP CODE ___ TELEPHONE (Include Area Code) ( )   ZIP CODE ___ TELEPHONE (Include Area Code) ( )

9. OTHER INSURED'S NAME (Last Name, First Name, Middle Initial)

10. IS PATIENT'S CONDITION RELATED TO:

11. INSURED'S POLICY GROUP OR FECA NUMBER

a. OTHER INSURED'S POLICY OR GROUP NUMBER

a. EMPLOYMENT? (Current or Previous) ☐ YES ☐ NO

a. INSURED'S DATE OF BIRTH MM | DD | YY   **SEX** M ☐ F ☐

b. RESERVED FOR NUCC USE

b. AUTO ACCIDENT? ☐ YES ☐ NO PLACE (State) ___

b. OTHER CLAIM ID (Designated by NUCC)

c. RESERVED FOR NUCC USE

c. OTHER ACCIDENT? ☐ YES ☐ NO

c. INSURANCE PLAN NAME OR PROGRAM NAME

d. INSURANCE PLAN NAME OR PROGRAM NAME

10d. CLAIM CODES (Designated by NUCC)

d. IS THERE ANOTHER HEALTH BENEFIT PLAN? ☐ YES ☐ NO *If yes*, complete items 9, 9a, and 9d.

READ BACK OF FORM BEFORE COMPLETING & SIGNING THIS FORM.

12. PATIENT'S OR AUTHORIZED PERSON'S SIGNATURE I authorize the release of any medical or other information necessary to process this claim. I also request payment of government benefits either to myself or to the party who accepts assignment below.

SIGNED ___ DATE ___

13. INSURED'S OR AUTHORIZED PERSON'S SIGNATURE I authorize payment of medical benefits to the undersigned physician or supplier for services described below.

SIGNED ___

14. DATE OF CURRENT ILLNESS, INJURY, or PREGNANCY (LMP) MM | DD | YY QUAL.

15. OTHER DATE QUAL. MM | DD | YY

16. DATES PATIENT UNABLE TO WORK IN CURRENT OCCUPATION FROM MM | DD | YY TO MM | DD | YY

17. NAME OF REFERRING PROVIDER OR OTHER SOURCE 17a. ___ 17b. NPI ___

18. HOSPITALIZATION DATES RELATED TO CURRENT SERVICES FROM MM | DD | YY TO MM | DD | YY

19. ADDITIONAL CLAIM INFORMATION (Designated by NUCC)

20. OUTSIDE LAB? ☐ YES ☐ NO $ CHARGES

21. DIAGNOSIS OR NATURE OF ILLNESS OR INJURY Relate A-L to service line below (24E) ICD Ind. ___

A. ___ B. ___ C. ___ D. ___
E. ___ F. ___ G. ___ H. ___
I. ___ J. ___ K. ___ L. ___

22. RESUBMISSION CODE ___ ORIGINAL REF. NO. ___

23. PRIOR AUTHORIZATION NUMBER

24. A. DATE(S) OF SERVICE From MM DD YY To MM DD YY	B. PLACE OF SERVICE	C. EMG	D. PROCEDURES, SERVICES, OR SUPPLIES (Explain Unusual Circumstances) CPT/HCPCS MODIFIER	E. DIAGNOSIS POINTER	F. $ CHARGES	G. DAYS OR UNITS	H. EPSDT Family Plan	I. ID. QUAL.	J. RENDERING PROVIDER ID. #
1								NPI	
2								NPI	
3								NPI	
4								NPI	
5								NPI	
6								NPI	

25. FEDERAL TAX I.D. NUMBER SSN ☐ EIN ☐

26. PATIENT'S ACCOUNT NO.

27. ACCEPT ASSIGNMENT? (For govt. claims, see back) ☐ YES ☐ NO

28. TOTAL CHARGE $

29. AMOUNT PAID $

30. Rsvd. for NUCC Use

31. SIGNATURE OF PHYSICIAN OR SUPPLIER INCLUDING DEGREES OR CREDENTIALS (I certify that the statements on the reverse apply to this bill and are made a part thereof.)

SIGNED ___ DATE ___

32. SERVICE FACILITY LOCATION INFORMATION a. NPI b.

33. BILLING PROVIDER INFO & PH # ( ) a. NPI b.

NUCC Instruction Manual available at: www.nucc.org **PLEASE PRINT OR TYPE** APPROVED OMB-0938-1197 FORM 1500 (02-12)

Clear Form

Figure 12-10

© 2018 Pearson Education, Inc.

REVIEW QUESTIONS

MATCHING

Choose the correct answer and write its corresponding letter in the space provided.

a. Medicare Part A
b. Respite care
c. Medicare secondary payer (MSP)
d. Crossover
e. GA

1. _____ The reassignment of the gaps in coverage that eliminates the need for filing a separate claim with Medigap
2. _____ Covers inpatient facility costs
3. _____ Care given to a hospice patient to allow the usual caregiver time to rest
4. _____ Term used when Medicare is not responsible for paying a claim first
5. _____ Modifier used on a claim form to identify that a patient has signed an ABN and that it is on file with the provider

MULTIPLE CHOICE

Circle the letter of the choice that best completes each statement or answers the question.

1. What is another name for Medicare Part C?
   a. Medigap
   b. MediCal
   c. Medicare Advantage
   d. None of the above

2. Which of the following is *not* covered by Medicare Parts A and B?
   a. Long-term care
   b. Routine dental care
   c. Routine eye care
   d. All of the above

3. Which of the following is considered medically necessary?
   a. An elective procedure
   b. An experimental or investigational procedure
   c. An essential treatment
   d. None of the above

4. Who receives a Medicare Summary Notice?
   a. Medicare beneficiaries
   b. Patients
   c. Providers
   d. Both a and b

5. What is the name of the form that Medicare will send a provider to request additional information or documentation for a claim to be processed?
   a. Advanced Beneficiary Notice
   b. Medicare Development Letter
   c. Remittance Advice Notice
   d. Explanation of Benefits Notice

© 2018 Pearson Education, Inc.

SHORT ANSWER

Provide the correct response to each question that follows.

1. a. What are coinsurance days?

    _____
    _____
    _____

    b. What are the criteria for Medicare basic days?

    _____
    _____
    _____

2. What is the difference between a fee-for-service and a managed care plan?

    _____
    _____
    _____

3. Define the 72-hour rule/3-day payment window rule.

    _____
    _____
    _____

4. What should be documented in FL 20 when an independent laboratory provides an EKG or obtains a specimen from a homebound or institutionalized patient?

    _____
    _____

5. What is the result of entering a dollar amount in FL 29?

    _____
    _____
    _____

TRUE/FALSE

Identify each statement as true (T) or false (F).

1. _____ Medicare plans can be either fee-for-service or managed care.
2. _____ A nonparticipating provider can choose to accept Medicare assignment.
3. _____ An ABN does not need to be signed for every questionably covered service.
4. _____ Selling or sharing Medicare health insurance claim numbers is considered fraud.
5. _____ Routinely waiving coinsurance and/or deductibles for Medicare patients is not subject to fraud penalties.

CHAPTER 13
Medicaid Medical Billing

CHAPTER OBJECTIVES

After reading this chapter, the student should be able to:

1. Understand the requirements for qualifying to receive Medicaid benefits.
2. Determine the schedule of benefits the Medicaid recipient will receive.
3. Discuss the method of verifying Medicaid benefits.
4. Submit a Medicaid claim and decipher claim status.

CHAPTER OUTLINE

Medicaid Guidelines

Eligibility Groups
   Categorically Needy
   Medically Needy
   Special Groups

Children's Health Insurance Program Reauthorization Act (CHIPRA)

Scope of Medicaid Services
   PACE

Amount and Duration of Medicaid Services

Payment for Medicaid Services

Medicaid Growth Trends
   Affordable Care Act Projections

The Medicaid–Medicare Relationship (Medi–Medi)

Medicaid Managed Care

Medicaid Verification

Medicaid Claims Filing
   Time Limits for Submitting Claims
   Appeal Time Limits
   Newborn Claim Hints

Completing the CMS-1500 Form for Medicaid (Primary)
   Practice Exercises

© 2018 Pearson Education, Inc.

KEY TERMS

Using the highlighted terms and glossary in the textbook, define the following terms.

1. categorically needy _____

_____

2. Children's Health Insurance Program (CHIP) _____

_____

3. Children's Health Insurance Program Reauthorization Act (CHIPRA) _____

_____

4. Early and Periodic Screening, Diagnostic and Treatment (EPSDT) _____

_____

5. Federal Medicaid Assistant Percentages (FMAP) _____

_____

6. medically needy _____

_____

7. Medi–Medi _____

_____

8. payer of last resort _____

_____

9. restricted status _____

_____

10. spend-down program _____

_____

11. State Children's Health Insurance Program (SCHIP) _____

_____

12. Supplemental Security Income (SSI) _____

_____

13. Temporary Assistance for Needy Families (TANF) _____

_____

14. Welfare Reform Bill _____

_____

CRITICAL THINKING QUESTIONS

Using the knowledge you have gained from reading the textbook, apply critical thinking skills to answer the following questions.

1. What is the federal government's involvement in the Medicaid program, and how does this compare with each state's involvement?

1. _____

2. _____

© 2018 Pearson Education, Inc.

3. _____

4. _____

2. a. What are the three groups that are eligible for Medicaid, under federal law?

   1. _____

   2. _____

   3. _____

   b. What six groups are considered to be categorically needy to qualify for Medicaid?

   1. _____

   2. _____

   3. _____

   4. _____

   5. _____

   6. _____

   c. Define a medically needy person.

   _____

   _____

   _____

3. Answer the following questions related to the Welfare Reform Bill:

   a. A patient, Christine Richards, is born to her mother, who receives Medicaid. Her mother is a legal alien. Does Christine qualify for Medicaid? Why or why not?

   _____

   _____

   _____

   _____

   _____

   b. If this patient had not been born in this country and just came here as an alien, would she qualify for Medicaid right now? Why or why not?

   _____

   _____

   _____

   _____

   c. Who determines TANF eligibility?

   _____

   _____

   _____

   _____

4. a. What are the 14 mandatory services that states must provide to Medicaid recipients?

1. _____

2. _____

3. _____

4. _____

5. _____

6. _____

7. _____

8. _____

9. _____

10. _____

11. _____

12. _____

13. _____

14. _____

b. What do you believe will be the future of Medicaid in 10 years? Discuss your answer with the class.

_____

_____

_____

_____

5. a. You filed a Medicaid claim 60 days after the services were provided. Was this claim submitted within Medicaid's allowed time period? Why or why not?

_____

_____

_____

b. If the medical biller accidentally overlooked a Medicaid claim that had not been filed within the allowed time period, what should he do?

_____

_____

_____

_____

c. The medical biller receives a denied Medicaid claim for a patient's account and decides to appeal. What is the allowed time period to submit this appeal?

_____

_____

© 2018 Pearson Education, Inc.

d. The medical biller has just received a denial for a Medicaid claim that she filed for a patient. The medical biller inspects the claim and realizes that she entered the wrong ID# for the patient. She corrects the claim and resubmits it. What is the time period allowed by Medicaid to resubmit this claim?

_____

_____

PRACTICE EXERCISES

1. Using the form locator information written out on your index cards, complete the following activity. Flag those FLs that would be filled out differently for Medicaid patients.

2. Case studies are provided for additional practice in completing the CMS-1500 claim form for Medicaid physician outpatient billing. By applying what you have learned in your student text, accurately code and complete each case study. Patient demographics and a brief case history are provided. Complete the cases based on the following criteria:

   - All patients have release of information and assignment of benefits signatures on file. Assignment of benefits is required by most states for Medicaid. SOF is not required in Item 13.

   - All providers accept assignment for Medicaid, by law. Item 27 should not be marked.

   - The group practice is the billing entity.

   - The national transition to NPI numbers is complete, and legacy PINs of individual payers are no longer used. If legacy PINS are still being used by your state Medicaid program, your instructor may provide you with Medicaid PINs in addition to the NPI.

   - 2017 ICD-10-CM and CPT codes are used.

   - Use eight-digit dates for birthdates. Use six-digit dates for all other dates.

   - All street names should be entered with standard postal abbreviations, even if they are spelled out on the source documents.

   - Enter the ICD-10 codes in the order they appear on the encounter form.

   - When entering CPT codes, enter the E/M code first. Enter remaining codes in descending price order.

To complete each case study, you must determine the correct fees. Refer to the Capital City Medical Fee Schedule, which is located after each case's source documents. Use the blank CMS-1500 form provided after each case.

   a. Using the source documents, the Capital City Medical Fee Schedule (Figure 13-1), and the blank CMS-1500 form provided (Figure 13-2), complete the following case study for patient Michael Schultz (Case 13-1):

CASE 13-1

Capital City Medical—123 Unknown Boulevard, Capital City, NY 12345-2222 (555) 555-1234

Phil Wells, MD, Mannie Mends, MD, Bette R. Soone, MD

Patient Information Form

Tax ID: 75-0246810

Group NPI: 1513171216

Patient Information:

Name: (Last, First) <u>Schultz, Michael</u>　　☒ Male　❑ Female　Birth Date: <u>10/01/1971</u>

Address: <u>84 Marble St, Capital City, NY 12345</u>　　　　Phone: (555) <u>555-6918</u>

Social Security Number: <u>723-44-4142</u>　　　　Full-Time Student:　❑ Yes　☒ No

Marital Status:　☒ Single　❑ Married　❑ Divorced　❑ Other

Employment:

Employer: <u>Buy Now Mart</u>　　　　Phone: (555) <u>555-5989</u>

Address: <u>914 W. Washington St. Capital City, NY 12345</u>

Condition Related to:　❑ Auto Accident　❑ Employment　❑ Other Accident

Date of Accident: _____　State: _____

Emergency Contact: _____ **Phone: ( )** _____

Primary Insurance: <u>Medicaid</u>　　　　Phone: ( ) _____

Address: <u>4875 Capital Blvd, Capital City, NY 12345</u>

Insurance Policyholder's Name: <u>Same</u>　　　❑ M ❑ F DOB: _____

Address: _____

Phone: ( ) _____ Relationship to Insured: ☒ Self ❑ Spouse ❑ Child ❑ Other

Employer: _____ Phone: ( ) _____

Employer's Address: _____

Policy/ID No: <u>0002316983333</u> Group No: _____ Percent Covered: ____% Copay Amt: $<u>5.00</u>

Secondary Insurance: _____ Phone: ( ) _____

Address: _____

Insurance Policyholder's Name: _____ ❑ M ❑ F DOB: _____

Address: _____

Phone: ( ) _____ Relationship to Insured: ❑ Self ❑ Spouse ❑ Child ❑ Other

Employer: _____ Phone: ( ) _____

Employer's Address: _____

Policy/ID No: _____ Group No: _____ Percent Covered: ____% Copay Amt: $_____

Reason for Visit: <u>I can't sleep and I'm stressed.</u>

Known Allergies: _____

Referred by: _____

© 2018 Pearson Education, Inc.

CASE 13-1
SOAP

06/10/20XX
Assignment of Benefits: Y
Signature on File: Y
Referring Physician: N

S: Michael Schultz presents with complaints of not being able to sleep for 2 weeks. He is stressed because he has been taking care of his sick mother and working. He feels overwhelmed.

O: On exam, Pt. gets nervous and anxious. His vitals are stable. Physical findings are unremarkable. Labs are normal.

A: 1. Generalized Anxiety—F41.1
2. Insomnia due to stress—F51.02

P: 1. Start Xanax.
2. Start Levapro.
3. Return in 2 weeks.

_____

Phil Wells, MD
Family Practice
NPI: 1234567890

CASE 13-1

Patient Name <u>Michael Schultz</u>

Capital City Medical
123 Unknown Boulevard, Capital City, NY 12345-2222

Date of Service
<u>06-10-20XX</u>

New Patient			Arthrocentesis/Aspiration/Injection			Laboratory		
Problem Focused	99201		Small Joint		20600	Amylase	82150	
Expanded Problem, Focused	99202		Interm Joint		20605	B12	82607	
Detailed	99203		Major Joint		20610	CBC & Diff	85025	X
Comprehensive	99204		**Other Invasive/Noninvasive**			Comp Metabolic Panel	80053	
Comprehensive/High Complex	99205		Audiometry		92552	Chlamydia Screen	87110	
Well Exam Infant (up to 12 mos.)	99381		Cast Application			Cholesterol	82465	
Well Exam 1–4 yrs.	99382		Location Long Short			Digoxin	80162	
Well Exam 5–11 yrs.	99383		Catheterization		51701	Electrolytes	80051	X
Well Exam 12–17 yrs.	99384		Circumcision		54150	Ferritin	82728	
Well Exam 18–39 yrs.	99385		Colposcopy		57452	Folate	82746	
Well Exam 40–64 yrs.	99386		Colposcopy w/Biopsy		57454	GC Screen	87070	
			Cryosurgery Premalignant Lesion			Glucose	82947	
			Location (s):			Glucose 1 HR	82950	
			Cryosurgery Warts			Glycosylated HGB A1C	83036	
Established Patient			Location (s):			HCT	85014	
Post-Op Follow Up Visit	99024		Curettement Lesion			HDL	83718	
Minimum	99211		Single		11055	Hep BSAG	87340	
Problem Focused	99212		2–4		11056	Hepatitis panel, acute	80074	
Expanded Problem Focused	99213	X	>4		11057	HGB	85018	
Detailed	99214		Diaphragm Fitting		57170	HIV	86703	
Comprehensive/High Complex	99215		Ear Irrigation		69210	Iron & TIBC	83550	
Well Exam Infant (up to 12 mos.)	99391		ECG		93000	Kidney Profile	80069	
Well exam 1–4 yrs.	99392		Endometrial Biopsy		58100	Lead	83655	
Well Exam 5–11 yrs.	99393		Exc. Lesion Malignant			Liver Profile	80076	
Well Exam 12–17 yrs.	99394		Benign			Mono Test	86308	
Well Exam 18–39 yrs.	99395		Location			Pap Smear	88155	
Well Exam 40–64 yrs.	99396		Exc. Skin Tags (1–15)		11200	Pregnancy Test	84703	
Obstetrics			Each Additional 10		11201	Obstetric Panel	80055	
Total OB Care	59400		Fracture Treatment			Pro Time	85610	
Injections			Loc			PSA	84153	
Administration Sub. / IM	90772		w/Reduc	w/o Reduc		RPR	86592	
Drug			I & D Abscess Single/Simple		10060	Sed. Rate	85651	X
Dosage			Multiple or Comp		10061	Stool Culture	87045	
Allergy	95115		I & D Pilonidal Cyst Simple		10080	Stool O & P	87177	
Cocci Skin Test	86490		Pilonidal Cyst Complex		10081	Strep Screen	87880	
DPT	90701		IV Therapy—To One Hour		90760	Theophylline	80198	
Hemophilus	90646		Each Additional Hour		90761	Thyroid Uptake	84479	
Influenza	90658		Laceration Repair			TSH	84443	
MMR	90707		Location Size Simp/Comp			Urinalysis	81000	
OPV	90712		Laryngoscopy		31505	Urine Culture	87088	
Pneumovax	90732		Oximetry		94760	Drawing Fee	36415	X
TB Skin Test	86580		Punch Biopsy			Specimen Collection	99000	
TD	90718		Rhythm Strip		93040	**Other:**		
Unlisted Immun	90749		Treadmill		93015			
Tetanus Toxoid	90703		Trigger Point or Tendon Sheath Inj.		20550			
Vaccine/Toxoid Admin <8 Yr Old w/ Counseling	90465							
Vaccine/Toxoid Administration for Adult	90471		Tympanometry		92567			

Diagnosis/ICD-10: F41.1, F51.02

I acknowledge receipt of medical services and authorize the release of any medical information necessary to process this claim for healthcare payment only. I do authorize payment to the provider.

Patient Signature <u>Michael Schultz</u>

Total Estimated Charges: _____

Payment Amount: _____

Next Appointment: _____

Figure 13-1

Capital City Medical
Fee Schedule

New Patient OV		Punch Biopsy various codes	$80
Problem Focused 99201	$45	Nebulizer various codes	$45
Expanded Problem Focused 99202	$65	Cast Application various codes	$85
Detailed 99203	$85	Laryngoscopy 31505	$255
Comprehensive 99204	$105	Audiometry 92552	$85
Comprehensive/High Complex 99205	$115	Tympanometry 92567	$85
Well Exam infant (less than 1 year) 99381	$45	Ear Irrigation 69210	$25
Well Exam 1–4 yrs. 99382	$50	Diaphragm Fitting 57170	$30
Well Exam 5–11 yrs. 99383	$55	IV Therapy (up to one hour) 90760	$65
Well Exam 12–17 yrs. 99384	$65	Each additional hour 90761	$50
Well Exam 18–39 yrs. 99385	$85	Oximetry 94760	$10
Well Exam 40–64 yrs. 99386	$105	ECG 93000	$75
Established Patient OV		Holter Monitor various codes	$170
Post Op Follow Up Visit 99024	$0	Rhythm Strip 93040	$60
Minimum 99211	$35	Treadmill 93015	$375
Problem Focused 99212	$45	Cocci Skin Test 86490	$20
Expanded Problem Focused 99213	$55	X-ray, spine, chest, bone—any area various codes	$275
Detailed 99214	$65	Avulsion Nail 11730	$200
Comprehensive/High Complex 99215	$75	**Laboratory**	
Well exam infant (less than 1 year) 99391	$35	Amylase 82150	$40
Well Exam 1–4 yrs. 99392	$40	B12 82607	$30
Well Exam 5–11 yrs. 99393	$45	CBC & Diff 85025	$95
Well Exam 12–17 yrs. 99394	$55	Comp Metabolic Panel 80053	$75
Well Exam 18–39 yrs. 99395	$65	Chlamydia Screen 87110	$70
Well Exam 40–64 yrs. 99396	$75	Cholestrerol 82465	$75
Obstetrics		Digoxin 80162	$40
Total OB Care 59400	$1700	Electrolytes 80051	$70
Injections		Estrogen, Total 82672	$50
Administration 90772	$10	Ferritin 82728	$40
Allergy 95115	$35	Folate 82746	$30
DPT 90701	$50	GC Screen 87070	$60
Drug various codes	$35	Glucose 82947	$35
Influenza 90658	$25	Glycosylated HGB A1C 83036	$45
MMR 90707	$50	HCT 85014	$30
OPV 90712	$40	HDL 83718	$35
Pneumovax 90732	$35	HGB 85018	$30
TB Skin Test 86580	$15	Hep BSAG 83740	$40
TD 90718	$40	Hepatitis panel, acute 80074	$95
Tetanus Toxoid 90703	$40	HIV 86703	$100
Vaccine/Toxoid Administration for Younger Than 8 Years Old w/ counseling 90465	$10	Iron & TIBC 83550	$45
		Kidney Profile 80069	$95
Vaccine/Toxoid Administration for Adult 90471	$10	Lead 83665	$55
Arthrocentesis/Aspiration/Injection		Lipase 83690	$40
Small Joint 20600	$50	Lipid Panel 80061	$95
Interm Joint 20605	$60	Liver Profile 80076	$95
Major Joint 20610	$70	Mono Test 86308	$30
Trigger Point/Tendon Sheath Inj. 20550	$90	Pap Smear 88155	$90
Other Invasive/Noninvasive Procedures		Pap Collection/Supervision 88142	$95
Catheterization 51701	$55	Pregnancy Test 84703	$90
Circumcision 54150	$150	Obstetric Panel 80055	$85
Colposcopy 57452	$225	Pro Time 85610	$50
Colposcopy w/Biopsy 57454	$250	PSA 84153	$50
Cryosurgery Premalignant Lesion various codes	$160	RPR 86592	$55
Endometrial Biopsy 58100	$190	Sed. Rate 85651	$50
Excision Lesion Malignant various codes	$145	Stool Culture 87045	$80
Excision Lesion Benign various codes	$125	Stool O & P 87177	$105
Curettement Lesion		Strep Screen 87880	$35
Single 11055	$70	Theophylline 80198	$40
2–4 11056	$80	Thyroid Uptake 84479	$75
>4 11057	$90	TSH 84443	$50
Excision Skin Tags (1–15) 11200	$55	Urinalysis 81000	$35
Each Additional 10 11201	$30	Urine Culture 87088	$80
I & D Abscess Single/Simple 10060	$75	Drawing Fee 36415	$15
Multiple/Complex 10061	$95	Specimen Collection 99000	$10
I & D Pilonidal Cyst Simple 10080	$105		
I & D Pilonidal Cyst Complex 10081	$130		
Laceration Repair various codes	$60		

HEALTH INSURANCE CLAIM FORM

APPROVED BY NATIONAL UNIFORM CLAIM COMMITTEE (NUCC) 02/12

PICA

PICA

1. MEDICARE	MEDICAID	TRICARE	CHAMPVA	GROUP HEALTH PLAN	FECA BLK LUNG	OTHER	1a. INSURED'S I.D. NUMBER (For Program in Item 1)
[X] (Medicare#)	(Medicaid#)	(ID#/DoD#)	(Member ID#)	(ID#)	(ID#)	(ID#)	

2. PATIENT'S NAME (Last Name, First Name, Middle Initial)

3. PATIENT'S BIRTH DATE MM DD YY SEX M ☐ F ☐

4. INSURED'S NAME (Last Name, First Name, Middle Initial)

5. PATIENT'S ADDRESS (No., Street)

6. PATIENT RELATIONSHIP TO INSURED Self ☐ Spouse ☐ Child ☐ Other ☐

7. INSURED'S ADDRESS (No., Street)

CITY   STATE

8. RESERVED FOR NUCC USE

CITY   STATE

ZIP CODE   TELEPHONE (Include Area Code) ( )

ZIP CODE   TELEPHONE (Include Area Code) ( )

9. OTHER INSURED'S NAME (Last Name, First Name, Middle Initial)

10. IS PATIENT'S CONDITION RELATED TO:

11. INSURED'S POLICY GROUP OR FECA NUMBER

a. OTHER INSURED'S POLICY OR GROUP NUMBER

a. EMPLOYMENT? (Current or Previous) ☐ YES ☐ NO

a. INSURED'S DATE OF BIRTH MM DD YY SEX M ☐ F ☐

b. RESERVED FOR NUCC USE

b. AUTO ACCIDENT? PLACE (State) ☐ YES ☐ NO

b. OTHER CLAIM ID (Designated by NUCC)

c. RESERVED FOR NUCC USE

c. OTHER ACCIDENT? ☐ YES ☐ NO

c. INSURANCE PLAN NAME OR PROGRAM NAME

d. INSURANCE PLAN NAME OR PROGRAM NAME

10d. CLAIM CODES (Designated by NUCC)

d. IS THERE ANOTHER HEALTH BENEFIT PLAN? ☐ YES ☐ NO *If yes*, complete items 9, 9a, and 9d.

READ BACK OF FORM BEFORE COMPLETING & SIGNING THIS FORM.
12. PATIENT'S OR AUTHORIZED PERSON'S SIGNATURE I authorize the release of any medical or other information necessary to process this claim. I also request payment of government benefits either to myself or to the party who accepts assignment below.

SIGNED _____ DATE _____

13. INSURED'S OR AUTHORIZED PERSON'S SIGNATURE I authorize payment of medical benefits to the undersigned physician or supplier for services described below.

SIGNED _____

14. DATE OF CURRENT ILLNESS, INJURY, or PREGNANCY (LMP) MM DD YY QUAL.

15. OTHER DATE QUAL. MM DD YY

16. DATES PATIENT UNABLE TO WORK IN CURRENT OCCUPATION FROM MM DD YY TO MM DD YY

17. NAME OF REFERRING PROVIDER OR OTHER SOURCE 17a. 17b. NPI

18. HOSPITALIZATION DATES RELATED TO CURRENT SERVICES FROM MM DD YY TO MM DD YY

19. ADDITIONAL CLAIM INFORMATION (Designated by NUCC)

20. OUTSIDE LAB? ☐ YES ☐ NO $ CHARGES

21. DIAGNOSIS OR NATURE OF ILLNESS OR INJURY Relate A-L to service line below (24E) ICD Ind.

A. _____ B. _____ C. _____ D. _____
E. _____ F. _____ G. _____ H. _____
I. _____ J. _____ K. _____ L. _____

22. RESUBMISSION CODE ORIGINAL REF. NO.

23. PRIOR AUTHORIZATION NUMBER

24. A. DATE(S) OF SERVICE From MM DD YY To MM DD YY	B. PLACE OF SERVICE	C. EMG	D. PROCEDURES, SERVICES, OR SUPPLIES (Explain Unusual Circumstances) CPT/HCPCS MODIFIER	E. DIAGNOSIS POINTER	F. $ CHARGES	G. DAYS OR UNITS	H. EPSDT Family Plan	I. ID. QUAL	J. RENDERING PROVIDER ID #
1								NPI	
2								NPI	
3								NPI	
4								NPI	
5								NPI	
6								NPI	

25. FEDERAL TAX I.D. NUMBER SSN EIN

26. PATIENT'S ACCOUNT NO.

27. ACCEPT ASSIGNMENT? (For govt. claims, see back) ☐ YES ☐ NO

28. TOTAL CHARGE $

29. AMOUNT PAID $

30. Rsvd. for NUCC Use

31. SIGNATURE OF PHYSICIAN OR SUPPLIER INCLUDING DEGREES OR CREDENTIALS (I certify that the statements on the reverse apply to this bill and are made a part thereof.)

SIGNED _____ DATE _____

32. SERVICE FACILITY LOCATION INFORMATION

a. NPI b.

33. BILLING PROVIDER INFO & PH # ( )

a. NPI b.

NUCC Instruction Manual available at: www.nucc.org   **PLEASE PRINT OR TYPE**   APPROVED OMB-0938-1197 FORM 1500 (02-12)

Clear Form

CARRIER

PATIENT AND INSURED INFORMATION

PHYSICIAN OR SUPPLIER INFORMATION

Figure 13-2

b. Using the source documents, the Capital City Medical Fee Schedule (Figure 13-3), and the blank CMS-1500 form provided (Figure 13-4), complete the following case study for patient Brenda Bloom (Case 13-2):

CASE 13-2

Capital City Medical—123 Unknown Boulevard, Capital City, NY 12345-2222 (555) 555-1234 Phil Wells, MD, Mannie Mends, MD, Bette R. Soone, MD	Patient Information Form Tax ID: 75-0246810 Group NPI: 1513171216

Patient Information:

Name: (Last, First) Bloom, Brenda ☐ Male ☒ Female Birth Date: 12/09/1944

Address: 51 Calico St, Township, NY 12345 Phone: (555) 555-4255

Social Security Number: 133-12-0019 Full-Time Student: ☐ Yes ☒ No

Marital Status: ☐ Single ☐ Married ☒ Divorced ☐ Other

Employment:

Employer: Retired Phone: ( )

Address:

Condition Related to: ☐ Auto Accident ☐ Employment ☐ Other Accident

Date of Accident: State:

Emergency Contact: **Phone: ( )**

Primary Insurance: Medicaid Phone: ( )

Address: P. O. Box 9834, Capital City, NY 12345

Insurance Policyholder's Name: Same ☐ M ☐ F DOB:

Address:

Phone: ( ) Relationship to Insured: ☒ Self ☐ Spouse ☐ Child ☐ Other

Employer: Phone: ( )

Employer's Address:

Policy/ID No: 366736530A Group No: Percent Covered: 80 % Copay Amt: $

Secondary Insurance: Medicaid Phone: ( )

Address: 4875 Capital Blvd, Capital City, NY 12345

Insurance Policyholder's Name: Same ☐ M ☐ F DOB:

Address:

Phone: ( ) Relationship to Insured: ☒ Self ☐ Spouse ☐ Child ☐ Other

Employer: Phone: ( )

Employer's Address:

Policy/ID No: 0002566499883 Group No: Percent Covered: % Copay Amt: $ 5.00

Reason for Visit: I am here for a checkup on my high blood pressure and cholesterol.

Known Allergies:

Referred by:

09/21/20XX
Assignment of Benefits: Y
Signature on File: Y
Referring Physician: N

S: Brenda Bloom is being seen today for a regular checkup on her high blood pressure and triglycerides.

O: She presents with no new problems. Her BP in office was 132/86. Review of recent lab showed significant improvement in her triglycerides.

A: 1. HTN—I10
2. Hypertriglyceridemia—E78.1

P: 1. Continue cholesterol meds.
2. Return in 3 months.

_____
Phil Wells, MD
Family Practice
NPI: 1234567890

© 2018 Pearson Education, Inc.

CASE 13-2

Patient Name Brenda Bloom

Capital City Medical
123 Unknown Boulevard, Capital City, NY 12345-2222

Date of Service
09-21-20XX

New Patient			Arthrocentesis/Aspiration/Injection			Laboratory		
Problem Focused	99201		Small Joint		20600	Amylase	82150	
Expanded Problem, Focused	99202		Interm Joint		20605	B12	82607	
Detailed	99203		Major Joint		20610	CBC & Diff	85025	
Comprehensive	99204		**Other Invasive/Noninvasive**			Comp Metabolic Panel	80053	
Comprehensive/High Complex	99205		Audiometry		92552	Chlamydia Screen	87110	
Well Exam Infant (up to 12 mos.)	99381		Cast Application			Cholesterol	82465	X
Well Exam 1–4 yrs.	99382		Location Long Short			Digoxin	80162	
Well Exam 5–11 yrs.	99383		Catheterization		51701	Electrolytes	80051	
Well Exam 12–17 yrs.	99384		Circumcision		54150	Ferritin	82728	
Well Exam 18–39 yrs.	99385		Colposcopy		57452	Folate	82746	
Well Exam 40–64 yrs.	99386		Colposcopy w/Biopsy		57454	GC Screen	87070	
			Cryosurgery Premalignant Lesion			Glucose	82947	
			Location (s):			Glucose 1 HR	82950	
						Glycosylated HGB A1C	83036	
Established Patient			Cryosurgery Warts			HCT	85014	
Post-Op Follow Up Visit	99024		Location (s):			HDL	83718	
Minimum	99211		Curettement Lesion			Hep BSAG	87340	
Problem Focused	99212		Single		11055	Hepatitis panel, acute	80074	
Expanded Problem Focused	99213	X	2–4		11056	HGB	85018	
Detailed	99214		>4		11057	HIV	86703	
Comprehensive/High Complex	99215		Diaphragm Fitting		57170	Iron & TIBC	83550	
Well Exam Infant (up to 12 mos.)	99391		Ear Irrigation		69210	Kidney Profile	80069	
Well exam 1–4 yrs.	99392		ECG		93000	Lead	83655	
Well Exam 5–11 yrs.	99393		Endometrial Biopsy		58100	Liver Profile	80076	
Well Exam 12–17 yrs.	99394		Exc. Lesion Malignant			Mono Test	86308	
Well Exam 18–39 yrs.	99395		Benign			Pap Smear	88155	
Well Exam 40–64 yrs.	99396		Location			Pregnancy Test	84703	
Obstetrics			Exc. Skin Tags (1–15)		11200	Obstetric Panel	80055	
Total OB Care	59400		Each Additional 10		11201	Pro Time	85610	
Injections			Fracture Treatment			PSA	84153	
Administration Sub. / IM	90772		Loc			RPR	86592	
Drug			w/Reduc	w/o Reduc		Sed. Rate	85651	
Dosage			I & D Abscess Single/Simple		10060	Stool Culture	87045	
Allergy	95115		Multiple or Comp		10061	Stool O & P	87177	
Cocci Skin Test	86490		I & D Pilonidal Cyst Simple		10080	Strep Screen	87880	
DPT	90701		Pilonidal Cyst Complex		10081	Theophylline	80198	
Hemophilus	90646		IV Therapy—To One Hour		90760	Thyroid Uptake	84479	
Influenza	90658		Each Additional Hour		90761	TSH	84443	
MMR	90707		Laceration Repair			Urinalysis	81000	
OPV	90712		Location Size Simp/Comp			Urine Culture	87088	
Pneumovax	90732		Laryngoscopy		31505	Drawing Fee	36415	X
TB Skin Test	86580		Oximetry		94760	Specimen Collection	99000	
TD	90718		Punch Biopsy			**Other:**		
Unlisted Immun	90749		Rhythm Strip		93040			
Tetanus Toxoid	90703		Treadmill		93015			
Vaccine/Toxoid Admin <8 Yr Old w/ Counseling	90465		Trigger Point or Tendon Sheath Inj.		20550			
Vaccine/Toxoid Administration for Adult	90471		Tympanometry		92567			

Diagnosis/ICD-10: I10, E78.1

I acknowledge receipt of medical services and authorize the release of any medical information necessary to process this claim for healthcare payment only. I do authorize payment to the provider.

Total Estimated Charges: _____

Payment Amount: _____

Patient Signature _Brenda Bloom_

Next Appointment: _____

Figure 13-3

Capital City Medical
Fee Schedule

New Patient OV			Punch Biopsy various codes	$80
Problem Focused 99201	$45		Nebulizer various codes	$45
Expanded Problem Focused 99202	$65		Cast Application various codes	$85
Detailed 99203	$85		Laryngoscopy 31505	$255
Comprehensive 99204	$105		Audiometry 92552	$85
Comprehensive/High Complex 99205	$115		Tympanometry 92567	$85
Well Exam infant (less than 1 year) 99381	$45		Ear Irrigation 69210	$25
Well Exam 1–4 yrs. 99382	$50		Diaphragm Fitting 57170	$30
Well Exam 5–11 yrs. 99383	$55		IV Therapy (up to one hour) 90760	$65
Well Exam 12–17 yrs. 99384	$65		Each additional hour 90761	$50
Well Exam 18–39 yrs. 99385	$85		Oximetry 94760	$10
Well Exam 40–64 yrs. 99386	$105		ECG 93000	$75
Established Patient OV			Holter Monitor various codes	$170
Post Op Follow Up Visit 99024	$0		Rhythm Strip 93040	$60
Minimum 99211	$35		Treadmill 93015	$375
Problem Focused 99212	$45		Cocci Skin Test 86490	$20
Expanded Problem Focused 99213	$55		X-ray, spine, chest, bone—any area various codes	$275
Detailed 99214	$65		Avulsion Nail 11730	$200
Comprehensive/High Complex 99215	$75		**Laboratory**	
Well exam infant (less than 1 year) 99391	$35		Amylase 82150	$40
Well Exam 1–4 yrs. 99392	$40		B12 82607	$30
Well Exam 5–11 yrs. 99393	$45		CBC & Diff 85025	$95
Well Exam 12–17 yrs. 99394	$55		Comp Metabolic Panel 80053	$75
Well Exam 18–39 yrs. 99395	$65		Chlamydia Screen 87110	$70
Well Exam 40–64 yrs. 99396	$75		Cholestrerol 82465	$75
Obstetrics			Digoxin 80162	$40
Total OB Care 59400	$1700		Electrolytes 80051	$70
Injections			Estrogen, Total 82672	$50
Administration 90772	$10		Ferritin 82728	$40
Allergy 95115	$35		Folate 82746	$30
DPT 90701	$50		GC Screen 87070	$60
Drug various codes	$35		Glucose 82947	$35
Influenza 90658	$25		Glycosylated HGB A1C 83036	$45
MMR 90707	$50		HCT 85014	$30
OPV 90712	$40		HDL 83718	$35
Pneumovax 90732	$35		HGB 85018	$30
TB Skin Test 86580	$15		Hep BSAG 83740	$40
TD 90718	$40		Hepatitis panel, acute 80074	$95
Tetanus Toxoid 90703	$40		HIV 86703	$100
Vaccine/Toxoid Administration for Younger			Iron & TIBC 83550	$45
Than 8 Years Old w/ counseling 90465	$10		Kidney Profile 80069	$95
Vaccine/Toxoid Administration for Adult 90471	$10		Lead 83665	$55
Arthrocentesis/Aspiration/Injection			Lipase 83690	$40
Small Joint 20600	$50		Lipid Panel 80061	$95
Interm Joint 20605	$60		Liver Profile 80076	$95
Major Joint 20610	$70		Mono Test 86308	$30
Trigger Point/Tendon Sheath Inj. 20550	$90		Pap Smear 88155	$90
Other Invasive/Noninvasive Procedures			Pap Collection/Supervision 88142	$95
Catheterization 51701	$55		Pregnancy Test 84703	$90
Circumcision 54150	$150		Obstetric Panel 80055	$85
Colposcopy 57452	$225		Pro Time 85610	$50
Colposcopy w/Biopsy 57454	$250		PSA 84153	$50
Cryosurgery Premalignant Lesion various codes	$160		RPR 86592	$55
Endometrial Biopsy 58100	$190		Sed. Rate 85651	$50
Excision Lesion Malignant various codes	$145		Stool Culture 87045	$80
Excision Lesion Benign various codes	$125		Stool O & P 87177	$105
Curettement Lesion			Strep Screen 87880	$35
Single 11055	$70		Theophylline 80198	$40
2–4 11056	$80		Thyroid Uptake 84479	$75
>4 11057	$90		TSH 84443	$50
Excision Skin Tags (1–15) 11200	$55		Urinalysis 81000	$35
Each Additional 10 11201	$30		Urine Culture 87088	$80
I & D Abscess Single/Simple 10060	$75		Drawing Fee 36415	$15
Multiple/Complex 10061	$95		Specimen Collection 99000	$10
I & D Pilonidal Cyst Simple 10080	$105			
I & D Pilonidal Cyst Complex 10081	$130			
Laceration Repair various codes	$60			

HEALTH INSURANCE CLAIM FORM

APPROVED BY NATIONAL UNIFORM CLAIM COMMITTEE (NUCC) 02/12

| | PICA | | | | | | | PICA | | |

1. MEDICARE ☒ (Medicare#)   MEDICAID ☐ (Medicaid#)   TRICARE ☐ (ID#/DoD#)   CHAMPVA ☐ (Member ID#)   GROUP HEALTH PLAN ☐ (ID#)   FECA BLK LUNG ☐ (ID#)   OTHER ☐ (ID#)   **1a. INSURED'S I.D. NUMBER** (For Program in Item 1)

2. PATIENT'S NAME (Last Name, First Name, Middle Initial)

3. PATIENT'S BIRTH DATE MM | DD | YY   SEX M ☐ F ☐

4. INSURED'S NAME (Last Name, First Name, Middle Initial)

5. PATIENT'S ADDRESS (No., Street)

6. PATIENT RELATIONSHIP TO INSURED Self ☐ Spouse ☐ Child ☐ Other ☐

7. INSURED'S ADDRESS (No., Street)

CITY   STATE

8. RESERVED FOR NUCC USE

CITY   STATE

ZIP CODE   TELEPHONE (Include Area Code) ( )

ZIP CODE   TELEPHONE (Include Area Code) ( )

9. OTHER INSURED'S NAME (Last Name, First Name, Middle Initial)

10. IS PATIENT'S CONDITION RELATED TO:

11. INSURED'S POLICY GROUP OR FECA NUMBER

a. OTHER INSURED'S POLICY OR GROUP NUMBER

a. EMPLOYMENT? (Current or Previous) ☐ YES ☐ NO

a. INSURED'S DATE OF BIRTH MM | DD | YY   SEX M ☐ F ☐

b. RESERVED FOR NUCC USE

b. AUTO ACCIDENT? ☐ YES ☐ NO   PLACE (State)

b. OTHER CLAIM ID (Designated by NUCC)

c. RESERVED FOR NUCC USE

c. OTHER ACCIDENT? ☐ YES ☐ NO

c. INSURANCE PLAN NAME OR PROGRAM NAME

d. INSURANCE PLAN NAME OR PROGRAM NAME

10d. CLAIM CODES (Designated by NUCC)

d. IS THERE ANOTHER HEALTH BENEFIT PLAN? ☐ YES ☐ NO *If yes,* complete items 9, 9a, and 9d.

READ BACK OF FORM BEFORE COMPLETING & SIGNING THIS FORM.
12. PATIENT'S OR AUTHORIZED PERSON'S SIGNATURE I authorize the release of any medical or other information necessary to process this claim. I also request payment of government benefits either to myself or to the party who accepts assignment below.

SIGNED _____ DATE _____

13. INSURED'S OR AUTHORIZED PERSON'S SIGNATURE I authorize payment of medical benefits to the undersigned physician or supplier for services described below.

SIGNED _____

14. DATE OF CURRENT ILLNESS, INJURY, or PREGNANCY (LMP) MM | DD | YY QUAL.

15. OTHER DATE QUAL. | MM | DD | YY

16. DATES PATIENT UNABLE TO WORK IN CURRENT OCCUPATION FROM MM | DD | YY TO MM | DD | YY

17. NAME OF REFERRING PROVIDER OR OTHER SOURCE

17a.
17b. NPI

18. HOSPITALIZATION DATES RELATED TO CURRENT SERVICES FROM MM | DD | YY TO MM | DD | YY

19. ADDITIONAL CLAIM INFORMATION (Designated by NUCC)

20. OUTSIDE LAB? ☐ YES ☐ NO $ CHARGES

21. DIAGNOSIS OR NATURE OF ILLNESS OR INJURY Relate A-L to service line below (24E)   ICD Ind. |

A. |___ B. |___ C. |___ D. |___
E. |___ F. |___ G. |___ H. |___
I. |___ J. |___ K. |___ L. |___

22. RESUBMISSION CODE   ORIGINAL REF. NO.

23. PRIOR AUTHORIZATION NUMBER

24. A. DATE(S) OF SERVICE						B. PLACE OF SERVICE	C. EMG	D. PROCEDURES, SERVICES, OR SUPPLIES (Explain Unusual Circumstances) CPT/HCPCS	MODIFIER	E. DIAGNOSIS POINTER	F. $ CHARGES	G. DAYS OR UNITS	H. EPSDT Family Plan	I. ID. QUAL	J. RENDERING PROVIDER ID. #
From MM	DD	YY	To MM	DD	YY										
1														NPI	
2														NPI	
3														NPI	
4														NPI	
5														NPI	
6														NPI	

25. FEDERAL TAX I.D. NUMBER   SSN ☐ EIN ☐

26. PATIENT'S ACCOUNT NO.

27. ACCEPT ASSIGNMENT? (For govt. claims, see back) ☐ YES ☐ NO

28. TOTAL CHARGE $

29. AMOUNT PAID $

30. Rsvd. for NUCC Use

31. SIGNATURE OF PHYSICIAN OR SUPPLIER INCLUDING DEGREES OR CREDENTIALS (I certify that the statements on the reverse apply to this bill and are made a part thereof.)

SIGNED _____ DATE _____

32. SERVICE FACILITY LOCATION INFORMATION

a. NPI   b.

33. BILLING PROVIDER INFO & PH # ( )

a. NPI   b.

NUCC Instruction Manual available at: www.nucc.org   **PLEASE PRINT OR TYPE**   APPROVED OMB-0938-1197 FORM 1500 (02-12)

Clear Form

Figure 13-4

c. Using the source documents, the Capital City Medical Fee Schedule (Figure 13-5), and the blank CMS-1500 form provided (Figure 13-6), complete the following case study for patient Blake McComb (Case 13-3):

CASE 13-3

Capital City Medical—123 Unknown Boulevard, Capital City, NY 12345-2222 (555) 555-1234	Patient Information Form
Phil Wells, MD, Mannie Mends, MD, Bette R. Soone, MD	Tax ID: 75-0246810 Group NPI: 1513171216

Patient Information:

Name: (Last, First) McComb, Blake   ☒ Male ☐ Female   Birth Date: 05/21/1966

Address: 6054 Spelling Rd., Capital City, NY 12345   Phone: (555) 555-9451

Social Security Number: 855-06-5872   Full-Time Student: ☐ Yes ☒ No

Marital Status: ☐ Single ☐ Married ☒ Divorced ☐ Other

Employment:

Employer: Yummy's Bakery Shop   Phone: (555) 555-6200

Address: 14 Mt. Royal Blvd., Capital City, NY 12345

Condition Related to: ☐ Auto Accident ☐ Employment ☐ Other Accident

Date of Accident: _____ State: _____

Emergency Contact: _____ **Phone: ( )** _____

Primary Insurance: Medicaid   Phone: ( ) _____

Address: 4875 Capital Blvd, Capital City, NY 12345

Insurance Policyholder's Name: Same   ☐ M ☐ F DOB: _____

Address: _____

Phone: ( ) _____ Relationship to Insured: ☒ Self ☐ Spouse ☐ Child ☐ Other

Employer: _____ Phone: ( ) _____

Employer's Address: _____

Policy/ID No: 03656499533   Group No: _____ Percent Covered: ____% Copay Amt: $ 5.00

Secondary Insurance: _____ Phone: ( ) _____

Address: _____

Insurance Policyholder's Name: _____ ☐ M ☐ F DOB: _____

Address: _____

Phone: ( ) _____ Relationship to Insured: ☐ Self ☐ Spouse ☐ Child ☐ Other

Employer: _____ Phone: ( ) _____

Employer's Address: _____

Policy/ID No: _____ Group No: _____ Percent Covered: ____% Copay Amt: $ _____

Reason for Visit: I am here for a hearing test.

Known Allergies: _____

Referred by: _____

CASE 13-3
SOAP

●

01/29/20XX
Assignment of Benefits: Y
Signature on File: Y
Referring Physician: N

S: Blake McComb is a new patient who is here for a hearing test. He is concerned that he may be experiencing some hearing loss.

O: Pt. is generally in good health. He is alert and oriented ×3. His mood is upbeat. Audiometry shows no signs of hearing loss in either ear. He is alert to all tone levels. Nose and throat present clear. There is no impacted cerumen bilaterally.

A: 1. Hearing exam—Z01.10

P: 1. Return in 1 month for PE.

_____

Phil Wells, MD
Family Practice
NPI: 1234567890

CASE 13-3

Patient Name Blake McComb

Capital City Medical
123 Unknown Boulevard, Capital City, NY 12345-2222

Date of Service
01-29-20XX

New Patient			Arthrocentesis/Aspiration/Injection			Laboratory	
Problem Focused	99201		Small Joint		20600	Amylase	82150
Expanded Problem, Focused	99202	X	Small Joint		20600	B12	82607
Detailed	99203		Interm Joint		20605	CBC & Diff	85025
Comprehensive	99204		Major Joint		20610	Comp Metabolic Panel	80053
Comprehensive/High Complex	99205		**Other Invasive/Noninvasive**			Chlamydia Screen	87110
Well Exam Infant (up to 12 mos.)	99381		Audiometry	92552	X	Cholesterol	82465
Well Exam 1–4 yrs.	99382		Cast Application			Digoxin	80162
Well Exam 5–11 yrs.	99383		Location Long Short			Electrolytes	80051
Well Exam 12–17 yrs.	99384		Catheterization		51701	Ferritin	82728
Well Exam 18–39 yrs.	99385		Circumcision		54150	Folate	82746
Well Exam 40–64 yrs.	99386		Colposcopy		57452	GC Screen	87070
			Colposcopy w/Biopsy		57454	Glucose	82947
			Cryosurgery Premalignant Lesion			Glucose 1 HR	82950
			Location (s):			Glycosylated HGB A1C	83036
Established Patient			Cryosurgery Warts			HCT	85014
Post-Op Follow Up Visit	99024		Location (s):			HDL	83718
Minimum	99211		Curettement Lesion			Hep BSAG	87340
Problem Focused	99212		Single		11055	Hepatitis panel, acute	80074
Expanded Problem Focused	99213		2–4		11056	HGB	85018
Detailed	99214		>4		11057	HIV	86703
Comprehensive/High Complex	99215		Diaphragm Fitting		57170	Iron & TIBC	83550
Well Exam Infant (up to 12 mos.)	99391		Ear Irrigation		69210	Kidney Profile	80069
Well exam 1–4 yrs.	99392		ECG		93000	Lead	83655
Well Exam 5–11 yrs.	99393		Endometrial Biopsy		58100	Liver Profile	80076
Well Exam 12–17 yrs.	99394		Exc. Lesion Malignant			Mono Test	86308
Well Exam 18–39 yrs.	99395		Benign			Pap Smear	88155
Well Exam 40–64 yrs.	99396		Location			Pregnancy Test	84703
Obstetrics			Exc. Skin Tags (1–15)		11200	Obstetric Panel	80055
Total OB Care	59400		Each Additional 10		11201	Pro Time	85610
Injections			Fracture Treatment			PSA	84153
Administration Sub. / IM	90772		Loc			RPR	86592
Drug			w/Reduc		w/o Reduc	Sed. Rate	85651
Dosage			I & D Abscess Single/Simple		10060	Stool Culture	87045
Allergy	95115		Multiple or Comp		10061	Stool O & P	87177
Cocci Skin Test	86490		I & D Pilonidal Cyst Simple		10080	Strep Screen	87880
DPT	90701		Pilonidal Cyst Complex		10081	Theophylline	80198
Hemophilus	90646		IV Therapy—To One Hour		90760	Thyroid Uptake	84479
Influenza	90658		Each Additional Hour		90761	TSH	84443
MMR	90707		Laceration Repair			Urinalysis	81000
OPV	90712		Location Size Simp/Comp			Urine Culture	87088
Pneumovax	90732		Laryngoscopy		31505	Drawing Fee	36415
TB Skin Test	86580		Oximetry		94760	Specimen Collection	99000
TD	90718		Punch Biopsy			**Other:**	
Unlisted Immun	90749		Rhythm Strip		93040		
Tetanus Toxoid	90703		Treadmill		93015		
Vaccine/Toxoid Admin <8 Yr Old w/ Counseling	90465		Trigger Point or Tendon Sheath Inj.		20550		
Vaccine/Toxoid Administration for Adult	90471		Tympanometry		92567		

Diagnosis/ICD-10: Z01.10

I acknowledge receipt of medical services and authorize the release of any medical information necessary to process this claim for healthcare payment only. I do authorize payment to the provider.

Patient Signature _Blake McComb_

Total Estimated Charges: _____

Payment Amount: _____

Next Appointment: _____

Figure 13-5

Capital City Medical
Fee Schedule

New Patient OV		Punch Biopsy various codes	$80
Problem Focused 99201	$45	Nebulizer various codes	$45
Expanded Problem Focused 99202	$65	Cast Application various codes	$85
Detailed 99203	$85	Laryngoscopy 31505	$255
Comprehensive 99204	$105	Audiometry 92552	$85
Comprehensive/High Complex 99205	$115	Tympanometry 92567	$85
Well Exam infant (less than 1 year) 99381	$45	Ear Irrigation 69210	$25
Well Exam 1–4 yrs. 99382	$50	Diaphragm Fitting 57170	$30
Well Exam 5–11 yrs. 99383	$55	IV Therapy (up to one hour) 90760	$65
Well Exam 12–17 yrs. 99384	$65	Each additional hour 90761	$50
Well Exam 18–39 yrs. 99385	$85	Oximetry 94760	$10
Well Exam 40–64 yrs. 99386	$105	ECG 93000	$75
Established Patient OV		Holter Monitor various codes	$170
Post Op Follow Up Visit 99024	$0	Rhythm Strip 93040	$60
Minimum 99211	$35	Treadmill 93015	$375
Problem Focused 99212	$45	Cocci Skin Test 86490	$20
Expanded Problem Focused 99213	$55	X-ray, spine, chest, bone—any area various codes	$275
Detailed 99214	$65	Avulsion Nail 11730	$200
Comprehensive/High Complex 99215	$75	**Laboratory**	
Well exam infant (less than 1 year) 99391	$35	Amylase 82150	$40
Well Exam 1–4 yrs. 99392	$40	B12 82607	$30
Well Exam 5–11 yrs. 99393	$45	CBC & Diff 85025	$95
Well Exam 12–17 yrs. 99394	$55	Comp Metabolic Panel 80053	$75
Well Exam 18–39 yrs. 99395	$65	Chlamydia Screen 87110	$70
Well Exam 40–64 yrs. 99396	$75	Cholestrerol 82465	$75
Obstetrics		Digoxin 80162	$40
Total OB Care 59400	$1700	Electrolytes 80051	$70
Injections		Estrogen, Total 82672	$50
Administration 90772	$10	Ferritin 82728	$40
Allergy 95115	$35	Folate 82746	$30
DPT 90701	$50	GC Screen 87070	$60
Drug various codes	$35	Glucose 82947	$35
Influenza 90658	$25	Glycosylated HGB A1C 83036	$45
MMR 90707	$50	HCT 85014	$30
OPV 90712	$40	HDL 83718	$35
Pneumovax 90732	$35	HGB 85018	$30
TB Skin Test 86580	$15	Hep BSAG 83740	$40
TD 90718	$40	Hepatitis panel, acute 80074	$95
Tetanus Toxoid 90703	$40	HIV 86703	$100
Vaccine/Toxoid Administration for Younger		Iron & TIBC 83550	$45
Than 8 Years Old w/ counseling 90465	$10	Kidney Profile 80069	$95
Vaccine/Toxoid Administration for Adult 90471	$10	Lead 83665	$55
Arthrocentesis/Aspiration/Injection		Lipase 83690	$40
Small Joint 20600	$50	Lipid Panel 80061	$95
Interm Joint 20605	$60	Liver Profile 80076	$95
Major Joint 20610	$70	Mono Test 86308	$30
Trigger Point/Tendon Sheath Inj. 20550	$90	Pap Smear 88155	$90
Other Invasive/Noninvasive Procedures		Pap Collection/Supervision 88142	$95
Catheterization 51701	$55	Pregnancy Test 84703	$90
Circumcision 54150	$150	Obstetric Panel 80055	$85
Colposcopy 57452	$225	Pro Time 85610	$50
Colposcopy w/Biopsy 57454	$250	PSA 84153	$50
Cryosurgery Premalignant Lesion various codes	$160	RPR 86592	$55
Endometrial Biopsy 58100	$190	Sed. Rate 85651	$50
Excision Lesion Malignant various codes	$145	Stool Culture 87045	$80
Excision Lesion Benign various codes	$125	Stool O & P 87177	$105
Curettement Lesion		Strep Screen 87880	$35
Single 11055	$70	Theophylline 80198	$40
2–4 11056	$80	Thyroid Uptake 84479	$75
>4 11057	$90	TSH 84443	$50
Excision Skin Tags (1–15) 11200	$55	Urinalysis 81000	$35
Each Additional 10 11201	$30	Urine Culture 87088	$80
I & D Abscess Single/Simple 10060	$75	Drawing Fee 36415	$15
Multiple/Complex 10061	$95	Specimen Collection 99000	$10
I & D Pilonidal Cyst Simple 10080	$105		
I & D Pilonidal Cyst Complex 10081	$130		
Laceration Repair various codes	$60		

HEALTH INSURANCE CLAIM FORM

APPROVED BY NATIONAL UNIFORM CLAIM COMMITTEE (NUCC) 02/12

☐☐ PICA

PICA ☐☐

1. MEDICARE	MEDICAID	TRICARE	CHAMPVA	GROUP HEALTH PLAN	FECA BLK LUNG	OTHER	1a. INSURED'S I.D. NUMBER (For Program in Item 1)
☒ (Medicare#)	☐ (Medicaid#)	☐ (ID#/DoD#)	☐ (Member ID#)	☐ (ID#)	☐ (ID#)	☐ (ID#)	

2. PATIENT'S NAME (Last Name, First Name, Middle Initial)

3. PATIENT'S BIRTH DATE MM | DD | YY   SEX M ☐ F ☐

4. INSURED'S NAME (Last Name, First Name, Middle Initial)

5. PATIENT'S ADDRESS (No., Street)

6. PATIENT RELATIONSHIP TO INSURED Self ☐ Spouse ☐ Child ☐ Other ☐

7. INSURED'S ADDRESS (No., Street)

CITY | STATE

8. RESERVED FOR NUCC USE

CITY | STATE

ZIP CODE | TELEPHONE (Include Area Code) ( )

ZIP CODE | TELEPHONE (Include Area Code) ( )

9. OTHER INSURED'S NAME (Last Name, First Name, Middle Initial)

10. IS PATIENT'S CONDITION RELATED TO:

11. INSURED'S POLICY GROUP OR FECA NUMBER

a. OTHER INSURED'S POLICY OR GROUP NUMBER

a. EMPLOYMENT? (Current or Previous) ☐ YES ☐ NO

a. INSURED'S DATE OF BIRTH MM | DD | YY   SEX M ☐ F ☐

b. RESERVED FOR NUCC USE

b. AUTO ACCIDENT? ☐ YES ☐ NO PLACE (State)

b. OTHER CLAIM ID (Designated by NUCC)

c. RESERVED FOR NUCC USE

c. OTHER ACCIDENT? ☐ YES ☐ NO

c. INSURANCE PLAN NAME OR PROGRAM NAME

d. INSURANCE PLAN NAME OR PROGRAM NAME

10d. CLAIM CODES (Designated by NUCC)

d. IS THERE ANOTHER HEALTH BENEFIT PLAN? ☐ YES ☐ NO If yes, complete items 9, 9a, and 9d.

READ BACK OF FORM BEFORE COMPLETING & SIGNING THIS FORM.

12. PATIENT'S OR AUTHORIZED PERSON'S SIGNATURE I authorize the release of any medical or other information necessary to process this claim. I also request payment of government benefits either to myself or to the party who accepts assignment below.

SIGNED _____ DATE _____

13. INSURED'S OR AUTHORIZED PERSON'S SIGNATURE I authorize payment of medical benefits to the undersigned physician or supplier for services described below.

SIGNED _____

14. DATE OF CURRENT ILLNESS, INJURY, or PREGNANCY (LMP) MM | DD | YY   QUAL.

15. OTHER DATE QUAL. MM | DD | YY

16. DATES PATIENT UNABLE TO WORK IN CURRENT OCCUPATION FROM MM | DD | YY TO MM | DD | YY

17. NAME OF REFERRING PROVIDER OR OTHER SOURCE

17a.
17b. NPI

18. HOSPITALIZATION DATES RELATED TO CURRENT SERVICES FROM MM | DD | YY TO MM | DD | YY

19. ADDITIONAL CLAIM INFORMATION (Designated by NUCC)

20. OUTSIDE LAB? ☐ YES ☐ NO $ CHARGES

21. DIAGNOSIS OR NATURE OF ILLNESS OR INJURY Relate A-L to service line below (24E) ICD Ind.

A. ____ B. ____ C. ____ D. ____
E. ____ F. ____ G. ____ H. ____
I. ____ J. ____ K. ____ L. ____

22. RESUBMISSION CODE | ORIGINAL REF. NO.

23. PRIOR AUTHORIZATION NUMBER

24. A. DATE(S) OF SERVICE From MM DD YY — To MM DD YY	B. PLACE OF SERVICE	C. EMG	D. PROCEDURES, SERVICES, OR SUPPLIES (Explain Unusual Circumstances) CPT/HCPCS	MODIFIER	E. DIAGNOSIS POINTER	F. $ CHARGES	G. DAYS OR UNITS	H. EPSDT Family Plan	I. ID. QUAL	J. RENDERING PROVIDER ID. #
1										NPI
2										NPI
3										NPI
4										NPI
5										NPI
6										NPI

25. FEDERAL TAX I.D. NUMBER SSN ☐ EIN ☐

26. PATIENT'S ACCOUNT NO.

27. ACCEPT ASSIGNMENT? (For govt. claims, see back) ☐ YES ☐ NO

28. TOTAL CHARGE $

29. AMOUNT PAID $

30. Rsvd. for NUCC Use

31. SIGNATURE OF PHYSICIAN OR SUPPLIER INCLUDING DEGREES OR CREDENTIALS (I certify that the statements on the reverse apply to this bill and are made a part thereof.)

SIGNED _____ DATE _____

32. SERVICE FACILITY LOCATION INFORMATION

a. NPI b.

33. BILLING PROVIDER INFO & PH # ( )

a. NPI b.

NUCC Instruction Manual available at: www.nucc.org

PLEASE PRINT OR TYPE

APPROVED OMB-0938-1197 FORM 1500 (02-12)

Clear Form

CARRIER

PATIENT AND INSURED INFORMATION

PHYSICIAN OR SUPPLIER INFORMATION

Figure 13-6

© 2018 Pearson Education, Inc.

d. Using the source documents, the Capital City Medical Fee Schedule (Figure 13-7), and the blank CMS-1500 form provided (Figure 13-8), complete the following case study for patient Jim Hill (Case 13-4):

CASE 13-4

Capital City Medical—123 Unknown Boulevard, Capital City, NY 12345-2222 (555) 555-1234	Patient Information Form
	Tax ID: 75-0246810
Phil Wells, MD, Mannie Mends, MD, Bette R. Soone, MD	Group NPI: 1513171216

Patient Information:

Name: (Last, First) Hill, Jim   ☒ Male ☐ Female   Birth Date: 03/18/1961

Address: 736 Hillcrest St, Capital City, NY 12345   Phone: (555) 555-6176

Social Security Number: 592-70-2833   Full-Time Student: ☐ Yes ☐ No

Marital Status: ☒ Single ☐ Married ☐ Divorced ☐ Other

Employment:

Employer: Retired   Phone: ( )

Address:

Condition Related to: ☐ Auto Accident ☐ Employment ☐ Other Accident

Date of Accident: _____ State: _____

Emergency Contact: _____ Phone: ( ) _____

Primary Insurance: Medicare   Phone: ( )

Address: P. O. Box 9834, Capital City, NY 12345

Insurance Policyholder's Name: Same   ☐ M ☐ F DOB: _____

Address:

Phone: ( ) _____ Relationship to Insured: ☒ Self ☐ Spouse ☐ Child ☐ Other

Employer: _____ Phone: ( ) _____

Employer's Address:

Policy/ID No: 720191114A   Group No: _____ Percent Covered: 80 % Copay Amt: $ _____

Secondary Insurance: Medicaid   Phone: ( )

Address: 4875 Capital Blvd, Capital City, NY 12345

Insurance Policyholder's Name: Same   ☐ M ☐ F DOB: _____

Address:

Phone: ( ) _____ Relationship to Insured: ☒ Self ☐ Spouse ☐ Child ☐ Other

Employer: _____ Phone: ( ) _____

Employer's Address:

Policy/ID No: 35255566874   Group No: _____ Percent Covered: ___% Copay Amt: $ 5.00

Reason for Visit: Checkup for kidney disease

Known Allergies: _____

Referred by: _____

CASE 13-4
SOAP

06/11/20XX
Assignment of Benefits: Y
Signature on File: Y
Referring Physician: N

S: Jim Hill is in for his regular CRF check. He complains of feeling down. He says he hasn't been himself lately.

O: Kidney values are stable. BP: 155/100. He admits that he has lost all interest in leaving the house. He is sleeping in excess of 10 hours a day, and he is barely eating. Pt. has lost 12 lbs. in the last month. He denies any suicidal thoughts. Kidney profile is stable.

A: 1. Stage 1 CRF with hypertensive nephropathy—I12.9, N18.1
　　 2. Depression, mental—F32.9

P: 1. Start Prozac once daily.
　　 2. Refill lopressor.
　　 3. Return in 2 weeks for evaluation of Prozac and depression.

_____

Phil Wells, MD
Family Practice
NPI: 1234567890

© 2018 Pearson Education, Inc.

CASE 13-4

Patient Name Jim Hill

Capital City Medical
123 Unknown Boulevard, Capital City, NY 12345-2222

Date of Service
06-11-20XX

New Patient			Arthrocentesis/Aspiration/Injection			Laboratory		
Problem Focused	99201		Small Joint		20600	Amylase	82150	
Expanded Problem, Focused	99202		Interm Joint		20605	B12	82607	
Detailed	99203		Major Joint		20610	CBC & Diff	85025	
Comprehensive	99204		**Other Invasive/Noninvasive**			Comp Metabolic Panel	80053	
Comprehensive/High Complex	99205		Audiometry		92552	Chlamydia Screen	87110	
Well Exam Infant (up to 12 mos.)	99381		Cast Application			Cholesterol	82465	
Well Exam 1–4 yrs.	99382		Location Long Short			Digoxin	80162	
Well Exam 5–11 yrs.	99383		Catheterization		51701	Electrolytes	80051	
Well Exam 12–17 yrs.	99384		Circumcision		54150	Ferritin	82728	
Well Exam 18–39 yrs.	99385		Colposcopy		57452	Folate	82746	
Well Exam 40–64 yrs.	99386		Colposcopy w/Biopsy		57454	GC Screen	87070	
			Cryosurgery Premalignant Lesion			Glucose	82947	
			Location (s):			Glucose 1 HR	82950	
						Glycosylated HGB A1C	83036	
Established Patient			Cryosurgery Warts			HCT	85014	
Post-Op Follow Up Visit	99024		Location (s):			HDL	83718	
Minimum	99211		Curettement Lesion			Hep BSAG	87340	
Problem Focused	99212		Single		11055	Hepatitis panel, acute	80074	
Expanded Problem Focused	99213	X	2–4		11056	HGB	85018	
Detailed	99214		>4		11057	HIV	86703	
Comprehensive/High Complex	99215		Diaphragm Fitting		57170	Iron & TIBC	83550	
Well Exam Infant (up to 12 mos.)	99391		Ear Irrigation		69210	Kidney Profile	80069	X
Well exam 1–4 yrs.	99392		ECG		93000	Lead	83655	
Well Exam 5–11 yrs.	99393		Endometrial Biopsy		58100	Liver Profile	80076	
Well Exam 12–17 yrs.	99394		Exc. Lesion Malignant			Mono Test	86308	
Well Exam 18–39 yrs.	99395		Benign			Pap Smear	88155	
Well Exam 40–64 yrs.	99396		Location			Pregnancy Test	84703	
Obstetrics			Exc. Skin Tags (1–15)		11200	Obstetric Panel	80055	
Total OB Care	59400		Each Additional 10		11201	Pro Time	85610	
Injections			Fracture Treatment			PSA	84153	
Administration Sub. / IM	90772		Loc			RPR	86592	
Drug			w/Reduc w/o Reduc			Sed. Rate	85651	
Dosage			I & D Abscess Single/Simple		10060	Stool Culture	87045	
Allergy	95115		Multiple or Comp		10061	Stool O & P	87177	
Cocci Skin Test	86490		I & D Pilonidal Cyst Simple		10080	Strep Screen	87880	
DPT	90701		Pilonidal Cyst Complex		10081	Theophylline	80198	
Hemophilus	90646		IV Therapy—To One Hour		90760	Thyroid Uptake	84479	
Influenza	90658		Each Additional Hour		90761	TSH	84443	
MMR	90707		Laceration Repair			Urinalysis	81000	
OPV	90712		Location Size Simp/Comp			Urine Culture	87088	
Pneumovax	90732		Laryngoscopy		31505	Drawing Fee	36415	X
TB Skin Test	86580		Oximetry		94760	Specimen Collection	99000	
TD	90718		Punch Biopsy			**Other:**		
Unlisted Immun	90749		Rhythm Strip		93040			
Tetanus Toxoid	90703		Treadmill		93015			
Vaccine/Toxoid Admin <8 Yr Old w/ Counseling	90465		Trigger Point or Tendon Sheath Inj.		20550			
Vaccine/Toxoid Administration for Adult	90471		Tympanometry		92567			

Diagnosis/ICD-10: I12.9, N18.1, F32.9

I acknowledge receipt of medical services and authorize the release of any medical information necessary to process this claim for healthcare payment only. I do authorize payment to the provider.

Total Estimated Charges: _____

Payment Amount: _____

Patient Signature Jim Hill _____

Next Appointment: _____

Figure 13-7

Capital City Medical
Fee Schedule

New Patient OV			Punch Biopsy various codes	$80
Problem Focused 99201	$45		Nebulizer various codes	$45
Expanded Problem Focused 99202	$65		Cast Application various codes	$85
Detailed 99203	$85		Laryngoscopy 31505	$255
Comprehensive 99204	$105		Audiometry 92552	$85
Comprehensive/High Complex 99205	$115		Tympanometry 92567	$85
Well Exam infant (less than 1 year) 99381	$45		Ear Irrigation 69210	$25
Well Exam 1–4 yrs. 99382	$50		Diaphragm Fitting 57170	$30
Well Exam 5–11 yrs. 99383	$55		IV Therapy (up to one hour) 90760	$65
Well Exam 12–17 yrs. 99384	$65		Each additional hour 90761	$50
Well Exam 18–39 yrs. 99385	$85		Oximetry 94760	$10
Well Exam 40–64 yrs. 99386	$105		ECG 93000	$75
Established Patient OV			Holter Monitor various codes	$170
Post Op Follow Up Visit 99024	$0		Rhythm Strip 93040	$60
Minimum 99211	$35		Treadmill 93015	$375
Problem Focused 99212	$45		Cocci Skin Test 86490	$20
Expanded Problem Focused 99213	$55		X-ray, spine, chest, bone—any area various codes	$275
Detailed 99214	$65		Avulsion Nail 11730	$200
Comprehensive/High Complex 99215	$75		**Laboratory**	
Well exam infant (less than 1 year) 99391	$35		Amylase 82150	$40
Well Exam 1–4 yrs. 99392	$40		B12 82607	$30
Well Exam 5–11 yrs. 99393	$45		CBC & Diff 85025	$95
Well Exam 12–17 yrs. 99394	$55		Comp Metabolic Panel 80053	$75
Well Exam 18–39 yrs. 99395	$65		Chlamydia Screen 87110	$70
Well Exam 40–64 yrs. 99396	$75		Cholestrerol 82465	$75
Obstetrics			Digoxin 80162	$40
Total OB Care 59400	$1700		Electrolytes 80051	$70
Injections			Estrogen, Total 82672	$50
Administration 90772	$10		Ferritin 82728	$40
Allergy 95115	$35		Folate 82746	$30
DPT 90701	$50		GC Screen 87070	$60
Drug various codes	$35		Glucose 82947	$35
Influenza 90658	$25		Glycosylated HGB A1C 83036	$45
MMR 90707	$50		HCT 85014	$30
OPV 90712	$40		HDL 83718	$35
Pneumovax 90732	$35		HGB 85018	$30
TB Skin Test 86580	$15		Hep BSAG 83740	$40
TD 90718	$40		Hepatitis panel, acute 80074	$95
Tetanus Toxoid 90703	$40		HIV 86703	$100
Vaccine/Toxoid Administration for Younger			Iron & TIBC 83550	$45
Than 8 Years Old w/ counseling 90465	$10		Kidney Profile 80069	$95
Vaccine/Toxoid Administration for Adult 90471	$10		Lead 83665	$55
Arthrocentesis/Aspiration/Injection			Lipase 83690	$40
Small Joint 20600	$50		Lipid Panel 80061	$95
Interm Joint 20605	$60		Liver Profile 80076	$95
Major Joint 20610	$70		Mono Test 86308	$30
Trigger Point/Tendon Sheath Inj. 20550	$90		Pap Smear 88155	$90
Other Invasive/Noninvasive Procedures			Pap Collection/Supervision 88142	$95
Catheterization 51701	$55		Pregnancy Test 84703	$90
Circumcision 54150	$150		Obstetric Panel 80055	$85
Colposcopy 57452	$225		Pro Time 85610	$50
Colposcopy w/Biopsy 57454	$250		PSA 84153	$50
Cryosurgery Premalignant Lesion various codes	$160		RPR 86592	$55
Endometrial Biopsy 58100	$190		Sed. Rate 85651	$50
Excision Lesion Malignant various codes	$145		Stool Culture 87045	$80
Excision Lesion Benign various codes	$125		Stool O & P 87177	$105
Curettement Lesion			Strep Screen 87880	$35
Single 11055	$70		Theophylline 80198	$40
2–4 11056	$80		Thyroid Uptake 84479	$75
>4 11057	$90		TSH 84443	$50
Excision Skin Tags (1–15) 11200	$55		Urinalysis 81000	$35
Each Additional 10 11201	$30		Urine Culture 87088	$80
I & D Abscess Single/Simple 10060	$75		Drawing Fee 36415	$15
Multiple/Complex 10061	$95		Specimen Collection 99000	$10
I & D Pilonidal Cyst Simple 10080	$105			
I & D Pilonidal Cyst Complex 10081	$130			
Laceration Repair various codes	$60			

HEALTH INSURANCE CLAIM FORM

APPROVED BY NATIONAL UNIFORM CLAIM COMMITTEE (NUCC) 02/12

PICA ☐☐☐   **PICA** ☐☐☐

1. MEDICARE ☒ (Medicare#)	MEDICAID ☐ (Medicaid#)	TRICARE ☐ (ID#/DoD#)	CHAMPVA ☐ (Member ID#)	GROUP HEALTH PLAN ☐ (ID#)	FECA BLK LUNG ☐ (ID#)	OTHER ☐ (ID#)	1a. INSURED'S I.D. NUMBER (For Program in Item 1)

2. PATIENT'S NAME (Last Name, First Name, Middle Initial)	3. PATIENT'S BIRTH DATE MM	DD	YY SEX M☐ F☐	4. INSURED'S NAME (Last Name, First Name, Middle Initial)

5. PATIENT'S ADDRESS (No., Street) | 6. PATIENT RELATIONSHIP TO INSURED Self☐ Spouse☐ Child☐ Other☐ | 7. INSURED'S ADDRESS (No., Street)

CITY | STATE | 8. RESERVED FOR NUCC USE | CITY | STATE

ZIP CODE | TELEPHONE (Include Area Code) ( ) | ZIP CODE | TELEPHONE (Include Area Code) ( )

9. OTHER INSURED'S NAME (Last Name, First Name, Middle Initial) | 10. IS PATIENT'S CONDITION RELATED TO: | 11. INSURED'S POLICY GROUP OR FECA NUMBER

a. OTHER INSURED'S POLICY OR GROUP NUMBER | a. EMPLOYMENT? (Current or Previous) YES☐ NO☐ | a. INSURED'S DATE OF BIRTH MM | DD | YY SEX M☐ F☐

b. RESERVED FOR NUCC USE | b. AUTO ACCIDENT? YES☐ NO☐ PLACE (State) | b. OTHER CLAIM ID (Designated by NUCC)

c. RESERVED FOR NUCC USE | c. OTHER ACCIDENT? YES☐ NO☐ | c. INSURANCE PLAN NAME OR PROGRAM NAME

d. INSURANCE PLAN NAME OR PROGRAM NAME | 10d. CLAIM CODES (Designated by NUCC) | d. IS THERE ANOTHER HEALTH BENEFIT PLAN? YES☐ NO☐ *If yes, complete items 9, 9a, and 9d.*

READ BACK OF FORM BEFORE COMPLETING & SIGNING THIS FORM.
12. PATIENT'S OR AUTHORIZED PERSON'S SIGNATURE I authorize the release of any medical or other information necessary to process this claim. I also request payment of government benefits either to myself or to the party who accepts assignment below.

SIGNED _____ DATE _____

13. INSURED'S OR AUTHORIZED PERSON'S SIGNATURE I authorize payment of medical benefits to the undersigned physician or supplier for services described below.

SIGNED _____

14. DATE OF CURRENT ILLNESS, INJURY, or PREGNANCY (LMP) MM	DD	YY QUAL.	15. OTHER DATE QUAL. MM	DD	YY	16. DATES PATIENT UNABLE TO WORK IN CURRENT OCCUPATION MM	DD	YY FROM TO MM	DD	YY

17. NAME OF REFERRING PROVIDER OR OTHER SOURCE | 17a. | 17b. NPI | 18. HOSPITALIZATION DATES RELATED TO CURRENT SERVICES MM | DD | YY FROM TO MM | DD | YY

19. ADDITIONAL CLAIM INFORMATION (Designated by NUCC) | 20. OUTSIDE LAB? YES☐ NO☐ $ CHARGES

21. DIAGNOSIS OR NATURE OF ILLNESS OR INJURY Relate A-L to service line below (24E) ICD Ind. | 22. RESUBMISSION CODE ORIGINAL REF. NO.
A. _____ B. _____ C. _____ D. _____
E. _____ F. _____ G. _____ H. _____
I. _____ J. _____ K. _____ L. _____ | 23. PRIOR AUTHORIZATION NUMBER

24. A. DATE(S) OF SERVICE From MM DD YY To MM DD YY	B. PLACE OF SERVICE	C. EMG	D. PROCEDURES, SERVICES, OR SUPPLIES (Explain Unusual Circumstances) CPT/HCPCS MODIFIER	E. DIAGNOSIS POINTER	F. $ CHARGES	G. DAYS OR UNITS	H. EPSDT Family Plan	I. ID. QUAL	J. RENDERING PROVIDER ID. #
1									NPI
2									NPI
3									NPI
4									NPI
5									NPI
6									NPI

25. FEDERAL TAX I.D. NUMBER SSN EIN	26. PATIENT'S ACCOUNT NO.	27. ACCEPT ASSIGNMENT? (For govt. claims, see back) YES☐ NO☐	28. TOTAL CHARGE $	29. AMOUNT PAID $	30. Rsvd. for NUCC Use

31. SIGNATURE OF PHYSICIAN OR SUPPLIER INCLUDING DEGREES OR CREDENTIALS (I certify that the statements on the reverse apply to this bill and are made a part thereof.) SIGNED _____ DATE _____	32. SERVICE FACILITY LOCATION INFORMATION a. NPI b.	33. BILLING PROVIDER INFO & PH # ( ) a. NPI b.

NUCC Instruction Manual available at: www.nucc.org | **PLEASE PRINT OR TYPE** | APPROVED OMB-0938-1197 FORM 1500 (02-12)

Clear Form

Vertical right margin: CARRIER — PATIENT AND INSURED INFORMATION — PHYSICIAN OR SUPPLIER INFORMATION

Figure 13-8

e. Using the source documents, the Capital City Medical Fee Schedule (Figure 13-9), and the blank CMS-1500 form provided (Figure 13-10), complete the following case study for patient Jenny Powers (Case 13-5):

CASE 13-5

Capital City Medical—123 Unknown Boulevard, Capital City, NY 12345-2222 (555) 555-1234 Phil Wells, MD, Mannie Mends, MD, Bette R. Soone, MD	Patient Information Form Tax ID: 75-0246810 Group NPI: 1513171216

Patient Information:

Name: (Last, First) Powers, Jenny   ❑ Male ☒ Female   Birth Date: 06/23/1985

Address: 512 Melba St, Capital City, NY 12345   Phone: (555) 555-6008

Social Security Number: 142-19-7757   Full-Time Student: ☒ Yes ❑ No

Marital Status: ☒ Single ❑ Married ❑ Divorced ❑ Other

Employment:

Employer: _____ Phone: ( ) _____

Address: _____

Condition Related to: ❑ Auto Accident ❑ Employment ❑ Other Accident

Date of Accident: _____ State: _____

Emergency Contact: _____ **Phone: ( )** _____

Primary Insurance: Medicaid   Phone: ( ) _____

Address: 4875 Capital Blvd, Capital City, NY 12345

Insurance Policyholder's Name: Same   ❑ M ❑ F DOB: _____

Address: _____

Phone: ( ) _____ Relationship to Insured: ☒ Self ❑ Spouse ❑ Child ❑ Other

Employer: _____ Phone: ( ) _____

Employer's Address: _____

Policy/ID No: 6684431000   Group No: _____ Percent Covered: ___% Copay Amt: $ 5.00

Secondary Insurance: _____ Phone: ( ) _____

Address: _____

Insurance Policyholder's Name: _____ ❑ M ❑ F DOB: _____

Address: _____

Phone: ( ) _____ Relationship to Insured: ❑ Self ❑ Spouse ❑ Child ❑ Other

Employer: _____ Phone: ( ) _____

Employer's Address: _____

Policy/ID No: _____ Group No: _____ Percent Covered: ___% Copay Amt: $ _____

Reason for Visit: I am here for a follow-up on my colonoscopy.

Known Allergies: _____

Referred by: _____

CASE 13-5
SOAP

07/17/20XX
Assignment of Benefits: Y
Signature on File: Y
Referring Physician: N

S: Jenny Powers is being seen today to review the results of her recent colonoscopy. She has been having periods of diarrhea alternating with constipation.

O: The colonoscopy shows no signs of polyps or inflammation to the diverticula. There is no evidence of hemorrhoids. Pt. does present with tenderness in the right lower quadrant.

A: 1. IBS with constipation—K58.1

P: 1. Start fiber supplement.
   2. Pamphlets on diet and stress management given.
   3. Return in 4 months.

_____
Phil Wells, MD
Family Practice
NPI: 1234567890

CASE 13-5

Patient Name Jenny Powers

Capital City Medical
123 Unknown Boulevard, Capital City, NY 12345-2222

Date of Service 07-17-20XX

New Patient			Arthrocentesis/Aspiration/Injection		Laboratory	
Problem Focused	99201		Arthrocentesis/Aspiration/Injection		Amylase	82150
Expanded Problem, Focused	99202		Small Joint	20600	B12	82607
Detailed	99203		Interm Joint	20605	CBC & Diff	85025
Comprehensive	99204		Major Joint	20610	Comp Metabolic Panel	80053
Comprehensive/High Complex	99205		**Other Invasive/Noninvasive**		Chlamydia Screen	87110
Well Exam Infant (up to 12 mos.)	99381		Audiometry	92552	Cholesterol	82465
Well Exam 1–4 yrs.	99382		Cast Application		Digoxin	80162
Well Exam 5–11 yrs.	99383		Location Long Short		Electrolytes	80051
Well Exam 12–17 yrs.	99384		Catheterization	51701	Ferritin	82728
Well Exam 18–39 yrs.	99385		Circumcision	54150	Folate	82746
Well Exam 40–64 yrs.	99386		Colposcopy	57452	GC Screen	87070
			Colposcopy w/Biopsy	57454	Glucose	82947
			Cryosurgery Premalignant Lesion		Glucose 1 HR	82950
			Location (s):		Glycosylated HGB A1C	83036
Established Patient			Cryosurgery Warts		HCT	85014
Post-Op Follow Up Visit	99024	X	Location (s):		HDL	83718
Minimum	99211		Curettement Lesion		Hep BSAG	87340
Problem Focused	99212		Single	11055	Hepatitis panel, acute	80074
Expanded Problem Focused	99213	X	2–4	11056	HGB	85018
Detailed	99214		>4	11057	HIV	86703
Comprehensive/High Complex	99215		Diaphragm Fitting	57170	Iron & TIBC	83550
Well Exam Infant (up to 12 mos.)	99391		Ear Irrigation	69210	Kidney Profile	80069
Well exam 1–4 yrs.	99392		ECG	93000	Lead	83655
Well Exam 5–11 yrs.	99393		Endometrial Biopsy	58100	Liver Profile	80076
Well Exam 12–17 yrs.	99394		Exc. Lesion Malignant		Mono Test	86308
Well Exam 18–39 yrs.	99395		Benign		Pap Smear	88155
Well Exam 40–64 yrs.	99396		Location		Pregnancy Test	84703
Obstetrics			Exc. Skin Tags (1–15)	11200	Obstetric Panel	80055
Total OB Care	59400		Each Additional 10	11201	Pro Time	85610
Injections			Fracture Treatment		PSA	84153
Administration Sub. / IM	90772		Loc		RPR	86592
Drug			w/Reduc w/o Reduc		Sed. Rate	85651
Dosage			I & D Abscess Single/Simple	10060	Stool Culture	87045
Allergy	95115		Multiple or Comp	10061	Stool O & P	87177
Cocci Skin Test	86490		I & D Pilonidal Cyst Simple	10080	Strep Screen	87880
DPT	90701		Pilonidal Cyst Complex	10081	Theophylline	80198
Hemophilus	90646		IV Therapy—To One Hour	90760	Thyroid Uptake	84479
Influenza	90658		Each Additional Hour	90761	TSH	84443
MMR	90707		Laceration Repair		Urinalysis	81000
OPV	90712		Location Size Simp/Comp		Urine Culture	87088
Pneumovax	90732		Laryngoscopy	31505	Drawing Fee	36415
TB Skin Test	86580		Oximetry	94760	Specimen Collection	99000
TD	90718		Punch Biopsy		**Other:**	
Unlisted Immun	90749		Rhythm Strip	93040		
Tetanus Toxoid	90703		Treadmill	93015		
Vaccine/Toxoid Admin <8 Yr Old w/ Counseling	90465		Trigger Point or Tendon Sheath Inj.	20550		
Vaccine/Toxoid Administration for Adult	90471		Tympanometry	92567		

Diagnosis/ICD-10: K58.1

I acknowledge receipt of medical services and authorize the release of any medical information necessary to process this claim for healthcare payment only. I do authorize payment to the provider.

Total Estimated Charges: _____

Payment Amount: _____

Patient Signature _Jenny Powers_____

Next Appointment: _____

Figure 13-9

Capital City Medical
Fee Schedule

New Patient OV		Punch Biopsy various codes	$80
Problem Focused 99201	$45	Nebulizer various codes	$45
Expanded Problem Focused 99202	$65	Cast Application various codes	$85
Detailed 99203	$85	Laryngoscopy 31505	$255
Comprehensive 99204	$105	Audiometry 92552	$85
Comprehensive/High Complex 99205	$115	Tympanometry 92567	$85
Well Exam infant (less than 1 year) 99381	$45	Ear Irrigation 69210	$25
Well Exam 1–4 yrs. 99382	$50	Diaphragm Fitting 57170	$30
Well Exam 5–11 yrs. 99383	$55	IV Therapy (up to one hour) 90760	$65
Well Exam 12–17 yrs. 99384	$65	Each additional hour 90761	$50
Well Exam 18–39 yrs. 99385	$85	Oximetry 94760	$10
Well Exam 40–64 yrs. 99386	$105	ECG 93000	$75
Established Patient OV		Holter Monitor various codes	$170
Post Op Follow Up Visit 99024	$0	Rhythm Strip 93040	$60
Minimum 99211	$35	Treadmill 93015	$375
Problem Focused 99212	$45	Cocci Skin Test 86490	$20
Expanded Problem Focused 99213	$55	X-ray, spine, chest, bone—any area various codes	$275
Detailed 99214	$65	Avulsion Nail 11730	$200
Comprehensive/High Complex 99215	$75	**Laboratory**	
Well exam infant (less than 1 year) 99391	$35	Amylase 82150	$40
Well Exam 1–4 yrs. 99392	$40	B12 82607	$30
Well Exam 5–11 yrs. 99393	$45	CBC & Diff 85025	$95
Well Exam 12–17 yrs. 99394	$55	Comp Metabolic Panel 80053	$75
Well Exam 18–39 yrs. 99395	$65	Chlamydia Screen 87110	$70
Well Exam 40–64 yrs. 99396	$75	Cholestrerol 82465	$75
Obstetrics		Digoxin 80162	$40
Total OB Care 59400	$1700	Electrolytes 80051	$70
Injections		Estrogen, Total 82672	$50
Administration 90772	$10	Ferritin 82728	$40
Allergy 95115	$35	Folate 82746	$30
DPT 90701	$50	GC Screen 87070	$60
Drug various codes	$35	Glucose 82947	$35
Influenza 90658	$25	Glycosylated HGB A1C 83036	$45
MMR 90707	$50	HCT 85014	$30
OPV 90712	$40	HDL 83718	$35
Pneumovax 90732	$35	HGB 85018	$30
TB Skin Test 86580	$15	Hep BSAG 83740	$40
TD 90718	$40	Hepatitis panel, acute 80074	$95
Tetanus Toxoid 90703	$40	HIV 86703	$100
Vaccine/Toxoid Administration for Younger		Iron & TIBC 83550	$45
Than 8 Years Old w/ counseling 90465	$10	Kidney Profile 80069	$95
Vaccine/Toxoid Administration for Adult 90471	$10	Lead 83665	$55
Arthrocentesis/Aspiration/Injection		Lipase 83690	$40
Small Joint 20600	$50	Lipid Panel 80061	$95
Interm Joint 20605	$60	Liver Profile 80076	$95
Major Joint 20610	$70	Mono Test 86308	$30
Trigger Point/Tendon Sheath Inj. 20550	$90	Pap Smear 88155	$90
Other Invasive/Noninvasive Procedures		Pap Collection/Supervision 88142	$95
Catheterization 51701	$55	Pregnancy Test 84703	$90
Circumcision 54150	$150	Obstetric Panel 80055	$85
Colposcopy 57452	$225	Pro Time 85610	$50
Colposcopy w/Biopsy 57454	$250	PSA 84153	$50
Cryosurgery Premalignant Lesion various codes	$160	RPR 86592	$55
Endometrial Biopsy 58100	$190	Sed. Rate 85651	$50
Excision Lesion Malignant various codes	$145	Stool Culture 87045	$80
Excision Lesion Benign various codes	$125	Stool O & P 87177	$105
Curettement Lesion		Strep Screen 87880	$35
Single 11055	$70	Theophylline 80198	$40
2–4 11056	$80	Thyroid Uptake 84479	$75
>4 11057	$90	TSH 84443	$50
Excision Skin Tags (1–15) 11200	$55	Urinalysis 81000	$35
Each Additional 10 11201	$30	Urine Culture 87088	$80
I & D Abscess Single/Simple 10060	$75	Drawing Fee 36415	$15
Multiple/Complex 10061	$95	Specimen Collection 99000	$10
I & D Pilonidal Cyst Simple 10080	$105		
I & D Pilonidal Cyst Complex 10081	$130		
Laceration Repair various codes	$60		

HEALTH INSURANCE CLAIM FORM

APPROVED BY NATIONAL UNIFORM CLAIM COMMITTEE (NUCC) 02/12

| | PICA | PICA | | |

CARRIER

1. MEDICARE ☐ (Medicare#) MEDICAID ☐ (Medicaid#) TRICARE ☐ (ID#/DoD#) CHAMPVA ☐ (Member ID#) GROUP HEALTH PLAN ☐ (ID#) FECA BLK LUNG ☐ (ID#) OTHER ☐ (ID#) — ☒ (Medicare#)

1a. INSURED'S I.D. NUMBER (For Program in Item 1)

2. PATIENT'S NAME (Last Name, First Name, Middle Initial)

3. PATIENT'S BIRTH DATE MM DD YY SEX M ☐ F ☐

4. INSURED'S NAME (Last Name, First Name, Middle Initial)

5. PATIENT'S ADDRESS (No., Street)

6. PATIENT RELATIONSHIP TO INSURED   Self ☐ Spouse ☐ Child ☐ Other ☐

7. INSURED'S ADDRESS (No., Street)

CITY   STATE

8. RESERVED FOR NUCC USE

CITY   STATE

ZIP CODE   TELEPHONE (Include Area Code) ( )

ZIP CODE   TELEPHONE (Include Area Code) ( )

9. OTHER INSURED'S NAME (Last Name, First Name, Middle Initial)

10. IS PATIENT'S CONDITION RELATED TO:

11. INSURED'S POLICY GROUP OR FECA NUMBER

a. OTHER INSURED'S POLICY OR GROUP NUMBER

a. EMPLOYMENT? (Current or Previous) YES ☐ NO ☐

a. INSURED'S DATE OF BIRTH MM DD YY SEX M ☐ F ☐

b. RESERVED FOR NUCC USE

b. AUTO ACCIDENT? YES ☐ NO ☐ PLACE (State)

b. OTHER CLAIM ID (Designated by NUCC)

c. RESERVED FOR NUCC USE

c. OTHER ACCIDENT? YES ☐ NO ☐

c. INSURANCE PLAN NAME OR PROGRAM NAME

d. INSURANCE PLAN NAME OR PROGRAM NAME

10d. CLAIM CODES (Designated by NUCC)

d. IS THERE ANOTHER HEALTH BENEFIT PLAN? YES ☐ NO ☐ If yes, complete items 9, 9a, and 9d.

PATIENT AND INSURED INFORMATION

READ BACK OF FORM BEFORE COMPLETING & SIGNING THIS FORM.
12. PATIENT'S OR AUTHORIZED PERSON'S SIGNATURE I authorize the release of any medical or other information necessary to process this claim. I also request payment of government benefits either to myself or to the party who accepts assignment below.

SIGNED _____   DATE _____

13. INSURED'S OR AUTHORIZED PERSON'S SIGNATURE I authorize payment of medical benefits to the undersigned physician or supplier for services described below.

SIGNED _____

14. DATE OF CURRENT ILLNESS, INJURY, or PREGNANCY (LMP) MM DD YY QUAL.

15. OTHER DATE QUAL. MM DD YY

16. DATES PATIENT UNABLE TO WORK IN CURRENT OCCUPATION MM DD YY FROM   TO MM DD YY

17. NAME OF REFERRING PROVIDER OR OTHER SOURCE

17a.
17b. NPI

18. HOSPITALIZATION DATES RELATED TO CURRENT SERVICES MM DD YY FROM   TO MM DD YY

19. ADDITIONAL CLAIM INFORMATION (Designated by NUCC)

20. OUTSIDE LAB? YES ☐ NO ☐ $ CHARGES

21. DIAGNOSIS OR NATURE OF ILLNESS OR INJURY Relate A-L to service line below (24E) ICD Ind.

A. ___ B. ___ C. ___ D. ___
E. ___ F. ___ G. ___ H. ___
I. ___ J. ___ K. ___ L. ___

22. RESUBMISSION CODE   ORIGINAL REF. NO.

23. PRIOR AUTHORIZATION NUMBER

24. A. DATE(S) OF SERVICE					B. PLACE OF SERVICE	C. EMG	D. PROCEDURES, SERVICES, OR SUPPLIES (Explain Unusual Circumstances)		E. DIAGNOSIS POINTER	F. $ CHARGES	G. DAYS OR UNITS	H. EPSDT Family Plan	I. ID. QUAL.	J. RENDERING PROVIDER ID. #
From MM DD YY		To MM DD YY					CPT/HCPCS	MODIFIER						
1														NPI
2														NPI
3														NPI
4														NPI
5														NPI
6														NPI

PHYSICIAN OR SUPPLIER INFORMATION

25. FEDERAL TAX I.D. NUMBER   SSN ☐ EIN ☐

26. PATIENT'S ACCOUNT NO.

27. ACCEPT ASSIGNMENT? (For govt. claims, see back) YES ☐ NO ☐

28. TOTAL CHARGE $

29. AMOUNT PAID $

30. Rsvd for NUCC Use

31. SIGNATURE OF PHYSICIAN OR SUPPLIER INCLUDING DEGREES OR CREDENTIALS (I certify that the statements on the reverse apply to this bill and are made a part thereof.)

SIGNED _____   DATE _____

32. SERVICE FACILITY LOCATION INFORMATION

a. NPI   b.

33. BILLING PROVIDER INFO & PH # ( )

a. NPI   b.

NUCC Instruction Manual available at: www.nucc.org   **PLEASE PRINT OR TYPE**   APPROVED OMB-0938-1197 FORM 1500 (02-12)

Clear Form

Figure 13-10

© 2018 Pearson Education, Inc.

REVIEW QUESTIONS

MATCHING

Choose the correct answer and write its corresponding letter in the space provided.

a. Immigrants
b. Payer of last resort
c. Spend down
d. Cost share
e. Medi–Medi

1. _____ Incurring medical expenses that result in income being reduced to or below a state's medically needy income level

2. _____ When a person is a beneficiary of both Medicaid and Medicare

3. _____ When an insurance plan requires an enrollee to pay toward coverage

4. _____ After 1996 are ineligible for Medicaid for 5 years

5. _____ States that Medicare is always the primary plan when a patient also has Medicaid

MULTIPLE CHOICE

Circle the letter of the choice that best completes the statement or answers the question.

1. Who funds Medicaid?
   a. State government
   b. Federal government
   c. Both a and b
   d. None of the above

2. Under what condition is a provider not allowed to bill a Medicaid recipient for an uncovered service?
   a. Preauthorization was not obtained.
   b. If a service was performed and the patient knew that it may not be covered.
   c. An ABN was signed by the patient for the uncovered service.
   d. Both a and c

3. When should Medicaid coverage be verified?
   a. At each visit
   b. Once a year
   c. Every six months
   d. Every quarter

4. Which of the following would be categorically needy?
   a. Caretakers of children under 18
   b. Recipients of adoptions assistance
   c. Adults within a certain income
   d. All of the above

5. What is another name for the Welfare Reform Bill?
   a. The Personal Responsibility and Work Opportunity Reconciliation Act of 1996
   b. The Balanced Budget Act of 1997
   c. The Ticket to Work and Work Incentives Improvement Act of 1999
   d. All of the above

SHORT ANSWER

Provide the correct response to each question that follows.

1. What law allows continued Medicaid coverage for disabled persons who are still able to work?

   _____

   _____

2. What is TANF?

   _____

   _____

3. Is a PCP required for Medicaid coverage?

   _____

   _____

4. What is the function of a care coordinator?

   _____

   _____

   _____

5. What are three ways to verify Medicaid coverage for a patient?

   1. _____

   2. _____

   3. _____

TRUE/FALSE

Identify each statement as true (T) or false (F).

1. _____ Medical services under Medicaid do not have any out-of-pocket expenses for patients.

2. _____ Emergency services and family planning services covered under Medicaid do not have any out-of-pocket expenses for patients.

3. _____ The federal government has set payment caps for the SCHIP, QI, and DSH programs.

4. _____ A Medicaid recipient may have the choice of an HMO plan.

5. _____ The Affordable Care Act will begin to limit Medicaid coverage.

© 2018 Pearson Education, Inc.

CHAPTER 14
TRICARE Medical Billing

CHAPTER OBJECTIVES

After reading this chapter, the student should be able to:

1. Determine eligibility for TRICARE participants.
2. Identify different types of benefits available to veterans and their family members.
3. Submit claims to TRICARE using the CMS-1500 and the UB-04 (CMS-1450) forms.

CHAPTER OUTLINE

TRICARE
>   *TRICARE Eligibility*
>   *The Patient's Financial Responsibilities*
>   *Timely Filing*
>   *Penalties and Interest Charges*
>   *Authorized Providers*
>   *Preauthorization*

TRICARE Standard and TRICARE Extra

TRICARE Prime

TRICARE Prime Remote

TRICARE Senior Prime/TRICARE for Life
>   *TRICARE Reform*

CHAMPVA

Submitting Claims to TRICARE

Completing the CMS-1500 Form for TRICARE (Primary)

Confidential and Sensitive Information

KEY TERMS

Using the highlighted terms and glossary in the textbook, define the following terms.

1. beneficiary _____

_____

2. catastrophic cap _____

_____

© 2018 Pearson Education, Inc.

3. Civilian Health and Medical Program of the Department of Veterans Affairs (CHAMPVA) _____

_____

4. Civilian Health and Medical Program of the Uniformed Services (CHAMPUS) _____

_____

5. cost share _____

_____

6. Defense Enrollment Eligibility Reporting System (DEERS) _____

_____

7. military treatment facility (MTF) _____

_____

8. nonavailability statement (NAS) _____

_____

9. Palmetto Government Benefits Administrators (PGBA) _____

_____

10. primary care manager (PCM) _____

_____

11. sponsor _____

_____

12. TRICARE _____

_____

13. TRICARE Extra _____

_____

14. TRICARE for Life (TFL) _____

_____

15. TRICARE Prime _____

_____

16. TRICARE Prime Remote (TPR) _____

_____

17. TRICARE Reserve Retired (TRR) _____

_____

18. TRICARE Reserve Select (TRS) _____

_____

19. TRICARE Senior Prime _____

_____

20. TRICARE Standard _____

_____

21. TRICARE Young Adult (TYA) _____

_____

22. Wisconsin Physicians Services (WPS) _____

_____

© 2018 Pearson Education, Inc.

CRITICAL THINKING QUESTIONS

Using the knowledge you have gained from reading the textbook, apply critical thinking skills to answer the following questions.

1. a. Merle Verlock is covered by TRICARE Prime. In your own words, briefly describe his plan.

    _____

    _____

    _____

    _____

    b. Explain Merle's medical access standards (wait time for appointment/care) under TRICARE Prime for the following types of care:

    1. Urgent care

        _____

    2. Routine care

        _____

        _____

    3. Referred specialty care

        _____

        _____

    4. Wellness/Preventive care

        _____

        _____

        _____

2. Jane Smith is covered by TRICARE Reserve Select. Explain how this plan works.

    _____

    _____

    _____

    _____

3. Brandon McGregory is reading over his TRICARE benefits package For TRICARE Prime, what are the consequences of not seeing a provider at an MTF, if he has one available?

    _____

    _____

    _____

4. a. Jaylynn Ramsey, who is not active duty personnel or a veteran of war, is choosing a TRICARE plan. She wants to pick the plan that allows her to access civilian medical facilities/providers as her primary healthcare. Which TRICARE plan is the best choice for Jaylynn?

_____

_____

b. Jaylynn's 67-year-old uncle, Jessie Ramsey, is also choosing a TRICARE plan. He is also Medicare eligible. Which TRICARE plan is the best choice for Jessie?

_____

_____

c. Laurel Orlando is currently an active duty marine. Which TRICARE plan is the best choice for her husband and two children?

_____

_____

5. Cedric Malcolm has CHAMPVA and needs to obtain care at the nearest VA facility. Using the Internet, locate the VA Hospital's website. Where is the closest VA Hospital in your area that Cedric can go to?

_____

_____

PRACTICE EXERCISES

1. Using the form locator information written out on your index cardsfrom a prior chapter, complete the following activity. Flag those FLs that would be filled out differently for TRICARE patients.

2. Case studies are provided for additional practice in completing the CMS-1500 claim form for TRICARE physician outpatient billing. By applying what you have learned in your student text, accurately code and complete each case study. Patient demographics and a brief case history are provided. Complete the cases based on the following criteria:

   * All patients have release of information and assignment of benefit signatures on file.

   * All providers are participating and accept assignment.

   * The group practice is the billing entity.

   * The national transition to NPI numbers is complete, and legacy PINs of individual payers are no longer used.

   * 2017 ICD-10-CM and CPT codes are used.

   * Use eight-digit dates for birthdates. Use six digit dates for all other dates.

   * All street names should be entered using standard postal abbreviations, even if they are spelled out on the source documents.

   * Enter ICD-10 codes in the order they appear on the encounter form.

   * When entering CPT codes, enter the E/M code first. Enter remaining codes in descending price order.

In order to determine the correct fees, refer to the Capital City Medical Fee Schedule, which is located after each case's source documents. Use the blank CMS-1500 form provided after each case.

a. Using the source documents, the Capital City Medical Fee Schedule (Figure 14-1), and the blank CMS-1500 form provided (Figure 14-2), complete the following case study for patient Staci Pratt (Case 14-1):

© 2018 Pearson Education, Inc.

CASE 14-1

Capital City Medical—123 Unknown Boulevard, Capital City, NY 12345-2222 (555) 555-1234	Patient Information Form
	Tax ID: 75-0246810
Phil Wells, MD, Mannie Mends, MD, Bette R. Soone, MD	Group NPI: 1513171216

Patient Information:

Name: (Last, First) <u>Pratt, Staci</u>   ❑ Male   ☒ Female   Birth Date: <u>05/30/1970</u>

Address: <u>7 Garfield Ave, Capital City, NY 12345</u>   Phone: <u>(555) 555-3701</u>

Social Security Number: <u>201-21-2802</u>   Full-Time Student: ❑ Yes   ☒ No

Marital Status: ❑ Single   ☒ Married   ❑ Divorced   ❑ Other

- - - - - - - - - -

Employment:

Employer: <u>Township Memorial Hospital</u>   Phone: <u>(555) 555-0700</u>

Address: <u>780 Shady Street, Township, NY 12345</u>

Condition Related to: ❑ Auto Accident   ❑ Employment   ❑ Other Accident

Date of Accident: _____ State: _____

Emergency Contact: _____ **Phone: ( )** _____

- - - - - - - - - -

Primary Insurance: <u>Tricare</u>   Phone: ( ) _____

Address: <u>7594 Forces-Run Rd, Militaryville, NY 12345</u>

Insurance Policyholder's Name: <u>Same</u>   ❑ M ❑ F DOB: _____

Address: _____

Phone: _____ Relationship to Insured: ☒ Self   ❑ Spouse   ❑ Child   ❑ Other

Employer: _____ Phone: ( ) _____

Employer's Address: _____

Policy/ID No: <u>201212802</u>   Group No: _____ Percent Covered: ___% Copay Amt: $<u>35.00</u>

- - - - - - - - - -

Secondary Insurance: _____ Phone: ( ) _____

Address: _____

Insurance Policyholder's Name: _____ ❑ M ❑ F DOB: _____

Address: _____

Phone: _____ Relationship to Insured: ❑ Self   ❑ Spouse   ❑ Child   ❑ Other

Employer: _____ Phone: ( ) _____

Employer's Address: _____

Policy/ID No: _____ Group No: _____ Percent Covered: ___% Copay Amt: $_____

- - - - - - - - - -

Reason for Visit: <u>Physical examination for Army Reserves.</u>

Known Allergies: _____

Referred by: _____

CASE 14-1
SOAP

06/17/20XX
Assignment of Benefits: Y
Signature on File: Y
Referring Physician: N

S: Staci Pratt is here today for a physical examination, including a pap smear and gynecological exam. She has no complaints. This is her yearly exam for the Army Reserves.

O: Pt. denies any recent problems. Her vitals are stable. Physical exam is unremarkable. Labs are negative for any disease process. She is cleared.

A: 1. Physical/Gynecological exam for Army Reserves—Z01.419

P: 1. Cleared for Army status.
   2. Return p.r.n.

_____

Phil Wells, MD
Family Practice
NPI: 1234567890

© 2018 Pearson Education, Inc.

CASE 14-1

Patient Name Staci Pratt

Capital City Medical
123 Unknown Boulevard, Capital City, NY 12345-2222

Date of Service
06-17-20XX

New Patient			Arthrocentesis/Aspiration/Injection			Laboratory	
Problem Focused	99201		Small Joint	20600		Amylase	82150
Expanded Problem, Focused	99202		Interm Joint	20605		B12	82607
Detailed	99203		Major Joint	20610		CBC & Diff	85025
Comprehensive	99204		**Other Invasive/Noninvasive**			Comp Metabolic Panel	80053
Comprehensive/High Complex	99205		Audiometry	92552		Chlamydia Screen	87110
Well Exam Infant (up to 12 mos.)	99381		Cast Application			Cholesterol	82465
Well Exam 1–4 yrs.	99382		Location Long Short			Digoxin	80162
Well Exam 5–11 yrs.	99383		Catheterization	51701		Electrolytes	80051
Well Exam 12–17 yrs.	99384		Circumcision	54150		Ferritin	82728
Well Exam 18–39 yrs.	99385		Colposcopy	57452		Folate	82746
Well Exam 40–64 yrs.	99386		Colposcopy w/Biopsy	57454		GC Screen	87070
			Cryosurgery Premalignant Lesion			Glucose	82947
			Location (s):			Glucose 1 HR	82950
			Cryosurgery Warts			Glycosylated HGB A1C	83036
Established Patient			Location (s):			HCT	85014
Post-Op Follow Up Visit	99024		Curettement Lesion			HDL	83718
Minimum	99211		Single	11055		Hep BSAG	87340
Problem Focused	99212		2–4	11056		Hepatitis panel, acute	80074
Expanded Problem Focused	99213		>4	11057		HGB	85018
Detailed	99214		Diaphragm Fitting	57170		HIV	86703
Comprehensive/High Complex	99215		Ear Irrigation	69210		Iron & TIBC	83550
Well Exam Infant (up to 12 mos.)	99391		ECG	93000		Kidney Profile	80069
Well exam 1–4 yrs.	99392		Endometrial Biopsy	58100		Lead	83655
Well Exam 5–11 yrs.	99393		Exc. Lesion Malignant			Liver Profile	80076
Well Exam 12–17 yrs.	99394					Mono Test	86308
Well Exam 18–39 yrs.	99395	X	Benign			Pap Smear	88155
Well Exam 40–64 yrs.	99396		Location			Pregnancy Test	84703
Obstetrics			Exc. Skin Tags (1–15)	11200		Obstetric Panel	80055
Total OB Care	59400		Each Additional 10	11201		Pro Time	85610
Injections			Fracture Treatment			PSA	84153
Administration Sub. / IM	90772		Loc			RPR	86592
Drug			w/Reduc w/o Reduc			Sed. Rate	85651
Dosage			I & D Abscess Single/Simple	10060		Stool Culture	87045
Allergy	95115		Multiple or Comp	10061		Stool O & P	87177
Cocci Skin Test	86490		I & D Pilonidal Cyst Simple	10080		Strep Screen	87880
DPT	90701		Pilonidal Cyst Complex	10081		Theophylline	80198
Hemophilus	90646		IV Therapy—To One Hour	90760		Thyroid Uptake	84479
Influenza	90658		Each Additional Hour	90761		TSH	84443
MMR	90707		Laceration Repair			Urinalysis	81000	X
OPV	90712		Location Size Simp/Comp			Urine Culture	87088
Pneumovax	90732		Laryngoscopy	31505		Drawing Fee	36415
TB Skin Test	86580		Oximetry	94760		Specimen Collection	99000
TD	90718		Punch Biopsy			**Other:**	
Unlisted Immun	90749		Rhythm Strip	93040			
Tetanus Toxoid	90703		Treadmill	93015			
Vaccine/Toxoid Admin <8 Yr Old w/ Counseling	90465		Trigger Point or Tendon Sheath Inj.	20550			
Vaccine/Toxoid Administration for Adult	90471		Tympanometry	92567			

Diagnosis/ICD-10: Z01.419

I acknowledge receipt of medical services and authorize the release of any medical information necessary to process this claim for healthcare payment only. I do authorize payment to the provider.

Patient Signature Staci Pratt

Total Estimated Charges: _____

Payment Amount: _____

Next Appointment: _____

Figure 14-1

Capital City Medical
Fee Schedule

New Patient OV

Problem Focused 99201	$45
Expanded Problem Focused 99202	$65
Detailed 99203	$85
Comprehensive 99204	$105
Comprehensive/High Complex 99205	$115
Well Exam infant (less than 1 year) 99381	$45
Well Exam 1–4 yrs. 99382	$50
Well Exam 5–11 yrs. 99383	$55
Well Exam 12–17 yrs. 99384	$65
Well Exam 18–39 yrs. 99385	$85
Well Exam 40–64 yrs. 99386	$105

Established Patient OV

Post Op Follow Up Visit 99024	$0
Minimum 99211	$35
Problem Focused 99212	$45
Expanded Problem Focused 99213	$55
Detailed 99214	$65
Comprehensive/High Complex 99215	$75
Well exam infant (less than 1 year) 99391	$35
Well Exam 1–4 yrs. 99392	$40
Well Exam 5–11 yrs. 99393	$45
Well Exam 12–17 yrs. 99394	$55
Well Exam 18–39 yrs. 99395	$65
Well Exam 40–64 yrs. 99396	$75

Obstetrics

Total OB Care 59400	$1700

Injections

Administration 90772	$10
Allergy 95115	$35
DPT 90701	$50
Drug various codes	$35
Influenza 90658	$25
MMR 90707	$50
OPV 90712	$40
Pneumovax 90732	$35
TB Skin Test 86580	$15
TD 90718	$40
Tetanus Toxoid 90703	$40
Vaccine/Toxoid Administration for Younger Than 8 Years Old w/ counseling 90465	$10
Vaccine/Toxoid Administration for Adult 90471	$10

Arthrocentesis/Aspiration/Injection

Small Joint 20600	$50
Interm Joint 20605	$60
Major Joint 20610	$70
Trigger Point/Tendon Sheath Inj. 20550	$90

Other Invasive/Noninvasive Procedures

Catheterization 51701	$55
Circumcision 54150	$150
Colposcopy 57452	$225
Colposcopy w/Biopsy 57454	$250
Cryosurgery Premalignant Lesion various codes	$160
Endometrial Biopsy 58100	$190
Excision Lesion Malignant various codes	$145
Excision Lesion Benign various codes	$125
Curettement Lesion	
Single 11055	$70
2–4 11056	$80
>4 11057	$90
Excision Skin Tags (1–15) 11200	$55
Each Additional 10 11201	$30
I & D Abscess Single/Simple 10060	$75
Multiple/Complex 10061	$95
I & D Pilonidal Cyst Simple 10080	$105
I & D Pilonidal Cyst Complex 10081	$130
Laceration Repair various codes	$60

Punch Biopsy various codes	$80
Nebulizer various codes	$45
Cast Application various codes	$85
Laryngoscopy 31505	$255
Audiometry 92552	$85
Tympanometry 92567	$85
Ear Irrigation 69210	$25
Diaphragm Fitting 57170	$30
IV Therapy (up to one hour) 90760	$65
Each additional hour 90761	$50
Oximetry 94760	$10
ECG 93000	$75
Holter Monitor various codes	$170
Rhythm Strip 93040	$60
Treadmill 93015	$375
Cocci Skin Test 86490	$20
X-ray, spine, chest, bone—any area various codes	$275
Avulsion Nail 11730	$200

Laboratory

Amylase 82150	$40
B12 82607	$30
CBC & Diff 85025	$95
Comp Metabolic Panel 80053	$75
Chlamydia Screen 87110	$70
Cholestrerol 82465	$75
Digoxin 80162	$40
Electrolytes 80051	$70
Estrogen, Total 82672	$50
Ferritin 82728	$40
Folate 82746	$30
GC Screen 87070	$60
Glucose 82947	$35
Glycosylated HGB A1C 83036	$45
HCT 85014	$30
HDL 83718	$35
HGB 85018	$30
Hep BSAG 83740	$40
Hepatitis panel, acute 80074	$95
HIV 86703	$100
Iron & TIBC 83550	$45
Kidney Profile 80069	$95
Lead 83665	$55
Lipase 83690	$40
Lipid Panel 80061	$95
Liver Profile 80076	$95
Mono Test 86308	$30
Pap Smear 88155	$90
Pap Collection/Supervision 88142	$95
Pregnancy Test 84703	$90
Obstetric Panel 80055	$85
Pro Time 85610	$50
PSA 84153	$50
RPR 86592	$55
Sed. Rate 85651	$50
Stool Culture 87045	$80
Stool O & P 87177	$105
Strep Screen 87880	$35
Theophylline 80198	$40
Thyroid Uptake 84479	$75
TSH 84443	$50
Urinalysis 81000	$35
Urine Culture 87088	$80
Drawing Fee 36415	$15
Specimen Collection 99000	$10

HEALTH INSURANCE CLAIM FORM

APPROVED BY NATIONAL UNIFORM CLAIM COMMITTEE (NUCC) 02/12

| | | PICA | | | | | | | | PICA | | |

1. MEDICARE	MEDICAID	TRICARE	CHAMPVA	GROUP HEALTH PLAN	FECA BLK LUNG	OTHER	1a. INSURED'S I.D. NUMBER	(For Program in Item 1)
[X] (Medicare#)	(Medicaid#)	(ID#/DoD#)	(Member ID#)	(ID#)	(ID#)	(ID#)		

2. PATIENT'S NAME (Last Name, First Name, Middle Initial)

3. PATIENT'S BIRTH DATE MM | DD | YY   SEX   M [ ]   F [ ]

4. INSURED'S NAME (Last Name, First Name, Middle Initial)

5. PATIENT'S ADDRESS (No., Street)

6. PATIENT RELATIONSHIP TO INSURED   Self [ ]   Spouse [ ]   Child [ ]   Other [ ]

7. INSURED'S ADDRESS (No., Street)

CITY   STATE

8. RESERVED FOR NUCC USE

CITY   STATE

ZIP CODE   TELEPHONE (Include Area Code)   ( )

ZIP CODE   TELEPHONE (Include Area Code)   ( )

9. OTHER INSURED'S NAME (Last Name, First Name, Middle Initial)

10. IS PATIENT'S CONDITION RELATED TO:

11. INSURED'S POLICY GROUP OR FECA NUMBER

a. OTHER INSURED'S POLICY OR GROUP NUMBER

a. EMPLOYMENT? (Current or Previous)   YES [ ]   NO [ ]

a. INSURED'S DATE OF BIRTH MM | DD | YY   SEX   M [ ]   F [ ]

b. RESERVED FOR NUCC USE

b. AUTO ACCIDENT?   YES [ ]   NO [ ]   PLACE (State)

b. OTHER CLAIM ID (Designated by NUCC)

c. RESERVED FOR NUCC USE

c. OTHER ACCIDENT?   YES [ ]   NO [ ]

c. INSURANCE PLAN NAME OR PROGRAM NAME

d. INSURANCE PLAN NAME OR PROGRAM NAME

10d. CLAIM CODES (Designated by NUCC)

d. IS THERE ANOTHER HEALTH BENEFIT PLAN?   YES [ ]   NO [ ]   *If yes, complete items 9, 9a, and 9d.*

READ BACK OF FORM BEFORE COMPLETING & SIGNING THIS FORM.

12. PATIENT'S OR AUTHORIZED PERSON'S SIGNATURE I authorize the release of any medical or other information necessary to process this claim. I also request payment of government benefits either to myself or to the party who accepts assignment below.

SIGNED _____ DATE _____

13. INSURED'S OR AUTHORIZED PERSON'S SIGNATURE I authorize payment of medical benefits to the undersigned physician or supplier for services described below.

SIGNED _____

14. DATE OF CURRENT ILLNESS, INJURY, or PREGNANCY (LMP) MM | DD | YY   QUAL.

15. OTHER DATE QUAL. | MM | DD | YY

16. DATES PATIENT UNABLE TO WORK IN CURRENT OCCUPATION FROM MM | DD | YY   TO MM | DD | YY

17. NAME OF REFERRING PROVIDER OR OTHER SOURCE   17a.   17b. NPI

18. HOSPITALIZATION DATES RELATED TO CURRENT SERVICES FROM MM | DD | YY   TO MM | DD | YY

19. ADDITIONAL CLAIM INFORMATION (Designated by NUCC)

20. OUTSIDE LAB?   YES [ ]   NO [ ] $ CHARGES

21. DIAGNOSIS OR NATURE OF ILLNESS OR INJURY Relate A-L to service line below (24E)   ICD Ind. |

A. _____ B. _____ C. _____ D. _____
E. _____ F. _____ G. _____ H. _____
I. _____ J. _____ K. _____ L. _____

22. RESUBMISSION CODE   ORIGINAL REF. NO.

23. PRIOR AUTHORIZATION NUMBER

24. A. DATE(S) OF SERVICE						B. PLACE OF SERVICE	C. EMG	D. PROCEDURES, SERVICES, OR SUPPLIES (Explain Unusual Circumstances)		E. DIAGNOSIS POINTER	F. $ CHARGES	G. DAYS OR UNITS	H. EPSDT Family Plan	I. ID. QUAL	J. RENDERING PROVIDER ID. #
From MM	DD	YY	To MM	DD	YY			CPT/HCPCS	MODIFIER						
1														NPI	
2														NPI	
3														NPI	
4														NPI	
5														NPI	
6														NPI	

25. FEDERAL TAX I.D. NUMBER   SSN [ ] EIN [ ]

26. PATIENT'S ACCOUNT NO.

27. ACCEPT ASSIGNMENT? (For govt. claims, see back)   YES [ ]   NO [ ]

28. TOTAL CHARGE $

29. AMOUNT PAID $

30. Rsvd. for NUCC Use

31. SIGNATURE OF PHYSICIAN OR SUPPLIER INCLUDING DEGREES OR CREDENTIALS (I certify that the statements on the reverse apply to this bill and are made a part thereof.)

SIGNED _____ DATE _____

32. SERVICE FACILITY LOCATION INFORMATION

a. NPI   b.

33. BILLING PROVIDER INFO & PH # ( )

a. NPI   b.

NUCC Instruction Manual available at: www.nucc.org   **PLEASE PRINT OR TYPE**   APPROVED OMB-0938-1197 FORM 1500 (02-12)

Clear Form

Figure 14-2

© 2018 Pearson Education, Inc.

b. Using the source documents, the Capital City Medical Fee Schedule (Figure 14-3), and the blank CMS-1500 form provided (Figure 14-4), complete the following case study for patient Jackson Trenton (Case 14-2):

CASE 14-2

Capital City Medical—123 Unknown Boulevard, Capital City, NY 12345-2222 (555) 555-1234	Patient Information Form
Phil Wells, MD, Mannie Mends, MD, Bette R. Soone, MD	Tax ID: 75-0246810 Group NPI: 1513171216

Patient Information:

Name: (Last, First) Trenton, Jackson ☒ Male ☐ Female Birth Date: 03/12/1942

Address: 319 W. Sun Ct, Township, NY 12345 Phone: (555) 555-7221

Social Security Number: 756-87-2918 Full-Time Student: ☐ Yes ☒ No

Marital Status: ☐ Single ☐ Married ☒ Divorced ☐ Other

Employment:

Employer: Retired Phone: ( )

Address:

Condition Related to: ☐ Auto Accident ☐ Employment ☐ Other Accident

Date of Accident: State:

Emergency Contact: **Phone: ( )**

Primary Insurance: CHAMPVA Phone: ( )

Address: P. O Box 4586, Capital City, NY 12345

Insurance Policyholder's Name: Same ☐ M ☐ F DOB:

Address:

Phone: Relationship to Insured: ☒ Self ☐ Spouse ☐ Child ☐ Other

Employer: Phone: ( )

Employer's Address:

Policy/ID No: 756872918 Group No: Percent Covered: 100 % Copay Amt: $

Secondary Insurance: Phone: ( )

Address:

Insurance Policyholder's Name: ☐ M ☐ F DOB:

Address:

Phone: Relationship to Insured: ☐ Self ☐ Spouse ☐ Child ☐ Other

Employer: Phone: ( )

Employer's Address:

Policy/ID No: Group No: Percent Covered: ___% Copay Amt: $

Reason for Visit: Follow-up on post-traumatic stress disorder.

Known Allergies:

Referred by:

CASE 14–2
● SOAP

01/12/20XX
Assignment of Benefits: Y
Signature on File: Y
Referring Physician: N

S: Jackson Trenton is seen today for a check on his post-traumatic stress disorder.

O: Pt. denies any problems with medication. He needs a refill on Lorazepam.

A: 1. Post-traumatic stress disorder—F43.10

P: 1. Continue medications.
    2. Return in 1 month.

_____

Phil Wells, MD
Family Practice
NPI: 1234567890

CASE 14-2

Patient Name: Jackson Trenton

Capital City Medical
123 Unknown Boulevard, Capital City, NY 12345-2222

Date of Service: 01-12-20XX

New Patient		
Problem Focused	99201	
Expanded Problem, Focused	99202	
Detailed	99203	
Comprehensive	99204	
Comprehensive/High Complex	99205	
Well Exam Infant (up to 12 mos.)	99381	
Well Exam 1–4 yrs.	99382	
Well Exam 5–11 yrs.	99383	
Well Exam 12–17 yrs.	99384	
Well Exam 18–39 yrs.	99385	
Well Exam 40–64 yrs.	99386	

Established Patient		
Post-Op Follow Up Visit	99024	
Minimum	99211	
Problem Focused	99212	X
Expanded Problem Focused	99213	
Detailed	99214	
Comprehensive/High Complex	99215	
Well Exam Infant (up to 12 mos.)	99391	
Well exam 1–4 yrs.	99392	
Well Exam 5–11 yrs.	99393	
Well Exam 12–17 yrs.	99394	
Well Exam 18–39 yrs.	99395	
Well Exam 40–64 yrs.	99396	

Obstetrics		
Total OB Care	59400	

Injections		
Administration Sub. / IM	90772	
Drug		
Dosage		
Allergy	95115	
Cocci Skin Test	86490	
DPT	90701	
Hemophilus	90646	
Influenza	90658	
MMR	90707	
OPV	90712	
Pneumovax	90732	
TB Skin Test	86580	
TD	90718	
Unlisted Immun	90749	
Tetanus Toxoid	90703	
Vaccine/Toxoid Admin <8 Yr Old w/ Counseling	90465	
Vaccine/Toxoid Administration for Adult	90471	

Diagnosis/ICD-10: F43.10

Arthrocentesis/Aspiration/Injection		
Small Joint		20600
Interm Joint		20605
Major Joint		20610

Other Invasive/Noninvasive		
Audiometry		92552
Cast Application		
Location Long Short		
Catheterization		51701
Circumcision		54150
Colposcopy		57452
Colposcopy w/Biopsy		57454
Cryosurgery Premalignant Lesion		
Location (s):		
Cryosurgery Warts		
Location (s):		
Curettement Lesion		
Single		11055
2–4		11056
>4		11057
Diaphragm Fitting		57170
Ear Irrigation		69210
ECG		93000
Endometrial Biopsy		58100
Exc. Lesion Malignant		
Benign		
Location		
Exc. Skin Taqs (1–15)		11200
Each Additional 10		11201
Fracture Treatment		
Loc		
w/Reduc w/o Reduc		
I & D Abscess Single/Simple		10060
Multiple or Comp		10061
I & D Pilonidal Cyst Simple		10080
Pilonidal Cyst Complex		10081
IV Therapy—To One Hour		90760
Each Additional Hour		90761
Laceration Repair		
Location Size Simp/Comp		
Laryngoscopy		31505
Oximetry		94760
Punch Biopsy		
Rhythm Strip		93040
Treadmill		93015
Trigger Point or Tendon Sheath Inj.		20550
Tympanometry		92567

Laboratory	
Amylase	82150
B12	82607
CBC & Diff	85025
Comp Metabolic Panel	80053
Chlamydia Screen	87110
Cholesterol	82465
Digoxin	80162
Electrolytes	80051
Ferritin	82728
Folate	82746
GC Screen	87070
Glucose	82947
Glucose 1 HR	82950
Glycosylated HGB A1C	83036
HCT	85014
HDL	83718
Hep BSAG	87340
Hepatitis panel, acute	80074
HGB	85018
HIV	86703
Iron & TIBC	83550
Kidney Profile	80069
Lead	83655
Liver Profile	80076
Mono Test	86308
Pap Smear	88155
Pregnancy Test	84703
Obstetric Panel	80055
Pro Time	85610
PSA	84153
RPR	86592
Sed. Rate	85651
Stool Culture	87045
Stool O & P	87177
Strep Screen	87880
Theophylline	80198
Thyroid Uptake	84479
TSH	84443
Urinalysis	81000
Urine Culture	87088
Drawing Fee	36415
Specimen Collection	99000
Other:	

I acknowledge receipt of medical services and authorize the release of any medical information necessary to process this claim for healthcare payment only. I do authorize payment to the provider.

Patient Signature: Jackson Trenton

Total Estimated Charges: _____

Payment Amount: _____

Next Appointment: _____

Figure 14-3

Capital City Medical
Fee Schedule

New Patient OV			Punch Biopsy various codes	$80
Problem Focused 99201	$45		Nebulizer various codes	$45
Expanded Problem Focused 99202	$65		Cast Application various codes	$85
Detailed 99203	$85		Laryngoscopy 31505	$255
Comprehensive 99204	$105		Audiometry 92552	$85
Comprehensive/High Complex 99205	$115		Tympanometry 92567	$85
Well Exam infant (less than 1 year) 99381	$45		Ear Irrigation 69210	$25
Well Exam 1–4 yrs. 99382	$50		Diaphragm Fitting 57170	$30
Well Exam 5–11 yrs. 99383	$55		IV Therapy (up to one hour) 90760	$65
Well Exam 12–17 yrs. 99384	$65		Each additional hour 90761	$50
Well Exam 18–39 yrs. 99385	$85		Oximetry 94760	$10
Well Exam 40–64 yrs. 99386	$105		ECG 93000	$75
Established Patient OV			Holter Monitor various codes	$170
Post Op Follow Up Visit 99024	$0		Rhythm Strip 93040	$60
Minimum 99211	$35		Treadmill 93015	$375
Problem Focused 99212	$45		Cocci Skin Test 86490	$20
Expanded Problem Focused 99213	$55		X-ray, spine, chest, bone—any area various codes	$275
Detailed 99214	$65		Avulsion Nail 11730	$200
Comprehensive/High Complex 99215	$75		**Laboratory**	
Well exam infant (less than 1 year) 99391	$35		Amylase 82150	$40
Well Exam 1–4 yrs. 99392	$40		B12 82607	$30
Well Exam 5–11 yrs. 99393	$45		CBC & Diff 85025	$95
Well Exam 12–17 yrs. 99394	$55		Comp Metabolic Panel 80053	$75
Well Exam 18–39 yrs. 99395	$65		Chlamydia Screen 87110	$70
Well Exam 40–64 yrs. 99396	$75		Cholestrerol 82465	$75
Obstetrics			Digoxin 80162	$40
Total OB Care 59400	$1700		Electrolytes 80051	$70
Injections			Estrogen, Total 82672	$50
Administration 90772	$10		Ferritin 82728	$40
Allergy 95115	$35		Folate 82746	$30
DPT 90701	$50		GC Screen 87070	$60
Drug various codes	$35		Glucose 82947	$35
Influenza 90658	$25		Glycosylated HGB A1C 83036	$45
MMR 90707	$50		HCT 85014	$30
OPV 90712	$40		HDL 83718	$35
Pneumovax 90732	$35		HGB 85018	$30
TB Skin Test 86580	$15		Hep BSAG 83740	$40
TD 90718	$40		Hepatitis panel, acute 80074	$95
Tetanus Toxoid 90703	$40		HIV 86703	$100
Vaccine/Toxoid Administration for Younger			Iron & TIBC 83550	$45
Than 8 Years Old w/ counseling 90465	$10		Kidney Profile 80069	$95
Vaccine/Toxoid Administration for Adult 90471	$10		Lead 83665	$55
Arthrocentesis/Aspiration/Injection			Lipase 83690	$40
Small Joint 20600	$50		Lipid Panel 80061	$95
Interm Joint 20605	$60		Liver Profile 80076	$95
Major Joint 20610	$70		Mono Test 86308	$30
Trigger Point/Tendon Sheath Inj. 20550	$90		Pap Smear 88155	$90
Other Invasive/Noninvasive Procedures			Pap Collection/Supervision 88142	$95
Catheterization 51701	$55		Pregnancy Test 84703	$90
Circumcision 54150	$150		Obstetric Panel 80055	$85
Colposcopy 57452	$225		Pro Time 85610	$50
Colposcopy w/Biopsy 57454	$250		PSA 84153	$50
Cryosurgery Premalignant Lesion various codes	$160		RPR 86592	$55
Endometrial Biopsy 58100	$190		Sed. Rate 85651	$50
Excision Lesion Malignant various codes	$145		Stool Culture 87045	$80
Excision Lesion Benign various codes	$125		Stool O & P 87177	$105
Curettement Lesion			Strep Screen 87880	$35
Single 11055	$70		Theophylline 80198	$40
2–4 11056	$80		Thyroid Uptake 84479	$75
>4 11057	$90		TSH 84443	$50
Excision Skin Tags (1–15) 11200	$55		Urinalysis 81000	$35
Each Additional 10 11201	$30		Urine Culture 87088	$80
I & D Abscess Single/Simple 10060	$75		Drawing Fee 36415	$15
Multiple/Complex 10061	$95		Specimen Collection 99000	$10
I & D Pilonidal Cyst Simple 10080	$105			
I & D Pilonidal Cyst Complex 10081	$130			
Laceration Repair various codes	$60			

HEALTH INSURANCE CLAIM FORM

APPROVED BY NATIONAL UNIFORM CLAIM COMMITTEE (NUCC) 02/12

| | PICA | | | | | | | | | | PICA | | |

1. MEDICARE	MEDICAID	TRICARE	CHAMPVA	GROUP HEALTH PLAN	FECA BLK LUNG	OTHER	1a. INSURED'S I.D. NUMBER	(For Program in Item 1)
☒ (Medicare#)	(Medicaid#)	(ID#/DoD#)	(Member ID#)	(ID#)	(ID#)	(ID#)		

2. PATIENT'S NAME (Last Name, First Name, Middle Initial)

3. PATIENT'S BIRTH DATE MM | DD | YY   SEX   M ☐   F ☐

4. INSURED'S NAME (Last Name, First Name, Middle Initial)

5. PATIENT'S ADDRESS (No., Street)

6. PATIENT RELATIONSHIP TO INSURED   Self ☐   Spouse ☐   Child ☐   Other ☐

7. INSURED'S ADDRESS (No., Street)

CITY | STATE

8. RESERVED FOR NUCC USE

CITY | STATE

ZIP CODE | TELEPHONE (Include Area Code) ( )

ZIP CODE | TELEPHONE (Include Area Code) ( )

9. OTHER INSURED'S NAME (Last Name, First Name, Middle Initial)

10. IS PATIENT'S CONDITION RELATED TO:

11. INSURED'S POLICY GROUP OR FECA NUMBER

a. OTHER INSURED'S POLICY OR GROUP NUMBER

a. EMPLOYMENT? (Current or Previous)   YES ☐   NO ☐

a. INSURED'S DATE OF BIRTH MM | DD | YY   SEX   M ☐   F ☐

b. RESERVED FOR NUCC USE

b. AUTO ACCIDENT?   PLACE (State)   YES ☐   NO ☐

b. OTHER CLAIM ID (Designated by NUCC)

c. RESERVED FOR NUCC USE

c. OTHER ACCIDENT?   YES ☐   NO ☐

c. INSURANCE PLAN NAME OR PROGRAM NAME

d. INSURANCE PLAN NAME OR PROGRAM NAME

10d. CLAIM CODES (Designated by NUCC)

d. IS THERE ANOTHER HEALTH BENEFIT PLAN?   YES ☐   NO ☐   If yes, complete items 9, 9a, and 9d.

READ BACK OF FORM BEFORE COMPLETING & SIGNING THIS FORM.
12. PATIENT'S OR AUTHORIZED PERSON'S SIGNATURE I authorize the release of any medical or other information necessary to process this claim. I also request payment of government benefits either to myself or to the party who accepts assignment below.

SIGNED _____ DATE _____

13. INSURED'S OR AUTHORIZED PERSON'S SIGNATURE I authorize payment of medical benefits to the undersigned physician or supplier for services described below.

SIGNED _____

14. DATE OF CURRENT ILLNESS, INJURY, or PREGNANCY (LMP) MM | DD | YY   QUAL.

15. OTHER DATE QUAL.   MM | DD | YY

16. DATES PATIENT UNABLE TO WORK IN CURRENT OCCUPATION FROM MM | DD | YY   TO MM | DD | YY

17. NAME OF REFERRING PROVIDER OR OTHER SOURCE   17a.   17b. NPI

18. HOSPITALIZATION DATES RELATED TO CURRENT SERVICES FROM MM | DD | YY   TO MM | DD | YY

19. ADDITIONAL CLAIM INFORMATION (Designated by NUCC)

20. OUTSIDE LAB?   YES ☐   NO ☐ $ CHARGES

21. DIAGNOSIS OR NATURE OF ILLNESS OR INJURY Relate A-L to service line below (24E)   ICD Ind.

A. |___| B. |___| C. |___| D. |___|
E. |___| F. |___| G. |___| H. |___|
I. |___| J. |___| K. |___| L. |___|

22. RESUBMISSION CODE   ORIGINAL REF. NO.

23. PRIOR AUTHORIZATION NUMBER

24. A. DATE(S) OF SERVICE						B. PLACE OF SERVICE	C. EMG	D. PROCEDURES, SERVICES, OR SUPPLIES (Explain Unusual Circumstances) CPT/HCPCS MODIFIER	E. DIAGNOSIS POINTER	F. $ CHARGES	G. DAYS OR UNITS	H. EPSDT Family Plan	I. ID. QUAL.	J. RENDERING PROVIDER ID. #
From MM	DD	YY	To MM	DD	YY									
1													NPI	
2													NPI	
3													NPI	
4													NPI	
5													NPI	
6													NPI	

25. FEDERAL TAX I.D. NUMBER   SSN EIN ☐

26. PATIENT'S ACCOUNT NO.

27. ACCEPT ASSIGNMENT? (For govt. claims, see back)   YES ☐   NO ☐

28. TOTAL CHARGE $

29. AMOUNT PAID $

30. Rsvd. for NUCC Use

31. SIGNATURE OF PHYSICIAN OR SUPPLIER INCLUDING DEGREES OR CREDENTIALS (I certify that the statements on the reverse apply to this bill and are made a part thereof.)

SIGNED _____ DATE _____

32. SERVICE FACILITY LOCATION INFORMATION

a. NPI   b.

33. BILLING PROVIDER INFO & PH # ( )

a. NPI   b.

Clear Form

PATIENT AND INSURED INFORMATION

PHYSICIAN OR SUPPLIER INFORMATION

Figure 14-4

© 2018 Pearson Education, Inc.

c. Using the source documents, the Capital City Medical Fee Schedule (Figure 14-5), and the blank CMS-1500 form provided (Figure 14-6), complete the following case study for patient Stephanie Reagan (Case 14-3):

CASE 14-3

Capital City Medical—123 Unknown Boulevard, Capital City, NY 12345-2222 (555) 555-1234

Phil Wells, MD, Mannie Mends, MD, Bette R. Soone, MD

Patient Information Form

Tax ID: 75-0246810

Group NPI: 1513171216

Patient Information:

Name: (Last, First) Reagan, Stephanie   ❑ Male ☒ Female   Birth Date: 09/10/1984

Address: 11 Twilight Ct., Capital City, NY 12345   Phone: (555) 555-4179

Social Security Number: 877-93-1688   Full-Time Student: ❑ Yes ☒ No

Marital Status: ❑ Single ☒ Married ❑ Divorced ❑ Other

Employment:

Employer: The Bullpen Sports Bar   Phone: (555) 555-2290

Address: 79 Point Plaza, Capital City, NY 12345

Condition Related to: ❑ Auto Accident ❑ Employment ❑ Other Accident

Date of Accident: _____ State: _____

Emergency Contact: _____ **Phone: ( )** _____

Primary Insurance: Tricare   Phone: ( ) _____

Address: 7594 Forces-Run Rd, Militaryville, NY 12345

Insurance Policyholder's Name: Calvin Reagan   ☒ M ❑ F DOB: 03/12/1983

Address: Same

Phone: _____ Relationship to Insured: ❑ Self ☒ Spouse ❑ Child ❑ Other

Employer: U. S. Air Force   Phone: ( ) _____

Employer's Address: 196, Airport Rd, Capital City, NY 12345

Policy/ID No: 333-48-1076   Group No: _____ Percent Covered: ___% Copay Amt: $35.00

Secondary Insurance: _____   Phone: ( ) _____

Address: _____

Insurance Policyholder's Name: _____   ❑ M ❑ F DOB: _____

Address: _____

Phone: _____ Relationship to Insured: ❑ Self ❑ Spouse ❑ Child ❑ Other

Employer: _____   Phone: ( ) _____

Employer's Address: _____

Policy/ID No: _____ Group No: _____ Percent Covered: ___% Copay Amt: $_____

Reason for Visit: I think that I have a yeast infection.

Known Allergies: _____

Referred by: _____

Figure 14-5

Capital City Medical
Fee Schedule

New Patient OV			Punch Biopsy various codes	$80
Problem Focused 99201	$45		Nebulizer various codes	$45
Expanded Problem Focused 99202	$65		Cast Application various codes	$85
Detailed 99203	$85		Laryngoscopy 31505	$255
Comprehensive 99204	$105		Audiometry 92552	$85
Comprehensive/High Complex 99205	$115		Tympanometry 92567	$85
Well Exam infant (less than 1 year) 99381	$45		Ear Irrigation 69210	$25
Well Exam 1–4 yrs. 99382	$50		Diaphragm Fitting 57170	$30
Well Exam 5–11 yrs. 99383	$55		IV Therapy (up to one hour) 90760	$65
Well Exam 12–17 yrs. 99384	$65		Each additional hour 90761	$50
Well Exam 18–39 yrs. 99385	$85		Oximetry 94760	$10
Well Exam 40–64 yrs. 99386	$105		ECG 93000	$75
Established Patient OV			Holter Monitor various codes	$170
Post Op Follow Up Visit 99024	$0		Rhythm Strip 93040	$60
Minimum 99211	$35		Treadmill 93015	$375
Problem Focused 99212	$45		Cocci Skin Test 86490	$20
Expanded Problem Focused 99213	$55		X-ray, spine, chest, bone—any area various codes	$275
Detailed 99214	$65		Avulsion Nail 11730	$200
Comprehensive/High Complex 99215	$75		**Laboratory**	
Well exam infant (less than 1 year) 99391	$35		Amylase 82150	$40
Well Exam 1–4 yrs. 99392	$40		B12 82607	$30
Well Exam 5–11 yrs. 99393	$45		CBC & Diff 85025	$95
Well Exam 12–17 yrs. 99394	$55		Comp Metabolic Panel 80053	$75
Well Exam 18–39 yrs. 99395	$65		Chlamydia Screen 87110	$70
Well Exam 40–64 yrs. 99396	$75		Cholestrerol 82465	$75
Obstetrics			Digoxin 80162	$40
Total OB Care 59400	$1700		Electrolytes 80051	$70
Injections			Estrogen, Total 82672	$50
Administration 90772	$10		Ferritin 82728	$40
Allergy 95115	$35		Folate 82746	$30
DPT 90701	$50		GC Screen 87070	$60
Drug various codes	$35		Glucose 82947	$35
Influenza 90658	$25		Glycosylated HGB A1C 83036	$45
MMR 90707	$50		HCT 85014	$30
OPV 90712	$40		HDL 83718	$35
Pneumovax 90732	$35		HGB 85018	$30
TB Skin Test 86580	$15		Hep BSAG 83740	$40
TD 90718	$40		Hepatitis panel, acute 80074	$95
Tetanus Toxoid 90703	$40		HIV 86703	$100
Vaccine/Toxoid Administration for Younger			Iron & TIBC 83550	$45
Than 8 Years Old w/ counseling 90465	$10		Kidney Profile 80069	$95
Vaccine/Toxoid Administration for Adult 90471	$10		Lead 83665	$55
Arthrocentesis/Aspiration/Injection			Lipase 83690	$40
Small Joint 20600	$50		Lipid Panel 80061	$95
Interm Joint 20605	$60		Liver Profile 80076	$95
Major Joint 20610	$70		Mono Test 86308	$30
Trigger Point/Tendon Sheath Inj. 20550	$90		Pap Smear 88155	$90
Other Invasive/Noninvasive Procedures			Pap Collection/Supervision 88142	$95
Catheterization 51701	$55		Pregnancy Test 84703	$90
Circumcision 54150	$150		Obstetric Panel 80055	$85
Colposcopy 57452	$225		Pro Time 85610	$50
Colposcopy w/Biopsy 57454	$250		PSA 84153	$50
Cryosurgery Premalignant Lesion various codes	$160		RPR 86592	$55
Endometrial Biopsy 58100	$190		Sed. Rate 85651	$50
Excision Lesion Malignant various codes	$145		Stool Culture 87045	$80
Excision Lesion Benign various codes	$125		Stool O & P 87177	$105
Curettement Lesion			Strep Screen 87880	$35
Single 11055	$70		Theophylline 80198	$40
2–4 11056	$80		Thyroid Uptake 84479	$75
>4 11057	$90		TSH 84443	$50
Excision Skin Tags (1–15) 11200	$55		Urinalysis 81000	$35
Each Additional 10 11201	$30		Urine Culture 87088	$80
I & D Abscess Single/Simple 10060	$75		Drawing Fee 36415	$15
Multiple/Complex 10061	$95		Specimen Collection 99000	$10
I & D Pilonidal Cyst Simple 10080	$105			
I & D Pilonidal Cyst Complex 10081	$130			
Laceration Repair various codes	$60			

HEALTH INSURANCE CLAIM FORM

APPROVED BY NATIONAL UNIFORM CLAIM COMMITTEE (NUCC) 02/12

| | PICA | | | | | | | PICA | | |

1. MEDICARE	MEDICAID	TRICARE	CHAMPVA	GROUP HEALTH PLAN	FECA BLK LUNG	OTHER	1a. INSURED'S I.D. NUMBER	(For Program in Item 1)
[X] (Medicare#)	(Medicaid#)	(ID#/DoD#)	(Member ID#)	(ID#)	(ID#)	(ID#)		

2. PATIENT'S NAME (Last Name, First Name, Middle Initial)

3. PATIENT'S BIRTH DATE MM DD YY **SEX** M □ F □

4. INSURED'S NAME (Last Name, First Name, Middle Initial)

5. PATIENT'S ADDRESS (No., Street)

6. PATIENT RELATIONSHIP TO INSURED Self □ Spouse □ Child □ Other □

7. INSURED'S ADDRESS (No., Street)

CITY / STATE

8. RESERVED FOR NUCC USE

CITY / STATE

ZIP CODE / TELEPHONE (Include Area Code) ( )

ZIP CODE / TELEPHONE (Include Area Code) ( )

9. OTHER INSURED'S NAME (Last Name, First Name, Middle Initial)

10. IS PATIENT'S CONDITION RELATED TO:

11. INSURED'S POLICY GROUP OR FECA NUMBER

a. OTHER INSURED'S POLICY OR GROUP NUMBER

a. EMPLOYMENT? (Current or Previous) YES □ NO □

a. INSURED'S DATE OF BIRTH MM DD YY **SEX** M □ F □

b. RESERVED FOR NUCC USE

b. AUTO ACCIDENT? YES □ NO □ PLACE (State)

b. OTHER CLAIM ID (Designated by NUCC)

c. RESERVED FOR NUCC USE

c. OTHER ACCIDENT? YES □ NO □

c. INSURANCE PLAN NAME OR PROGRAM NAME

d. INSURANCE PLAN NAME OR PROGRAM NAME

10d. CLAIM CODES (Designated by NUCC)

d. IS THERE ANOTHER HEALTH BENEFIT PLAN? YES □ NO □ *If yes,* complete items 9, 9a, and 9d.

READ BACK OF FORM BEFORE COMPLETING & SIGNING THIS FORM.
12. PATIENT'S OR AUTHORIZED PERSON'S SIGNATURE I authorize the release of any medical or other information necessary to process this claim. I also request payment of government benefits either to myself or to the party who accepts assignment below.

SIGNED _____ DATE _____

13. INSURED'S OR AUTHORIZED PERSON'S SIGNATURE I authorize payment of medical benefits to the undersigned physician or supplier for services described below.

SIGNED _____

14. DATE OF CURRENT ILLNESS, INJURY, or PREGNANCY (LMP) MM DD YY QUAL.

15. OTHER DATE QUAL. MM DD YY

16. DATES PATIENT UNABLE TO WORK IN CURRENT OCCUPATION FROM MM DD YY TO MM DD YY

17. NAME OF REFERRING PROVIDER OR OTHER SOURCE
17a.
17b. NPI

18. HOSPITALIZATION DATES RELATED TO CURRENT SERVICES FROM MM DD YY TO MM DD YY

19. ADDITIONAL CLAIM INFORMATION (Designated by NUCC)

20. OUTSIDE LAB? YES □ NO □ $ CHARGES

21. DIAGNOSIS OR NATURE OF ILLNESS OR INJURY Relate A-L to service line below (24E) ICD Ind.

A. ___ B. ___ C. ___ D. ___
E. ___ F. ___ G. ___ H. ___
I. ___ J. ___ K. ___ L. ___

22. RESUBMISSION CODE ___ ORIGINAL REF. NO.

23. PRIOR AUTHORIZATION NUMBER

24. A. DATE(S) OF SERVICE From MM DD YY To MM DD YY	B. PLACE OF SERVICE	C. EMG	D. PROCEDURES, SERVICES, OR SUPPLIES (Explain Unusual Circumstances) CPT/HCPCS MODIFIER	E. DIAGNOSIS POINTER	F. $ CHARGES	G. DAYS OR UNITS	H. EPSDT Family Plan	I. ID. QUAL	J. RENDERING PROVIDER ID. #
1									NPI
2									NPI
3									NPI
4									NPI
5									NPI
6									NPI

25. FEDERAL TAX I.D. NUMBER SSN EIN

26. PATIENT'S ACCOUNT NO.

27. ACCEPT ASSIGNMENT? (For govt. claims, see back) YES □ NO □

28. TOTAL CHARGE $

29. AMOUNT PAID $

30. Rsvd. for NUCC Use

31. SIGNATURE OF PHYSICIAN OR SUPPLIER INCLUDING DEGREES OR CREDENTIALS (I certify that the statements on the reverse apply to this bill and are made a part thereof.)

SIGNED _____ DATE _____

32. SERVICE FACILITY LOCATION INFORMATION

a. NPI b.

33. BILLING PROVIDER INFO & PH # ( )

a. NPI b.

NUCC Instruction Manual available at: www.nucc.org

PLEASE PRINT OR TYPE

APPROVED OMB-0938-1197 FORM 1500 (02-12)

Clear Form

Figure 14-6

d. Using the source documents, the Capital City Medical Fee Schedule (Figure 14-7), and the blank CMS-1500 form provided (Figure 14-8), complete the following case study for patient Allen Won (Case 14-4):

CASE 14-4

Capital City Medical—123 Unknown Boulevard, Capital City, NY 12345-2222 (555) 555-1234	Patient Information Form
	Tax ID: 75-0246810
Phil Wells, MD, Mannie Mends, MD, Bette R. Soone, MD	Group NPI: 1513171216

Patient Information:

Name: (Last, First) Won, Allen ☒ Male ☐ Female Birth Date: 08/14/2002

Address: 448 Sunset Ln, Capital City, NY 12345 Phone: (555) 555-5312

Social Security Number: 505-72-6853 Full-Time Student: ☒ Yes ☐ No

Marital Status: ☐ Single ☐ Married ☐ Divorced ☐ Other

Employment:

Employer: _____ Phone: ( ) _____

Address: _____

Condition Related to: ☐ Auto Accident ☐ Employment ☐ Other Accident

Date of Accident: _____ State: _____

Emergency Contact: _____ **Phone: ( )** _____

Primary Insurance: Tricare Phone: ( ) _____

Address: 7594 Forces-Run Rd, Militaryville, NY 12345

Insurance Policyholder's Name: Victor Won ☒ M ☐ F DOB: 04/24/1986

Address: Same

Phone: _____ Relationship to Insured: ☐ Self ☐ Spouse ☒ Child ☐ Other

Employer: U.S. Marine Corp. Phone: ( ) _____

Employer's Address: 1819 Base Ave, Capital City, NY 12345

Policy/ID No: 983-50-5983 Group No: _____ Percent Covered: ___% Copay Amt: $35.00

Secondary Insurance: _____ Phone: ( ) _____

Address: _____

Insurance Policyholder's Name: _____ ☐ M ☐ F DOB: _____

Address: _____

Phone: _____ Relationship to Insured: ☐ Self ☐ Spouse ☐ Child ☐ Other

Employer: _____ Phone: ( ) _____

Employer's Address: _____

Policy/ID No: _____ Group No: _____ Percent Covered: ___% Copay Amt: $_____

Reason for Visit: My son has head lice.

Known Allergies: _____

Referred by: _____

CASE 14-4
SOAP

04/16/20XX
Assignment of Benefits: Y
Signature on File: Y
Referring Physician: N

S: Allen Won presents in the office today for head lice. He may have gotten it from a classmate who was sent home on Monday for the same problem.

O: There is evidence of lice eggs on the scalp. Skin presents unremarkable, without rash or lacerations.

A: 1. Pediculus capitis—B85.0

P: 1. Lindane shampoo daily.
   2. Keep clothes and linens clean.
   3. Mother told that it may take more than one treatment to rid the head of lice. Mother was advised to shave Allen's head, for best results.

Phil Wells, MD
Family Practice
NPI: 1234567890

CASE 14-4

Patient Name Allen Won

Capital City Medical
123 Unknown Boulevard, Capital City, NY 12345-2222

Date of Service
04-16-20XX

New Patient			Arthrocentesis/Aspiration/Injection			Laboratory	
Problem Focused	99201		Arthrocentesis/Aspiration/Injection			Amylase	82150
Expanded Problem, Focused	99202		Small Joint		20600	B12	82607
Detailed	99203		Interm Joint		20605	CBC & Diff	85025
Comprehensive	99204		Major Joint		20610	Comp Metabolic Panel	80053
Comprehensive/High Complex	99205		**Other Invasive/Noninvasive**			Chlamydia Screen	87110
Well Exam Infant (up to 12 mos.)	99381		Audiometry		92552	Cholesterol	82465
Well Exam 1–4 yrs.	99382		Cast Application			Digoxin	80162
Well Exam 5–11 yrs.	99383		Location Long Short			Electrolytes	80051
Well Exam 12–17 yrs.	99384		Catheterization		51701	Ferritin	82728
Well Exam 18–39 yrs.	99385		Circumcision		54150	Folate	82746
Well Exam 40–64 yrs.	99386		Colposcopy		57452	GC Screen	87070
			Colposcopy w/Biopsy		57454	Glucose	82947
			Cryosurgery Premalignant Lesion			Glucose 1 HR	82950
			Location (s):			Glycosylated HGB A1C	83036
Established Patient			Cryosurgery Warts			HCT	85014
Post-Op Follow Up Visit	99024		Location (s):			HDL	83718
Minimum	99211		Curettement Lesion			Hep BSAG	87340
Problem Focused	99212	X	Single		11055	Hepatitis panel, acute	80074
Expanded Problem Focused	99213		2–4		11056	HGB	85018
Detailed	99214		>4		11057	HIV	86703
Comprehensive/High Complex	99215		Diaphragm Fitting		57170	Iron & TIBC	83550
Well Exam Infant (up to 12 mos.)	99391		Ear Irrigation		69210	Kidney Profile	80069
Well exam 1–4 yrs.	99392		ECG		93000	Lead	83655
Well Exam 5–11 yrs.	99393		Endometrial Biopsy		58100	Liver Profile	80076
Well Exam 12–17 yrs.	99394		Exc. Lesion Malignant			Mono Test	86308
Well Exam 18–39 yrs.	99395		Benign			Pap Smear	88155
Well Exam 40–64 yrs.	99396		Location			Pregnancy Test	84703
Obstetrics			Exc. Skin Tags (1–15)		11200	Obstetric Panel	80055
Total OB Care	59400		Each Additional 10		11201	Pro Time	85610
Injections			Fracture Treatment			PSA	84153
Administration Sub. / IM	90772		Loc			RPR	86592
Drug			w/Reduc		w/o Reduc	Sed. Rate	85651
Dosage			I & D Abscess Single/Simple		10060	Stool Culture	87045
Allergy	95115		Multiple or Comp		10061	Stool O & P	87177
Cocci Skin Test	86490		I & D Pilonidal Cyst Simple		10080	Strep Screen	87880
DPT	90701		Pilonidal Cyst Complex		10081	Theophylline	80198
Hemophilus	90646		IV Therapy—To One Hour		90760	Thyroid Uptake	84479
Influenza	90658		Each Additional Hour		90761	TSH	84443
MMR	90707		Laceration Repair			Urinalysis	81000
OPV	90712		Location Size Simp/Comp			Urine Culture	87088
Pneumovax	90732		Laryngoscopy		31505	Drawing Fee	36415
TB Skin Test	86580		Oximetry		94760	Specimen Collection	99000
TD	90718		Punch Biopsy			**Other:**	
Unlisted Immun	90749		Rhythm Strip		93040		
Tetanus Toxoid	90703		Treadmill		93015		
Vaccine/Toxoid Admin <8 Yr Old w/ Counseling	90465		Trigger Point or Tendon Sheath Inj.		20550		
Vaccine/Toxoid Administration for Adult	90471		Tympanometry		92567		

Diagnosis/ICD-10: B85.0

I acknowledge receipt of medical services and authorize the release of any medical information necessary to process this claim for healthcare payment only. I do authorize payment to the provider.

Total Estimated Charges: _____

Payment Amount: _____

Patient Signature *Victor Won*

Next Appointment: _____

Figure 14-7

Capital City Medical
Fee Schedule

New Patient OV		Punch Biopsy various codes	$80
Problem Focused 99201	$45	Nebulizer various codes	$45
Expanded Problem Focused 99202	$65	Cast Application various codes	$85
Detailed 99203	$85	Laryngoscopy 31505	$255
Comprehensive 99204	$105	Audiometry 92552	$85
Comprehensive/High Complex 99205	$115	Tympanometry 92567	$85
Well Exam infant (less than 1 year) 99381	$45	Ear Irrigation 69210	$25
Well Exam 1–4 yrs. 99382	$50	Diaphragm Fitting 57170	$30
Well Exam 5–11 yrs. 99383	$55	IV Therapy (up to one hour) 90760	$65
Well Exam 12–17 yrs. 99384	$65	Each additional hour 90761	$50
Well Exam 18–39 yrs. 99385	$85	Oximetry 94760	$10
Well Exam 40–64 yrs. 99386	$105	ECG 93000	$75
Established Patient OV		Holter Monitor various codes	$170
Post Op Follow Up Visit 99024	$0	Rhythm Strip 93040	$60
Minimum 99211	$35	Treadmill 93015	$375
Problem Focused 99212	$45	Cocci Skin Test 86490	$20
Expanded Problem Focused 99213	$55	X-ray, spine, chest, bone—any area various codes	$275
Detailed 99214	$65	Avulsion Nail 11730	$200
Comprehensive/High Complex 99215	$75	**Laboratory**	
Well exam infant (less than 1 year) 99391	$35	Amylase 82150	$40
Well Exam 1–4 yrs. 99392	$40	B12 82607	$30
Well Exam 5–11 yrs. 99393	$45	CBC & Diff 85025	$95
Well Exam 12–17 yrs. 99394	$55	Comp Metabolic Panel 80053	$75
Well Exam 18–39 yrs. 99395	$65	Chlamydia Screen 87110	$70
Well Exam 40–64 yrs. 99396	$75	Cholestrerol 82465	$75
Obstetrics		Digoxin 80162	$40
Total OB Care 59400	$1700	Electrolytes 80051	$70
Injections		Estrogen, Total 82672	$50
Administration 90772	$10	Ferritin 82728	$40
Allergy 95115	$35	Folate 82746	$30
DPT 90701	$50	GC Screen 87070	$60
Drug various codes	$35	Glucose 82947	$35
Influenza 90658	$25	Glycosylated HGB A1C 83036	$45
MMR 90707	$50	HCT 85014	$30
OPV 90712	$40	HDL 83718	$35
Pneumovax 90732	$35	HGB 85018	$30
TB Skin Test 86580	$15	Hep BSAG 83740	$40
TD 90718	$40	Hepatitis panel, acute 80074	$95
Tetanus Toxoid 90703	$40	HIV 86703	$100
Vaccine/Toxoid Administration for Younger		Iron & TIBC 83550	$45
Than 8 Years Old w/ counseling 90465	$10	Kidney Profile 80069	$95
Vaccine/Toxoid Administration for Adult 90471	$10	Lead 83665	$55
Arthrocentesis/Aspiration/Injection		Lipase 83690	$40
Small Joint 20600	$50	Lipid Panel 80061	$95
Interm Joint 20605	$60	Liver Profile 80076	$95
Major Joint 20610	$70	Mono Test 86308	$30
Trigger Point/Tendon Sheath Inj. 20550	$90	Pap Smear 88155	$90
Other Invasive/Noninvasive Procedures		Pap Collection/Supervision 88142	$95
Catheterization 51701	$55	Pregnancy Test 84703	$90
Circumcision 54150	$150	Obstetric Panel 80055	$85
Colposcopy 57452	$225	Pro Time 85610	$50
Colposcopy w/Biopsy 57454	$250	PSA 84153	$50
Cryosurgery Premalignant Lesion various codes	$160	RPR 86592	$55
Endometrial Biopsy 58100	$190	Sed. Rate 85651	$50
Excision Lesion Malignant various codes	$145	Stool Culture 87045	$80
Excision Lesion Benign various codes	$125	Stool O & P 87177	$105
Curettement Lesion		Strep Screen 87880	$35
Single 11055	$70	Theophylline 80198	$40
2–4 11056	$80	Thyroid Uptake 84479	$75
>4 11057	$90	TSH 84443	$50
Excision Skin Tags (1–15) 11200	$55	Urinalysis 81000	$35
Each Additional 10 11201	$30	Urine Culture 87088	$80
I & D Abscess Single/Simple 10060	$75	Drawing Fee 36415	$15
Multiple/Complex 10061	$95	Specimen Collection 99000	$10
I & D Pilonidal Cyst Simple 10080	$105		
I & D Pilonidal Cyst Complex 10081	$130		
Laceration Repair various codes	$60		

HEALTH INSURANCE CLAIM FORM

APPROVED BY NATIONAL UNIFORM CLAIM COMMITTEE (NUCC) 02/12

CARRIER

| | PICA | | | | | | | | | | PICA | |

1. MEDICARE ☒ (Medicare#) MEDICAID ☐ (Medicaid#) TRICARE ☐ (ID#/DoD#) CHAMPVA ☐ (Member ID#) GROUP HEALTH PLAN ☐ (ID#) FECA BLK LUNG ☐ (ID#) OTHER ☐ (ID#)

1a. INSURED'S I.D. NUMBER (For Program in Item 1)

2. PATIENT'S NAME (Last Name, First Name, Middle Initial)

3. PATIENT'S BIRTH DATE MM DD YY   SEX M☐ F☐

4. INSURED'S NAME (Last Name, First Name, Middle Initial)

5. PATIENT'S ADDRESS (No., Street)

6. PATIENT RELATIONSHIP TO INSURED Self☐ Spouse☐ Child☐ Other☐

7. INSURED'S ADDRESS (No., Street)

CITY   STATE

8. RESERVED FOR NUCC USE

CITY   STATE

ZIP CODE   TELEPHONE (Include Area Code) (   )

ZIP CODE   TELEPHONE (Include Area Code) (   )

9. OTHER INSURED'S NAME (Last Name, First Name, Middle Initial)

10. IS PATIENT'S CONDITION RELATED TO:

11. INSURED'S POLICY GROUP OR FECA NUMBER

a. OTHER INSURED'S POLICY OR GROUP NUMBER

a. EMPLOYMENT? (Current or Previous) YES☐ NO☐

a. INSURED'S DATE OF BIRTH MM DD YY   SEX M☐ F☐

b. RESERVED FOR NUCC USE

b. AUTO ACCIDENT? YES☐ NO☐ PLACE (State)

b. OTHER CLAIM ID (Designated by NUCC)

c. RESERVED FOR NUCC USE

c. OTHER ACCIDENT? YES☐ NO☐

c. INSURANCE PLAN NAME OR PROGRAM NAME

d. INSURANCE PLAN NAME OR PROGRAM NAME

10d. CLAIM CODES (Designated by NUCC)

d. IS THERE ANOTHER HEALTH BENEFIT PLAN? YES☐ NO☐ If yes, complete items 9, 9a, and 9d.

READ BACK OF FORM BEFORE COMPLETING & SIGNING THIS FORM.
12. PATIENT'S OR AUTHORIZED PERSON'S SIGNATURE I authorize the release of any medical or other information necessary to process this claim. I also request payment of government benefits either to myself or to the party who accepts assignment below.

SIGNED _____ DATE _____

13. INSURED'S OR AUTHORIZED PERSON'S SIGNATURE I authorize payment of medical benefits to the undersigned physician or supplier for services described below.

SIGNED _____

14. DATE OF CURRENT ILLNESS, INJURY, or PREGNANCY (LMP) MM DD YY   QUAL.

15. OTHER DATE QUAL.   MM DD YY

16. DATES PATIENT UNABLE TO WORK IN CURRENT OCCUPATION FROM MM DD YY TO MM DD YY

17. NAME OF REFERRING PROVIDER OR OTHER SOURCE 17a. 17b. NPI

18. HOSPITALIZATION DATES RELATED TO CURRENT SERVICES FROM MM DD YY TO MM DD YY

19. ADDITIONAL CLAIM INFORMATION (Designated by NUCC)

20. OUTSIDE LAB? YES☐ NO☐ $ CHARGES

21. DIAGNOSIS OR NATURE OF ILLNESS OR INJURY Relate A-L to service line below (24E) ICD Ind.

A. ___ B. ___ C. ___ D. ___
E. ___ F. ___ G. ___ H. ___
I. ___ J. ___ K. ___ L. ___

22. RESUBMISSION CODE   ORIGINAL REF. NO.

23. PRIOR AUTHORIZATION NUMBER

24. A. DATE(S) OF SERVICE From MM DD YY To MM DD YY	B. PLACE OF SERVICE	C. EMG	D. PROCEDURES, SERVICES, OR SUPPLIES (Explain Unusual Circumstances) CPT/HCPCS MODIFIER	E. DIAGNOSIS POINTER	F. $ CHARGES	G. DAYS OR UNITS	H. EPSDT Family Plan	I. ID. QUAL	J. RENDERING PROVIDER ID. #
1									NPI
2									NPI
3									NPI
4									NPI
5									NPI
6									NPI

25. FEDERAL TAX I.D. NUMBER   SSN EIN ☐

26. PATIENT'S ACCOUNT NO.

27. ACCEPT ASSIGNMENT? (For govt. claims, see back) YES☐ NO☐

28. TOTAL CHARGE $

29. AMOUNT PAID $

30. Rsvd. for NUCC Use

31. SIGNATURE OF PHYSICIAN OR SUPPLIER INCLUDING DEGREES OR CREDENTIALS (I certify that the statements on the reverse apply to this bill and are made a part thereof.)

SIGNED _____ DATE _____

32. SERVICE FACILITY LOCATION INFORMATION a. NPI b.

33. BILLING PROVIDER INFO & PH # (   ) a. NPI b.

PATIENT AND INSURED INFORMATION

PHYSICIAN OR SUPPLIER INFORMATION

NUCC Instruction Manual available at: www.nucc.org   **PLEASE PRINT OR TYPE**   APPROVED OMB-0938-1197 FORM 1500 (02-12)

Clear Form

Figure 14-8

© 2018 Pearson Education, Inc.

e. Using the source documents, the Capital City Medical Fee Schedule (Figure 14-9), and the blank CMS-1500 form provided (Figure 14-10), complete the following case study for patient Gerardo Lamos (Case 14-5):

CASE 14-5

Capital City Medical—123 Unknown Boulevard, Capital City, NY 12345-2222 (555) 555-1234	Patient Information Form
Phil Wells, MD, Mannie Mends, MD, Bette R. Soone, MD	Tax ID: 75-0246810
	Group NPI: 1513171216

Patient Information:

Name: (Last, First) Lamos, Gerardo   ☒ Male ☐ Female Birth Date: 01/21/1944

Address: 6270 Meyer Ave, Capital City, NY 12345   Phone: (555) 555-0590

Social Security Number: 431-00-8131   Full-Time Student: ☐ Yes ☐ No

Marital Status: ☐ Single ☒ Married ☐ Divorced ☐ Other

Employment:

Employer: Retired   Phone: ( )

Address:

Condition Related to: ☐ Auto Accident ☐ Employment ☐ Other Accident

Date of Accident: State:

Emergency Contact: **Phone: ( )**

Primary Insurance: CHAMPVA   Phone: ( )

Address: P. O Box 4586, Capital City, NY 12345

Insurance Policyholder's Name: Same   ☐ M ☐ F DOB:

Address:

Phone: Relationship to Insured: ☒ Self ☐ Spouse ☐ Child ☐ Other

Employer: Phone: ( )

Employer's Address:

Policy/ID No: 431008131   Group No: Percent Covered: 100 % Copay Amt: $

Secondary Insurance: Phone: ( )

Address:

Insurance Policyholder's Name: ☐ M ☐ F DOB:

Address:

Phone: Relationship to Insured: ☐ Self ☐ Spouse ☐ Child ☐ Other

Employer: Phone: ( )

Employer's Address:

Policy/ID No: Group No: Percent Covered: % Copay Amt: $

Reason for Visit: I think that my bronchitis is back.

Known Allergies:

Referred by:

CASE 14-5
SOAP

02/01/20XX
Assignment of Benefits: Y
Signature on File: Y
Referring Physician: N

S: Gerardo Lamos is being seen because of possible recurrence of bronchitis. He says that his chest hurts, and that he has a productive cough.

O: There is no fever present. Chest sounds congested on A&P. No wheezing, rubs, or rhonchi. Nose and oropharynx are clear. Throat does appear red due to coughing.

A: 1. Chronic bronchitis—J42

P: 1. Avelox one daily with food.
2. Guaifenesin, one twice a day.
3. Finish all medications.

_____

Phil Well, MD
Family Practice
NPI: 1234567890

© 2018 Pearson Education, Inc.

CASE 14-5

Patient Name Gerardo Lamos

Capital City Medical
123 Unknown Boulevard, Capital City, NY 12345-2222

Date of Service
02-01-20XX

New Patient			Other Invasive/Noninvasive			Laboratory	
Problem Focused	99201		Arthrocentesis/Aspiration/Injection			Amylase	82150
Expanded Problem, Focused	99202		Small Joint		20600	B12	82607
Detailed	99203		Interm Joint		20605	CBC & Diff	85025
Comprehensive	99204		Major Joint		20610	Comp Metabolic Panel	80053
Comprehensive/High Complex	99205		**Other Invasive/Noninvasive**			Chlamydia Screen	87110
Well Exam Infant (up to 12 mos.)	99381		Audiometry		92552	Cholesterol	82465
Well Exam 1–4 yrs.	99382		Cast Application			Digoxin	80162
Well Exam 5–11 yrs.	99383		Location Long Short			Electrolytes	80051
Well Exam 12–17 yrs.	99384		Catheterization		51701	Ferritin	82728
Well Exam 18–39 yrs.	99385		Circumcision		54150	Folate	82746
Well Exam 40–64 yrs.	99386		Colposcopy		57452	GC Screen	87070
			Colposcopy w/Biopsy		57454	Glucose	82947
			Cryosurgery Premalignant Lesion			Glucose 1 HR	82950
			Location (s):			Glycosylated HGB A1C	83036
Established Patient			Cryosurgery Warts			HCT	85014
Post-Op Follow Up Visit	99024		Location (s):			HDL	83718
Minimum	99211		Curettement Lesion			Hep BSAG	87340
Problem Focused	99212	X	Single		11055	Hepatitis panel, acute	80074
Expanded Problem Focused	99213		2–4		11056	HGB	85018
Detailed	99214		>4		11057	HIV	86703
Comprehensive/High Complex	99215		Diaphragm Fitting		57170	Iron & TIBC	83550
Well Exam Infant (up to 12 mos.)	99391		Ear Irrigation		69210	Kidney Profile	80069
Well exam 1–4 yrs.	99392		ECG		93000	Lead	83655
Well Exam 5–11 yrs.	99393		Endometrial Biopsy		58100	Liver Profile	80076
Well Exam 12–17 yrs.	99394		Exc. Lesion Malignant			Mono Test	86308
Well Exam 18–39 yrs.	99395		Benign			Pap Smear	88155
Well Exam 40–64 yrs.	99396		Location			Pregnancy Test	84703
Obstetrics			Exc. Skin Tags (1–15)		11200	Obstetric Panel	80055
Total OB Care	59400		Each Additional 10		11201	Pro Time	85610
Injections			Fracture Treatment			PSA	84153
Administration Sub. / IM	90772		Loc			RPR	86592
Drug			w/Reduc w/o Reduc			Sed. Rate	85651
Dosage			I & D Abscess Single/Simple		10060	Stool Culture	87045
Allergy	95115		Multiple or Comp		10061	Stool O & P	87177
Cocci Skin Test	86490		I & D Pilonidal Cyst Simple		10080	Strep Screen	87880
DPT	90701		Pilonidal Cyst Complex		10081	Theophylline	80198
Hemophilus	90646		IV Therapy—To One Hour		90760	Thyroid Uptake	84479
Influenza	90658		Each Additional Hour		90761	TSH	84443
MMR	90707		Laceration Repair			Urinalysis	81000
OPV	90712		Location Size Simp/Comp			Urine Culture	87088
Pneumovax	90732		Laryngoscopy		31505	Drawing Fee	36415
TB Skin Test	86580		Oximetry		94760	Specimen Collection	99000
TD	90718		Punch Biopsy			**Other:**	
Unlisted Immun	90749		Rhythm Strip		93040		
Tetanus Toxoid	90703		Treadmill		93015		
Vaccine/Toxoid Admin <8 Yr Old w/ Counseling	90465		Trigger Point or Tendon Sheath Inj.		20550		
Vaccine/Toxoid Administration for Adult	90471		Tympanometry		92567		

Diagnosis/ICD-10: J42

I acknowledge receipt of medical services and authorize the release of any medical information necessary to process this claim for healthcare payment only. I do authorize payment to the provider.

Patient Signature *Gerardo Lamos*

Total Estimated Charges: _____

Payment Amount: _____

Next Appointment: _____

Figure 14-9

Capital City Medical
Fee Schedule

New Patient OV			Punch Biopsy various codes	$80
Problem Focused 99201	$45		Nebulizer various codes	$45
Expanded Problem Focused 99202	$65		Cast Application various codes	$85
Detailed 99203	$85		Laryngoscopy 31505	$255
Comprehensive 99204	$105		Audiometry 92552	$85
Comprehensive/High Complex 99205	$115		Tympanometry 92567	$85
Well Exam infant (less than 1 year) 99381	$45		Ear Irrigation 69210	$25
Well Exam 1–4 yrs. 99382	$50		Diaphragm Fitting 57170	$30
Well Exam 5–11 yrs. 99383	$55		IV Therapy (up to one hour) 90760	$65
Well Exam 12–17 yrs. 99384	$65		Each additional hour 90761	$50
Well Exam 18–39 yrs. 99385	$85		Oximetry 94760	$10
Well Exam 40–64 yrs. 99386	$105		ECG 93000	$75
Established Patient OV			Holter Monitor various codes	$170
Post Op Follow Up Visit 99024	$0		Rhythm Strip 93040	$60
Minimum 99211	$35		Treadmill 93015	$375
Problem Focused 99212	$45		Cocci Skin Test 86490	$20
Expanded Problem Focused 99213	$55		X-ray, spine, chest, bone—any area various codes	$275
Detailed 99214	$65		Avulsion Nail 11730	$200
Comprehensive/High Complex 99215	$75		**Laboratory**	
Well exam infant (less than 1 year) 99391	$35		Amylase 82150	$40
Well Exam 1–4 yrs. 99392	$40		B12 82607	$30
Well Exam 5–11 yrs. 99393	$45		CBC & Diff 85025	$95
Well Exam 12–17 yrs. 99394	$55		Comp Metabolic Panel 80053	$75
Well Exam 18–39 yrs. 99395	$65		Chlamydia Screen 87110	$70
Well Exam 40–64 yrs. 99396	$75		Cholestrerol 82465	$75
Obstetrics			Digoxin 80162	$40
Total OB Care 59400	$1700		Electrolytes 80051	$70
Injections			Estrogen, Total 82672	$50
Administration 90772	$10		Ferritin 82728	$40
Allergy 95115	$35		Folate 82746	$30
DPT 90701	$50		GC Screen 87070	$60
Drug various codes	$35		Glucose 82947	$35
Influenza 90658	$25		Glycosylated HGB A1C 83036	$45
MMR 90707	$50		HCT 85014	$30
OPV 90712	$40		HDL 83718	$35
Pneumovax 90732	$35		HGB 85018	$30
TB Skin Test 86580	$15		Hep BSAG 83740	$40
TD 90718	$40		Hepatitis panel, acute 80074	$95
Tetanus Toxoid 90703	$40		HIV 86703	$100
Vaccine/Toxoid Administration for Younger Than 8 Years Old w/ counseling 90465	$10		Iron & TIBC 83550	$45
			Kidney Profile 80069	$95
Vaccine/Toxoid Administration for Adult 90471	$10		Lead 83665	$55
Arthrocentesis/Aspiration/Injection			Lipase 83690	$40
Small Joint 20600	$50		Lipid Panel 80061	$95
Interm Joint 20605	$60		Liver Profile 80076	$95
Major Joint 20610	$70		Mono Test 86308	$30
Trigger Point/Tendon Sheath Inj. 20550	$90		Pap Smear 88155	$90
Other Invasive/Noninvasive Procedures			Pap Collection/Supervision 88142	$95
Catheterization 51701	$55		Pregnancy Test 84703	$90
Circumcision 54150	$150		Obstetric Panel 80055	$85
Colposcopy 57452	$225		Pro Time 85610	$50
Colposcopy w/Biopsy 57454	$250		PSA 84153	$50
Cryosurgery Premalignant Lesion various codes	$160		RPR 86592	$55
Endometrial Biopsy 58100	$190		Sed. Rate 85651	$50
Excision Lesion Malignant various codes	$145		Stool Culture 87045	$80
Excision Lesion Benign various codes	$125		Stool O & P 87177	$105
Curettement Lesion			Strep Screen 87880	$35
Single 11055	$70		Theophylline 80198	$40
2–4 11056	$80		Thyroid Uptake 84479	$75
>4 11057	$90		TSH 84443	$50
Excision Skin Tags (1–15) 11200	$55		Urinalysis 81000	$35
Each Additional 10 11201	$30		Urine Culture 87088	$80
I & D Abscess Single/Simple 10060	$75		Drawing Fee 36415	$15
Multiple/Complex 10061	$95		Specimen Collection 99000	$10
I & D Pilonidal Cyst Simple 10080	$105			
I & D Pilonidal Cyst Complex 10081	$130			
Laceration Repair various codes	$60			

HEALTH INSURANCE CLAIM FORM

APPROVED BY NATIONAL UNIFORM CLAIM COMMITTEE (NUCC) 02/12

| | PICA | | | | | | | | | PICA | |

1. MEDICARE	MEDICAID	TRICARE	CHAMPVA	GROUP HEALTH PLAN	FECA BLK LUNG	OTHER	1a. INSURED'S I.D. NUMBER	(For Program in Item 1)
☒ (Medicare#)	(Medicaid#)	(ID#/DoD#)	(Member ID#)	(ID#)	(ID#)	(ID#)		

2. PATIENT'S NAME (Last Name, First Name, Middle Initial)

3. PATIENT'S BIRTH DATE MM | DD | YY **SEX** M☐ F☐

4. INSURED'S NAME (Last Name, First Name, Middle Initial)

5. PATIENT'S ADDRESS (No., Street)

6. PATIENT RELATIONSHIP TO INSURED Self☐ Spouse☐ Child☐ Other☐

7. INSURED'S ADDRESS (No., Street)

CITY | STATE

8. RESERVED FOR NUCC USE

CITY | STATE

ZIP CODE | TELEPHONE (Include Area Code) ( )

ZIP CODE | TELEPHONE (Include Area Code) ( )

9. OTHER INSURED'S NAME (Last Name, First Name, Middle Initial)

10. IS PATIENT'S CONDITION RELATED TO:

11. INSURED'S POLICY GROUP OR FECA NUMBER

a. OTHER INSURED'S POLICY OR GROUP NUMBER

a. EMPLOYMENT? (Current or Previous) YES☐ NO☐

a. INSURED'S DATE OF BIRTH MM | DD | YY **SEX** M☐ F☐

b. RESERVED FOR NUCC USE

b. AUTO ACCIDENT? YES☐ NO☐ PLACE (State)

b. OTHER CLAIM ID (Designated by NUCC)

c. RESERVED FOR NUCC USE

c. OTHER ACCIDENT? YES☐ NO☐

c. INSURANCE PLAN NAME OR PROGRAM NAME

d. INSURANCE PLAN NAME OR PROGRAM NAME

10d. CLAIM CODES (Designated by NUCC)

d. IS THERE ANOTHER HEALTH BENEFIT PLAN? YES☐ NO☐ *If yes, complete items 9, 9a, and 9d.*

READ BACK OF FORM BEFORE COMPLETING & SIGNING THIS FORM.
12. PATIENT'S OR AUTHORIZED PERSON'S SIGNATURE I authorize the release of any medical or other information necessary to process this claim. I also request payment of government benefits either to myself or to the party who accepts assignment below.

SIGNED _____ DATE _____

13. INSURED'S OR AUTHORIZED PERSON'S SIGNATURE I authorize payment of medical benefits to the undersigned physician or supplier for services described below.

SIGNED _____

14. DATE OF CURRENT ILLNESS, INJURY, or PREGNANCY (LMP) MM | DD | YY QUAL.

15. OTHER DATE QUAL. MM | DD | YY

16. DATES PATIENT UNABLE TO WORK IN CURRENT OCCUPATION FROM MM | DD | YY TO MM | DD | YY

17. NAME OF REFERRING PROVIDER OR OTHER SOURCE

17a. | 17b. NPI

18. HOSPITALIZATION DATES RELATED TO CURRENT SERVICES FROM MM | DD | YY TO MM | DD | YY

19. ADDITIONAL CLAIM INFORMATION (Designated by NUCC)

20. OUTSIDE LAB? YES☐ NO☐ $ CHARGES

21. DIAGNOSIS OR NATURE OF ILLNESS OR INJURY Relate A-L to service line below (24E) ICD Ind. |

A. ____ B. ____ C. ____ D. ____
E. ____ F. ____ G. ____ H. ____
I. ____ J. ____ K. ____ L. ____

22. RESUBMISSION CODE | ORIGINAL REF. NO.

23. PRIOR AUTHORIZATION NUMBER

24. A. DATE(S) OF SERVICE From MM DD YY To MM DD YY	B. PLACE OF SERVICE	C. EMG	D. PROCEDURES, SERVICES, OR SUPPLIES (Explain Unusual Circumstances) CPT/HCPCS MODIFIER	E. DIAGNOSIS POINTER	F. $ CHARGES	G. DAYS OR UNITS	H. EPSDT Family Plan	I. ID. QUAL	J. RENDERING PROVIDER ID. #
1									NPI
2									NPI
3									NPI
4									NPI
5									NPI
6									NPI

25. FEDERAL TAX I.D. NUMBER SSN☐ EIN☐

26. PATIENT'S ACCOUNT NO.

27. ACCEPT ASSIGNMENT? (For govt. claims, see back) YES☐ NO☐

28. TOTAL CHARGE $

29. AMOUNT PAID $

30. Rsvd. for NUCC Use

31. SIGNATURE OF PHYSICIAN OR SUPPLIER INCLUDING DEGREES OR CREDENTIALS (I certify that the statements on the reverse apply to this bill and are made a part thereof.)

SIGNED _____ DATE _____

32. SERVICE FACILITY LOCATION INFORMATION

a. NPI | b.

33. BILLING PROVIDER INFO & PH # ( )

a. NPI | b.

NUCC Instruction Manual available at: www.nucc.org   **PLEASE PRINT OR TYPE**   APPROVED OMB-0938-1197 FORM 1500 (02-12)

Clear Form

Figure 14-10

3. Using the information from Chapter 14 in your student text, complete the following table by comparing the TRICARE plans:

	TRICARE Standard/Extra	TRICARE Prime/Prime Remote
Type of Program		
Availability		
Enrollment		
Enrollment fees		
Costs		
Provider choices		
MTF priority		
Primary care managers		
Referral and authorization requirements		
Clinical preventive care		

© 2018 Pearson Education, Inc.

REVIEW QUESTIONS

MATCHING

Choose the correct answer and write its corresponding letter in the space provided.

a. HCF
b. Nonavailability statement
c. Catastrophic cap
d. DEERS
e. CHAMPUS

1. _____ Database listing all eligible TRICARE recipients and their status of TRICARE coverage
2. _____ Former title of TRICARE
3. _____ An electronic document stating that a specific service required for a TRICARE patient is not provided at a nearby MTF, allowing for civilian medical services
4. _____ Assist the patient with the referral or preauthorization process.
5. _____ A limit placed on the total amount of medical expenses

MULTIPLE CHOICE

Circle the letter of the choice that best completes the statement or answers the question.

1. When does the TRICARE fiscal year begin?
   a. October 1
   b. January 1
   c. July 1
   d. January 15

2. For how many days is a NAS valid after the initial issuing date?
   a. 90 days
   b. 30 days
   c. 15 days
   d. 60 days

3. A non-par can charge how much for a visit?
   a. Up to 90% of charges
   b. Up to 100% of charges
   c. Up to 115% of charges
   d. None of the above

4. The active duty service member under TRICARE is known as the _____.
   a. sponsor
   b. beneficiary
   c. Both a and b
   d. None of the above

5. An individual who qualifies for TRICARE under an active duty service member is known as the _____.
   a. sponsor
   b. beneficiary
   c. Both a and b
   d. None of the above

SHORT ANSWER

Provide the correct response to each question that follows.

1. What are the five TRICARE programs?

   1. _____
   2. _____
   3. _____
   4. _____
   5. _____

2. When might an NAS need to be filed?

   _____

3. What claim form is used by TRICARE and CHAMPVA for the following services?

   Inpatient _____

   Outpatient _____

4. How would the medical office specialist determine where to send a claim for the following programs?

   TRICARE

   _____

   _____

   _____

   CHAMPVA

   _____

   _____

   _____

5. a. Who is covered under CHAMPVA?

   _____

   _____

   b. To have CHAMPVA cover medical services, what type of facility must be used?

   _____

   c. What is required if a veteran wants to obtain community medical treatment?

   _____

   _____

   d. Do all medical services for veterans need approval prior to treatment?

   _____

© 2018 Pearson Education, Inc.

TRUE/FALSE

Identify each statement as true (T) or false (F).

1. _____ All referrals and authorizations must be arranged by a TRICARE primary care manager (PCM) to ensure coverage of services to be provided.

2. _____ TRICARE Prime Remote is offered only in the United States and does not require enrollment in this program.

3. _____ If a patient has another type of insurance, Tricare is secondary.

4. _____ CHAMPVA is the primary payer to Medicare for services covered by both programs.

5. _____ MTF services do not vary per facility.

CHAPTER 15
Explanation of Benefits and Payment Adjudication

CHAPTER OBJECTIVES

After reading this chapter, the student should be able to:

1. Define the steps for filing a medical claim.
2. Understand the importance of the Explanation of Benefits and Electronic Remittance Advice forms.
3. Calculate accurate payment by a carrier or third-party payer.
4. Make adjustments to patient accounts.
5. Review reason codes.

CHAPTER OUTLINE

Steps for Filing a Medical Claim

Claims Process

Determining the Fees
  Charge-Based Fee Structures
  Resource-Based Fee Structures

History of the Resource-Based Relative Value Scale

The RBRVS System

The Medicare conversion factor

Determining the Medicare Fee

Allowed Charges

Payers' Policies

Capitation

Value-based Reimbursement

Calculations of Patient Charges
  Deductible
  Copayments
  Coinsurance
  Excluded Services

Balance Billing

Processing an Explanation of Benefits
  Information on an EOB/ERA

Reviewing Claims Information

KEY TERMS

Using the highlighted terms and glossary in the textbook, define the following terms.

1. adjudication _____

_____

2. adjustment _____

_____

3. allowed charge _____

_____

4. appeal _____

_____

5. balance billing _____

_____

6. capitation plan _____

_____

7. charge-based fees _____

_____

8. conversion factor _____

_____

9. coordination of benefits (COB) _____

_____

10. Electronic Remittance Advice (ERA) _____

_____

11. excluded services _____

_____

12. Explanation of Benefits (EOB) _____

_____

13. Geographic Practice Cost Index (GPCI) _____

_____

14. lifetime maximum _____

_____

15. manual review _____

_____

© 2018 Pearson Education, Inc.

16. Medicare conversion factor (MCF) _____

_____

17. Medicare Fee Schedule (MFS) _____

_____

18. nationally uniform relative value _____

_____

19. out-of-pocket expenses _____

_____

20. pending claim _____

_____

21. per member per month (PMPM) _____

_____

22. reason codes _____

_____

23. relative value unit (RVU) _____

_____

24. remark codes _____

_____

25. resource-based fees _____

_____

26. resource-based relative value scale (RBRVS) _____

_____

27. retention schedule _____

_____

28. turnaround time _____

_____

29. usual, customary, and reasonable (UCR) _____

_____

30. withhold _____

_____

31. write-offs _____

_____

CRITICAL THINKING QUESTIONS

Using the knowledge you have gained from reading the textbook, apply critical thinking skills to answer the following questions.

1. Before an EOB is received, what steps must be completed by the medical office specialist?

    1. _____

    2. _____

3. _____

4. _____

5. _____

6. _____

7. _____

8. _____

2. a. The insurance carrier has determined that a provided service is covered, but there is no reimbursement paid to the rendering provider. Will an EOB still be sent out? If so, who will receive the EOB? _____

   b. Refer to the preceding question. Would an ERA be sent out? If so, who will receive the ERA?

   _____

3. You are a claim examiner and have decided that a claim needs to be pulled for a manual review. What would you request from the rendering medical provider to help you to determine whether the claim should be paid or denied?

   _____

   _____

4. You are a medical billing specialist and have just received an EOB from an insurance carrier. What information is listed on the EOB?

   _____

   _____

   _____

   _____

   _____

5. a. As the medical office specialist, you have just received an EOB on patient Irma Winslott. What steps must be taken before you post this information?

   _____

   _____

   _____

   _____

   b. Once you have taken the steps described in your answer to the previous question and accuracy has been established, where would you post this information?

   _____

   _____

   c. If an error has been identified on Irma's EOB, what is the first step to locating the error?

   _____

   _____

© 2018 Pearson Education, Inc.

d. Irma's claim has been sent back to the office as denied, and it is clear that this claim should have been paid. What should you do to obtain payment?

_____

_____

_____

PRACTICE EXERCISES

1. a. Using the information in Chapter 15 of your student text, determine the Medicare allowed fee for the following geographical areas by using the GPCIs and conversion factor for 2017, which is 35.8887:

Locality	Work GPCI	Practice Expense GPCI	Malpractice Expense GPCI
Capital City	1.050	1.042	0.155
Township	1.020	1.106	0.080

Code	Work RVU	Practice RVU	Malpractice RVU
99203	1.25	1.16	0.20
99213	0.94	0.98	0.15

    b. Use the initial 2017 conversion factor of 35.8887 to complete the following:

	Capital City	Township
99203:		
99213:		

2. Using the given information, calculate the following charges:

Mason Winston was seen in the office today for immunizations. The total charges are $100. The allowed amount is $80. His benefits pay 80 percent. His policy has a deductible of $25.

Usual Charge _____

Allowed Charge _____

Deductible _____

Policy pays _____ of the allowed charge after deductible, which is _____.

Patient responsible for the _____ of the allowed charge plus the deductible, which is _____.

Provider writes off the difference between the usual and allowed _____.

3. On the following examples of information provided in an explanation of benefits, complete the tables with the payment information given for each:

    a.

Physician charges	Allowed Amounts	Insurance Pays	Deductible
75.00	52.00	80%	150.00*
145.00	103.00		
110.00	86.00		

	Charge	Adjustment	Allowed	Deductible	Co-pay	Ins. Pays	Coinsurance
	$	$	$	$	$	$	$
	$	$	$	$	$	$	$
	$	$	$	$	$	$	$
TOTALS	$	$	$	$	$	$	$

*Deductible not met.

Balance due from patient:

Patient's deductible: $_____

Patient's coinsurance: $_____

Total due: $_____

Total insurance pays: $_____

Total physician write-off: $_____

b.

Physician Charges	Allowed Amounts	Insurance Pays	Deductible
3,625.00	75%	70%	350.00*

	Charge	Adjustment	Allowed	Deductible	Copay	Ins. Pays	Coinsurance
	$	$	$	$	$	$	$
TOTALS	$	$	$	$	$	$	$

*$50.00 of deductible has been met.

Balance due from patient:

Patient's deductible: $_____

Patient's coinsurance: $_____

Total due: $_____

Total insurance pays: $_____

Total physician write-off: $_____

© 2018 Pearson Education, Inc.

4. a. Complete the following EOB:

Today's Date

Payer Name & Address

Health Insurance Co.
777 Corporate Way
Capital City, NY 12345

Provider's Name & Address

Phil Wells, M.D.
123 Unknown Boulevard
Capital City, TX 12345

This statement covers payments for the following patient(s):

Claim Detail Section (*Hint:* If there are numbers in the "SEE REMARKS" column, see the Remarks Section for an explanation.)

Patient Name: McGee, Regina	**Patient Account #:** RM0562
Patient ID#: 319-91-6257	**Insured's Name:** McGee, Regina
Group #: 55216	
Provider Name: Phil Wells, M.D.	**Inventory #:** 44597 **Claim Control #:** 28940

Service Date(s)	Procedure	Charges	Adjustment	Allowed	Co-pay	Deduct/Not Covered	Coins	Paid At.	Provider Paid/ Remarks
07/09/2007	99213 OV	55.00		32.00	0.00	0.00		80%	
07/09/2007	69210 Ear Irr.	25.00		10.00	0.00	0.00		80%	
TOTALS									

BALANCE DUE FROM PATIENT: PT'S DED/NOT COV $_____

PT'S COINS. $_____

031 Met Maximum Limit

PAYMENT SUMMARY SECTION (Totals)

Charges	Adjustment	Allowed	Copay	Deduct/Not Covered	Coins	Total Paid

THIS IS NOT A BILL

© 2018 Pearson Education, Inc.

b. Answer the following questions Regina has concerning her EOB:

1. What does it mean when the statement "THIS IS NOT A BILL" appears on the EOB?

_____

_____

_____

_____

2. Explain to Regina what the difference is between the copay and deductible.

_____

_____

_____

_____

3. Explain to Regina what the Deduct/Not Covered column means.

_____

_____

_____

_____

4. Explain to Regina why there is a difference between the allowed charge and the insurance carrier's actual payment.

_____

_____

_____

_____

© 2018 Pearson Education, Inc.

5. Using the EOB provided, fill in the following information:

Health Insurance Company

Health Insurance HMO

777 Corporate Way

Capital City, WI 12345

800-555-9876

Explanation of Benefits

Insured Name:	Gavin Retort
Insured ID/SS#:	505-11-3223
Policy:	
Claim Number:	LP-60042-003
Control Number:	208652144
Date:	01/31/08

Below Is an Explanation of Benefits for your Medical Coverage

Patient: Gavin Retort **Patient ID/SS#:** 505-11-3223

Provider Name: Phil Wells, M.D. **Patient Account #:** GR375100

Service Code	Service Description	Service Date(s)	Provider Charge	Allowed Amount	Discount Amount	Not Covered	Deductible	Copay	Pay At	Remarks	Amount Paid
99386	Well Exam	01/16/08	$105.00	$77.60	$27.40	$0.00	$0.00	$20.00	100%	0054	$57.60
TOTALS			$105.00	$77.60	$27.40	$0.00	$0.00	$20.00			$47.60

Remarks

0054 PPO-Preferred Provider benefits applied. Your provider has agreed to the negotiated rate in accordance with the Private Healthcare Systems provider agreement. You should not be billed for this amount.

Payment Summary

Payment Sent To:	Phil Wells, M.D.
Payment Amount:	$67.60
Payment Date:	01/31/08
Patient's Portion:	$20.00

Total Payment Summary

Payment(s) Sent To:	Phil Wells, M.D.
Total Payment Amount:	$67.60
Payment Date:	01/31/08
***TOTAL PATIENT PORTION:**	**$20.00**

Insurance company name: _____

Patient's name: _____

Patient's ID: _____

Provider's name: _____

Date of service: _____

Total charge: _____

Procedure(s): _____

Copay: _____

Deductible: _____

Coinsurance due from patient: _____

Allowed amount: _____

Discount amount: _____

Noncovered items: _____

Rate of benefit (%): _____

Amount paid: _____

Remarks: _____

Outcome: ☐ Bill patient balance ☐ Call carrier

☐ Appeal ☐ Claim paid in full

REVIEW QUESTIONS

MATCHING

Choose the correct answer and write its corresponding letter in the space provided.

a. discount amount
b. deductible
c. allowed charges
d. coinsurance
e. adjustment

1. _____ Difference between provider charges and allowed amount; amount physician must write off

2. _____ Maximum allowed amount for a covered charge that includes the amount both the insurance carrier and the patient will pay

3. _____ Amount of money owed by a patient every year that must be met before health insurance pays at 100 percent

4. _____ The percentage of money owed by a patient for provided medical services

5. _____ A positive or negative change to a patient's account balance, including corrections and write-offs

MULTIPLECHOICE

Circle the letter of the choice that best completes the statement or answers the question.

1. Which of the following is stated on an EOB?
   a. The status of a claim
   b. The patient's demographics, including services provided
   c. Charges, adjustments, and any patient out-of-pocket expenses
   d. All of the above

2. Which of the following is a reason that a manually reviewed claim would be denied?
   a. Lack of required preauthorization
   b. Lack of medical necessity
   c. Lack of eligibility for a reported procedure
   d. All of the above

3. What is balance billing?
   a. Accepting allowed amount
   b. Billing patient for amount left after
   c. Billing patient for discounted amount
   d. Both b and c

4. The act of billing a patient for any monetary amount left after the insurance carrier has made payment is known as _____.
   a. adjudication
   b. balance billing
   c. turn-around billing
   d. direct payment

5. EOB explanation codes often used by insurance carriers are also known as _____.
   a. reason codes
   b. direct codes
   c. remark codes
   d. Both a and c

© 2018 Pearson Education, Inc.

SHORT ANSWER

Provide the correct response to each question that follows.

1. What are four examples of a patient's out-of-pocket expenses?
   1. _____
   2. _____
   3. _____
   4. _____

2. When should a patient's out-of-pocket expenses be collected? _____

3. What is an ERA? _____

4. What are the three explanations for the status of a claim?
   1. _____
   2. _____
   3. _____

5. Answer the following questions related to RBRVS calculations for reimbursement:
   a. Briefly explain the three cost elements related to the National Uniform Relative Value.
      1. Provider's work _____
      _____

      2. Practice expense _____
      _____

      3. Professional liability insurance _____
      _____

   b. Briefly explain the Geographic Practice Cost Index (GPCI). _____
   _____

   c. Briefly explain the Nationally Uniform Conversion Factor. _____
   _____

   d. How often is the Nationally Uniform Conversion Factor updated? _____
   _____

TRUE/FALSE

Identify each statement as true (T) or false (F).

1. _____ More than one patient can be listed on an EOB.

2. _____ A dated front and back copy of the patient's insurance card should be filed in the patient's medical chart.

3. _____ A lockbox service helps with faster collection of payments.

4. _____ A nonparticipating provider can bill a patient for fees not covered by the insurance carrier's allowed charge.

5. _____ A participating provider can bill a patient for fees not covered by the insurance carrier's allowed charge.

CHAPTER 16

Refunds, Follow-Up, and Appeals

CHAPTER OBJECTIVES

After reading this chapter, the student should be able to:

1. Understand reimbursement follow-up.
2. Know the common problems and solutions for denied or delayed payments.
3. Use problem-solving and communication skills to answer patients' questions about claims.
4. Format medical records with proper documentation.
5. Understand the appeals process and register a formal appeal.
6. Understand ERISA rules and regulations.
7. Write letters of appeal on denied claims.
8. Understand refund guidelines.
9. Rebill insurance claims.
10. Discuss the three levels of Medicare appeals.
11. Calculate and issue refunds.

CHAPTER OUTLINE

Electronically filing claims

Claims Rejection Follow-Up

Rebilling

Denied or Delayed Payments

Answering Patients' Questions about Claims

Claim Rejection Appeal

Peer Review

State Insurance Commissioner

Carrier Audits

Documentation
Documentation Guidelines
SOAP Record-Keeping Format

Necessity of Appeals

Registering a Formal Appeal

The Appeals Process
Reason Codes That Require a Formal Appeal

KEY TERMS

Using the highlighted terms and glossary in the textbook, define the following terms.

1. administrative law judge (ALJ) hearing _____

   _____

2. documentation _____

   _____

3. Employee Retirement Income Security Act (ERISA) of 1974 _____

   _____

4. follow-up _____

   _____

5. insurance commissioner _____

   _____

6. peer review _____

   _____

7. qualified independent contractors (QICs) _____

   _____

8. redetermination _____

   _____

9. SOAP format _____

   _____

© 2018 Pearson Education, Inc.

CRITICAL THINKING QUESTIONS

Using the knowledge you have gained from reading the textbook, apply critical thinking skills to answer the following questions.

1. Answer the following questions related to responding to a patient's questions about a claim:

   a. Mr. Tim calls, and he is upset about a bill that he received from your clinic. What should you do first, and why? _____

   _____

   _____

   b. When looking up Mr. Tim's information, you find the claim was denied, and the reason was stated as no coverage at the time of service. What should you do?

   _____

   _____

   _____

   _____

   _____

2. Identify a solution for each given scenario when a claim needs to be rebilled.

   a. A patient was seen by a podiatrist for pain in his right heel. An X-ray was taken that showed evidence of a heel spur. The physician documented a cortisone injection in the right heel in the patient's chart, but forgot to document the injection on the superbill. A week after the claim submittal, you determine that the cortisone injection wasn't billed. What should be done to receive reimbursement for the injection?

   _____

   _____

   _____

   _____

   b. A patient had two different ultrasounds for a related problem within 2 weeks of each other. She had a pelvic ultrasound on May 13 and a transvaginal ultrasound on May 24. You discover that the transvaginal ultrasound was never billed. What should be done to receive reimbursement for the second ultrasound?

   _____

   _____

   _____

   _____

3. a. Who is notified by an insurance carrier when a claim has been denied?

   _____

   b. You are sending an appeal letter to an insurance carrier for a denied claim to be reconsidered for reimbursement. What is the first step that must be taken before you begin to write the appeal letter?

   _____

   _____

   _____

c. You have received a denied claim letter from Max Cambridge's insurance carrier. What types of actions should be taken to assure Mr. Cambridge that you are making your best effort in seeking a resolution to this problem?

_____

_____

_____

4. Part of your job description is to ensure that an insurance audit runs smoothly. What are the three main steps to avoid problems during an insurance audit?

1. _____

2. _____

3. _____

5. Answer the following questions regarding researching the validity of a refund request by an insurance carrier or patient:

a. An insurance carrier sends a request for a refund because a patient's coverage was canceled prior to the date that services were rendered. What should you do before preparing the refund?

_____

_____

_____

b. An insurance carrier sends a request for a refund because of an overpayment. What should you do before preparing the refund?

_____

_____

_____

c. An insurance carrier sends a request for a refund because it paid as the primary payer when it should have paid as the secondary payer. What should you do before preparing the refund?

_____

_____

_____

d. A patient requests a refund for overpayment of her Medicare deductible for the year. She forgot that she had previously paid the deductible 2 weeks ago at another physician's office. After contacting Medicare, you find out that she has in fact paid the deductible previous to her appointment at your office. What should you do?

_____

_____

_____

e. A patient prepays for services that end up being covered by his insurance carrier. What should you do before preparing the refund?

_____

_____

_____

© 2018 Pearson Education, Inc.

PRACTICE EXERCISES

1. a. Using the information presented in Chapter 16 of your student text, read the given items and determine what part of the SOAP format each is. Write S for subjective, O for objective, A for assessment, and P for plan, in the spaces provided.

   1. Cymbalta 60 mg qday. _____

   2. Patient states he has had right upper abdominal pain for 3 days. _____

   3. CBC and CMP were run to check for kidney infection. _____

   4. Primary complaint is regarding left knee pain for 1 month. _____

   5. It was determined that the patient has atrial fibrillation. _____

   b. In your own words, explain the difference between subjective and objective data.

   _____

   _____

   _____

   _____

2. Read the given scenarios and decide whether each query can be responded to by telephone or by written appeal. Provide your answers in the spaces shown.

   a. An insurance carrier sends a letter of request to a patient for an update on the patient's address.

   _____

   b. An insurance carrier contacts the office for additional clinical documentation to process a claim.

   _____

   c. An emergency procedure was performed without preauthorization.

   _____

   d. A claim was denied because the procedure was not considered to be medically necessary. The physician believes that it was.

   _____

3. Read the following delayed or denied claim scenarios, decide what would be the appropriate solution for each, and provide your answers in the spaces shown.

   a. A patient has a surgical procedure that didn't have the required preauthorization.

   _____

   _____

   b. A patient is seen for a preexisting condition that is not covered by the insurance carrier.

   _____

   _____

4. In the following space, write an appeal for patient Mary Thompson. She had an abdominal and a pelvic CT performed that the insurance carrier ruled as medically unnecessary. She recently had an abdominopelvic ultrasound, which was negative for any disease process, but she still complains of severe pain in her abdomen. Be sure to use positive reinforcement within your appeal letter.

   _____

   _____

   _____

_____

_____

_____

_____

_____

_____

_____

_____

_____

_____

_____

_____

_____

_____

_____

_____

_____

_____

_____

_____

_____

_____

_____

_____

_____

_____

_____

_____

_____

_____

_____

_____

5. A patient requests a refund on his $200 deductible. He forgot that he paid it previously at his last appointment. You check his records, and he has, in fact, paid it twice this year. He does have an outstanding balance of $80 with your office. What is the amount that the patient will receive for a refund?

_____

© 2018 Pearson Education, Inc.

MATCHING

Choose the correct answer and write its corresponding letter in the space provided.

a. peer review
b. insurance commissioner
c. redetermination
d. denied claim
e. claim appeal

1. _____ An unbiased group of physicians that determines adequate payment for provided medical services after an appeal has been denied by an insurance carrier

2. _____ Medicare review of a first-level appealed claim

3. _____ Written request for a review of a denied claim that asks an insurance carrier to reconsider reimbursement for rendered medical services

4. _____ Regulates insurance companies and serves as a liaison between the patient and carrier and between the physician and carrier; can aid in settling complaints related to claim reimbursement

5. _____ A claim that is not paid by the insurance carrier due to issues such as lack of coverage, preexisting conditions, or non-covered benefit

MULTIPLE CHOICE

Circle the letter of the choice that best completes the statement or answers the question.

1. Which of the following is a reason that an insurance carrier may ask a medical provider to rebill?
   a. Missing or incomplete claim information
   b. Errors on a claim
   c. A service provided was not medically necessary
   d. Both a and b

2. Overpayment can occur for all of the following reasons *except:*
   a. the patient pays too much.
   b. both payers pay as primary.
   c. both patient and payer pay at the same time.
   d. None of the above

3. Who can file a complaint with the Insurance Commissioner?
   a. The patient
   b. The physician
   c. The insurance carrier
   d. Both a and b

4. Which of the following is an acceptable signature on an appeal letter?
   a. Signature of the provider on the claim form only, but not on the appeal letter
   b. Actual signature or stamped signature of the provider or authorized employee
   c. Signature of the provider represented by the signature and initials of an authorized employee
   d. Both b and c

5. A wrongful retention of an insurance carrier's overpayment is known as _____.
   a. Conversion
   b. Contestment
   c. Reception
   d. Both a and c

SHORT ANSWER

Provide the correct response to each question that follows.

1. Why is it important to alert the payer if you are rebilling a claim?

   _____
   _____
   _____

2. List two ways that follow-up of an outstanding claim can be accomplished.

   1. _____
      _____
   2. _____

3. a. What is a disallowance?

      _____
      _____

   b. When appealing a disallowance, the medical office specialist should include what important information?

      _____
      _____

4. Name six persons to whom to redirect an appeal and why.

   1. _____
      _____
   2. _____
      _____
   3. _____
      _____
   4. _____
      _____
   5. _____
      _____
   6. _____
      _____

© 2018 Pearson Education, Inc.

5. What are three reasons that an overpayment from an insurance carrier can occur?

1. _____

2. _____

3. _____

TRUE/FALSE

Identify each statement as true (T) or false (F).

1. _____ An insurance claim must be monitored until payment is received.

2. _____ If a claim states that the patient's coverage has been cancelled, the medical office specialist should rebill.

3. _____ Valid court rulings and federal and state laws should be used as references in appeal letters.

4. _____ The medical office specialist should always research a refund requested by an insurance carrier before submitting the refund.

5. _____ Insurance carriers are not allowed to automatically recoup overpayments that were issued to a medical provider.

CHAPTER 17
Workers' Compensation

CHAPTER OBJECTIVES

After reading this chapter, the student should be able to:

1. Understand the history of workers' compensation.
2. Distinguish between federal workers' compensation and state workers' compensation.
3. List the classifications of a work-related injury.
4. Know injured workers' responsibilities and rights.
5. Understand the responsibility of the treating doctor/physician of record.
6. Understand the role of an ombudsman in assisting with claims.
7. Know the four types of workers' compensation benefits.
8. Discuss the different types of disability.
9. Accurately complete a CMS-1500 form for a workers' compensation claim.
10. Determine the workers' compensation fee based on the Medicare Fee Schedule.

CHAPTER OUTLINE

Benefits and Compensation Termination
    Types of Government Disability Policies

Verifying Insurance Benefits

Preauthorization
    Requirements for the Preauthorization Request

Filing Insurance Claims

Completing the CMS-1500 for Workers' Compensation Claims

Independent Review Organizations
    How to Obtain an Independent Review
    The IRO Decision

Medical Records

Fraud
    Penalties
    Medical Provider Fraud

Calculating Reimbursements

KEY TERMS

Using the highlighted terms and glossary in the textbook, define the following terms.

1. Admission of liability _____

   _____

2. burial benefits _____

   _____

3. death benefits _____

   _____

4. designated doctor _____

   _____

5. disability _____

   _____

6. disability compensation programs _____

   _____

7. District of Columbia Workers' Compensation Act _____

   _____

8. Employer's First Report of Injury or Illness _____

   _____

9. Energy Employees' Occupational Illness Compensation Program Act (EEOICP) ___

   _____

   _____

10. Federal Coal Mine Health and Safety Act (Black Lung Benefits Reform Act) ___

   _____

   _____

© 2018 Pearson Education, Inc.

11. Federal Employees' Compensation Act (FECA) _____
_____

12. final report _____
_____

13. fraud indicators _____
_____

14. impairment _____
_____

15. impairment income benefits _____
_____

16. impairment rating _____
_____

17. income benefits _____
_____

18. independent review organization (IRO) _____
_____

19. lifetime income benefits _____
_____

20. Longshore and Harbor Workers' Compensation Act (LHWCA) _____
_____

21. maximum medical improvement _____

22. medical benefits _____

23. Notice of Contest _____
_____

24. occupational diseases and illnesses _____
_____

25. Occupational Safety and Health Act _____
_____

26. Occupational Safety and Health Administration (OSHA) _____
_____

27. Office of Workers' Compensation Programs (OWCP) _____
_____

28. ombudsmen _____
_____

29. physician of record _____
_____

30. Social Security Disability Insurance (SSDI) _____
_____

31. treating doctor _____

_____

32. Veteran's Disability Compensation _____

_____

33. Veteran's Disability Pension Benefits _____

_____

34. vocational rehabilitation _____

_____

35. Work Status Report _____

_____

CRITICAL THINKING QUESTIONS

Using the knowledge you have gained from reading the textbook, apply critical thinking skills to answer the following questions.

1. In the following scenarios, determine what type of income benefit each patient qualifies for:

   a. Injured worker Melissa McCain was in an accident in a work vehicle, which resulted in amputation of both legs as a result of injuries sustained. What type of income benefits does she qualify for?

   _____

   b. Injured worker Joe Williams was injured at work and assigned an impairment rating of 18%. He is earning 80% less than the state wage and did not take a lump sum payment of impairment income benefits. What type of income benefits does he qualify for?

   _____

   c. Injured worker Howard White was burned on the hand and has been off for 7 days. What type of income benefit does he qualify for?

   _____

2. a. You have just made an initial appointment for Jackie Alberto for a workers' compensation appointment. How would you verify that she is covered under a workers' compensation plan?

   _____

   _____

   b. Injured worker Miles Wetherby has not filed an injury report with his employer. Can his regular health insurance plan cover his visit to your office for this injury?

   _____

   _____

   _____

© 2018 Pearson Education, Inc.

3. After reading each given scenario, determine whether each injury would be either covered or not covered by workers' compensation insurance. Write *C* for covered and *NC* for not covered in the spaces provided.

   a. Rodger Ludwig injures his back while helping a patient onto the exam table.

   _____

   b. Marissa Javen trips and sprains her left ankle while getting on the elevator at work.

   _____

   c. Henry Wakeman cuts off the tip of his right index finger while using the meat slicer at work. He had stopped at the bar before his shift that day and had a few shots of whiskey.

   _____

   d. Bret Galloway is a welder. Lately, he has been experiencing moderate pain and numbness in his left arm, especially near the elbow. After examination, it is determined that he has cubital tunnel.

   _____

   e. Eddie Mann works in an automotive shop. He has been warned on many occasions that he is to wear safety glasses when performing certain procedures, yet he fails to abide by the rules because the glasses are "too uncomfortable." A piece of metal suddenly embeds in his left eye and scratches the cornea significantly.

   _____

   f. Elise Stanton is a mail carrier. Yesterday while working, a straight-end wind broke a branch off a tree and struck her in the head, causing a mild contusion.

   _____

4. Read the given statements and determine the type of workers' compensation fraud being committed for each scenario presented. Write whether each indicates *employer fraud*, *employee fraud*, *attorney fraud*, or *medical provider fraud* in the spaces provided.

   a. A single procedure is unbundled when billed.

   _____

   b. A suspicious injury occurs right before punch-out time on Friday afternoon.

   _____

   c. Reporting a smaller amount of payroll than what is true.

   _____

   d. Underutilization.

   _____

   e. A worker who is under workers' compensation has been bartending full time. His friend owns the bar, so he is being paid "off the books."

   _____

   f. A worker who has claimed a back injury was seen moving a couch into his house.

   _____

   g. An attorney charges for an unexplainable number of hours worked with the injured workers' case.

   _____

© 2018 Pearson Education, Inc.

5. a. What would you do if you suspected that a patient was committing workers' compensation fraud? Would you notify anyone? If so, whom?

_____

_____

_____

b. An injured worker is being investigated by the local district attorney for possible workers' compensation fraud. She has been receiving both medical and income benefits. She is compensated $2500 per month by the state. If she is found guilty of workers' compensation fraud, what penalties can she encounter? What type of crime is this considered to be?

_____

_____

_____

_____

_____

PRACTICE EXERCISES

1. Using the form locator information written out on your index cards from a prior chapter, complete the following activity. Flag those FLs that would be filled out differently for workers' compensation patients.

2. Follow the directions in your student text on calculating the workers' compensation reimbursement for the CPT codes listed, and use your state to complete this exercise.

CPT Code	MFS	WC
99202		
99203		
99201		
99211		
99213		
99214		

© 2018 Pearson Education, Inc.

3. The given case studies are provided for additional practice in completing the CMS-1500 claim form for workers' compensation physician outpatient billing. By applying what you have learned in your student text, accurately code and complete each case study. Patient demographics and a brief case history are provided. Complete the cases on the basis of the following assumptions:

- All patients have release of information and assignment of benefit signatures on file as a condition for workers' compensation. Items 12 and 13 should not be completed.

- All providers are participating and accept assignment by law. Item 27 should not be marked.

- The group practice is the billing entity.

- The national transition to NPI numbers is complete, and legacy PINs of individual payers are no longer used. If legacy PINS are still being used by your state's workers' compensation program, your instructor may provide legacy PINs in addition to the NPI.

- 2017 ICD-10-CM and CPT codes are used.

- Use eight-digit dates for birthdates. Use six-digit dates for all other dates.

- All street names should be entered with standard postal abbreviations, even if they are spelled out on the source documents.

- Enter ICD-10 codes in the order they appear on the encounter form.

- When entering CPT codes, enter the E/M code first. Enter remaining CPT codes in descending price order.

- Enter the workers' compensation assigned claim number in Item 1a. (Requirements will vary by state.)

Complete each case study. To determine the correct fees, refer to the Capital City Medical Fee Schedule, which is located after each case's source documents. Use the blank CMS-1500 form provided after each case.

a. Using the source documents, the Capital City Medical Fee Schedule (Figure 17-1), and the blank CMS-1500 form provided (Figure 17-2), complete the following case study for patient Zoe Rocco (Case 17-1):

CASE 17-1

Capital City Medical—123 Unknown Boulevard, Capital City, NY 12345-2222 (555) 555-1234	Patient Information Form
Phil Wells, MD, Mannie Mends, MD, Bette R. Soone, MD	Tax ID: 75-0246810
	Group NPI: 1513171216

Patient Information:

Name: (Last, First) Rocco, Zoe   ☒ Male   ☐ Female   Birth Date: 01/04/1968

Address: 431 Mason Dr, Capital City, NY 12345   Phone: (555) 555-4334

Social Security Number: 361-71-6650   Full-Time Student: ☐ Yes ☒ No

Marital Status: ☐ Single ☒ Married ☐ Divorced ☐ Other

Employment:

Employer: Quality Steel Company   Phone: (555) 555-7835

Address: 600 Silver Rd, Capital City, NY 12345

Condition Related to: ☐ Auto Accident ☒ Employment ☐ Other Accident

Date of Accident: 09/19/20XX   State: Township

Emergency Contact: _____ **Phone: ( )** _____

Primary Insurance: Capital Workers' Compensation Insurance Co.   Phone: ( ) _____

Address: 40 Hurt Rd, Capital City, NY 12345

Insurance Policyholder's Name: _____ ☐ M ☐ F DOB: _____

Address: _____

Phone: _____ Relationship to Insured: ☒ Self ☐ Spouse ☐ Child ☐ Other

Employer: _____   Phone: ( ) _____

Employer's Address: _____

Policy/ID No: WCZR5742 ____ Group No: ____ Percent Covered: ____% Copay Amt: $____

Secondary Insurance: _____ Phone: ( ) _____

Address: _____

Insurance Policyholder's Name: _____ ☐ M ☐ F DOB: _____

Address: _____

Phone: _____ Relationship to Insured: ☐ Self ☐ Spouse ☐ Child ☐ Other

Employer: _____   Phone: ( ) _____

Employer's Address: _____

Policy/ID No: _____ Group No: ____ Percent Covered: ____% Copay Amt: $____

Reason for Visit: I have been having extreme pain in my right elbow.

Known Allergies: _____

Referred by: _____

© 2018 Pearson Education, Inc.

CASE 17-1
● SOAP

09/20/20XX
Assignment of Benefits: Y
Signature on File: Y
Referring Physician: N

S: New patient Zoe Rocco is complaining of severe pain in his right elbow, which began a week ago.

O: Pt. has limited ROM in the right elbow. It is sensitive to touch. No redness, ulcerations, or rash is present. Pt. does have numbness and tingling. It is described as an "aching" pain. He is a steel polisher, full time.

A: 1. Cubital tunnel, right elbow—G56.21

P: 1. Start pt. on Ibuprofen one ×3 days.
2. Obtain EMG of the right extremity.
3. Return in 1 week to discuss results.
4. Off of work until further notice.
5. Refer to Mannie Mends, MD, for possible surgical repair of the ulnar nerve.
6. Please bill his workers' compensation. His info is as follows:
Capital Workers' Compensation Insurance Co.
40 Hurt Rd.
Capital City, NY 12345
Claim#WCZR5742
7. Phil Wells, MD state license#-MD-123456-L

_____

Phil Wells, MD
Family Practice
NPI: 1234567890

CASE 17-1

Patient Name Zoe Rocco

Capital City Medical
123 Unknown Boulevard, Capital City, NY 12345-2222

Date of Service
09-20-20XX

New Patient			Arthrocentesis/Aspiration/Injection			Laboratory	
Problem Focused	99201		Small Joint	20600		Amylase	82150
Expanded Problem, Focused	99202		Interm Joint	20605		B12	82607
Detailed	99203	X	Major Joint	20610		CBC & Diff	85025
Comprehensive	99204		**Other Invasive/Noninvasive**			Comp Metabolic Panel	80053
Comprehensive/High Complex	99205		Audiometry	92552		Chlamydia Screen	87110
Well Exam Infant (up to 12 mos.)	99381		Cast Application			Cholesterol	82465
Well Exam 1–4 yrs.	99382		Location Long Short			Digoxin	80162
Well Exam 5–11 yrs.	99383		Catheterization	51701		Electrolytes	80051
Well Exam 12–17 yrs.	99384		Circumcision	54150		Ferritin	82728
Well Exam 18–39 yrs.	99385		Colposcopy	57452		Folate	82746
Well Exam 40–64 yrs.	99386		Colposcopy w/Biopsy	57454		GC Screen	87070
			Cryosurgery Premalignant Lesion			Glucose	82947
			Location (s):			Glucose 1 HR	82950
			Cryosurgery Warts			Glycosylated HGB A1C	83036
Established Patient			Location (s):			HCT	85014
Post-Op Follow Up Visit	99024		Curettement Lesion			HDL	83718
Minimum	99211		Single	11055		Hep BSAG	87340
Problem Focused	99212		2–4	11056		Hepatitis panel, acute	80074
Expanded Problem Focused	99213		>4	11057		HGB	85018
Detailed	99214		Diaphragm Fitting	57170		HIV	86703
Comprehensive/High Complex	99215		Ear Irrigation	69210		Iron & TIBC	83550
Well Exam Infant (up to 12 mos.)	99391		ECG	93000		Kidney Profile	80069
Well exam 1–4 yrs.	99392		Endometrial Biopsy	58100		Lead	83655
Well Exam 5–11 yrs.	99393		Exc. Lesion Malignant			Liver Profile	80076
Well Exam 12–17 yrs.	99394		Benign			Mono Test	86308
Well Exam 18–39 yrs.	99395		Location			Pap Smear	88155
Well Exam 40–64 yrs.	99396		Exc. Skin Tags (1–15)	11200		Pregnancy Test	84703
Obstetrics			Each Additional 10	11201		Obstetric Panel	80055
Total OB Care	59400		Fracture Treatment			Pro Time	85610
Injections			Loc			PSA	84153
Administration Sub. / IM	90772		w/Reduc w/o Reduc			RPR	86592
Drug			I & D Abscess Single/Simple	10060		Sed. Rate	85651
Dosage			Multiple or Comp	10061		Stool Culture	87045
Allergy	95115		I & D Pilonidal Cyst Simple	10080		Stool O & P	87177
Cocci Skin Test	86490		Pilonidal Cyst Complex	10081		Strep Screen	87880
DPT	90701		IV Therapy—To One Hour	90760		Theophylline	80198
Hemophilus	90646		Each Additional Hour	90761		Thyroid Uptake	84479
Influenza	90658		Laceration Repair			TSH	84443
MMR	90707		Location Size Simp/Comp			Urinalysis	81000
OPV	90712		Laryngoscopy	31505		Urine Culture	87088
Pneumovax	90732		Oximetry	94760		Drawing Fee	36415
TB Skin Test	86580		Punch Biopsy			Specimen Collection	99000
TD	90718		Rhythm Strip	93040		**Other:**	
Unlisted Immun	90749		Treadmill	93015			
Tetanus Toxoid	90703		Trigger Point or Tendon Sheath Inj.	20550			
Vaccine/Toxoid Admin <8 Yr Old w/ Counseling	90465						
Vaccine/Toxoid Administration for Adult	90471		Tympanometry	92567			

Diagnosis/ICD-10: G56.21

I acknowledge receipt of medical services and authorize the release of any medical information necessary to process this claim for healthcare payment only. I do authorize payment to the provider.

Total Estimated Charges: _____

Payment Amount: _____

Patient Signature Zoe Rocco _____

Next Appointment: _____

Figure 17-1

Capital City Medical
Fee Schedule

New Patient OV			Punch Biopsy various codes	$80
Problem Focused 99201	$45		Nebulizer various codes	$45
Expanded Problem Focused 99202	$65		Cast Application various codes	$85
Detailed 99203	$85		Laryngoscopy 31505	$255
Comprehensive 99204	$105		Audiometry 92552	$85
Comprehensive/High Complex 99205	$115		Tympanometry 92567	$85
Well Exam infant (less than 1 year) 99381	$45		Ear Irrigation 69210	$25
Well Exam 1–4 yrs. 99382	$50		Diaphragm Fitting 57170	$30
Well Exam 5–11 yrs. 99383	$55		IV Therapy (up to one hour) 90760	$65
Well Exam 12–17 yrs. 99384	$65		Each additional hour 90761	$50
Well Exam 18–39 yrs. 99385	$85		Oximetry 94760	$10
Well Exam 40–64 yrs. 99386	$105		ECG 93000	$75
Established Patient OV			Holter Monitor various codes	$170
Post Op Follow Up Visit 99024	$0		Rhythm Strip 93040	$60
Minimum 99211	$35		Treadmill 93015	$375
Problem Focused 99212	$45		Cocci Skin Test 86490	$20
Expanded Problem Focused 99213	$55		X-ray, spine, chest, bone—any area various codes	$275
Detailed 99214	$65		Avulsion Nail 11730	$200
Comprehensive/High Complex 99215	$75		**Laboratory**	
Well exam infant (less than 1 year) 99391	$35		Amylase 82150	$40
Well Exam 1–4 yrs. 99392	$40		B12 82607	$30
Well Exam 5–11 yrs. 99393	$45		CBC & Diff 85025	$95
Well Exam 12–17 yrs. 99394	$55		Comp Metabolic Panel 80053	$75
Well Exam 18–39 yrs. 99395	$65		Chlamydia Screen 87110	$70
Well Exam 40–64 yrs. 99396	$75		Cholestrerol 82465	$75
Obstetrics			Digoxin 80162	$40
Total OB Care 59400	$1700		Electrolytes 80051	$70
Injections			Estrogen, Total 82672	$50
Administration 90772	$10		Ferritin 82728	$40
Allergy 95115	$35		Folate 82746	$30
DPT 90701	$50		GC Screen 87070	$60
Drug various codes	$35		Glucose 82947	$35
Influenza 90658	$25		Glycosylated HGB A1C 83036	$45
MMR 90707	$50		HCT 85014	$30
OPV 90712	$40		HDL 83718	$35
Pneumovax 90732	$35		HGB 85018	$30
TB Skin Test 86580	$15		Hep BSAG 83740	$40
TD 90718	$40		Hepatitis panel, acute 80074	$95
Tetanus Toxoid 90703	$40		HIV 86703	$100
Vaccine/Toxoid Administration for Younger Than 8 Years Old w/ counseling 90465	$10		Iron & TIBC 83550	$45
			Kidney Profile 80069	$95
Vaccine/Toxoid Administration for Adult 90471	$10		Lead 83665	$55
Arthrocentesis/Aspiration/Injection			Lipase 83690	$40
Small Joint 20600	$50		Lipid Panel 80061	$95
Interm Joint 20605	$60		Liver Profile 80076	$95
Major Joint 20610	$70		Mono Test 86308	$30
Trigger Point/Tendon Sheath Inj. 20550	$90		Pap Smear 88155	$90
Other Invasive/Noninvasive Procedures			Pap Collection/Supervision 88142	$95
Catheterization 51701	$55		Pregnancy Test 84703	$90
Circumcision 54150	$150		Obstetric Panel 80055	$85
Colposcopy 57452	$225		Pro Time 85610	$50
Colposcopy w/Biopsy 57454	$250		PSA 84153	$50
Cryosurgery Premalignant Lesion various codes	$160		RPR 86592	$55
Endometrial Biopsy 58100	$190		Sed. Rate 85651	$50
Excision Lesion Malignant various codes	$145		Stool Culture 87045	$80
Excision Lesion Benign various codes	$125		Stool O & P 87177	$105
Curettement Lesion			Strep Screen 87880	$35
Single 11055	$70		Theophylline 80198	$40
2–4 11056	$80		Thyroid Uptake 84479	$75
>4 11057	$90		TSH 84443	$50
Excision Skin Tags (1–15) 11200	$55		Urinalysis 81000	$35
Each Additional 10 11201	$30		Urine Culture 87088	$80
I & D Abscess Single/Simple 10060	$75		Drawing Fee 36415	$15
Multiple/Complex 10061	$95		Specimen Collection 99000	$10
I & D Pilonidal Cyst Simple 10080	$105			
I & D Pilonidal Cyst Complex 10081	$130			
Laceration Repair various codes	$60			

HEALTH INSURANCE CLAIM FORM

APPROVED BY NATIONAL UNIFORM CLAIM COMMITTEE (NUCC) 02/12

| | PICA | | | | | | | | PICA | |

1. MEDICARE	MEDICAID	TRICARE	CHAMPVA	GROUP HEALTH PLAN	FECA BLK LUNG	OTHER	1a. INSURED'S I.D. NUMBER	(For Program in Item 1)
[X] (Medicare#)	(Medicaid#)	(ID#/DoD#)	(Member ID#)	(ID#)	(ID#)	(ID#)		

2. PATIENT'S NAME (Last Name, First Name, Middle Initial)

3. PATIENT'S BIRTH DATE MM DD YY   SEX M [ ] F [ ]

4. INSURED'S NAME (Last Name, First Name, Middle Initial)

5. PATIENT'S ADDRESS (No., Street)

6. PATIENT RELATIONSHIP TO INSURED
Self [ ] Spouse [ ] Child [ ] Other [ ]

7. INSURED'S ADDRESS (No., Street)

CITY   STATE

8. RESERVED FOR NUCC USE

CITY   STATE

ZIP CODE   TELEPHONE (Include Area Code) ( )

ZIP CODE   TELEPHONE (Include Area Code) ( )

9. OTHER INSURED'S NAME (Last Name, First Name, Middle Initial)

10. IS PATIENT'S CONDITION RELATED TO:

11. INSURED'S POLICY GROUP OR FECA NUMBER

a. OTHER INSURED'S POLICY OR GROUP NUMBER

a. EMPLOYMENT? (Current or Previous) YES [ ] NO [ ]

a. INSURED'S DATE OF BIRTH MM DD YY   SEX M [ ] F [ ]

b. RESERVED FOR NUCC USE

b. AUTO ACCIDENT?   PLACE (State) YES [ ] NO [ ]

b. OTHER CLAIM ID (Designated by NUCC)

c. RESERVED FOR NUCC USE

c. OTHER ACCIDENT? YES [ ] NO [ ]

c. INSURANCE PLAN NAME OR PROGRAM NAME

d. INSURANCE PLAN NAME OR PROGRAM NAME

10d. CLAIM CODES (Designated by NUCC)

d. IS THERE ANOTHER HEALTH BENEFIT PLAN?
YES [ ] NO [ ] If yes, complete items 9, 9a, and 9d.

READ BACK OF FORM BEFORE COMPLETING & SIGNING THIS FORM.
12. PATIENT'S OR AUTHORIZED PERSON'S SIGNATURE I authorize the release of any medical or other information necessary to process this claim. I also request payment of government benefits either to myself or to the party who accepts assignment below.

SIGNED _____ DATE _____

13. INSURED'S OR AUTHORIZED PERSON'S SIGNATURE I authorize payment of medical benefits to the undersigned physician or supplier for services described below.

SIGNED _____

14. DATE OF CURRENT ILLNESS, INJURY, or PREGNANCY (LMP) MM DD YY QUAL.

15. OTHER DATE QUAL. MM DD YY

16. DATES PATIENT UNABLE TO WORK IN CURRENT OCCUPATION MM DD YY FROM   TO MM DD YY

17. NAME OF REFERRING PROVIDER OR OTHER SOURCE

17a.
17b. NPI

18. HOSPITALIZATION DATES RELATED TO CURRENT SERVICES MM DD YY FROM   TO MM DD YY

19. ADDITIONAL CLAIM INFORMATION (Designated by NUCC)

20. OUTSIDE LAB? YES [ ] NO [ ] $ CHARGES

21. DIAGNOSIS OR NATURE OF ILLNESS OR INJURY Relate A-L to service line below (24E) ICD Ind. [ ]

A. ____ B. ____ C. ____ D. ____
E. ____ F. ____ G. ____ H. ____
I. ____   J. ____ K. ____ L. ____

22. RESUBMISSION CODE   ORIGINAL REF. NO.

23. PRIOR AUTHORIZATION NUMBER

24. A. DATE(S) OF SERVICE						B. PLACE OF SERVICE	C. EMG	D. PROCEDURES, SERVICES, OR SUPPLIES (Explain Unusual Circumstances) CPT/HCPCS MODIFIER	E. DIAGNOSIS POINTER	F. $ CHARGES	G. DAYS OR UNITS	H. EPSDT Family Plan	I. ID QUAL.	J. RENDERING PROVIDER ID. #
From MM	DD	YY	To MM	DD	YY									
1													NPI	
2													NPI	
3													NPI	
4													NPI	
5													NPI	
6													NPI	

25. FEDERAL TAX I.D. NUMBER   SSN EIN [ ]

26. PATIENT'S ACCOUNT NO.

27. ACCEPT ASSIGNMENT? (For govt. claims, see back) YES [ ] NO [ ]

28. TOTAL CHARGE $

29. AMOUNT PAID $

30. Rsvd. for NUCC Use

31. SIGNATURE OF PHYSICIAN OR SUPPLIER INCLUDING DEGREES OR CREDENTIALS (I certify that the statements on the reverse apply to this bill and are made a part thereof.)

SIGNED _____ DATE _____

32. SERVICE FACILITY LOCATION INFORMATION

a. NPI   b.

33. BILLING PROVIDER INFO & PH # ( )

a. NPI   b.

NUCC Instruction Manual available at: www.nucc.org   **PLEASE PRINT OR TYPE**   APPROVED OMB-0938-1197 FORM 1500 (02-12)

Clear Form

CARRIER

PATIENT AND INSURED INFORMATION

PHYSICIAN OR SUPPLIER INFORMATION

Figure 17-2

© 2018 Pearson Education, Inc.

b. Using the source documents, the Capital City Medical Fee Schedule (Figure 17-3), and the blank CMS-1500 form provided (Figure 17-4), complete the following case study for patient Fritz Patrick (Case 17-2):

CASE 17-2

Capital City Medical—123 Unknown Boulevard, Capital City, NY 12345-2222 (555) 555-1234	**Patient Information Form**
	Tax ID: 75-0246810
Phil Wells, MD, Mannie Mends, MD, Bette R. Soone, MD	**Group NPI: 1513171216**

Patient Information:

Name: (Last, First) Patrick, Fritz   ☒ Male ☐ Female Birth Date: 02/22/1959

Address: 795 Moon Rd, Township, NY 12345   Phone: (555) 555-9909

Social Security Number: 271-88-4567   Full-Time Student: ☐ Yes ☒ No

Marital Status: ☒ Single ☐ Married ☐ Divorced ☐ Other

Employment:

Employer: Retired   Phone: ( )

Address:

Condition Related to: ☐ Auto Accident ☒ Employment ☐ Other Accident

Date of Accident: _____ State: _____

Emergency Contact: _____ **Phone: ( )** _____

Primary Insurance: Black Lung Workers' Compensation   Phone: ( )

Address: 88 Injury Center, Capital City, NY 12345

Insurance Policyholder's Name: _____ ☐ M ☐ F DOB: _____

Address:

Phone: _____ Relationship to Insured: ☒ Self ☐ Spouse ☐ Child ☐ Other

Employer: _____ Phone: ( ) _____

Employer's Address:

Policy/ID No: 271884567 ____ Group No: _____ Percent Covered: ___% Copay Amt: $_____

Secondary Insurance: _____ Phone: ( ) _____

Address:

Insurance Policyholder's Name: _____ ☐ M ☐ F DOB: _____

Address:

Phone: _____ Relationship to Insured: ☐ Self ☐ Spouse ☐ Child ☐ Other

Employer: _____ Phone: ( ) _____

Employer's Address:

Policy/ID No: _____ Group No: _____ Percent Covered: ___% Copay Amt: $_____

Reason for Visit: I am here for a follow-up on coal dust in my lungs.

Known Allergies: _____

Referred by: _____

CASE 17-2
SOAP

11/16/20XX
Assignment of Benefits: Y
Signature on File: Y
Referring Physician: N

S: Fritz Patrick presents in the office today for a checkup on his black lung disease.

O: He has no new complaints. He does use oxygen and his nebulizer as directed. He presents as stable.

A: 1. Pneumoconiosis (coal miners)—J60

P: 1. Continue meds and oxygen.
    2. Return in 3 months.
    3. Phil Wells, MD state license#-MD-123456-L

_____

Phil Wells, MD
Family Practice
NPI: 1234567890

© 2018 Pearson Education, Inc.

CASE 17-2

Patient Name Fritz Patrick

Capital City Medical
123 Unknown Boulevard, Capital City, NY 12345-2222

Date of Service
11-18-20XX

New Patient			Other Invasive/Noninvasive		Laboratory		
Problem Focused	99201		Arthrocentesis/Aspiration/Injection		Amylase	82150
Expanded Problem, Focused	99202		Small Joint	20600	B12	82607
Detailed	99203		Interm Joint	20605	CBC & Diff	85025
Comprehensive	99204		Major Joint	20610	Comp Metabolic Panel	80053
Comprehensive/High Complex	99205		**Other Invasive/Noninvasive**		Chlamydia Screen	87110
Well Exam Infant (up to 12 mos.)	99381		Audiometry	92552	Cholesterol	82465
Well Exam 1–4 yrs.	99382		Cast Application		Digoxin	80162
Well Exam 5–11 yrs.	99383		Location Long Short		Electrolytes	80051
Well Exam 12–17 yrs.	99384		Catheterization	51701	Ferritin	82728
Well Exam 18–39 yrs.	99385		Circumcision	54150	Folate	82746
Well Exam 40–64 yrs.	99386		Colposcopy	57452	GC Screen	87070
			Colposcopy w/Biopsy	57454	Glucose	82947
			Cryosurgery Premalignant Lesion		Glucose 1 HR	82950
			Location (s):		Glycosylated HGB A1C	83036
Established Patient			Cryosurgery Warts		HCT	85014
Post-Op Follow Up Visit	99024		Location (s):		HDL	83718
Minimum	99211		Curettement Lesion		Hep BSAG	87340
Problem Focused	99212	X	Single	11055	Hepatitis panel, acute	80074
Expanded Problem Focused	99213		2–4	11056	HGB	85018
Detailed	99214		>4	11057	HIV	86703
Comprehensive/High Complex	99215		Diaphragm Fitting	57170	Iron & TIBC	83550
Well Exam Infant (up to 12 mos.)	99391		Ear Irrigation	69210	Kidney Profile	80069
Well exam 1–4 yrs.	99392		ECG	93000	Lead	83655
Well Exam 5–11 yrs.	99393		Endometrial Biopsy	58100	Liver Profile	80076
Well Exam 12–17 yrs.	99394		Exc. Lesion Malignant		Mono Test	86308
Well Exam 18–39 yrs.	99395		Benign		Pap Smear	88155
Well Exam 40–64 yrs.	99396		Location		Pregnancy Test	84703
Obstetrics			Exc. Skin Tags (1–15)	11200	Obstetric Panel	80055
Total OB Care	59400		Each Additional 10	11201	Pro Time	85610
Injections			Fracture Treatment		PSA	84153
Administration Sub. / IM	90772		Loc		RPR	86592
Drug			w/Reduc w/o Reduc		Sed. Rate	85651
Dosage			I & D Abscess Single/Simple	10060	Stool Culture	87045
Allergy	95115		Multiple or Comp	10061	Stool O & P	87177
Cocci Skin Test	86490		I & D Pilonidal Cyst Simple	10080	Strep Screen	87880
DPT	90701		Pilonidal Cyst Complex	10081	Theophylline	80198
Hemophilus	90646		IV Therapy—To One Hour	90760	Thyroid Uptake	84479
Influenza	90658		Each Additional Hour	90761	TSH	84443
MMR	90707		Laceration Repair		Urinalysis	81000
OPV	90712		Location Size Simp/Comp		Urine Culture	87088
Pneumovax	90732		Laryngoscopy	31505	Drawing Fee	36415
TB Skin Test	86580		Oximetry	94760	Specimen Collection	99000
TD	90718		Punch Biopsy		**Other:**	
Unlisted Immun	90749		Rhythm Strip	93040		
Tetanus Toxoid	90703		Treadmill	93015		
Vaccine/Toxoid Admin <8 Yr Old w/ Counseling	90465		Trigger Point or Tendon Sheath Inj.	20550		
Vaccine/Toxoid Administration for Adult	90471		Tympanometry	92567		

Diagnosis/ICD-10: J60

I acknowledge receipt of medical services and authorize the release of any medical information necessary to process this claim for healthcare payment only. I do authorize payment to the provider.

Patient Signature Fritz Patrick

Total Estimated Charges: _____

Payment Amount: _____

Next Appointment: _____

Figure 17-3

Capital City Medical
Fee Schedule

New Patient OV				Punch Biopsy various codes	$80
Problem Focused 99201	$45			Nebulizer various codes	$45
Expanded Problem Focused 99202	$65			Cast Application various codes	$85
Detailed 99203	$85			Laryngoscopy 31505	$255
Comprehensive 99204	$105			Audiometry 92552	$85
Comprehensive/High Complex 99205	$115			Tympanometry 92567	$85
Well Exam infant (less than 1 year) 99381	$45			Ear Irrigation 69210	$25
Well Exam 1–4 yrs. 99382	$50			Diaphragm Fitting 57170	$30
Well Exam 5–11 yrs. 99383	$55			IV Therapy (up to one hour) 90760	$65
Well Exam 12–17 yrs. 99384	$65			Each additional hour 90761	$50
Well Exam 18–39 yrs. 99385	$85			Oximetry 94760	$10
Well Exam 40–64 yrs. 99386	$105			ECG 93000	$75
Established Patient OV				Holter Monitor various codes	$170
Post Op Follow Up Visit 99024	$0			Rhythm Strip 93040	$60
Minimum 99211	$35			Treadmill 93015	$375
Problem Focused 99212	$45			Cocci Skin Test 86490	$20
Expanded Problem Focused 99213	$55			X-ray, spine, chest, bone—any area various codes	$275
Detailed 99214	$65			Avulsion Nail 11730	$200
Comprehensive/High Complex 99215	$75			**Laboratory**	
Well exam infant (less than 1 year) 99391	$35			Amylase 82150	$40
Well Exam 1–4 yrs. 99392	$40			B12 82607	$30
Well Exam 5–11 yrs. 99393	$45			CBC & Diff 85025	$95
Well Exam 12–17 yrs. 99394	$55			Comp Metabolic Panel 80053	$75
Well Exam 18–39 yrs. 99395	$65			Chlamydia Screen 87110	$70
Well Exam 40–64 yrs. 99396	$75			Cholestrerol 82465	$75
Obstetrics				Digoxin 80162	$40
Total OB Care 59400	$1700			Electrolytes 80051	$70
Injections				Estrogen, Total 82672	$50
Administration 90772	$10			Ferritin 82728	$40
Allergy 95115	$35			Folate 82746	$30
DPT 90701	$50			GC Screen 87070	$60
Drug various codes	$35			Glucose 82947	$35
Influenza 90658	$25			Glycosylated HGB A1C 83036	$45
MMR 90707	$50			HCT 85014	$30
OPV 90712	$40			HDL 83718	$35
Pneumovax 90732	$35			HGB 85018	$30
TB Skin Test 86580	$15			Hep BSAG 83740	$40
TD 90718	$40			Hepatitis panel, acute 80074	$95
Tetanus Toxoid 90703	$40			HIV 86703	$100
Vaccine/Toxoid Administration for Younger				Iron & TIBC 83550	$45
Than 8 Years Old w/ counseling 90465	$10			Kidney Profile 80069	$95
Vaccine/Toxoid Administration for Adult 90471	$10			Lead 83665	$55
Arthrocentesis/Aspiration/Injection				Lipase 83690	$40
Small Joint 20600	$50			Lipid Panel 80061	$95
Interm Joint 20605	$60			Liver Profile 80076	$95
Major Joint 20610	$70			Mono Test 86308	$30
Trigger Point/Tendon Sheath Inj. 20550	$90			Pap Smear 88155	$90
Other Invasive/Noninvasive Procedures				Pap Collection/Supervision 88142	$95
Catheterization 51701	$55			Pregnancy Test 84703	$90
Circumcision 54150	$150			Obstetric Panel 80055	$85
Colposcopy 57452	$225			Pro Time 85610	$50
Colposcopy w/Biopsy 57454	$250			PSA 84153	$50
Cryosurgery Premalignant Lesion various codes	$160			RPR 86592	$55
Endometrial Biopsy 58100	$190			Sed. Rate 85651	$50
Excision Lesion Malignant various codes	$145			Stool Culture 87045	$80
Excision Lesion Benign various codes	$125			Stool O & P 87177	$105
Curettement Lesion				Strep Screen 87880	$35
Single 11055	$70			Theophylline 80198	$40
2–4 11056	$80			Thyroid Uptake 84479	$75
>4 11057	$90			TSH 84443	$50
Excision Skin Tags (1–15) 11200	$55			Urinalysis 81000	$35
Each Additional 10 11201	$30			Urine Culture 87088	$80
I & D Abscess Single/Simple 10060	$75			Drawing Fee 36415	$15
Multiple/Complex 10061	$95			Specimen Collection 99000	$10
I & D Pilonidal Cyst Simple 10080	$105				
I & D Pilonidal Cyst Complex 10081	$130				
Laceration Repair various codes	$60				

HEALTH INSURANCE CLAIM FORM

APPROVED BY NATIONAL UNIFORM CLAIM COMMITTEE (NUCC) 02/12

1. MEDICARE	MEDICAID	TRICARE	CHAMPVA	GROUP HEALTH PLAN	FECA BLK LUNG	OTHER	1a. INSURED'S I.D. NUMBER	(For Program in Item 1)
[X] (Medicare#)	[ ] (Medicaid#)	[ ] (ID#/DoD#)	[ ] (Member ID#)	[ ] (ID#)	[ ] (ID#)	[ ] (ID#)		

2. PATIENT'S NAME (Last Name, First Name, Middle Initial)	3. PATIENT'S BIRTH DATE MM DD YY SEX M [ ] F [ ]	4. INSURED'S NAME (Last Name, First Name, Middle Initial)

5. PATIENT'S ADDRESS (No., Street)	6. PATIENT RELATIONSHIP TO INSURED Self [ ] Spouse [ ] Child [ ] Other [ ]	7. INSURED'S ADDRESS (No., Street)
CITY STATE	8. RESERVED FOR NUCC USE	CITY STATE
ZIP CODE TELEPHONE (Include Area Code) ( )		ZIP CODE TELEPHONE (Include Area Code) ( )

9. OTHER INSURED'S NAME (Last Name, First Name, Middle Initial)	10. IS PATIENT'S CONDITION RELATED TO:	11. INSURED'S POLICY GROUP OR FECA NUMBER
a. OTHER INSURED'S POLICY OR GROUP NUMBER	a. EMPLOYMENT? (Current or Previous) [ ]YES [ ]NO	a. INSURED'S DATE OF BIRTH MM DD YY SEX M [ ] F [ ]
b. RESERVED FOR NUCC USE	b. AUTO ACCIDENT? PLACE (State) [ ]YES [ ]NO	b. OTHER CLAIM ID (Designated by NUCC)
c. RESERVED FOR NUCC USE	c. OTHER ACCIDENT? [ ]YES [ ]NO	c. INSURANCE PLAN NAME OR PROGRAM NAME
d. INSURANCE PLAN NAME OR PROGRAM NAME	10d. CLAIM CODES (Designated by NUCC)	d. IS THERE ANOTHER HEALTH BENEFIT PLAN? [ ]YES [ ]NO If yes, complete items 9, 9a, and 9d.

READ BACK OF FORM BEFORE COMPLETING & SIGNING THIS FORM.

12. PATIENT'S OR AUTHORIZED PERSON'S SIGNATURE I authorize the release of any medical or other information necessary to process this claim. I also request payment of government benefits either to myself or to the party who accepts assignment below. SIGNED _____ DATE _____	13. INSURED'S OR AUTHORIZED PERSON'S SIGNATURE I authorize payment of medical benefits to the undersigned physician or supplier for services described below. SIGNED _____

14. DATE OF CURRENT ILLNESS, INJURY, or PREGNANCY (LMP) MM DD YY QUAL.	15. OTHER DATE QUAL. MM DD YY	16. DATES PATIENT UNABLE TO WORK IN CURRENT OCCUPATION MM DD YY MM DD YY FROM TO
17. NAME OF REFERRING PROVIDER OR OTHER SOURCE	17a. 17b. NPI	18. HOSPITALIZATION DATES RELATED TO CURRENT SERVICES MM DD YY MM DD YY FROM TO

19. ADDITIONAL CLAIM INFORMATION (Designated by NUCC)	20. OUTSIDE LAB? [ ]YES [ ]NO $ CHARGES

21. DIAGNOSIS OR NATURE OF ILLNESS OR INJURY Relate A-L to service line below (24E) ICD Ind.	22. RESUBMISSION CODE ORIGINAL REF. NO.
A.___ B.___ C.___ D.___ E.___ F.___ G.___ H.___ I.___ J.___ K.___ L.___	23. PRIOR AUTHORIZATION NUMBER

24. A. DATE(S) OF SERVICE From To MM DD YY MM DD YY	B. PLACE OF SERVICE	C. EMG	D. PROCEDURES, SERVICES, OR SUPPLIES (Explain Unusual Circumstances) CPT/HCPCS MODIFIER	E. DIAGNOSIS POINTER	F. $ CHARGES	G. DAYS OR UNITS	H. EPSDT Family Plan	I. ID. QUAL	J. RENDERING PROVIDER ID. #
1									NPI
2									NPI
3									NPI
4									NPI
5									NPI
6									NPI

25. FEDERAL TAX I.D. NUMBER SSN EIN	26. PATIENT'S ACCOUNT NO.	27. ACCEPT ASSIGNMENT? (For govt. claims, see back) [ ]YES [ ]NO	28. TOTAL CHARGE $	29. AMOUNT PAID $	30. Rsvd. for NUCC Use
31. SIGNATURE OF PHYSICIAN OR SUPPLIER INCLUDING DEGREES OR CREDENTIALS (I certify that the statements on the reverse apply to this bill and are made a part thereof.) SIGNED ___ DATE ___	32. SERVICE FACILITY LOCATION INFORMATION a. NPI b.	33. BILLING PROVIDER INFO & PH # ( ) a. NPI b.			

NUCC Instruction Manual available at: www.nucc.org   **PLEASE PRINT OR TYPE**   APPROVED OMB-0938-1197 FORM 1500 (02-12)

Clear Form

CARRIER | PATIENT AND INSURED INFORMATION | PHYSICIAN OR SUPPLIER INFORMATION

Figure 17-4

c. Using the source documents, the Capital City Medical Fee Schedule (Figure 17-5), and the blank CMS-1500 form provided (Figure 17-6), complete the following case study for patient Nick Orelli (Case 17-3):

CASE 17-3

Capital City Medical—123 Unknown Boulevard, Capital City, NY 12345-2222 (555) 555-1234 Phil Wells, MD, Mannie Mends, MD, Bette R. Soone, MD	Patient Information Form Tax ID: 75-0246810 Group NPI: 1513171216

Patient Information:

Name: (Last, First) Orelli, Nick   ☒ Male ☐ Female Birth Date: 07/15/1964

Address: 41 Sixth Ave, Capital City, NY 12345   Phone: (555) 555-1867

Social Security Number: 387-81-5185   Full-Time Student: ☐ Yes ☒ No

Marital Status: ☐ Single ☒ Married ☐ Divorced ☐ Other

Employment:

Employer: Metal Recycle Co.   Phone: (555) 555-8438

Address: 2934 Balph Rd, Township, NY 12345

Condition Related to: ☐ Auto Accident ☒ Employment ☐ Other Accident

Date of Accident: 05/04/20XX   State: NY

Emergency Contact: _____ **Phone: ( )** _____

Primary Insurance: Employees Workers' Compensation Insurance Co. Phone: ( ) _____

Address: 1408 Baker Rd, Capital City, NY 12345

Insurance Policyholder's Name: _____ ☐ M ☐ F DOB: _____

Address: _____

Phone: _____ Relationship to Insured: ☒ Self ☐ Spouse ☐ Child ☐ Other

Employer: _____ Phone: ( ) _____

Employer's Address: _____

Policy/ID No: WCNO6496   Group No: ____ Percent Covered: ___% Copay Amt: $____

Secondary Insurance: _____ Phone: ( ) _____

Address: _____

Insurance Policyholder's Name: same _____ ☐ M ☐ F DOB: _____

Address: _____

Phone: _____ Relationship to Insured: ☐ Self ☐ Spouse ☐ Child ☐ Other

Employer: _____ Phone: ( ) _____

Employer's Address: _____

Policy/ID No: _____ Group No: ____ Percent Covered: ___% Copay Amt: $____

Reason for Visit: I burned my hand at work while welding.

Known Allergies: _____

Referred by: _____

CASE 17-3
● SOAP

05/04/20XX
Assignment of Benefits: Y
Signature on File: Y
Referring Physician: N

S: Nick Orelli is being seen for a burn on his left hand today. He was welding at work when his arm slipped, causing his welding torch to burn his left hand.

O: The exam reveals rubor on the back of his left hand. The area is blistered. It does not look infected at this time. He denies any other burns.

A: 1. Burn, back of left hand, 2nd degree—T23.262A
2. Welding torch burn—X08.8XXA

P: 1. Start oral antibiotics.
2. Antibiotic ointment twice daily.
3. Keep area clean and dry.
4. Change dressing twice a day, or if dirty or wet.
5. Return to office if infection occurs.
6. Return to work 05/08/20XX if there are no complications.
7. Please bill his workers' compensation. His info is as follows:
Employees' Workers' Compensation Insurance Co.
1408 Baker Road
Capital City, NY 12345
Claim#WCNO6496
8. Phil Wells, MD state license#-MD-123456-L

Phil Wells, MD
Family Practice
NPI: 1234567890

CASE 17-3

Patient Name Nick Orelli

Capital City Medical
123 Unknown Boulevard, Capital City, NY 12345-2222

Date of Service
05-04-20XX

New Patient			Other Invasive/Noninvasive etc.			Laboratory	
Problem Focused	99201		Arthrocentesis/Aspiration/Injection			Amylase	82150
Expanded Problem, Focused	99202		Small Joint	20600		B12	82607
Detailed	99203		Interm Joint	20605		CBC & Diff	85025
Comprehensive	99204		Major Joint	20610		Comp Metabolic Panel	80053
Comprehensive/High Complex	99205		**Other Invasive/Noninvasive**			Chlamydia Screen	87110
Well Exam Infant (up to 12 mos.)	99381		Audiometry	92552		Cholesterol	82465
Well Exam 1–4 yrs.	99382		Cast Application			Digoxin	80162
Well Exam 5–11 yrs.	99383		Location Long Short			Electrolytes	80051
Well Exam 12–17 yrs.	99384		Catheterization	51701		Ferritin	82728
Well Exam 18–39 yrs.	99385		Circumcision	54150		Folate	82746
Well Exam 40–64 yrs.	99386		Colposcopy	57452		GC Screen	87070
			Colposcopy w/Biopsy	57454		Glucose	82947
			Cryosurgery Premalignant Lesion			Glucose 1 HR	82950
			Location (s):			Glycosylated HGB A1C	83036
Established Patient			Cryosurgery Warts			HCT	85014
Post-Op Follow Up Visit	99024		Location (s):			HDL	83718
Minimum	99211		Curettement Lesion			Hep BSAG	87340
Problem Focused	99212		Single	11055		Hepatitis panel, acute	80074
Expanded Problem Focused	99213	X	2–4	11056		HGB	85018
Detailed	99214		>4	11057		HIV	86703
Comprehensive/High Complex	99215		Diaphragm Fitting	57170		Iron & TIBC	83550
Well Exam Infant (up to 12 mos.)	99391		Ear Irrigation	69210		Kidney Profile	80069
Well exam 1–4 yrs.	99392		ECG	93000		Lead	83655
Well Exam 5–11 yrs.	99393		Endometrial Biopsy	58100		Liver Profile	80076
Well Exam 12–17 yrs.	99394		Exc. Lesion Malignant			Mono Test	86308
Well Exam 18–39 yrs.	99395		Benign			Pap Smear	88155
Well Exam 40–64 yrs.	99396		Location			Pregnancy Test	84703
Obstetrics			Exc. Skin Taqs (1–15)	11200		Obstetric Panel	80055
Total OB Care	59400		Each Additional 10	11201		Pro Time	85610
Injections			Fracture Treatment			PSA	84153
Administration Sub. / IM	90772		Loc			RPR	86592
Drug			w/Reduc w/o Reduc			Sed. Rate	85651
Dosage			I & D Abscess Single/Simple	10060		Stool Culture	87045
Allergy	95115		Multiple or Comp	10061		Stool O & P	87177
Cocci Skin Test	86490		I & D Pilonidal Cyst Simple	10080		Strep Screen	87880
DPT	90701		Pilonidal Cyst Complex	10081		Theophylline	80198
Hemophilus	90646		IV Therapy—To One Hour	90760		Thyroid Uptake	84479
Influenza	90658		Each Additional Hour	90761		TSH	84443
MMR	90707		Laceration Repair			Urinalysis	81000
OPV	90712		Location Size Simp/Comp			Urine Culture	87088
Pneumovax	90732		Laryngoscopy	31505		Drawing Fee	36415
TB Skin Test	86580		Oximetry	94760		Specimen Collection	99000
TD	90718		Punch Biopsy			**Other:**	
Unlisted Immun	90749		Rhythm Strip	93040			
Tetanus Toxoid	90703		Treadmill	93015			
Vaccine/Toxoid Admin <8 Yr Old w/ Counseling	90465		Trigger Point or Tendon Sheath Inj.	20550			
Vaccine/Toxoid Administration for Adult	90471		Tympanometry	92567			

Diagnosis/ICD-10: T23.262A, X08.8XXA

I acknowledge receipt of medical services and authorize the release of any medical information necessary to process this claim for healthcare payment only. I do authorize payment to the provider.

Total Estimated Charges: _____

Payment Amount: _____

Patient Signature _Nick Orelli_

Next Appointment: _____

Figure 17-5

Capital City Medical
Fee Schedule

New Patient OV				
Problem Focused 99201	$45		Punch Biopsy various codes	$80
Expanded Problem Focused 99202	$65		Nebulizer various codes	$45
Detailed 99203	$85		Cast Application various codes	$85
Comprehensive 99204	$105		Laryngoscopy 31505	$255
Comprehensive/High Complex 99205	$115		Audiometry 92552	$85
Well Exam infant (less than 1 year) 99381	$45		Tympanometry 92567	$85
Well Exam 1–4 yrs. 99382	$50		Ear Irrigation 69210	$25
Well Exam 5–11 yrs. 99383	$55		Diaphragm Fitting 57170	$30
Well Exam 12–17 yrs. 99384	$65		IV Therapy (up to one hour) 90760	$65
Well Exam 18–39 yrs. 99385	$85		Each additional hour 90761	$50
Well Exam 40–64 yrs. 99386	$105		Oximetry 94760	$10
Established Patient OV			ECG 93000	$75
Post Op Follow Up Visit 99024	$0		Holter Monitor various codes	$170
Minimum 99211	$35		Rhythm Strip 93040	$60
Problem Focused 99212	$45		Treadmill 93015	$375
Expanded Problem Focused 99213	$55		Cocci Skin Test 86490	$20
Detailed 99214	$65		X-ray, spine, chest, bone—any area various codes	$275
Comprehensive/High Complex 99215	$75		Avulsion Nail 11730	$200
Well exam infant (less than 1 year) 99391	$35		**Laboratory**	
Well Exam 1–4 yrs. 99392	$40		Amylase 82150	$40
Well Exam 5–11 yrs. 99393	$45		B12 82607	$30
Well Exam 12–17 yrs. 99394	$55		CBC & Diff 85025	$95
Well Exam 18–39 yrs. 99395	$65		Comp Metabolic Panel 80053	$75
Well Exam 40–64 yrs. 99396	$75		Chlamydia Screen 87110	$70
Obstetrics			Cholestrerol 82465	$75
Total OB Care 59400	$1700		Digoxin 80162	$40
Injections			Electrolytes 80051	$70
Administration 90772	$10		Estrogen, Total 82672	$50
Allergy 95115	$35		Ferritin 82728	$40
DPT 90701	$50		Folate 82746	$30
Drug various codes	$35		GC Screen 87070	$60
Influenza 90658	$25		Glucose 82947	$35
MMR 90707	$50		Glycosylated HGB A1C 83036	$45
OPV 90712	$40		HCT 85014	$30
Pneumovax 90732	$35		HDL 83718	$35
TB Skin Test 86580	$15		HGB 85018	$30
TD 90718	$40		Hep BSAG 83740	$40
Tetanus Toxoid 90703	$40		Hepatitis panel, acute 80074	$95
Vaccine/Toxoid Administration for Younger Than 8 Years Old w/ counseling 90465	$10		HIV 86703	$100
			Iron & TIBC 83550	$45
Vaccine/Toxoid Administration for Adult 90471	$10		Kidney Profile 80069	$95
Arthrocentesis/Aspiration/Injection			Lead 83665	$55
Small Joint 20600	$50		Lipase 83690	$40
Interm Joint 20605	$60		Lipid Panel 80061	$95
Major Joint 20610	$70		Liver Profile 80076	$95
Trigger Point/Tendon Sheath Inj. 20550	$90		Mono Test 86308	$30
Other Invasive/Noninvasive Procedures			Pap Smear 88155	$90
Catheterization 51701	$55		Pap Collection/Supervision 88142	$95
Circumcision 54150	$150		Pregnancy Test 84703	$90
Colposcopy 57452	$225		Obstetric Panel 80055	$85
Colposcopy w/Biopsy 57454	$250		Pro Time 85610	$50
Cryosurgery Premalignant Lesion various codes	$160		PSA 84153	$50
Endometrial Biopsy 58100	$190		RPR 86592	$55
Excision Lesion Malignant various codes	$145		Sed. Rate 85651	$50
Excision Lesion Benign various codes	$125		Stool Culture 87045	$80
Curettement Lesion			Stool O & P 87177	$105
Single 11055	$70		Strep Screen 87880	$35
2–4 11056	$80		Theophylline 80198	$40
>4 11057	$90		Thyroid Uptake 84479	$75
Excision Skin Tags (1–15) 11200	$55		TSH 84443	$50
Each Additional 10 11201	$30		Urinalysis 81000	$35
I & D Abscess Single/Simple 10060	$75		Urine Culture 87088	$80
Multiple/Complex 10061	$95		Drawing Fee 36415	$15
I & D Pilonidal Cyst Simple 10080	$105		Specimen Collection 99000	$10
I & D Pilonidal Cyst Complex 10081	$130			
Laceration Repair various codes	$60			

HEALTH INSURANCE CLAIM FORM

APPROVED BY NATIONAL UNIFORM CLAIM COMMITTEE (NUCC) 02/12

☐☐ PICA

	PICA ☐☐

1. MEDICARE ☒ (Medicare#) **MEDICAID** ☐ (Medicaid#) **TRICARE** ☐ (ID#/DoD#) **CHAMPVA** ☐ (Member ID#) **GROUP HEALTH PLAN** ☐ (ID#) **FECA BLK LUNG** ☐ (ID#) **OTHER** ☐ (ID#) | **1a. INSURED'S I.D. NUMBER** (For Program in Item 1)

2. PATIENT'S NAME (Last Name, First Name, Middle Initial) | **3. PATIENT'S BIRTH DATE** MM ┊ DD ┊ YY **SEX** M ☐ F ☐ | **4. INSURED'S NAME (Last Name, First Name, Middle Initial)**

5. PATIENT'S ADDRESS (No., Street) | **6. PATIENT RELATIONSHIP TO INSURED** Self ☐ Spouse ☐ Child ☐ Other ☐ | **7. INSURED'S ADDRESS (No., Street)**

CITY | STATE | **8. RESERVED FOR NUCC USE** | CITY | STATE

ZIP CODE | TELEPHONE (Include Area Code) ( ) | ZIP CODE | TELEPHONE (Include Area Code) ( )

9. OTHER INSURED'S NAME (Last Name, First Name, Middle Initial) | **10. IS PATIENT'S CONDITION RELATED TO:** | **11. INSURED'S POLICY GROUP OR FECA NUMBER**

a. OTHER INSURED'S POLICY OR GROUP NUMBER | **a. EMPLOYMENT? (Current or Previous)** ☐ YES ☐ NO | **a. INSURED'S DATE OF BIRTH** MM ┊ DD ┊ YY **SEX** M ☐ F ☐

b. RESERVED FOR NUCC USE | **b. AUTO ACCIDENT?** PLACE (State) ☐ YES ☐ NO | **b. OTHER CLAIM ID (Designated by NUCC)**

c. RESERVED FOR NUCC USE | **c. OTHER ACCIDENT?** ☐ YES ☐ NO | **c. INSURANCE PLAN NAME OR PROGRAM NAME**

d. INSURANCE PLAN NAME OR PROGRAM NAME | **10d. CLAIM CODES (Designated by NUCC)** | **d. IS THERE ANOTHER HEALTH BENEFIT PLAN?** ☐ YES ☐ NO *If yes*, complete items 9, 9a, and 9d.

READ BACK OF FORM BEFORE COMPLETING & SIGNING THIS FORM.
12. PATIENT'S OR AUTHORIZED PERSON'S SIGNATURE I authorize the release of any medical or other information necessary to process this claim. I also request payment of government benefits either to myself or to the party who accepts assignment below.

SIGNED _____ DATE _____

13. INSURED'S OR AUTHORIZED PERSON'S SIGNATURE I authorize payment of medical benefits to the undersigned physician or supplier for services described below.

SIGNED _____

14. DATE OF CURRENT ILLNESS, INJURY, or PREGNANCY (LMP) MM ┊ DD ┊ YY QUAL | **15. OTHER DATE** QUAL ┊ MM ┊ DD ┊ YY | **16. DATES PATIENT UNABLE TO WORK IN CURRENT OCCUPATION** FROM MM ┊ DD ┊ YY TO MM ┊ DD ┊ YY

17. NAME OF REFERRING PROVIDER OR OTHER SOURCE | 17a. | 17b. NPI | **18. HOSPITALIZATION DATES RELATED TO CURRENT SERVICES** FROM MM ┊ DD ┊ YY TO MM ┊ DD ┊ YY

19. ADDITIONAL CLAIM INFORMATION (Designated by NUCC) | **20. OUTSIDE LAB?** ☐ YES ☐ NO $ CHARGES

21. DIAGNOSIS OR NATURE OF ILLNESS OR INJURY Relate A-L to service line below (24E) ICD Ind. ┊
A. |___| B. |___| C. |___| D. |___|
E. |___| F. |___| G. |___| H. |___|
I. |___| J. |___| K. |___| L. |___| | **22. RESUBMISSION CODE** | ORIGINAL REF. NO.

23. PRIOR AUTHORIZATION NUMBER

24. A. DATE(S) OF SERVICE From MM DD YY To MM DD YY	B. PLACE OF SERVICE	C. EMG	D. PROCEDURES, SERVICES, OR SUPPLIES (Explain Unusual Circumstances) CPT/HCPCS MODIFIER	E. DIAGNOSIS POINTER	F. $ CHARGES	G. DAYS OR UNITS	H. EPSDT Family Plan	I. ID. QUAL	J. RENDERING PROVIDER ID. #
1									NPI
2									NPI
3									NPI
4									NPI
5									NPI
6									NPI

25. FEDERAL TAX I.D. NUMBER SSN EIN ☐ ☐ | **26. PATIENT'S ACCOUNT NO.** | **27. ACCEPT ASSIGNMENT?** (For govt. claims, see back) ☐ YES ☐ NO | **28. TOTAL CHARGE** $ | **29. AMOUNT PAID** $ | **30. Rsvd. for NUCC Use**

31. SIGNATURE OF PHYSICIAN OR SUPPLIER INCLUDING DEGREES OR CREDENTIALS (I certify that the statements on the reverse apply to this bill and are made a part thereof.)

SIGNED _____ DATE _____ | **32. SERVICE FACILITY LOCATION INFORMATION** a. NPI   b. | **33. BILLING PROVIDER INFO & PH # ( )** a. NPI   b.

NUCC Instruction Manual available at: www.nucc.org   **PLEASE PRINT OR TYPE**   APPROVED OMB-0938-1197 FORM 1500 (02-12)

`Clear Form`

(side margins: CARRIER — PATIENT AND INSURED INFORMATION — PHYSICIAN OR SUPPLIER INFORMATION)

Figure 17-6

© 2018 Pearson Education, Inc.

d. Using the source documents, the Capital City Medical Fee Schedule (Figure 17-7), and the blank CMS-1500 form provided (Figure 17-8), complete the following case study for patient Gloria McMannis (Case 17-4):

CASE 17-4

Capital City Medical—123 Unknown Boulevard, Capital City, NY 12345-2222 (555) 555-1234

Phil Wells, MD, Mannie Mends, MD, Bette R. Soone, MD

Patient Information Form

Tax ID: 75-0246810

Group NPI: 1513171216

Patient Information:

Name: (Last, First) McMannis, Gloria   ☐ Male ☒ Female Birth Date: 11/09/1961

Address: 53 Homer St, Township, NY 12345   Phone: (555) 555-8613

Social Security Number: 695-08-2865   Full-Time Student: ☐ Yes ☒ No

Marital Status: ☒ Single ☐ Married ☐ Divorced ☐ Other

Employment:

Employer: Furniture Plus   Phone: (555) 555-5316

Address: 4592 Capital Square, Capital City, NY 12345

Condition Related to: ☐ Auto Accident ☒ Employment ☐ Other Accident

Date of Accident: 08/12/20XX   State: Capital City

Emergency Contact: _____   **Phone: ( )** _____

Primary Insurance: State Workers' Compensation Insurance Co.   Phone: ( ) _____

Address: 88 Injury Center, Capital City, NY 12345

Insurance Policyholder's Name: _____ ☐ M ☐ F DOB: _____

Address: _____

Phone: _____ Relationship to Insured: ☒ Self ☐ Spouse ☐ Child ☐ Other

Employer: _____ Phone: ( ) _____

Employer's Address: _____

Policy/ID No: WCGMO802   Group No: ____ Percent Covered: ___% Copay Amt: $____

Secondary Insurance: _____   Phone: ( ) _____

Address: _____

Insurance Policyholder's Name: _____ ☐ M ☐ F DOB: _____

Address: _____

Phone: _____ Relationship to Insured: ☐ Self ☐ Spouse ☐ Child ☐ Other

Employer: _____ Phone: ( ) _____

Employer's Address: _____

Policy/ID No: _____   Group No: ____ Percent Covered: ___% Copay Amt: $____

Reason for Visit: I hurt my back at work today while moving a couch.

Known Allergies: _____

Referred by: _____

CASE 17-4
SOAP

08/12/20XX
Assignment of Benefits: Y
Signature on File: Y
Referring Physician: N

S: New patient Gloria McMannis hurt her lower back at work today, while helping another employee move a couch.

O: Pt. complains of pain in the lumber region. It is tender to the touch. She states that the pain is an "8." The skin shows no bruising or lesions. She was wearing a lifting belt. Lumbar spine X-ray today shows swelling. There is no evidence of herniation or fracture.

A: 1. Back strain, lumbar—S39.012A
2. Injury during lifting/moving—X50.0XXA

P: 1. Naproxen 2 times/day.
2. Heating pad as needed.
3. Appointment in 1 week.
4. Return to work 08/15/20XX, only under light duty.
5. Please bill her workers' compensation. Her info is as follows:
State Workers' Compensation Insurance Co.
88 Injury Center
Capital City, NY 12345
Claim#WCGM0802
6. Phil Wells, MD state license#-MD-123456-L

_____

Phil Wells, MD
Family Practice
NPI: 1234567890

© 2018 Pearson Education, Inc.

CASE 17-4

Patient Name Gloria McMannis

Capital City Medical
123 Unknown Boulevard, Capital City, NY 12345-2222

Date of Service
08-12-20XX

New Patient			Other Invasive/Noninvasive			Laboratory	
Problem Focused	99201		Arthrocentesis/Aspiration/Injection			Amylase	82150
Expanded Problem, Focused	99202		Small Joint	20600		B12	82607
Detailed	99203	X	Interm Joint	20605		CBC & Diff	85025
Comprehensive	99204		Major Joint	20610		Comp Metabolic Panel	80053
Comprehensive/High Complex	99205		**Other Invasive/Noninvasive**			Chlamydia Screen	87110
Well Exam Infant (up to 12 mos.)	99381		Audiometry	92552		Cholesterol	82465
Well Exam 1–4 yrs.	99382		Cast Application			Digoxin	80162
Well Exam 5–11 yrs.	99383		Location Long Short			Electrolytes	80051
Well Exam 12–17 yrs.	99384		Catheterization	51701		Ferritin	82728
Well Exam 18–39 yrs.	99385		Circumcision	54150		Folate	82746
Well Exam 40–64 yrs.	99386		Colposcopy	57452		GC Screen	87070
			Colposcopy w/Biopsy	57454		Glucose	82947
			Cryosurgery Premalignant Lesion			Glucose 1 HR	82950
			Location (s):			Glycosylated HGB A1C	83036
Established Patient			Cryosurgery Warts			HCT	85014
Post-Op Follow Up Visit	99024		Location (s):			HDL	83718
Minimum	99211		Curettement Lesion			Hep BSAG	87340
Problem Focused	99212		Single	11055		Hepatitis panel, acute	80074
Expanded Problem Focused	99213		2–4	11056		HGB	85018
Detailed	99214		>4	11057		HIV	86703
Comprehensive/High Complex	99215		Diaphragm Fitting	57170		Iron & TIBC	83550
Well Exam Infant (up to 12 mos.)	99391		Ear Irrigation	69210		Kidney Profile	80069
Well exam 1–4 yrs.	99392		ECG	93000		Lead	83655
Well Exam 5–11 yrs.	99393		Endometrial Biopsy	58100		Liver Profile	80076
Well Exam 12–17 yrs.	99394		Exc. Lesion Malignant			Mono Test	86308
Well Exam 18–39 yrs.	99395		Benign			Pap Smear	88155
Well Exam 40–64 yrs.	99396		Location			Pregnancy Test	84703
Obstetrics			Exc. Skin Taqs (1–15)	11200		Obstetric Panel	80055
Total OB Care	59400		Each Additional 10	11201		Pro Time	85610
Injections			Fracture Treatment			PSA	84153
Administration Sub. / IM	90772		Loc			RPR	86592
Drug			w/Reduc w/o Reduc			Sed. Rate	85651
Dosage			I & D Abscess Single/Simple	10060		Stool Culture	87045
Allergy	95115		Multiple or Comp	10061		Stool O & P	87177
Cocci Skin Test	86490		I & D Pilonidal Cyst Simple	10080		Strep Screen	87880
DPT	90701		Pilonidal Cyst Complex	10081		Theophylline	80198
Hemophilus	90646		IV Therapy—To One Hour	90760		Thyroid Uptake	84479
Influenza	90658		Each Additional Hour	90761		TSH	84443
MMR	90707		Laceration Repair			Urinalysis	81000
OPV	90712		Location Size Simp/Comp			Urine Culture	87088
Pneumovax	90732		Laryngoscopy	31505		Drawing Fee	36415
TB Skin Test	86580		Oximetry	94760		Specimen Collection	99000
TD	90718		Punch Biopsy			**Other:**	
Unlisted Immun	90749		Rhythm Strip	93040		X-Ray L-Spine	72100	X
Tetanus Toxoid	90703		Treadmill	93015			
Vaccine/Toxoid Admin <8 Yr Old w/ Counseling	90465		Trigger Point or Tendon Sheath Inj.	20550			
Vaccine/Toxoid Administration for Adult	90471		Tympanometry	92567			

Diagnosis/ICD-10: S39.012A,
                              X50.0XXA

I acknowledge receipt of medical services and authorize the release of any medical information necessary to process this claim for healthcare payment only. I do authorize payment to the provider.

Patient Signature Gloria McMannis

Total Estimated Charges: _____

Payment Amount: _____

Next Appointment: _____

Figure 17-7

Capital City Medical
Fee Schedule

New Patient OV			Punch Biopsy various codes	$80
Problem Focused 99201	$45		Nebulizer various codes	$45
Expanded Problem Focused 99202	$65		Cast Application various codes	$85
Detailed 99203	$85		Laryngoscopy 31505	$255
Comprehensive 99204	$105		Audiometry 92552	$85
Comprehensive/High Complex 99205	$115		Tympanometry 92567	$85
Well Exam infant (less than 1 year) 99381	$45		Ear Irrigation 69210	$25
Well Exam 1–4 yrs. 99382	$50		Diaphragm Fitting 57170	$30
Well Exam 5–11 yrs. 99383	$55		IV Therapy (up to one hour) 90760	$65
Well Exam 12–17 yrs. 99384	$65		Each additional hour 90761	$50
Well Exam 18–39 yrs. 99385	$85		Oximetry 94760	$10
Well Exam 40–64 yrs. 99386	$105		ECG 93000	$75
Established Patient OV			Holter Monitor various codes	$170
Post Op Follow Up Visit 99024	$0		Rhythm Strip 93040	$60
Minimum 99211	$35		Treadmill 93015	$375
Problem Focused 99212	$45		Cocci Skin Test 86490	$20
Expanded Problem Focused 99213	$55		X-ray, spine, chest, bone—any area various codes	$275
Detailed 99214	$65		Avulsion Nail 11730	$200
Comprehensive/High Complex 99215	$75		**Laboratory**	
Well exam infant (less than 1 year) 99391	$35		Amylase 82150	$40
Well Exam 1–4 yrs. 99392	$40		B12 82607	$30
Well Exam 5–11 yrs. 99393	$45		CBC & Diff 85025	$95
Well Exam 12–17 yrs. 99394	$55		Comp Metabolic Panel 80053	$75
Well Exam 18–39 yrs. 99395	$65		Chlamydia Screen 87110	$70
Well Exam 40–64 yrs. 99396	$75		Cholestrerol 82465	$75
Obstetrics			Digoxin 80162	$40
Total OB Care 59400	$1700		Electrolytes 80051	$70
Injections			Estrogen, Total 82672	$50
Administration 90772	$10		Ferritin 82728	$40
Allergy 95115	$35		Folate 82746	$30
DPT 90701	$50		GC Screen 87070	$60
Drug various codes	$35		Glucose 82947	$35
Influenza 90658	$25		Glycosylated HGB A1C 83036	$45
MMR 90707	$50		HCT 85014	$30
OPV 90712	$40		HDL 83718	$35
Pneumovax 90732	$35		HGB 85018	$30
TB Skin Test 86580	$15		Hep BSAG 83740	$40
TD 90718	$40		Hepatitis panel, acute 80074	$95
Tetanus Toxoid 90703	$40		HIV 86703	$100
Vaccine/Toxoid Administration for Younger			Iron & TIBC 83550	$45
Than 8 Years Old w/ counseling 90465	$10		Kidney Profile 80069	$95
Vaccine/Toxoid Administration for Adult 90471	$10		Lead 83665	$55
Arthrocentesis/Aspiration/Injection			Lipase 83690	$40
Small Joint 20600	$50		Lipid Panel 80061	$95
Interm Joint 20605	$60		Liver Profile 80076	$95
Major Joint 20610	$70		Mono Test 86308	$30
Trigger Point/Tendon Sheath Inj. 20550	$90		Pap Smear 88155	$90
Other Invasive/Noninvasive Procedures			Pap Collection/Supervision 88142	$95
Catheterization 51701	$55		Pregnancy Test 84703	$90
Circumcision 54150	$150		Obstetric Panel 80055	$85
Colposcopy 57452	$225		Pro Time 85610	$50
Colposcopy w/Biopsy 57454	$250		PSA 84153	$50
Cryosurgery Premalignant Lesion various codes	$160		RPR 86592	$55
Endometrial Biopsy 58100	$190		Sed. Rate 85651	$50
Excision Lesion Malignant various codes	$145		Stool Culture 87045	$80
Excision Lesion Benign various codes	$125		Stool O & P 87177	$105
Curettement Lesion			Strep Screen 87880	$35
Single 11055	$70		Theophylline 80198	$40
2–4 11056	$80		Thyroid Uptake 84479	$75
>4 11057	$90		TSH 84443	$50
Excision Skin Tags (1–15) 11200	$55		Urinalysis 81000	$35
Each Additional 10 11201	$30		Urine Culture 87088	$80
I & D Abscess Single/Simple 10060	$75		Drawing Fee 36415	$15
Multiple/Complex 10061	$95		Specimen Collection 99000	$10
I & D Pilonidal Cyst Simple 10080	$105			
I & D Pilonidal Cyst Complex 10081	$130			
Laceration Repair various codes	$60			

HEALTH INSURANCE CLAIM FORM

APPROVED BY NATIONAL UNIFORM CLAIM COMMITTEE (NUCC) 02/12

↑ CARRIER →

| | PICA | | | | | | | | PICA | |

1. MEDICARE ☒ (Medicare#)   MEDICAID ☐ (Medicaid#)   TRICARE ☐ (ID#/DoD#)   CHAMPVA ☐ (Member ID#)   GROUP HEALTH PLAN ☐ (ID#)   FECA BLK LUNG ☐ (ID#)   OTHER ☐ (ID#)   **1a. INSURED'S I.D. NUMBER** (For Program in Item 1)

2. PATIENT'S NAME (Last Name, First Name, Middle Initial)

3. PATIENT'S BIRTH DATE MM | DD | YY   **SEX** M ☐ F ☐

4. INSURED'S NAME (Last Name, First Name, Middle Initial)

5. PATIENT'S ADDRESS (No., Street)

6. PATIENT RELATIONSHIP TO INSURED Self ☐ Spouse ☐ Child ☐ Other ☐

7. INSURED'S ADDRESS (No., Street)

CITY   STATE

8. RESERVED FOR NUCC USE

CITY   STATE

ZIP CODE   TELEPHONE (Include Area Code) ( )

ZIP CODE   TELEPHONE (Include Area Code) ( )

9. OTHER INSURED'S NAME (Last Name, First Name, Middle Initial)

10. IS PATIENT'S CONDITION RELATED TO:

11. INSURED'S POLICY GROUP OR FECA NUMBER

a. OTHER INSURED'S POLICY OR GROUP NUMBER

a. EMPLOYMENT? (Current or Previous) ☐ YES ☐ NO

a. INSURED'S DATE OF BIRTH MM | DD | YY   **SEX** M ☐ F ☐

b. RESERVED FOR NUCC USE

b. AUTO ACCIDENT? ☐ YES ☐ NO   PLACE (State)

b. OTHER CLAIM ID (Designated by NUCC)

c. RESERVED FOR NUCC USE

c. OTHER ACCIDENT? ☐ YES ☐ NO

c. INSURANCE PLAN NAME OR PROGRAM NAME

d. INSURANCE PLAN NAME OR PROGRAM NAME

10d. CLAIM CODES (Designated by NUCC)

d. IS THERE ANOTHER HEALTH BENEFIT PLAN? ☐ YES ☐ NO *If yes*, complete items 9, 9a, and 9d.

READ BACK OF FORM BEFORE COMPLETING & SIGNING THIS FORM.

12. PATIENT'S OR AUTHORIZED PERSON'S SIGNATURE I authorize the release of any medical or other information necessary to process this claim. I also request payment of government benefits either to myself or to the party who accepts assignment below.

SIGNED _____ DATE _____

13. INSURED'S OR AUTHORIZED PERSON'S SIGNATURE I authorize payment of medical benefits to the undersigned physician or supplier for services described below.

SIGNED _____

← PATIENT AND INSURED INFORMATION →

14. DATE OF CURRENT ILLNESS, INJURY, or PREGNANCY (LMP) MM | DD | YY   QUAL.

15. OTHER DATE QUAL. MM | DD | YY

16. DATES PATIENT UNABLE TO WORK IN CURRENT OCCUPATION FROM MM | DD | YY   TO MM | DD | YY

17. NAME OF REFERRING PROVIDER OR OTHER SOURCE   17a.   17b. NPI

18. HOSPITALIZATION DATES RELATED TO CURRENT SERVICES FROM MM | DD | YY   TO MM | DD | YY

19. ADDITIONAL CLAIM INFORMATION (Designated by NUCC)

20. OUTSIDE LAB? ☐ YES ☐ NO $ CHARGES

21. DIAGNOSIS OR NATURE OF ILLNESS OR INJURY Relate A-L to service line below (24E)   ICD Ind. |

A. |___   B. |___   C. |___   D. |___
E. |___   F. |___   G. |___   H. |___
I. |___   J. |___   K. |___   L. |___

22. RESUBMISSION CODE   ORIGINAL REF. NO.

23. PRIOR AUTHORIZATION NUMBER

24. A. DATE(S) OF SERVICE From MM DD YY — To MM DD YY	B. PLACE OF SERVICE	C. EMG	D. PROCEDURES, SERVICES, OR SUPPLIES (Explain Unusual Circumstances) CPT/HCPCS MODIFIER	E. DIAGNOSIS POINTER	F. $ CHARGES	G. DAYS OR UNITS	H. EPSDT Family Plan	I. ID. QUAL	J. RENDERING PROVIDER ID. #
1									NPI
2									NPI
3									NPI
4									NPI
5									NPI
6									NPI

25. FEDERAL TAX I.D. NUMBER   SSN ☐ EIN ☐

26. PATIENT'S ACCOUNT NO.

27. ACCEPT ASSIGNMENT? (For govt. claims, see back) ☐ YES ☐ NO

28. TOTAL CHARGE $

29. AMOUNT PAID $

30. Rsvd. for NUCC Use

31. SIGNATURE OF PHYSICIAN OR SUPPLIER INCLUDING DEGREES OR CREDENTIALS (I certify that the statements on the reverse apply to this bill and are made a part thereof.)

SIGNED _____ DATE _____

32. SERVICE FACILITY LOCATION INFORMATION a. NPI   b.

33. BILLING PROVIDER INFO & PH # ( )   a. NPI   b.

← PHYSICIAN OR SUPPLIER INFORMATION →

NUCC Instruction Manual available at: www.nucc.org   **PLEASE PRINT OR TYPE**   APPROVED OMB-0938-1197 FORM 1500 (02-12)

Clear Form

Figure 17-8

e. Using the source documents, the Capital City Medical Fee Schedule (Figure 17-9), and the blank CMS-1500 form provided (Figure 17-10), complete the following case study for patient Sasha Janiels (Case 17-5):

CASE 17-5

Capital City Medical—123 Unknown Boulevard, Capital City, NY 12345-2222 (555) 555-1234	Patient Information Form
	Tax ID: 75-0246810
Phil Wells, MD, Mannie Mends, MD, Bette R. Soone, MD	Group NPI: 1513171216

Patient Information:

Name: (Last, First) Janiels, Sasha ☐ Male ☒ Female Birth Date: 12/21/1958

Address: 981 Cross Rd, Capital City, NY 12345   Phone: (555) 555-1615

Social Security Number: 355-46-1161   Full-Time Student: ☐ Yes ☒ No

Marital Status: ☐ Single ☒ Married ☐ Divorced ☐ Other

Employment:

Employer: Capital City General Hospital   Phone: (555) 555-1000

Address: 1000 Cherry St, Capital City, NY 12345

Condition Related to: ☐ Auto Accident ☒ Employment ☐ Other Accident

Date of Accident: 06/26/20XX   State: NY

Emergency Contact: _____   **Phone: ( )** _____

Primary Insurance: State Workers' Compensation Insurance Co.   Phone: ( ) _____

Address: 88 Injury Center, Capital City, NY 12345

Insurance Policyholder's Name: _____ ☐ M ☐ F DOB: _____

Address: _____

Phone: _____ Relationship to Insured: ☒ Self ☐ Spouse ☐ Child ☐ Other

Employer: _____ Phone: ( ) _____

Employer's Address: _____

Policy/ID No: WCSJ1111   Group No: ____ Percent Covered: ___% Copay Amt: $____

Secondary Insurance: _____   Phone: ( ) _____

Address: _____

Insurance Policyholder's Name: _____ ☐ M ☐ F DOB: _____

Address: _____

Phone: _____ Relationship to Insured: ☐ Self ☐ Spouse ☐ Child ☐ Other

Employer: _____ Phone: ( ) _____

Employer's Address: _____

Policy/ID No: _____ Group No: ____ Percent Covered: ___% Copay Amt: $____

Reason for Visit: I accidentally had a fingerstick today after administering an injection.

Known Allergies: _____

Referred by: _____

CASE 17-5
SOAP

06/26/20XX
Assignment of Benefits: Y
Signature on File: Y
Referring Physician: N

S: Sasha Janiels is being seen today due to a needlestick accident after administering an injection of codeine to a patient. It is not known whether the patient has any bloodborne disease.

O: Pt. has a hypodermic needle puncture on her right middle finger. There is no infection at the site. Pt. has no history of any bloodborne diseases. All other systems are unremarkable. Mood and affect are anxious, but pleasant. This is normal, due to this recent event.

A: 1. Wound, hypodermic needle puncture of right middle finger—S61.212A
2. Accidental needlestick—L76.12

P: 1. HIV test today and in 6 months; Hepatitis panel today.
2. Follow up in 10 days for results.
3. May return to work tomorrow.
4. Please bill her workers' compensation. Her info is as follows:
State Workers' Compensation Insurance Co.
88 Injury Center
Capital City, NY 12345
Claim#WCSJ1111
5. Phil Wells, MD state license#-MD-123456-L

_____

Phil Wells, MD
Family Practice
NPI: 1234567890

CASE 17-5

Patient Name Sasha Janiels

Capital City Medical
123 Unknown Boulevard, Capital City, NY 12345-2222

Date of Service
06-26-20XX

New Patient			Arthrocentesis/Aspiration/Injection			Laboratory		
Problem Focused	99201		Small Joint	20600		Amylase	82150	
Expanded Problem, Focused	99202		Interm Joint	20605		B12	82607	
Detailed	99203		Major Joint	20610		CBC & Diff	85025	
Comprehensive	99204		**Other Invasive/Noninvasive**			Comp Metabolic Panel	80053	
Comprehensive/High Complex	99205		Audiometry	92552		Chlamydia Screen	87110	
Well Exam Infant (up to 12 mos.)	99381		Cast Application			Cholesterol	82465	
Well Exam 1–4 yrs.	99382		Location Long Short			Diqoxin	80162	
Well Exam 5–11 yrs.	99383		Catheterization	51701		Electrolytes	80051	
Well Exam 12–17 yrs.	99384		Circumcision	54150		Ferritin	82728	
Well Exam 18–39 yrs.	99385		Colposcopy	57452		Folate	82746	
Well Exam 40–64 yrs.	99386		Colposcopy w/Biopsy	57454		GC Screen	87070	
			Cryosurgery Premalignant Lesion			Glucose	82947	
			Location (s):			Glucose 1 HR	82950	
			Cryosurgery Warts			Glycosylated HGB A1C	83036	
Established Patient			Location (s):			HCT	85014	
Post-Op Follow Up Visit	99024		Curettement Lesion			HDL	83718	
Minimum	99211		Single	11055		Hep BSAG	87340	
Problem Focused	99212		2–4	11056		Hepatitis panel, acute	80074	X
Expanded Problem Focused	99213	X	>4	11057		HGB	85018	
Detailed	99214		Diaphragm Fitting	57170		HIV	86703	X
Comprehensive/High Complex	99215		Ear Irrigation	69210		Iron & TIBC	83550	
Well Exam Infant (up to 12 mos.)	99391		ECG	93000		Kidney Profile	80069	
Well exam 1–4 yrs.	99392		Endometrial Biopsy	58100		Lead	83655	
Well Exam 5–11 yrs.	99393		Exc. Lesion Malignant			Liver Profile	80076	
Well Exam 12–17 yrs.	99394		Benign			Mono Test	86308	
Well Exam 18–39 yrs.	99395		Location			Pap Smear	88155	
Well Exam 40–64 yrs.	99396		Exc. Skin Taqs (1–15)	11200		Pregnancy Test	84703	
Obstetrics			Each Additional 10	11201		Obstetric Panel	80055	
Total OB Care	59400		**Fracture Treatment**			Pro Time	85610	
Injections			Loc			PSA	84153	
Administration Sub. / IM	90772		w/Reduc w/o Reduc			RPR	86592	
Drug			I & D Abscess Single/Simple	10060		Sed. Rate	85651	
Dosage			Multiple or Comp	10061		Stool Culture	87045	
Allergy	95115		I & D Pilonidal Cyst Simple	10080		Stool O & P	87177	
Cocci Skin Test	86490		Pilonidal Cyst Complex	10081		Strep Screen	87880	
DPT	90701		IV Therapy—To One Hour	90760		Theophylline	80198	
Hemophilus	90646		Each Additional Hour	90761		Thyroid Uptake	84479	
Influenza	90658		Laceration Repair			TSH	84443	
MMR	90707		Location Size Simp/Comp			Urinalysis	81000	
OPV	90712		Laryngoscopy	31505		Urine Culture	87088	
Pneumovax	90732		Oximetry	94760		Drawing Fee	36415	X
TB Skin Test	86580		Punch Biopsy			Specimen Collection	99000	
TD	90718		Rhythm Strip	93040		**Other:**		
Unlisted Immun	90749		Treadmill	93015				
Tetanus Toxoid	90703		Trigger Point or Tendon Sheath Inj.	20550				
Vaccine/Toxoid Admin <8 Yr Old w/ Counseling	90465		Tympanometry	92567				
Vaccine/Toxoid Administration for Adult	90471							

Diagnosis/ICD-10: **S61.212A, L76.12**

I acknowledge receipt of medical services and authorize the release of any medical information necessary to process this claim for healthcare payment only. I do authorize payment to the provider.

Patient Signature Sasha Janiels

Total Estimated Charges: _____

Payment Amount: _____

Next Appointment: _____

Figure 17-9

Capital City Medical
Fee Schedule

New Patient OV				
Problem Focused 99201	$45		Punch Biopsy various codes	$80
Expanded Problem Focused 99202	$65		Nebulizer various codes	$45
Detailed 99203	$85		Cast Application various codes	$85
Comprehensive 99204	$105		Laryngoscopy 31505	$255
Comprehensive/High Complex 99205	$115		Audiometry 92552	$85
Well Exam infant (less than 1 year) 99381	$45		Tympanometry 92567	$85
Well Exam 1–4 yrs. 99382	$50		Ear Irrigation 69210	$25
Well Exam 5–11 yrs. 99383	$55		Diaphragm Fitting 57170	$30
Well Exam 12–17 yrs. 99384	$65		IV Therapy (up to one hour) 90760	$65
Well Exam 18–39 yrs. 99385	$85		Each additional hour 90761	$50
Well Exam 40–64 yrs. 99386	$105		Oximetry 94760	$10
Established Patient OV			ECG 93000	$75
Post Op Follow Up Visit 99024	$0		Holter Monitor various codes	$170
Minimum 99211	$35		Rhythm Strip 93040	$60
Problem Focused 99212	$45		Treadmill 93015	$375
Expanded Problem Focused 99213	$55		Cocci Skin Test 86490	$20
Detailed 99214	$65		X-ray, spine, chest, bone—any area various codes	$275
Comprehensive/High Complex 99215	$75		Avulsion Nail 11730	$200
Well exam infant (less than 1 year) 99391	$35		**Laboratory**	
Well Exam 1–4 yrs. 99392	$40		Amylase 82150	$40
Well Exam 5–11 yrs. 99393	$45		B12 82607	$30
Well Exam 12–17 yrs. 99394	$55		CBC & Diff 85025	$95
Well Exam 18–39 yrs. 99395	$65		Comp Metabolic Panel 80053	$75
Well Exam 40–64 yrs. 99396	$75		Chlamydia Screen 87110	$70
Obstetrics			Cholestrerol 82465	$75
Total OB Care 59400	$1700		Digoxin 80162	$40
Injections			Electrolytes 80051	$70
Administration 90772	$10		Estrogen, Total 82672	$50
Allergy 95115	$35		Ferritin 82728	$40
DPT 90701	$50		Folate 82746	$30
Drug various codes	$35		GC Screen 87070	$60
Influenza 90658	$25		Glucose 82947	$35
MMR 90707	$50		Glycosylated HGB A1C 83036	$45
OPV 90712	$40		HCT 85014	$30
Pneumovax 90732	$35		HDL 83718	$35
TB Skin Test 86580	$15		HGB 85018	$30
TD 90718	$40		Hep BSAG 83740	$40
Tetanus Toxoid 90703	$40		Hepatitis panel, acute 80074	$95
Vaccine/Toxoid Administration for Younger			HIV 86703	$100
Than 8 Years Old w/ counseling 90465	$10		Iron & TIBC 83550	$45
Vaccine/Toxoid Administration for Adult 90471	$10		Kidney Profile 80069	$95
Arthrocentesis/Aspiration/Injection			Lead 83665	$55
Small Joint 20600	$50		Lipase 83690	$40
Interm Joint 20605	$60		Lipid Panel 80061	$95
Major Joint 20610	$70		Liver Profile 80076	$95
Trigger Point/Tendon Sheath Inj. 20550	$90		Mono Test 86308	$30
Other Invasive/Noninvasive Procedures			Pap Smear 88155	$90
Catheterization 51701	$55		Pap Collection/Supervision 88142	$95
Circumcision 54150	$150		Pregnancy Test 84703	$90
Colposcopy 57452	$225		Obstetric Panel 80055	$85
Colposcopy w/Biopsy 57454	$250		Pro Time 85610	$50
Cryosurgery Premalignant Lesion various codes	$160		PSA 84153	$50
Endometrial Biopsy 58100	$190		RPR 86592	$55
Excision Lesion Malignant various codes	$145		Sed. Rate 85651	$50
Excision Lesion Benign various codes	$125		Stool Culture 87045	$80
Curettement Lesion			Stool O & P 87177	$105
Single 11055	$70		Strep Screen 87880	$35
2–4 11056	$80		Theophylline 80198	$40
>4 11057	$90		Thyroid Uptake 84479	$75
Excision Skin Tags (1–15) 11200	$55		TSH 84443	$50
Each Additional 10 11201	$30		Urinalysis 81000	$35
I & D Abscess Single/Simple 10060	$75		Urine Culture 87088	$80
Multiple/Complex 10061	$95		Drawing Fee 36415	$15
I & D Pilonidal Cyst Simple 10080	$105		Specimen Collection 99000	$10
I & D Pilonidal Cyst Complex 10081	$130			
Laceration Repair various codes	$60			

HEALTH INSURANCE CLAIM FORM

APPROVED BY NATIONAL UNIFORM CLAIM COMMITTEE (NUCC) 02/12

☐☐ PICA

PICA ☐☐☐

CARRIER

1. MEDICARE ☒ (Medicare#) MEDICAID ☐ (Medicaid#) TRICARE ☐ (ID#/DoD#) CHAMPVA ☐ (Member ID#) GROUP HEALTH PLAN ☐ (ID#) FECA BLK LUNG ☐ (ID#) OTHER ☐ (ID#)

1a. INSURED'S I.D. NUMBER (For Program in Item 1)

2. PATIENT'S NAME (Last Name, First Name, Middle Initial)

3. PATIENT'S BIRTH DATE MM | DD | YY SEX M ☐ F ☐

4. INSURED'S NAME (Last Name, First Name, Middle Initial)

5. PATIENT'S ADDRESS (No., Street)

6. PATIENT RELATIONSHIP TO INSURED Self ☐ Spouse ☐ Child ☐ Other ☐

7. INSURED'S ADDRESS (No., Street)

CITY STATE

8. RESERVED FOR NUCC USE

CITY STATE

ZIP CODE TELEPHONE (Include Area Code) (   )

ZIP CODE TELEPHONE (Include Area Code) (   )

9. OTHER INSURED'S NAME (Last Name, First Name, Middle Initial)

10. IS PATIENT'S CONDITION RELATED TO:

11. INSURED'S POLICY GROUP OR FECA NUMBER

a. OTHER INSURED'S POLICY OR GROUP NUMBER

a. EMPLOYMENT? (Current or Previous) YES ☐ NO ☐

a. INSURED'S DATE OF BIRTH MM | DD | YY SEX M ☐ F ☐

b. RESERVED FOR NUCC USE

b. AUTO ACCIDENT? YES ☐ NO ☐ PLACE (State)

b. OTHER CLAIM ID (Designated by NUCC)

c. RESERVED FOR NUCC USE

c. OTHER ACCIDENT? YES ☐ NO ☐

c. INSURANCE PLAN NAME OR PROGRAM NAME

d. INSURANCE PLAN NAME OR PROGRAM NAME

10d. CLAIM CODES (Designated by NUCC)

d. IS THERE ANOTHER HEALTH BENEFIT PLAN? YES ☐ NO ☐ If yes, complete items 9, 9a, and 9d.

READ BACK OF FORM BEFORE COMPLETING & SIGNING THIS FORM.

12. PATIENT'S OR AUTHORIZED PERSON'S SIGNATURE I authorize the release of any medical or other information necessary to process this claim. I also request payment of government benefits either to myself or to the party who accepts assignment below.

SIGNED _____ DATE _____

13. INSURED'S OR AUTHORIZED PERSON'S SIGNATURE I authorize payment of medical benefits to the undersigned physician or supplier for services described below.

SIGNED _____

PATIENT AND INSURED INFORMATION

14. DATE OF CURRENT ILLNESS, INJURY, or PREGNANCY (LMP) MM | DD | YY QUAL.

15. OTHER DATE QUAL. MM | DD | YY

16. DATES PATIENT UNABLE TO WORK IN CURRENT OCCUPATION MM | DD | YY FROM TO MM | DD | YY

17. NAME OF REFERRING PROVIDER OR OTHER SOURCE 17a. 17b. NPI

18. HOSPITALIZATION DATES RELATED TO CURRENT SERVICES MM | DD | YY FROM TO MM | DD | YY

19. ADDITIONAL CLAIM INFORMATION (Designated by NUCC)

20. OUTSIDE LAB? YES ☐ NO ☐ $ CHARGES

21. DIAGNOSIS OR NATURE OF ILLNESS OR INJURY Relate A-L to service line below (24E) ICD Ind. ___

A. ____ B. ____ C. ____ D. ____
E. ____ F. ____ G. ____ H. ____
I. ____ J. ____ K. ____ L. ____

22. RESUBMISSION CODE ____ ORIGINAL REF. NO. ____

23. PRIOR AUTHORIZATION NUMBER

24. A. DATE(S) OF SERVICE						B. PLACE OF SERVICE	C. EMG	D. PROCEDURES, SERVICES, OR SUPPLIES (Explain Unusual Circumstances)		E. DIAGNOSIS POINTER	F. $ CHARGES	G. DAYS OR UNITS	H. EPSDT Family Plan	I. ID. QUAL	J. RENDERING PROVIDER ID. #
From MM	DD	YY	To MM	DD	YY			CPT/HCPCS	MODIFIER						
1														NPI	
2														NPI	
3														NPI	
4														NPI	
5														NPI	
6														NPI	

25. FEDERAL TAX I.D. NUMBER SSN ☐ EIN ☐

26. PATIENT'S ACCOUNT NO.

27. ACCEPT ASSIGNMENT? (For govt. claims, see back) YES ☐ NO ☐

28. TOTAL CHARGE $

29. AMOUNT PAID $

30. Rsvd. for NUCC Use

31. SIGNATURE OF PHYSICIAN OR SUPPLIER INCLUDING DEGREES OR CREDENTIALS (I certify that the statements on the reverse apply to this bill and are made a part thereof.)

SIGNED _____ DATE _____

32. SERVICE FACILITY LOCATION INFORMATION

a. NPI b.

33. BILLING PROVIDER INFO & PH # (   )

a. NPI b.

PHYSICIAN OR SUPPLIER INFORMATION

NUCC Instruction Manual available at: www.nucc.org **PLEASE PRINT OR TYPE** APPROVED OMB-0938-1197 FORM 1500 (02-12)

Clear Form

Figure 17-10

© 2018 Pearson Education, Inc.

REVIEW QUESTIONS

MATCHING

Choose the correct answer and write its corresponding letter in the space provided.

a. occupational diseases and illnesses
b. impairment
c. FECA
d. OSHA
e. independent review

1. _____ Act that provides millions of workers with workers' compensation benefits
2. _____ Process of checking over healthcare services for the purpose of medical necessity
3. _____ Health problems due to exposure to a health hazard in the workplace (also known as nontraumatic injuries/illnesses)
4. _____ Enforces a safe working environment for employees
5. _____ Permanent physical damage to a worker's body resulting from a work-related injury/illness

MULTIPLE CHOICE

Circle the letter of the choice that best completes the statement or answers the question.

1. Which of the following is considered workers' compensation fraud?
   a. A worker who gets paid "under the table" while receiving workers' compensation benefits
   b. Boilerplate medical reports
   c. Product switching
   d. All of the above

2. Once an injured worker has been examined by a designated physician, which of the following is (are) the only person(s) involved in the case who is (are) allowed to have direct communication with this physician?
   a. The injured worker
   b. Representatives of the workers' compensation carrier
   c. The worker's attorney
   d. All of the above

3. Which of the following is considered a work-related injury?
   a. Repetitive motions such as typing
   b. Lung problems due to dust
   c. Loss of hearing due to loud noises
   d. All of the above

4. Which of the following is (are) *not* considered a work-related injury?
   a. A work injury that requires vocational rehabilitation
   b. A work injury that does not result in a disability
   c. An injury to a worker by another worker due to a personal conflict
   d. Both a and b

5. Which of the following can refer to a treating physician/physician of record?
   a. An injured worker's PCP who has been approved by the workers' compensation carrier
   b. A designated physician
   c. One who helps to resolve a worker's compensation claim dispute
   d. All of the above

SHORT ANSWER

Provide the correct response to each question that follows.

1. List the four types of worker's compensation income benefits.
   1. _____
   2. _____
   3. _____
   4. _____

2. What is the time limit for an injured worker or insurance carrier to dispute the maximum medical improvement date or the impairment rating?

   _____

3. What are the four types of workers' compensation benefits?
   1. _____
      _____
   2. _____
      _____
   3. _____
      _____
   4. _____
      _____

4. a. What important steps should be taken to ensure that a workers' compensation medical chart and related information are easily identified and retrieved?

   _____
   _____
   _____

   b. What important documentation should be included in an injured worker's medical chart?

   _____
   _____
   _____

© 2018 Pearson Education, Inc.

5. Name the six reasons for termination of temporary partial and temporary permanent disability benefits.

1. _____

2. _____

3. _____

4. _____

5. _____

6. _____

TRUE/FALSE

Identify each statement as true (T) or false (F).

1. _____ The medical office specialist does not need a workers' compensation case number to file a claim with the workers' compensation plan.

2. _____ An occupational injury/illness may develop over time.

3. _____ Temporary disability benefits will not be terminated if benefits are exhausted.

4. _____ An injured worker does not have to file a report of injury/illness with his/her employer for workers' compensation benefits to become effective.

5. _____ Each state governs and administers its own workers' compensation program.

Tests

TEST 1: IDENTIFY THE CORRECT DIAGNOSTIC CODE

Directions: Accurately code each given diagnosis with the correct ICD-10-CM/PCS code(s). Determine the correct number of codes for each scenario. Code external cause codes where applicable.

1. Admission for radiation (block delivery)
   ICD-10-CM Code(s) _____

2. Alcoholism complicating pregnancy, 20 weeks
   ICD-10-CM Code(s) _____

3. Aplastic anemia due to red cell aplasia (adult, acquired)
   ICD-10-CM Code(s) _____

4. Abdominal aortic aneurysm
   ICD-10-CM Code(s) _____

5. Childhood asthma, moderate persistent
   ICD-10-CM Code(s) _____

6. Right shoulder dislocation of NB; birth injury
   ICD-10-CM Code(s) _____

7. Sinus bradycardia
   ICD-10-CM Code(s) _____

8. Gonococcal balanitis
   ICD-10-CM Code(s) _____

9. Second-degree and third-degree burn to lower back due to fall into campfire in fire ring
   ICD-10-CM Code(s) _____

10. Routine follow-up for postpartum care
    ICD-10-CM Code(s) _____

11. Breech Cesarean delivery; single liveborn delivered
    ICD-10-CM Code(s) _____

12. Sacral decubitus, stage 2
    ICD-10-CM Code(s) _____

13. Hereditary macular degeneration
    ICD-10-CM Code(s) _____

14. Diabetes Mellitus II with cataracts
    ICD-10-CM Code(s) _____

15. Rash from allergic reaction to initial dose of penicillin; properly administered
    ICD-10-CM Code(s) _____

16. Postop paroxysmal atrial fibrillation
    ICD-10-CM Code(s) _____

17. Congestive heart failure

    ICD-10-CM Code(s) _____

18. Abnormal protein findings in urine

    ICD-10-CM Code(s) _____

19. Denture fitting

    ICD-10-CM Code(s) _____

20. Fracture, surgical neck of right humerus due to fall during roller skating

    ICD-10-CM Code(s) _____

21. Tension headache

    ICD-10-CM Code(s) _____

22. History of penicillin allergy

    ICD-10-CM Code(s) _____

23. Family history of polycystic kidney disease

    ICD-10-CM Code(s) _____

24. History of noncompliance to medical treatment

    ICD-10-CM Code(s) _____

25. Orthostatic hypotension

    ICD-10-CM Code(s) _____

26. Late effect, post-traumatic arthritis due to old left ankle sprain

    ICD-10-CM Code(s) _____

27. Primary neoplasm of stomach with secondary neoplasm of the spine

    ICD-10-CM Code(s) _____

28. Outcome, delivery of twins, both born alive (mother's chart)

    ICD-10-CM Code(s) _____

29. Melanoma on the skin of back

    ICD-10-CM Code(s) _____

30. Respiratory arrest after accidental overdose of dilaudid by nurse

    ICD-10-CM Code(s) _____

31. Food poisoning due to salmonella with gastroenteritis

    ICD-10-CM Code(s) _____

32. Late effect of facial droop due to stroke suffered 3 months ago

    ICD-10-CM Code(s) _____

33. End-stage kidney disease

    ICD-10-CM Code(s) _____

© 2018 Pearson Education, Inc.

TEST 2: CODING HOSPITAL PROCEDURES

Directions: Using the ICD-10-PCS manual, accurately code the following hospital procedures, determining the correct number of codes for each scenario:

1. Laparoscopic ablation of liver lesion

   ICD-10-PCS Code _____

2. Ileostomy

   ICD-10-PCS Code _____

3. Open appendicocecostomy

   ICD-10-PCS Code _____

4. Arthroplasty of right wrist, total

   ICD-10-PCS Code _____

5. Brush lung biopsy. LLL, via bronchoscopy

   ICD-10-PCS Code _____

6. Blood transfusion (autologous platelets) via peripheral vein

   ICD-10-PCS Code _____

7. Aortocoronary bypass using left greater saphenous vein graft

   ICD-10-PCS Code _____

8. Atrial cardioversion

   ICD-10-PCS Code _____

9. Swan-Ganz catheterization (monitoring only)

   ICD-10-PCS Code _____

10. Chemotherapy infusion via PICC line for cancer

    ICD-10-PCS Code _____

11. Vacuum extraction delivery with episiotomy

    ICD-10-PCS Code _____

12. Destruction of prostatic lesion by transurethral needle ablation

    ICD-10-PCS Code _____

13. Left heart TEE

    ICD-10-PCS Code _____

14. Steroid injection into left knee

    ICD-10-PCS Code _____

15. Laryngotracheoscopy

    ICD-10-PCS Code _____

16. Laparoscopic lysis of peritoneal adhesions

    ICD-10-PCS Code _____

17. Open mammoplasty with augmentation, left breast synthetic implant

    ICD-10-PCS Code _____

18. Bilateral femoral vein phlebography using high osmolar contrast

    ICD-10-PCS Code _____

19. X-ray of left knee; no contrast

    ICD-10-PCS Code _____

20. Creation of ventriculo-peritoneal shunt; open

    ICD-10-PCS Code _____

21. Laparoscopic partial ascending colon excision

    ICD-10-PCS Code _____

22. CT scan of head, no contrast

    ICD-10-PCS Code _____

23. Lacrimal gland drainage with tube insertion

    ICD-10-PCS Code _____

24. Cardiac stress test, thallium

    ICD-10-PCS Code _____

25. Bilateral retrograde pyelogram using low osmolar contrast

    ICD-10-PCS Code _____

© 2018 Pearson Education, Inc.

TEST 3: CODING OUTPATIENT PROCEDURES AND DIAGNOSES

Directions: Using the ICD-10-CM/PCS and the CPT® manuals, accurately code each given outpatient procedure and diagnosis. Include CPT modifiers as necessary. (These codes do not require an E/M code.)

1. A 17-year-old male has had chronic tonsillitis with adenitis since he was a toddler. He undergoes a tonsillectomy with adenectomy without any complications.

   Diagnosis code(s) ICD-10-CM: _____

   Procedure code(s) _____

2. An attending technician performs a sleep study on a patient who has not been sleeping well. The test reveals obstructive sleep apnea.

   Diagnosis code(s) ICD-10-CM: _____

   Procedure code(s) _____

3. During a physical examination, a patient's EKG reveals premature atrial contractions (PACs).

   Diagnosis code(s) ICD-10-CM: _____

   Procedure code(s) _____

4. A transurethral resection of the prostate is performed by an assistant surgeon on a patient with prostate cancer, primary. The surgery is performed by the electrosurgical technique.

   Diagnosis code(s) ICD-10-CM: _____

   Procedure code(s) _____

5. A female patient is admitted to the hospital for a right and left bundle branch block (R&L BBB). A dual chamber pacemaker with epicardial electrodes is inserted by endoscopy. The patient tolerates the procedure well. The cardiovascular surgeon informs the patient that he only performed the surgery, and that she is to follow up with her regular consulting cardiologist for postoperative care.

   Diagnosis code(s) ICD-10-CM: _____

   Procedure code(s) _____

6. Mrs. Packard is in the office today for her monthly vitamin B12 IV injection. She has a vitamin B12 deficiency.

   Diagnosis code(s) ICD-10-CM: _____

   Procedure code(s) _____

7. A patient presents with shortness of breath (SOB) and chest pain (CP). The EKG that is done in the office shows no abnormalities. The patient is sent home with a 24-hour Holter monitor that also is normal. The next day, a stress exercise conducted in the physician's office is stopped due to the occurrence of chest pain. Code for all services.

   Diagnosis code(s) ICD-10-CM: _____

   Procedure code(s) _____

8. Carolyn Ashbury has been having reflux esophagitis problems for 4 months. She has tried three different medicines that have provided no relief. Because Carolyn's mother had esophageal cancer, the physician performs a flexible esophagoscopy with biopsy.

   Diagnosis code(s) ICD-10-CM: _____

   Procedure code(s) _____

© 2018 Pearson Education, Inc.

9. A patient has injured his ulnar nerve of the wrist and hand. Neuroplasty of the ulnar nerve is performed to free it of scar tissue.

Diagnosis code(s) ICD-10-CM: _____

Procedure code(s) _____

10. A patient with an acute recurrent myocardial infarction (MI) 1 week ago has a right heart catheterization. This procedure includes contrast injection for the heart catheter with supervision, interpretation, and report for the imaging.

Diagnosis code(s) ICD-10-CM: _____

Procedure code(s) _____

11. Douglas Fuller suffered a complicated forehead wound due to striking his head against the corner of his bedroom dresser. He has an adjacent skin tissue transfer of 3 sq. cm to his forehead.

Diagnosis code(s) ICD-10-CM: _____

Procedure code(s) _____

12. A patient has simple destruction of vaginal venereal warts by laser surgery.

Diagnosis code(s) ICD-10-CM: _____

Procedure code(s) _____

13. Mr. Wallace has a repair to his diaphragm for a hiatal hernia. The procedure is done by thoracoabdominal approach.

Diagnosis code(s) ICD-10-CM: _____

Procedure code(s) _____

14. A patient is seen today for a psychological interview and evaluation. The patient has narcissistic personality disorder.

Diagnosis code(s) ICD-10-CM: _____

Procedure code(s) _____

15. A patient with acquired hydrocephalus undergoes a Tokildsen operation to create a brain shunt.

Diagnosis code(s) ICD-10-CM: _____

Procedure code(s) _____

© 2018 Pearson Education, Inc.

TEST 4: CODING OUTPATIENT RADIOLOGY AND/OR PATHOLOGY PROCEDURES AND DIAGNOSES

Directions: Using the ICD-10-CM/PCS and the CPT manuals, accurately code each given outpatient radiology and/or pathology procedure and diagnosis. Include CPT modifiers as necessary. (These codes do not require an E/M code.)

Radiology

1. A CT scan of the brain, without contrast, followed by contrast, with 3-D rendering and postprocessing, is performed on a patient with clonic epilepsy.

   Diagnosis code(s) ICD-10-CM: _____

   Procedure code(s) _____

2. A limited abdominal ultrasound (U/S) is performed on a patient with right upper quadrant abdominal pain.

   Diagnosis code(s) ICD-10-CM: _____

   Procedure code(s) _____

3. Rebecca DeMarco undergoes a DXA scan to evaluate her total body composition. She is at postmenopausal status and is having an osteoporosis screen.

   Diagnosis code(s) ICD-10-CM: _____

   Procedure code(s) _____

4. A B/L pulmonary angiography is performed to confirm an iatrogenic pulmonary embolism.

   Diagnosis code(s) ICD-10-CM: _____

   Procedure code(s) _____

5. Lucas Andrews, who has been experiencing shoulder pain and limited ROM, is ordered an MRI of the left shoulder. Films show a left rotator cuff tear.

   Diagnosis code(s) ICD-10-CM: _____

   Procedure code(s) _____

6. Eugene Vitale receives five radiation treatment management sessions for his papillary carcinoma thyroid cancer, in situ.

   Diagnosis code(s) ICD-10-CM: _____

   Procedure code(s) _____

Laboratory/Pathology

7. During surgery, the pathologist receives a specimen of the descending colon. He freezes one block and separates two frozen sections to examine. He makes a diagnosis of primary carcinoma and calls up the result to the operating room.

   Diagnosis code(s) ICD-10-CM: _____

   Procedure code(s) _____

8. Steven Palmer is seen today with complaints of frequent urination and excessive thirst. A urinalysis (U/A) dipstick and complete metabolic panel (CMP) are performed. Patient is ordered a glucose tolerance test, which will be performed by an outside lab.

   Diagnosis code(s) ICD-10-CM: _____

   Procedure code(s) _____

9. A patient experiencing headaches and nausea is admitted for carbon monoxide poisoning due to a gas leak in her home gas pipes. A qualitative carbon monoxide level is drawn three times in one day.

   Diagnosis code(s) ICD-10-CM: _____

   Procedure code(s) _____

10. A patient presents, complaining of the inability to stop bleeding. A platelet count assay, a partial thromboplastin time (PTT), and a clot factor VIII (vw factor, multimetric analysis) are drawn. Blood tests reveal hemophilia A.

    Diagnosis code(s) ICD-10-CM: _____

    Procedure code(s) _____

11. A stool sample is tested for Helicobacter pylori (*H. pylori*). Positive test results confirm the infection.

    Diagnosis code(s) ICD-10-CM: _____

    Procedure code(s) _____

12. Surgical pathology for sterilization by vasectomy is negative for disease process.

    Diagnosis code(s) ICD-10-CM: _____

    Procedure code(s) _____

13. Surgical pathology of a bone marrow biopsy is ordered for a patient with leukocytosis and a family history of leukemia.

    Diagnosis code(s) ICD-10-CM: _____

    Procedure code(s) _____

14. Blood typing for ABO, Rh, and MN is drawn for paternity testing.

    Diagnosis code(s) ICD-10-CM: _____

    Procedure code(s) _____

© 2018 Pearson Education, Inc.

TEST 5: CODING PROCEDURES AND DIAGNOSES, USING E/M CODES

Directions: Using the CPT and ICD-10-CM/PCS manuals, code each scenario with a diagnosis code and an E/M code. Code any applicable diagnoses and/or procedures. Include modifiers as appropriate.

1. Denise Cox sees her family physician for a routine checkup on hypothyroidism and migraines. She has no complaints. An EFP exam is performed, with the following results: Neck: Supple. Throat: No masses felt. BP: 108/74, P: 80. TSH is 2.4. Maxalt has reduced her migraine episodes. Increase Synthroid to 50 mcg. daily. MDM was of low complexity. Return in 3 months with another TSH. Total time spent: 15 minutes.

   Diagnosis code(s) ICD-10-CM: _____

   E/M code_____

   Procedure code(s)_____

2. Leonard Black is seeing his new PCP today. He is a 35-year-old African American male who has recently moved to the area. He does have HTN, benign. He is currently taking Diovan 80 mg daily. A full PE is conducted. On exam, BP: 124/80, P: 76. Wt: 186. Ht: 6⬚1⬚. HEENT: Normocephalic, atraumatic. Ears clear bilaterally. Eyes: Ecteric. Sclera is white. Nose: Clear. Throat: No masses. Neck: No bruits. Chest: Clear to A&P. No wheezes, rales, or rhonchi. Cardiovascular: S1, S2 present. No murmur. Abdomen: Soft, nontender. No masses felt. GI: Pt. denies heartburn and nausea. Bowel sounds are normal. MS: Normal ROM. No pain or swelling present. Skin: No breaks or bruises. Neurologic: A&O 33. Deep tendon refluxes are symmetrical. Psychiatric: Mood and affect upbeat. Labs (in office): Urinalysis by dipstick is negative for any disease process. CBC, automated, and diff normal values. Fasting lab prescription given. Patient to return for fasting lab results in 1 month.

   Diagnosis code(s) ICD-10-CM: _____

   E/M code_____

   Procedure code(s)_____

3. A patient who was admitted for osteomyelitis of the left thigh 2 days ago is seen by her attending physician. A problem-focused internal history and exam indicates that she is responding well to therapy.

   Diagnosis code(s) ICD-10-CM: _____

   E/M code_____

   Procedure code(s)_____

4. Dr. Melvin Gregory spends 45 minutes preparing hospital discharge orders for his patient. The patient, who has suffered a CVA with cerebral infarct, will be transferred to skilled nursing.

   Diagnosis code(s) ICD-10-CM: _____

   E/M code_____

   Procedure code(s)_____

5. Victoria Marshall is admitted to the hospital with acute cholecystitis and cholelithiasis. Her PCP orders Roger Marvin, M.D., General Surgeon, to evaluate Victoria's condition. He performs a comprehensive history and PE. MDM is MC. A recommendation for surgery is made to the PCP.

   Diagnosis code(s) ICD-10-CM: _____

   Procedure code(s)_____

   E/M code_____

© 2018 Pearson Education, Inc.

6. A patient with right heel pain is referred to an orthopedist. A detailed history reveals that the patient has congenital flat feet. A detailed exam is performed. Right heel X-rays show the presence of a heel spur and plantar fasciitis. The patient is ordered orthotics. A prescription for Ibuprofen is given. MDM is LC. The patient is to return in 1 month for reevaluation. A report is dictated to the PCP.

   Diagnosis code(s) ICD-10-CM: _____

   E/M code_____

   Procedure code(s)_____

7. A new patient, Ellen Armstrong, is being seen by Lois Garlock, M.D., Internal Medicine, for a rash on both forearms. In an EPF history, the patient states that the rash is itchy and has been spreading. She noticed the rash 2 days ago. An EPF examination is consistent with poison oak. The patient is administered intramuscular Depo-Medrol injection. The patient also is given a prescription for hydrocortisone 2.5% to apply topically to the infected area 2 times daily. The patient is advised to keep the area clean and to change bedding often. MDM SF.

   Diagnosis code(s) ICD-10-CM: _____

   E/M code_____

   Procedure code(s)_____

8. A physician delivers a total of 120 minutes of critical care for a patient in a hepatic coma.

   Diagnosis code(s) ICD-10-CM: _____

   E/M code_____

   Procedure code(s)_____

© 2018 Pearson Education, Inc.

TEST 6: EXPLANATION OF BENEFITS

Directions: Using the information provided on the Explanation of Benefits form that follows, calculate the total insurance payment to the rendering physician, payment owed by the patient, and appropriate adjustments. In addition, calculate the totals for each column and complete the Patient Summary section.

Today's Date: 11/02/2017

Payer Name & Address, Telephone #

HealthCo
777 Corporate Way
Capital City, NY 12345

Provider's Name & Address

Phil Wells, M.D.
123 Unknown Boulevard
Capital City, NY 12345

This statement covers payments for the following patient(s):

Claim Detail Section (If there are numbers in the "SEE REMARKS" column, see the Remarks section for explanation.)

Patient Name: Depinto, Janice	**Patient Account #:** JD85235	
Patient ID#: 710151933	**Insured's Name:** Depinto, Janice	
Group #: 65257		
Provider Name: Phil Wells, M.D.	**Inventory #:** 11454	**Claim Control #:** 91075

Service Date(s)	Procedure	Charges	Adjustment	Allowed	Co-pay	Deduct/Not Covered	Coins	Paid Amt.	Provider Paid	Remarks
9/27/2017	99213	55.00		38.00	0.00	0.00		80%		CO 045
9/27/2017	85025	95.00		65.00	0.00	0.00		80%		CO 045
9/27/2017	81000	35.00		30.00	0.00	0.00		80%		CO 045
9/27/2017	36415	15.00		12.00	0.00	0.00		80%		CO 045
TOTALS										

BALANCE DUE FROM PATIENT: PT'S DED/NOT COV $_____

PT'S COINS. $_____

045 Charges exceed contracted fee.

CO Contractual obligation—provider responsible

PAYMENT SUMMARY SECTION (TOTALS)

Charges	Adjustment	Allowed	Co-pay	Deduct/Not Covered	Coins	Total Paid

© 2018 Pearson Education, Inc.

TEST 7: EXPLANATION OF BENEFITS

Directions: Using the information provided on the Explanation of Benefits form that follows, calculate the total insurance payment to the rendering physician, payment owed by the patient, and appropriate adjustments. In addition, calculate the totals for each column and complete the Payment Summary section.

Today's Date: 03/20/2017

Payer Name & Address

| HealthCo |
| 777 Corporate Way |
| Capital City, NY 12345 |

Provider's Name & Address

| Phil Wells, M.D. |
| 123 Unknown Boulevard |
| Capital City, NY 12345 |

This statement covers payments for the following patient(s):

Claim Detail Section (If there are numbers in the "SEE REMARKS" column, see the Remarks section for explanation.)

Patient Name: Kendall, Marty	**Patient Account #:** MK65443	
Patient ID#: 685502020	**Insured's Name:** Kendall, Marty	
Group #: 86513		
Provider Name: Phil Wells, M.D.	**Inventory #:** 36374	**Claim Control #:** 75488

Service Date(s)	Procedure	Charges	Adjustment	Allowed	Co-pay	Deduct/Not Covered	Coins	Paid Amt.	Provider Paid	Remarks
02/16/2017	99202	65.00		50.00	0.00	50.00		80%		CO 045 PR 001
02/16/2017	93000	75.00		55.00	0.00			80%		CO 045
02/16/2017	85025	95.00		65.00	0.00			80%		CO 045
02/16/2017	36415	15.00		12.00	0.00			80%		CO 045
TOTALS										

BALANCE DUE FROM PATIENT: PT'S DED/NOT COV $_____

PT'S COINS. $_____

045 Charges exceed contracted fee.

001 Deductible amount

PR Patient responsible

CO Contractual obligation—provider responsible

PAYMENT SUMMARY SECTION (TOTALS)

Charges	Adjustment	Allowed	Co-pay	Deduct/Not Covered	Coins	Total Paid

© 2018 Pearson Education, Inc.

TEST 8: COMPLETE A MEDICARE CLAIM

Directions: Using the source documents provided for patient Elsie Spaulding and the Capital City Medical fee schedule (Figure 1), accurately complete a CMS-1500 claim form for Medicare. Use the blank CMS-1500 form provided (Figure 2).

Complete the case on the basis of the following criteria:

- All patients have release of information and assignment of benefit signatures on file.
- All providers are participating and accept assignment.
- The group practice is the billing entity.
- The national transition to NPI numbers is complete, and legacy PINs and UPINs are no longer used.
- 2017 ICD-10-CM/PCS and CPT codes are used.
- Use eight-digit dates for birthdates. Use six-digit dates for all other dates.
- All street names should be entered with standard postal abbreviations, even if they are spelled out on the source documents.
- Enter ICD-10 codes in the order in which they are listed on the encounter form.
- When entering CPT codes, enter the E/M code first. Enter remaining codes in descending price order.

Capital City Medical—123 Unknown Boulevard, Capital City, NY 12345-2222 (555) 555-1234

Phil Wells, MD, Mannie Mends, MD, Bette R. Soone, MD

Patient Information Form

Tax ID: 75-0246810

Group NPI: 1513171216

Patient Information:

Name: (Last, First) <u>Spaulding, Elsie</u>   ☐ Male   ☒ Female   Birth Date: <u>04/26/1947</u>

Address: <u>60 Pittsburgh Rd, Township, NY 12345</u>   Phone: (555) <u>555-0082</u>

Social Security Number: <u>949-29-7761</u>   Full-Time Student: ☐ Yes   ☒ No

Marital Status: ☐ Single   ☒ Married   ☐ Divorced   ☐ Other

Employment:

Employer: <u>Retired</u>   Phone: ( ) _____

Address: _____

Condition Related to: ☐ Auto Accident   ☐ Employment   ☐ Other Accident

Date of Accident: _____   State: _____

Emergency Contact: _____   **Phone: ( )** _____

Primary Insurance: <u>Medicare</u>   Phone: ( ) _____

Address: <u>P. O. Box 9834, Capital City, NY 12345</u>

Insurance Policyholder's Name: <u>Same</u>   ☐ M ☐ F DOB: _____

Address: _____

Phone: _____   Relationship to Insured: ☐ Self ☐ Spouse ☐ Child ☐ Other

Employer: _____   Phone: ( ) _____

Employer's Address: _____

Policy/ID No: <u>698915517A</u>   Group No: _____   Percent Covered: <u>80</u> % Copay Amt: $_____

Secondary Insurance: _____   Phone: ( ) _____

Address: _____

Insurance Policyholder's Name: _____   ☐ M ☐ F DOB: _____

Address: _____

Phone: _____   Relationship to Insured: ☐ Self ☐ Spouse ☐ Child ☐ Other

Employer: _____   Phone: ( ) _____

Employer's Address: _____

Policy/ID No: _____   Group No: _____   Percent Covered: ___% Copay Amt: $_____

Reason for Visit: <u>Here for lower back pain</u>

Known Allergies: _____

Referred by: _____

© 2018 Pearson Education, Inc.

11/04/20XX
Assignment of Benefits: Y
Signature on File: Y
Referring Physician: N

S: Elsie Spaulding is here to discuss the results of her spinal X-ray. She still has back pain constantly.
O: On exam, pt. still has lower back pain, especially with movement. X-ray shows degeneration in L4 1 L5 BP: 118/70, P: 68.
A: 1. Osteoarthritis lower back— M47.896
P: 1. Start Celebrex 200mg one p.o. q.d.
  2. Return in 1 month.

_____

Phil Wells, MD
Family Practice
NPI: 1234567890

TEST 8

Patient Name Elsie Spaulding

Capital City Medical
123 Unknown Boulevard, Capital City, NY 12345-2222

Date of Service
11-04-20XX

New Patient		Other Invasive/Noninvasive		Laboratory	
Problem Focused	99201	Arthrocentesis/Aspiration/Injection		Amylase	82150
Expanded Problem, Focused	99202	Small Joint	20600	B12	82607
Detailed	99203	Interm Joint	20605	CBC & Diff	85025
Comprehensive	99204	Major Joint	20610	Comp Metabolic Panel	80053
Comprehensive/High Complex	99205	**Other Invasive/Noninvasive**		Chlamydia Screen	87110
Well Exam Infant (up to 12 mos.)	99381	Audiometry	92552	Cholesterol	82465
Well Exam 1–4 yrs.	99382	Cast Application		Digoxin	80162
Well Exam 5–11 yrs.	99383	Location Long Short		Electrolytes	80051
Well Exam 12–17 yrs.	99384	Catheterization	51701	Ferritin	82728
Well Exam 18–39 yrs.	99385	Circumcision	54150	Folate	82746
Well Exam 40–64 yrs.	99386	Colposcopy	57452	GC Screen	87070
		Colposcopy w/Biopsy	57454	Glucose	82947
		Cryosurgery Premalignant Lesion		Glucose 1 HR	82950
		Location (s):		Glycosylated HGB A1C	83036
Established Patient		Cryosurgery Warts		HCT	85014
Post-Op Follow Up Visit	99024	Location (s):		HDL	83718
Minimum	99211	Curettement Lesion		Hep BSAG	87340
Problem Focused	99212	Single	11055	Hepatitis panel, acute	80074
Expanded Problem Focused	99213 X	2–4	11056	HGB	85018
Detailed	99214	>4	11057	HIV	86703
Comprehensive/High Complex	99215	Diaphragm Fitting	57170	Iron & TIBC	83550
Well Exam Infant (up to 12 mos.)	99391	Ear Irrigation	69210	Kidney Profile	80069
Well exam 1–4 yrs.	99392	ECG	93000	Lead	83655
Well Exam 5–11 yrs.	99393	Endometrial Biopsy	58100	Liver Profile	80076
Well Exam 12–17 yrs.	99394	Exc. Lesion Malignant		Mono Test	86308
Well Exam 18–39 yrs.	99395	Benign		Pap Smear	88155
Well Exam 40–64 yrs.	99396	Location		Pregnancy Test	84703
Obstetrics		Exc. Skin Tags (1–15)	11200	Obstetric Panel	80055
Total OB Care	59400	Each Additional 10	11201	Pro Time	85610
Injections		Fracture Treatment		PSA	84153
Administration Sub. / IM	90772	Loc		RPR	86592
Drug		w/Reduc w/o Reduc		Sed. Rate	85651
Dosage		I & D Abscess Single/Simple	10060	Stool Culture	87045
Allergy	95115	Multiple or Comp	10061	Stool O & P	87177
Cocci Skin Test	86490	I & D Pilonidal Cyst Simple	10080	Strep Screen	87880
DPT	90701	Pilonidal Cyst Complex	10081	Theophylline	80198
Hemophilus	90646	IV Therapy—To One Hour	90760	Thyroid Uptake	84479
Influenza	90658	Each Additional Hour	90761	TSH	84443
MMR	90707	Laceration Repair		Urinalysis	81000
OPV	90712	Location Size Simp/Comp		Urine Culture	87088
Pneumovax	90732	Laryngoscopy	31505	Drawing Fee	36415
TB Skin Test	86580	Oximetry	94760	Specimen Collection	99000
TD	90718	Punch Biopsy		**Other:**	
Unlisted Immun	90749	Rhythm Strip	93040		
Tetanus Toxoid	90703	Treadmill	93015		
Vaccine/Toxoid Admin <8 Yr Old w/ Counseling	90465	Trigger Point or Tendon Sheath Inj.	20550		
Vaccine/Toxoid Administration for Adult	90471	Tympanometry	92567		

Diagnosis/ICD-10: **M47.896**

I acknowledge receipt of medical services and authorize the release of any medical information necessary to process this claim for healthcare payment only. I do authorize payment to the provider.

Total Estimated Charges: _____

Payment Amount: _____

Patient Signature Elsie Spaulding

Next Appointment: _____

Figure 1

Capital City Medical
Fee Schedule

New Patient OV	
Problem Focused 99201	$45
Expanded Problem Focused 99202	$65
Detailed 99203	$85
Comprehensive 99204	$105
Comprehensive/High Complex 99205	$115
Well Exam infant (less than 1 year) 99381	$45
Well Exam 1–4 yrs. 99382	$50
Well Exam 5–11 yrs. 99383	$55
Well Exam 12–17 yrs. 99384	$65
Well Exam 18–39 yrs. 99385	$85
Well Exam 40–64 yrs. 99386	$105

Established Patient OV	
Post Op Follow Up Visit 99024	$0
Minimum 99211	$35
Problem Focused 99212	$45
Expanded Problem Focused 99213	$55
Detailed 99214	$65
Comprehensive/High Complex 99215	$75
Well exam infant (less than 1 year) 99391	$35
Well Exam 1–4 yrs. 99392	$40
Well Exam 5–11 yrs. 99393	$45
Well Exam 12–17 yrs. 99394	$55
Well Exam 18–39 yrs. 99395	$65
Well Exam 40–64 yrs. 99396	$75

Obstetrics	
Total OB Care 59400	$1700

Injections	
Administration 90772	$10
Allergy 95115	$35
DPT 90701	$50
Drug various codes	$35
Influenza 90658	$25
MMR 90707	$50
OPV 90712	$40
Pneumovax 90732	$35
TB Skin Test 86580	$15
TD 90718	$40
Tetanus Toxoid 90703	$40
Vaccine/Toxoid Administration for Younger Than 8 Years Old w/ counseling 90465	$10
Vaccine/Toxoid Administration for Adult 90471	$10

Arthrocentesis/Aspiration/Injection	
Small Joint 20600	$50
Interm Joint 20605	$60
Major Joint 20610	$70
Trigger Point/Tendon Sheath Inj. 20550	$90

Other Invasive/Noninvasive Procedures	
Catheterization 51701	$55
Circumcision 54150	$150
Colposcopy 57452	$225
Colposcopy w/Biopsy 57454	$250
Cryosurgery Premalignant Lesion various codes	$160
Endometrial Biopsy 58100	$190
Excision Lesion Malignant various codes	$145
Excision Lesion Benign various codes	$125
Curettement Lesion	
Single 11055	$70
2–4 11056	$80
>4 11057	$90
Excision Skin Tags (1–15) 11200	$55
Each Additional 10 11201	$30
I & D Abscess Single/Simple 10060	$75
Multiple/Complex 10061	$95
I & D Pilonidal Cyst Simple 10080	$105
I & D Pilonidal Cyst Complex 10081	$130
Laceration Repair various codes	$60

Punch Biopsy various codes	$80
Nebulizer various codes	$45
Cast Application various codes	$85
Laryngoscopy 31505	$255
Audiometry 92552	$85
Tympanometry 92567	$85
Ear Irrigation 69210	$25
Diaphragm Fitting 57170	$30
IV Therapy (up to one hour) 90760	$65
Each additional hour 90761	$50
Oximetry 94760	$10
ECG 93000	$75
Holter Monitor various codes	$170
Rhythm Strip 93040	$60
Treadmill 93015	$375
Cocci Skin Test 86490	$20
X-ray, spine, chest, bone—any area various codes	$275
Avulsion Nail 11730	$200

Laboratory	
Amylase 82150	$40
B12 82607	$30
CBC & Diff 85025	$95
Comp Metabolic Panel 80053	$75
Chlamydia Screen 87110	$70
Cholestrerol 82465	$75
Digoxin 80162	$40
Electrolytes 80051	$70
Estrogen, Total 82672	$50
Ferritin 82728	$40
Folate 82746	$30
GC Screen 87070	$60
Glucose 82947	$35
Glycosylated HGB A1C 83036	$45
HCT 85014	$30
HDL 83718	$35
HGB 85018	$30
Hep BSAG 83740	$40
Hepatitis panel, acute 80074	$95
HIV 86703	$100
Iron & TIBC 83550	$45
Kidney Profile 80069	$95
Lead 83665	$55
Lipase 83690	$40
Lipid Panel 80061	$95
Liver Profile 80076	$95
Mono Test 86308	$30
Pap Smear 88155	$90
Pap Collection/Supervision 88142	$95
Pregnancy Test 84703	$90
Obstetric Panel 80055	$85
Pro Time 85610	$50
PSA 84153	$50
RPR 86592	$55
Sed. Rate 85651	$50
Stool Culture 87045	$80
Stool O & P 87177	$105
Strep Screen 87880	$35
Theophylline 80198	$40
Thyroid Uptake 84479	$75
TSH 84443	$50
Urinalysis 81000	$35
Urine Culture 87088	$80
Drawing Fee 36415	$15
Specimen Collection 99000	$10

HEALTH INSURANCE CLAIM FORM

APPROVED BY NATIONAL UNIFORM CLAIM COMMITTEE (NUCC) 02/12

| | PICA | | | | | | | | | PICA | |

CARRIER

1. MEDICARE	MEDICAID	TRICARE	CHAMPVA	GROUP HEALTH PLAN	FECA BLK LUNG	OTHER	1a. INSURED'S I.D. NUMBER	(For Program in Item 1)
[X] (Medicare#)	[ ] (Medicaid#)	[ ] (ID#/DoD#)	[ ] (Member ID#)	[ ] (ID#)	[ ] (ID#)	[ ] (ID#)		

2. PATIENT'S NAME (Last Name, First Name, Middle Initial)

3. PATIENT'S BIRTH DATE   SEX
MM   DD   YY   M [ ]   F [ ]

4. INSURED'S NAME (Last Name, First Name, Middle Initial)

5. PATIENT'S ADDRESS (No., Street)

6. PATIENT RELATIONSHIP TO INSURED
Self [ ]   Spouse [ ]   Child [ ]   Other [ ]

7. INSURED'S ADDRESS (No., Street)

CITY   STATE

8. RESERVED FOR NUCC USE

CITY   STATE

ZIP CODE   TELEPHONE (Include Area Code)
(   )

ZIP CODE   TELEPHONE (Include Area Code)
(   )

9. OTHER INSURED'S NAME (Last Name, First Name, Middle Initial)

10. IS PATIENT'S CONDITION RELATED TO:

11. INSURED'S POLICY GROUP OR FECA NUMBER

a. OTHER INSURED'S POLICY OR GROUP NUMBER

a. EMPLOYMENT? (Current or Previous)
[ ] YES   [ ] NO

a. INSURED'S DATE OF BIRTH   SEX
MM   DD   YY   M [ ]   F [ ]

b. RESERVED FOR NUCC USE

b. AUTO ACCIDENT?   PLACE (State)
[ ] YES   [ ] NO

b. OTHER CLAIM ID (Designated by NUCC)

c. RESERVED FOR NUCC USE

c. OTHER ACCIDENT?
[ ] YES   [ ] NO

c. INSURANCE PLAN NAME OR PROGRAM NAME

d. INSURANCE PLAN NAME OR PROGRAM NAME

10d. CLAIM CODES (Designated by NUCC)

d. IS THERE ANOTHER HEALTH BENEFIT PLAN?
[ ] YES   [ ] NO   If yes, complete items 9, 9a, and 9d.

READ BACK OF FORM BEFORE COMPLETING & SIGNING THIS FORM.

12. PATIENT'S OR AUTHORIZED PERSON'S SIGNATURE I authorize the release of any medical or other information necessary to process this claim. I also request payment of government benefits either to myself or to the party who accepts assignment below.

SIGNED _____   DATE _____

13. INSURED'S OR AUTHORIZED PERSON'S SIGNATURE I authorize payment of medical benefits to the undersigned physician or supplier for services described below.

SIGNED _____

PATIENT AND INSURED INFORMATION

14. DATE OF CURRENT ILLNESS, INJURY, or PREGNANCY (LMP)
MM   DD   YY   QUAL.

15. OTHER DATE
QUAL.   MM   DD   YY

16. DATES PATIENT UNABLE TO WORK IN CURRENT OCCUPATION
FROM   MM   DD   YY   TO   MM   DD   YY

17. NAME OF REFERRING PROVIDER OR OTHER SOURCE
17a.
17b. NPI

18. HOSPITALIZATION DATES RELATED TO CURRENT SERVICES
FROM   MM   DD   YY   TO   MM   DD   YY

19. ADDITIONAL CLAIM INFORMATION (Designated by NUCC)

20. OUTSIDE LAB? $ CHARGES
[ ] YES   [ ] NO

21. DIAGNOSIS OR NATURE OF ILLNESS OR INJURY Relate A-L to service line below (24E)   ICD Ind. ___

22. RESUBMISSION CODE   ORIGINAL REF. NO.

A. _____   B. _____   C. _____   D. _____
E. _____   F. _____   G. _____   H. _____
I. _____   J. _____   K. _____   L. _____

23. PRIOR AUTHORIZATION NUMBER

24. A. DATE(S) OF SERVICE						B. PLACE OF SERVICE	C. EMG	D. PROCEDURES, SERVICES, OR SUPPLIES (Explain Unusual Circumstances) CPT/HCPCS	MODIFIER	E. DIAGNOSIS POINTER	F. $ CHARGES	G. DAYS OR UNITS	H. EPSDT Family Plan	I. ID. QUAL	J. RENDERING PROVIDER ID. #
From MM	DD	YY	To MM	DD	YY										
1															NPI
2															NPI
3															NPI
4															NPI
5															NPI
6															NPI

PHYSICIAN OR SUPPLIER INFORMATION

25. FEDERAL TAX I.D. NUMBER   SSN EIN

26. PATIENT'S ACCOUNT NO.

27. ACCEPT ASSIGNMENT? (For govt. claims, see back)
[ ] YES   [ ] NO

28. TOTAL CHARGE
$

29. AMOUNT PAID
$

30. Rsvd. for NUCC Use

31. SIGNATURE OF PHYSICIAN OR SUPPLIER INCLUDING DEGREES OR CREDENTIALS
(I certify that the statements on the reverse apply to this bill and are made a part thereof.)

SIGNED _____   DATE _____

32. SERVICE FACILITY LOCATION INFORMATION

a. NPI   b.

33. BILLING PROVIDER INFO & PH # (   )

a. NPI   b.

NUCC Instruction Manual available at: www.nucc.org   **PLEASE PRINT OR TYPE**   APPROVED OMB-0938-1197 FORM 1500 (02-12)

Clear Form

Figure 2

© 2018 Pearson Education, Inc.

TEST 9: COMPLETE A MEDICAID CLAIM

Directions: Using the source documents provided for patient Ty Nelson and the Capital City Medical fee schedule (Figure 3), accurately complete a CMS-1500 claim form for Medicaid. Use the blank CMS-1500 claim form provided (Figure 4).

Complete the case on the basis of the following criteria:

- All patients have release of information and assignment of benefit signatures on file. Assignment of benefits is required by most states for Medicaid. SOF is not required in Item 13.

- All providers accept assignment for Medicaid by law. Item 27 should not be marked.

- The group practice is the billing entity.

- The national transition to NPI numbers is complete, and legacy PINs of individual payers are no longer used. If legacy PINS are still being used by your state Medicaid program, your instructor may provide you with Medicaid PINs in addition to the NPI.

- 2017 ICD-10-CM/PCS and CPT codes are used.

- Use eight-digit dates for birthdates. Use six-digit dates for all other dates.

- All street names should be entered with standard postal abbreviations, even if they are spelled out on the source documents.

- Enter the ICD-10 codes in the order in which they appear on the encounter form.

- When entering CPT codes, enter the E/M code first. Enter remaining codes in descending price order.

TEST 9

Capital City Medical—123 Unknown Boulevard, Capital City,
NY 12345-2222 (555) 555-1234

Phil Wells, MD, Mannie Mends, MD, Bette R. Soone, MD

Patient Information Form

Tax ID: 75-0246810

Group NPI: 1513171216

Patient Information:

Name: (Last, First) <u>Nelson, Ty</u> ☒ Male ❑ Female Birth Date: <u>08/21/2006</u>

Address: <u>518 Moon Ave, Capital City, NY 12345</u> Phone: (555) <u>555-8168</u>

Social Security Number: <u>404-11-6786</u> Full-Time Student: ☒ Yes ❑ No

Marital Status: ☒ Single ❑ Married ❑ Divorced ❑ Other

- - -

Employment:

Employer: <u>Retired</u> Phone: ( ) _____

Address: _____

Condition Related to: ❑ Auto Accident ❑ Employment ❑ Other Accident

Date of Accident: _____ State: _____

Emergency Contact: _____ **Phone: ( )** _____

- - -

Primary Insurance: <u>Medicaid</u> Phone: ( ) _____

Address: <u>4875 Capital Blvd, Capital City, NY 12345</u>

Insurance Policyholder's Name: <u>Same</u> ❑ M ❑ F DOB: _____

Address: <u>Same</u>

Phone: _____ Relationship to Insured: ☒ Self ❑ Spouse ❑ Child ❑ Other

Employer: _____ Phone: ( ) _____

Employer's Address: _____

Policy/ID No: <u>8694631321</u> Group No: ____ Percent Covered: <u>80</u> % Copay Amt: $<u>5.00</u>

- - -

Secondary Insurance: _____ Phone: ( ) _____

Address: _____

Insurance Policyholder's Name: _____ ❑ M ❑ F DOB: _____

Address: _____

Phone: _____ Relationship to Insured: ❑ Self ❑ Spouse ❑ Child ❑ Other

Employer: _____ Phone: ( ) _____

Employer's Address: _____

Policy/ID No: _____ Group No: ____ Percent Covered: ____% Copay Amt: $____

- - -

Reason for Visit: <u>Annual checkup.</u>

Known Allergies: _____

Referred by: _____

© 2018 Pearson Education, Inc.

08/30/20XX
Assignment of Benefits: Y
Signature on File: Y
Referring Physician: N

S: Ty Nelson is here for his annual well check. His mom says she has no new complaints for him.
O: Pt. has developed normally. Chest is clear to A&P. There is no lymphadenopathy present. He is alert and oriented ×3.
A: 1. Well child— Z00.129
P: 1. Return p.r.n.

_____
Phil Wells, MD
Family Practice
NPI: 1234567890

TEST 9

Patient Name Ty Nelson

Capital City Medical
123 Unknown Boulevard, Capital City, NY 12345-2222

Date of Service
08-30-20XX

New Patient			Other Invasive/Noninvasive			Laboratory	
Problem Focused	99201		Arthrocentesis/Aspiration/Injection			Amylase	82150
Expanded Problem, Focused	99202		Small Joint		20600	B12	82607
Detailed	99203		Interm Joint		20605	CBC & Diff	85025
Comprehensive	99204		Major Joint		20610	Comp Metabolic Panel	80053
Comprehensive/High Complex	99205		**Other Invasive/Noninvasive**			Chlamydia Screen	87110
Well Exam Infant (up to 12 mos.)	99381		Audiometry		92552	Cholesterol	82465
Well Exam 1–4 yrs.	99382		Cast Application			Digoxin	80162
Well Exam 5–11 yrs.	99383		Location Long Short			Electrolytes	80051
Well Exam 12–17 yrs.	99384		Catheterization		51701	Ferritin	82728
Well Exam 18–39 yrs.	99385		Circumcision		54150	Folate	82746
Well Exam 40–64 yrs.	99386		Colposcopy		57452	GC Screen	87070
			Colposcopy w/Biopsy		57454	Glucose	82947
			Cryosurgery Premalignant Lesion			Glucose 1 HR	82950
			Location (s):			Glycosylated HGB A1C	83036
Established Patient			Cryosurgery Warts			HCT	85014
Post-Op Follow Up Visit	99024		Location (s):			HDL	83718
Minimum	99211		Curettement Lesion			Hep BSAG	87340
Problem Focused	99212		Single		11055	Hepatitis panel, acute	80074
Expanded Problem Focused	99213		2–4		11056	HGB	85018
Detailed	99214		>4		11057	HIV	86703
Comprehensive/High Complex	99215		Diaphragm Fitting		57170	Iron & TIBC	83550
Well Exam Infant (up to 12 mos.)	99391		Ear Irrigation		69210	Kidney Profile	80069
Well exam 1–4 yrs.	99392		ECG		93000	Lead	83655
Well Exam 5–11 yrs.	99393	X	Endometrial Biopsy		58100	Liver Profile	80076
Well Exam 12–17 yrs.	99394		Exc. Lesion Malignant			Mono Test	86308
Well Exam 18–39 yrs.	99395		Benign			]Pap Smear	88155
Well Exam 40–64 yrs.	99396		Location			Pregnancy Test	84703
Obstetrics			Exc. Skin Tags (1–15)		11200	Obstetric Panel	80055
Total OB Care	59400		Each Additional 10		11201	Pro Time	85610
Injections			Fracture Treatment			PSA	84153
Administration Sub. / IM	90772		Loc			RPR	86592
Drug			w/Reduc	w/o Reduc		Sed. Rate	85651
Dosage			I & D Abscess Single/Simple		10060	Stool Culture	87045
Allergy	95115		Multiple or Comp		10061	Stool O & P	87177
Cocci Skin Test	86490		I & D Pilonidal Cyst Simple		10080	Strep Screen	87880
DPT	90701		Pilonidal Cyst Complex		10081	Theophylline	80198
Hemophilus	90646		IV Therapy—To One Hour		90760	Thyroid Uptake	84479
Influenza	90658		Each Additional Hour		90761	TSH	84443
MMR	90707		Laceration Repair			Urinalysis	81000
OPV	90712		Location Size Simp/Comp			Urine Culture	87088
Pneumovax	90732		Laryngoscopy		31505	Drawing Fee	36415
TB Skin Test	86580		Oximetry		94760	Specimen Collection	99000
TD	90718		Punch Biopsy			**Other:**	
Unlisted Immun	90749		Rhythm Strip		93040		
Tetanus Toxoid	90703		Treadmill		93015		
Vaccine/Toxoid Admin <8 Yr Old w/ Counseling	90465		Trigger Point or Tendon Sheath Inj.		20550		
Vaccine/Toxoid Administration for Adult	90471		Tympanometry		92567		

Diagnosis/ICD-10: **Z00.129**

I acknowledge receipt of medical services and authorize the release of any medical information necessary to process this claim for healthcare payment only. I do authorize payment to the provider.

Patient Signature _Sydney Nelson_

Total Estimated Charges: _____

Payment Amount: _____

Next Appointment: _____

Figure 3

Capital City Medical
Fee Schedule

New Patient OV			Punch Biopsy various codes	$80
Problem Focused 99201	$45		Nebulizer various codes	$45
Expanded Problem Focused 99202	$65		Cast Application various codes	$85
Detailed 99203	$85		Laryngoscopy 31505	$255
Comprehensive 99204	$105		Audiometry 92552	$85
Comprehensive/High Complex 99205	$115		Tympanometry 92567	$85
Well Exam infant (less than 1 year) 99381	$45		Ear Irrigation 69210	$25
Well Exam 1–4 yrs. 99382	$50		Diaphragm Fitting 57170	$30
Well Exam 5–11 yrs. 99383	$55		IV Therapy (up to one hour) 90760	$65
Well Exam 12–17 yrs. 99384	$65		Each additional hour 90761	$50
Well Exam 18–39 yrs. 99385	$85		Oximetry 94760	$10
Well Exam 40–64 yrs. 99386	$105		ECG 93000	$75
Established Patient OV			Holter Monitor various codes	$170
Post Op Follow Up Visit 99024	$0		Rhythm Strip 93040	$60
Minimum 99211	$35		Treadmill 93015	$375
Problem Focused 99212	$45		Cocci Skin Test 86490	$20
Expanded Problem Focused 99213	$55		X-ray, spine, chest, bone—any area various codes	$275
Detailed 99214	$65		Avulsion Nail 11730	$200
Comprehensive/High Complex 99215	$75		**Laboratory**	
Well exam infant (less than 1 year) 99391	$35		Amylase 82150	$40
Well Exam 1–4 yrs. 99392	$40		B12 82607	$30
Well Exam 5–11 yrs. 99393	$45		CBC & Diff 85025	$95
Well Exam 12–17 yrs. 99394	$55		Comp Metabolic Panel 80053	$75
Well Exam 18–39 yrs. 99395	$65		Chlamydia Screen 87110	$70
Well Exam 40–64 yrs. 99396	$75		Cholestrerol 82465	$75
Obstetrics			Digoxin 80162	$40
Total OB Care 59400	$1700		Electrolytes 80051	$70
Injections			Estrogen, Total 82672	$50
Administration 90772	$10		Ferritin 82728	$40
Allergy 95115	$35		Folate 82746	$30
DPT 90701	$50		GC Screen 87070	$60
Drug various codes	$35		Glucose 82947	$35
Influenza 90658	$25		Glycosylated HGB A1C 83036	$45
MMR 90707	$50		HCT 85014	$30
OPV 90712	$40		HDL 83718	$35
Pneumovax 90732	$35		HGB 85018	$30
TB Skin Test 86580	$15		Hep BSAG 83740	$40
TD 90718	$40		Hepatitis panel, acute 80074	$95
Tetanus Toxoid 90703	$40		HIV 86703	$100
Vaccine/Toxoid Administration for Younger Than 8 Years Old w/ counseling 90465	$10		Iron & TIBC 83550	$45
			Kidney Profile 80069	$95
Vaccine/Toxoid Administration for Adult 90471	$10		Lead 83665	$55
Arthrocentesis/Aspiration/Injection			Lipase 83690	$40
Small Joint 20600	$50		Lipid Panel 80061	$95
Interm Joint 20605	$60		Liver Profile 80076	$95
Major Joint 20610	$70		Mono Test 86308	$30
Trigger Point/Tendon Sheath Inj. 20550	$90		Pap Smear 88155	$90
Other Invasive/Noninvasive Procedures			Pap Collection/Supervision 88142	$95
Catheterization 51701	$55		Pregnancy Test 84703	$90
Circumcision 54150	$150		Obstetric Panel 80055	$85
Colposcopy 57452	$225		Pro Time 85610	$50
Colposcopy w/Biopsy 57454	$250		PSA 84153	$50
Cryosurgery Premalignant Lesion various codes	$160		RPR 86592	$55
Endometrial Biopsy 58100	$190		Sed. Rate 85651	$50
Excision Lesion Malignant various codes	$145		Stool Culture 87045	$80
Excision Lesion Benign various codes	$125		Stool O & P 87177	$105
Curettement Lesion			Strep Screen 87880	$35
Single 11055	$70		Theophylline 80198	$40
2–4 11056	$80		Thyroid Uptake 84479	$75
>4 11057	$90		TSH 84443	$50
Excision Skin Tags (1–15) 11200	$55		Urinalysis 81000	$35
Each Additional 10 11201	$30		Urine Culture 87088	$80
I & D Abscess Single/Simple 10060	$75		Drawing Fee 36415	$15
Multiple/Complex 10061	$95		Specimen Collection 99000	$10
I & D Pilonidal Cyst Simple 10080	$105			
I & D Pilonidal Cyst Complex 10081	$130			
Laceration Repair various codes	$60			

HEALTH INSURANCE CLAIM FORM

APPROVED BY NATIONAL UNIFORM CLAIM COMMITTEE (NUCC) 02/12

| | PICA | | | | | | | PICA | |

1. MEDICARE ☒(Medicare#)   MEDICAID ☐(Medicaid#)   TRICARE ☐(ID#/DoD#)   CHAMPVA ☐(Member ID#)   GROUP HEALTH PLAN ☐(ID#)   FECA BLK LUNG ☐(ID#)   OTHER ☐(ID#)

1a. INSURED'S I.D. NUMBER (For Program in Item 1)

2. PATIENT'S NAME (Last Name, First Name, Middle Initial)

3. PATIENT'S BIRTH DATE MM DD YY   SEX M ☐ F ☐

4. INSURED'S NAME (Last Name, First Name, Middle Initial)

5. PATIENT'S ADDRESS (No., Street)

6. PATIENT RELATIONSHIP TO INSURED Self ☐ Spouse ☐ Child ☐ Other ☐

7. INSURED'S ADDRESS (No., Street)

CITY   STATE

8. RESERVED FOR NUCC USE

CITY   STATE

ZIP CODE   TELEPHONE (Include Area Code) ( )

ZIP CODE   TELEPHONE (Include Area Code) ( )

9. OTHER INSURED'S NAME (Last Name, First Name, Middle Initial)

10. IS PATIENT'S CONDITION RELATED TO:

11. INSURED'S POLICY GROUP OR FECA NUMBER

a. OTHER INSURED'S POLICY OR GROUP NUMBER

a. EMPLOYMENT? (Current or Previous) ☐ YES ☐ NO

a. INSURED'S DATE OF BIRTH MM DD YY   SEX M ☐ F ☐

b. RESERVED FOR NUCC USE

b. AUTO ACCIDENT? ☐ YES ☐ NO   PLACE (State)

b. OTHER CLAIM ID (Designated by NUCC)

c. RESERVED FOR NUCC USE

c. OTHER ACCIDENT? ☐ YES ☐ NO

c. INSURANCE PLAN NAME OR PROGRAM NAME

d. INSURANCE PLAN NAME OR PROGRAM NAME

10d. CLAIM CODES (Designated by NUCC)

d. IS THERE ANOTHER HEALTH BENEFIT PLAN? ☐ YES ☐ NO   If yes, complete items 9, 9a, and 9d.

READ BACK OF FORM BEFORE COMPLETING & SIGNING THIS FORM.
12. PATIENT'S OR AUTHORIZED PERSON'S SIGNATURE I authorize the release of any medical or other information necessary to process this claim. I also request payment of government benefits either to myself or to the party who accepts assignment below.

SIGNED _____   DATE _____

13. INSURED'S OR AUTHORIZED PERSON'S SIGNATURE I authorize payment of medical benefits to the undersigned physician or supplier for services described below.

SIGNED _____

14. DATE OF CURRENT ILLNESS, INJURY, or PREGNANCY (LMP) MM DD YY   QUAL.

15. OTHER DATE QUAL. MM DD YY

16. DATES PATIENT UNABLE TO WORK IN CURRENT OCCUPATION FROM MM DD YY   TO MM DD YY

17. NAME OF REFERRING PROVIDER OR OTHER SOURCE   17a.   17b. NPI

18. HOSPITALIZATION DATES RELATED TO CURRENT SERVICES FROM MM DD YY   TO MM DD YY

19. ADDITIONAL CLAIM INFORMATION (Designated by NUCC)

20. OUTSIDE LAB? ☐ YES ☐ NO $ CHARGES

21. DIAGNOSIS OR NATURE OF ILLNESS OR INJURY Relate A-L to service line below (24E)   ICD Ind.

A. ___ B. ___ C. ___ D. ___
E. ___ F. ___ G. ___ H. ___
I. ___ J. ___ K. ___ L. ___

22. RESUBMISSION CODE   ORIGINAL REF. NO.

23. PRIOR AUTHORIZATION NUMBER

24. A. DATE(S) OF SERVICE From MM DD YY To MM DD YY	B. PLACE OF SERVICE	C. EMG	D. PROCEDURES, SERVICES, OR SUPPLIES (Explain Unusual Circumstances) CPT/HCPCS MODIFIER	E. DIAGNOSIS POINTER	F. $ CHARGES	G. DAYS OR UNITS	H. EPSDT Family Plan	I. ID. QUAL	J. RENDERING PROVIDER ID. #
1									NPI
2									NPI
3									NPI
4									NPI
5									NPI
6									NPI

25. FEDERAL TAX I.D. NUMBER   SSN EIN ☐ ☐

26. PATIENT'S ACCOUNT NO.

27. ACCEPT ASSIGNMENT? (For govt. claims, see back) ☐ YES ☐ NO

28. TOTAL CHARGE $

29. AMOUNT PAID $

30. Rsvd. for NUCC Use

31. SIGNATURE OF PHYSICIAN OR SUPPLIER INCLUDING DEGREES OR CREDENTIALS (I certify that the statements on the reverse apply to this bill and are made a part thereof.)

SIGNED   DATE

32. SERVICE FACILITY LOCATION INFORMATION

a. NPI   b.

33. BILLING PROVIDER INFO & PH # ( )

a. NPI   b.

NUCC Instruction Manual available at: www.nucc.org   **PLEASE PRINT OR TYPE**   APPROVED OMB-0938-1197 FORM 1500 (02-12)

Clear Form

Figure 4

© 2018 Pearson Education, Inc.

TEST 10: COMPLETE A MEDI–MEDI CLAIM

Directions: Using the source documents provided for patient Calvin Frew, and the Capital City Medical fee schedule (Figure 5), accurately complete a CMS-1500 claim form for this Medi–Medi claim. Use the blank CMS-1500 claim form provided (Figure 6).

TEST 10

Capital City Medical—123 Unknown Boulevard, Capital City, NY 12345-2222 (555) 555-1234	**Patient Information Form**
	Tax ID: 75-0246810
Phil Wells, MD, Mannie Mends, MD, Bette R. Soone, MD	**Group NPI: 1513171216**

Patient Information:

Name: (Last, First) <u>Frew, Calvin</u> ☒ Male ☐ Female Birth Date: <u>12/29/1951</u>

Address: <u>721 Braden Ln, Capital City, NY 12345</u> Phone: (555) <u>555-6227</u>

Social Security Number: <u>303-03-1620</u> Full-Time Student: ☐ Yes ☒ No

Marital Status: ☐ Single ☐ Married ☒ Divorced ☐ Other

Employment:

Employer: <u>Retired</u> Phone: ( ) _____

Address: _____

Condition Related to: ☐ Auto Accident ☐ Employment ☐ Other Accident

Date of Accident: _____ State: _____

Emergency Contact: _____ Phone: ( ) _____

Primary Insurance: <u>Medicare</u> Phone: ( ) _____

Address: <u>P. O. Box 9834, Capital City, NY 12345</u>

Insurance Policyholder's Name: <u>Same</u> ☐ M ☐ F DOB: _____

Address: _____

Phone: _____ Relationship to Insured: ☒ Self ☐ Spouse ☐ Child ☐ Other

Employer: _____ Phone: ( ) _____

Employer's Address: _____

Policy/ID No: <u>521869954A</u> Group No: _____ Percent Covered: <u>80</u> % Copay Amt: $_____

Secondary Insurance: <u>Medicaid</u> Phone: ( ) _____

Address: <u>4875 Capital Blvd, Capital City, NY 12345</u>

Insurance Policyholder's Name: <u>Same</u> ☐ M ☐ F DOB: _____

Address: _____

Phone: _____ Relationship to Insured: ☒ Self ☐ Spouse ☐ Child ☐ Other

Employer: _____ Phone: ( ) _____

Employer's Address: _____

Policy/ID No: <u>00665843324998</u> Group No: _____ Percent Covered: ___% Copay Amt: $<u>5.00</u>

Reason for Visit: <u>I woke up this morning with pain in my right thumb</u>

Known Allergies: _____

Referred by: _____

TEST 10
SOAP

10/18/20XX
Assignment of Benefits: Y
Signature on File: Y
Referring Physician: N

S: Calvin Frew complains of pain in his right thumb since he woke up this morning. He can hardly move it.

O: Pt. denies any injury to his thumb. BP: 148/88. X-ray reveals dislocation. Put back in place without any complications.

A: 1. Right thumb dislocation— S63.104A

P: 1. Thumb placed back into joint successfully.
  2. Keep appointment in 1 month for blood pressure checkup.

_____

Phil Wells, MD
Family Practice
NPI: 1234567890

© 2018 Pearson Education, Inc.

TEST 10

Capital City Medical
123 Unknown Boulevard, Capital City, NY 12345-2222

Date of Service
10-18-20XX

New Patient			Arthrocentesis/Aspiration/Injection		Laboratory	
Problem Focused	99201				Amylase	82150
Expanded Problem, Focused	99202		Small Joint	20600	B12	82607
Detailed	99203		Interm Joint	20605	CBC & Diff	85025
Comprehensive	99204		Major Joint	20610	Comp Metabolic Panel	80053
Comprehensive/High Complex	99205		**Other Invasive/Noninvasive**		Chlamydia Screen	87110
Well Exam Infant (up to 12 mos.)	99381		Audiometry	92552	Cholesterol	82465
Well Exam 1–4 yrs.	99382		Cast Application		Digoxin	80162
Well Exam 5–11 yrs.	99383		Location Long Short		Electrolytes	80051
Well Exam 12–17 yrs.	99384		Catheterization	51701	Ferritin	82728
Well Exam 18–39 yrs.	99385		Circumcision	54150	Folate	82746
Well Exam 40–64 yrs.	99386		Colposcopy	57452	GC Screen	87070
			Colposcopy w/Biopsy	57454	Glucose	82947
			Cryosurgery Premalignant Lesion		Glucose 1 HR	82950
			Location (s):		Glycosylated HGB A1C	83036
Established Patient			Cryosurgery Warts		HCT	85014
Post-Op Follow Up Visit	99024		Location (s):		HDL	83718
Minimum	99211		Curettement Lesion		Hep BSAG	87340
Problem Focused	99212		Single	11055	Hepatitis panel, acute	80074
Expanded Problem Focused	99213	X	2–4	11056	HGB	85018
Detailed	99214		>4	11057	HIV	86703
Comprehensive/High Complex	99215		Diaphragm Fitting	57170	Iron & TIBC	83550
Well Exam Infant (up to 12 mos.)	99391		Ear Irrigation	69210	Kidney Profile	80069
Well exam 1–4 yrs.	99392		ECG	93000	Lead	83655
Well Exam 5–11 yrs.	99393		Endometrial Biopsy	58100	Liver Profile	80076
Well Exam 12–17 yrs.	99394		Exc. Lesion Malignant		Mono Test	86308
Well Exam 18–39 yrs.	99395		Benign		Pap Smear	88155
Well Exam 40–64 yrs.	99396		Location		Pregnancy Test	84703
Obstetrics			Exc. Skin Tags (1–15)	11200	Obstetric Panel	80055
Total OB Care	59400		Each Additional 10	11201	Pro Time	85610
Injections			Fracture Treatment		PSA	84153
Administration Sub. / IM	90772		Loc		RPR	86592
Drug			w/Reduc w/o Reduc		Sed. Rate	85651
Dosage			I & D Abscess Single/Simple	10060	Stool Culture	87045
Allergy	95115		Multiple or Comp	10061	Stool O & P	87177
Cocci Skin Test	86490		I & D Pilonidal Cyst Simple	10080	Strep Screen	87880
DPT	90701		Pilonidal Cyst Complex	10081	Theophylline	80198
Hemophilus	90646		IV Therapy—To One Hour	90760	Thyroid Uptake	84479
Influenza	90658		Each Additional Hour	90761	TSH	84443
MMR	90707		Laceration Repair		Urinalysis	81000
OPV	90712		Location Size Simp/Comp		Urine Culture	87088
Pneumovax	90732		Laryngoscopy	31505	Drawing Fee	36415
TB Skin Test	86580		Oximetry	94760	Specimen Collection	99000
TD	90718		Punch Biopsy		**Other:**	
Unlisted Immun	90749		Rhythm Strip	93040		
Tetanus Toxoid	90703		Treadmill	93015		
Vaccine/Toxoid Admin <8 Yr Old w/ Counseling	90465		Trigger Point or Tendon Sheath Inj.	20550		
Vaccine/Toxoid Administration for Adult	90471		Tympanometry	92567		

Diagnosis/ICD-10: **S63.104A**

I acknowledge receipt of medical services and authorize the release of any medical information necessary to process this claim for healthcare payment only. I do authorize payment to the provider.

Total Estimated Charges: _____

Payment Amount: _____

Patient Signature _Calvin Frew_____

Next Appointment: _____

Figure 5

Capital City Medical
Fee Schedule

New Patient OV			Punch Biopsy various codes	$80
Problem Focused 99201	$45		Nebulizer various codes	$45
Expanded Problem Focused 99202	$65		Cast Application various codes	$85
Detailed 99203	$85		Laryngoscopy 31505	$255
Comprehensive 99204	$105		Audiometry 92552	$85
Comprehensive/High Complex 99205	$115		Tympanometry 92567	$85
Well Exam infant (less than 1 year) 99381	$45		Ear Irrigation 69210	$25
Well Exam 1–4 yrs. 99382	$50		Diaphragm Fitting 57170	$30
Well Exam 5–11 yrs. 99383	$55		IV Therapy (up to one hour) 90760	$65
Well Exam 12–17 yrs. 99384	$65		Each additional hour 90761	$50
Well Exam 18–39 yrs. 99385	$85		Oximetry 94760	$10
Well Exam 40–64 yrs. 99386	$105		ECG 93000	$75
Established Patient OV			Holter Monitor various codes	$170
Post Op Follow Up Visit 99024	$0		Rhythm Strip 93040	$60
Minimum 99211	$35		Treadmill 93015	$375
Problem Focused 99212	$45		Cocci Skin Test 86490	$20
Expanded Problem Focused 99213	$55		X-ray, spine, chest, bone—any area various codes	$275
Detailed 99214	$65		Avulsion Nail 11730	$200
Comprehensive/High Complex 99215	$75		**Laboratory**	
Well exam infant (less than 1 year) 99391	$35		Amylase 82150	$40
Well Exam 1–4 yrs. 99392	$40		B12 82607	$30
Well Exam 5–11 yrs. 99393	$45		CBC & Diff 85025	$95
Well Exam 12–17 yrs. 99394	$55		Comp Metabolic Panel 80053	$75
Well Exam 18–39 yrs. 99395	$65		Chlamydia Screen 87110	$70
Well Exam 40–64 yrs. 99396	$75		Cholestrerol 82465	$75
Obstetrics			Digoxin 80162	$40
Total OB Care 59400	$1700		Electrolytes 80051	$70
Injections			Estrogen, Total 82672	$50
Administration 90772	$10		Ferritin 82728	$40
Allergy 95115	$35		Folate 82746	$30
DPT 90701	$50		GC Screen 87070	$60
Drug various codes	$35		Glucose 82947	$35
Influenza 90658	$25		Glycosylated HGB A1C 83036	$45
MMR 90707	$50		HCT 85014	$30
OPV 90712	$40		HDL 83718	$35
Pneumovax 90732	$35		HGB 85018	$30
TB Skin Test 86580	$15		Hep BSAG 83740	$40
TD 90718	$40		Hepatitis panel, acute 80074	$95
Tetanus Toxoid 90703	$40		HIV 86703	$100
Vaccine/Toxoid Administration for Younger			Iron & TIBC 83550	$45
Than 8 Years Old w/ counseling 90465	$10		Kidney Profile 80069	$95
Vaccine/Toxoid Administration for Adult 90471	$10		Lead 83665	$55
Arthrocentesis/Aspiration/Injection			Lipase 83690	$40
Small Joint 20600	$50		Lipid Panel 80061	$95
Interm Joint 20605	$60		Liver Profile 80076	$95
Major Joint 20610	$70		Mono Test 86308	$30
Trigger Point/Tendon Sheath Inj. 20550	$90		Pap Smear 88155	$90
Other Invasive/Noninvasive Procedures			Pap Collection/Supervision 88142	$95
Catheterization 51701	$55		Pregnancy Test 84703	$90
Circumcision 54150	$150		Obstetric Panel 80055	$85
Colposcopy 57452	$225		Pro Time 85610	$50
Colposcopy w/Biopsy 57454	$250		PSA 84153	$50
Cryosurgery Premalignant Lesion various codes	$160		RPR 86592	$55
Endometrial Biopsy 58100	$190		Sed. Rate 85651	$50
Excision Lesion Malignant various codes	$145		Stool Culture 87045	$80
Excision Lesion Benign various codes	$125		Stool O & P 87177	$105
Curettement Lesion			Strep Screen 87880	$35
Single 11055	$70		Theophylline 80198	$40
2–4 11056	$80		Thyroid Uptake 84479	$75
>4 11057	$90		TSH 84443	$50
Excision Skin Tags (1–15) 11200	$55		Urinalysis 81000	$35
Each Additional 10 11201	$30		Urine Culture 87088	$80
I & D Abscess Single/Simple 10060	$75		Drawing Fee 36415	$15
Multiple/Complex 10061	$95		Specimen Collection 99000	$10
I & D Pilonidal Cyst Simple 10080	$105			
I & D Pilonidal Cyst Complex 10081	$130			
Laceration Repair various codes	$60			

HEALTH INSURANCE CLAIM FORM

APPROVED BY NATIONAL UNIFORM CLAIM COMMITTEE (NUCC) 02/12

		PICA							PICA	

1. MEDICARE ☒ (Medicare#)   MEDICAID ☐ (Medicaid#)   TRICARE ☐ (ID#/DoD#)   CHAMPVA ☐ (Member ID#)   GROUP HEALTH PLAN ☐ (ID#)   FECA BLK LUNG ☐ (ID#)   OTHER ☐ (ID#)   **1a. INSURED'S I.D. NUMBER** (For Program in Item 1)

2 PATIENT'S NAME (Last Name, First Name, Middle Initial)

3. PATIENT'S BIRTH DATE MM | DD | YY   SEX M ☐ F ☐

4. INSURED'S NAME (Last Name, First Name, Middle Initial)

5. PATIENT'S ADDRESS (No., Street)

6. PATIENT RELATIONSHIP TO INSURED   Self ☐ Spouse ☐ Child ☐ Other ☐

7. INSURED'S ADDRESS (No., Street)

CITY   STATE

8. RESERVED FOR NUCC USE

CITY   STATE

ZIP CODE   TELEPHONE (Include Area Code) ( )

ZIP CODE   TELEPHONE (Include Area Code) ( )

9. OTHER INSURED'S NAME (Last Name, First Name, Middle Initial)

10. IS PATIENT'S CONDITION RELATED TO:

11. INSURED'S POLICY GROUP OR FECA NUMBER

a. OTHER INSURED'S POLICY OR GROUP NUMBER

a. EMPLOYMENT? (Current or Previous) YES ☐ NO ☐

a. INSURED'S DATE OF BIRTH MM | DD | YY   SEX M ☐ F ☐

b. RESERVED FOR NUCC USE

b. AUTO ACCIDENT? YES ☐ NO ☐   PLACE (State)

b. OTHER CLAIM ID (Designated by NUCC)

c. RESERVED FOR NUCC USE

c. OTHER ACCIDENT? YES ☐ NO ☐

c. INSURANCE PLAN NAME OR PROGRAM NAME

d. INSURANCE PLAN NAME OR PROGRAM NAME

10d. CLAIM CODES (Designated by NUCC)

d. IS THERE ANOTHER HEALTH BENEFIT PLAN? YES ☐ NO ☐ *If yes,* complete items 9, 9a, and 9d.

READ BACK OF FORM BEFORE COMPLETING & SIGNING THIS FORM.
12. PATIENT'S OR AUTHORIZED PERSON'S SIGNATURE I authorize the release of any medical or other information necessary to process this claim. I also request payment of government benefits either to myself or to the party who accepts assignment below.

SIGNED _____ DATE _____

13. INSURED'S OR AUTHORIZED PERSON'S SIGNATURE I authorize payment of medical benefits to the undersigned physician or supplier for services described below.

SIGNED _____

14. DATE OF CURRENT ILLNESS, INJURY, or PREGNANCY (LMP) MM | DD | YY   QUAL

15. OTHER DATE QUAL | MM | DD | YY

16. DATES PATIENT UNABLE TO WORK IN CURRENT OCCUPATION FROM MM | DD | YY TO MM | DD | YY

17. NAME OF REFERRING PROVIDER OR OTHER SOURCE   17a.   17b. NPI

18. HOSPITALIZATION DATES RELATED TO CURRENT SERVICES FROM MM | DD | YY TO MM | DD | YY

19. ADDITIONAL CLAIM INFORMATION (Designated by NUCC)

20. OUTSIDE LAB? YES ☐ NO ☐ $ CHARGES

21. DIAGNOSIS OR NATURE OF ILLNESS OR INJURY Relate A-L to service line below (24E)   ICD Ind.
A. |_____ B. |_____ C. |_____ D. |_____
E. |_____ F. |_____ G. |_____ H. |_____
I. |_____ J. |_____ K. |_____ L. |_____

22. RESUBMISSION CODE   ORIGINAL REF. NO.

23. PRIOR AUTHORIZATION NUMBER

24. A. DATE(S) OF SERVICE From MM DD YY To MM DD YY	B. PLACE OF SERVICE	C. EMG	D. PROCEDURES, SERVICES, OR SUPPLIES (Explain Unusual Circumstances) CPT/HCPCS MODIFIER	E. DIAGNOSIS POINTER	F. $ CHARGES	G. DAYS OR UNITS	H. EPSDT Family Plan	I. ID. QUAL	J. RENDERING PROVIDER ID. #
1									NPI
2									NPI
3									NPI
4									NPI
5									NPI
6									NPI

25. FEDERAL TAX I.D. NUMBER   SSN ☐ EIN ☐

26. PATIENT'S ACCOUNT NO.

27. ACCEPT ASSIGNMENT? (For govt. claims, see back) YES ☐ NO ☐

28. TOTAL CHARGE $

29. AMOUNT PAID $

30. Rsvd. for NUCC Use

31. SIGNATURE OF PHYSICIAN OR SUPPLIER INCLUDING DEGREES OR CREDENTIALS (I certify that the statements on the reverse apply to this bill and are made a part thereof.)

SIGNED _____ DATE _____

32. SERVICE FACILITY LOCATION INFORMATION
a. NPI   b.

33. BILLING PROVIDER INFO & PH # ( )
a. NPI   b.

NUCC Instruction Manual available at: www.nucc.org   **PLEASE PRINT OR TYPE**   APPROVED OMB-0938-1197 FORM 1500 (02-12)

Clear Form

Figure 6

© 2018 Pearson Education, Inc.

TEST 11: COMPLETE A TRICARE CLAIM

Directions: Using the source documents provided for patient Gracie Lloyd and the Capital City Medical fee schedule (Figure 7), accurately complete a CMS-1500 claim form for TRICARE. Use the blank CMS-1500 claim form provided (Figure 8).

Complete the case on the basis of the following criteria:

- All patients have release of information and assignment of benefit signatures on file.

- All providers are participating and accept assignment.

- The group practice is the billing entity.

- The national transition to NPI numbers is complete, and legacy PINs of individual payers are no longer used.

- 2017 ICD-10-CM/PCS and CPT codes are used.

- Use eight-digit dates for birthdates. Use six-digit dates for all other dates.

- All street names should be entered with standard postal abbreviations, even if they are spelled out on the source documents.

- Enter ICD-10 codes in the order in which they appear on the encounter form.

- When entering CPT codes, enter the E/M code first. Enter remaining codes in descending price order.

© 2018 Pearson Education, Inc.

TEST 11

Capital City Medical—123 Unknown Boulevard, Capital City, NY 12345-2222 (555) 555-1234	**Patient Information Form**
	Tax ID: 75-0246810
Phil Wells, MD, Mannie Mends, MD, Bette R. Soone, MD	**Group NPI: 1513171216**

Patient Information:

Name: (Last, First) <u>Lloyd, Gracie</u>   ☐ Male ☒ Female Birth Date: <u>11/03/1976</u>

Address: <u>630 Jefferson Base, Capital City, NY 12345</u>   Phone: (555) <u>555-3232</u>

Social Security Number: <u>619-42-8736</u>   Full-Time Student: ☐ Yes ☐ No

Marital Status: ☐ Single ☒ Married ☐ Divorced ☐ Other

Employment:

Employer: <u>Jefferson Base</u>   Phone: (555) <u>555-1600</u>

Address: <u>600 Jefferson Base, Capital City, NY 12345</u>

Condition Related to: ☐ Auto Accident ☐ Employment ☐ Other Accident

Date of Accident: _____ State: _____

Emergency Contact: _____ **Phone: ( )** _____

Primary Insurance: <u>Medicare</u>   Phone: ( ) _____

Address: <u>7594 Forces-Run Rd, Militaryville, NY 12345</u>

Insurance Policyholder's Name: <u>Same</u>   ☐ M ☐ F DOB: _____

Address: _____

Phone: _____ Relationship to Insured: ☒ Self ☐ Spouse ☐ Child ☐ Other

Employer: _____ Phone: ( ) _____

Employer's Address: _____

Policy/ID No: <u>619428736</u> Group No: _____ Percent Covered: <u>80</u> % Copay Amt: $<u>35.00</u>

Secondary Insurance: _____ Phone: ( ) _____

Address: _____

Insurance Policyholder's Name: _____ ☐ M ☐ F DOB: _____

Address: _____

Phone: _____ Relationship to Insured: ☐ Self ☐ Spouse ☐ Child ☐ Other

Employer: _____ Phone: ( ) _____

Employer's Address: _____

Policy/ID No: _____ Group No: _____ Percent Covered: ___% Copay Amt: $_____

Reason for Visit: <u>I think that I may be pregnant.</u> _____

Known Allergies: _____

Referred by: _____

TEST 11
SOAP

01/24/20XX
Assignment of Benefits: Y
Signature on File: Y
Referring Physician: N

S: Gracie Lloyd complains of missed menses ×2 weeks.

O: Pt. denies any N&V. Her last menstrual period was 12-10-20XX. She has one child, female, alive and well. She has no history of miscarriage or abortion.

A: 1. Absent menstruation— N91.2 Pregnancy test Z32.00

P: 1. Serum pregnancy today.
    2. Will call pt. with results.

_____

Phil Wells, MD
Family Practice
NPI: 1234567890

© 2018 Pearson Education, Inc.

TEST 11

Patient Name Gracie Lloyd

Capital City Medical
123 Unknown Boulevard, Capital City, NY 12345-2222

Date of Service
01-24-20XX

New Patient			Other Invasive/Noninvasive			Laboratory		
Problem Focused	99201		Arthrocentesis/Aspiration/Injection			Amylase	82150	
Expanded Problem, Focused	99202		Small Joint	20600		B12	82607	
Detailed	99203		Interm Joint	20605		CBC & Diff	85025	
Comprehensive	99204		Major Joint	20610		Comp Metabolic Panel	80053	
Comprehensive/High Complex	99205		**Other Invasive/Noninvasive**			Chlamydia Screen	87110	
Well Exam Infant (up to 12 mos.)	99381		Audiometry	92552		Cholesterol	82465	
Well Exam 1–4 yrs.	99382		Cast Application			Digoxin	80162	
Well Exam 5–11 yrs.	99383		Location Long Short			Electrolytes	80051	
Well Exam 12–17 yrs.	99384		Catheterization	51701		Ferritin	82728	
Well Exam 18–39 yrs.	99385		Circumcision	54150		Folate	82746	
Well Exam 40–64 yrs.	99386		Colposcopy	57452		GC Screen	87070	
			Colposcopy w/Biopsy	57454		Glucose	82947	
			Cryosurgery Premalignant Lesion			Glucose 1 HR	82950	
			Location (s):			Glycosylated HGB A1C	83036	
Established Patient			Cryosurgery Warts			HCT	85014	
Post-Op Follow Up Visit	99024		Location (s):			HDL	83718	
Minimum	99211		Curettement Lesion			Hep BSAG	87340	
Problem Focused	99212	X	Single	11055		Hepatitis panel, acute	80074	
Expanded Problem Focused	99213		2–4	11056		HGB	85018	
Detailed	99214		>4	11057		HIV	86703	
Comprehensive/High Complex	99215		Diaphragm Fitting	57170		Iron & TIBC	83550	
Well Exam Infant (up to 12 mos.)	99391		Ear Irrigation	69210		Kidney Profile	80069	
Well exam 1–4 yrs.	99392		ECG	93000		Lead	83655	
Well Exam 5–11 yrs.	99393		Endometrial Biopsy	58100		Liver Profile	80076	
Well Exam 12–17 yrs.	99394		Exc. Lesion Malignant			Mono Test	86308	
Well Exam 18–39 yrs.	99395		Benign			Pap Smear	88155	
Well Exam 40–64 yrs.	99396		Location			Pregnancy Test	84703	X
Obstetrics			Exc. Skin Tags (1–15)	11200		Obstetric Panel	80055	
Total OB Care	59400		Each Additional 10	11201		Pro Time	85610	
Injections			Fracture Treatment			PSA	84153	
Administration Sub. / IM	90772		Loc			RPR	86592	
Drug			w/Reduc w/o Reduc			Sed. Rate	85651	
Dosage			I & D Abscess Single/Simple	10060		Stool Culture	87045	
Allergy	95115		Multiple or Comp	10061		Stool O & P	87177	
Cocci Skin Test	86490		I & D Pilonidal Cyst Simple	10080		Strep Screen	87880	
DPT	90701		Pilonidal Cyst Complex	10081		Theophylline	80198	
Hemophilus	90646		IV Therapy—To One Hour	90760		Thyroid Uptake	84479	
Influenza	90658		Each Additional Hour	90761		TSH	84443	
MMR	90707		Laceration Repair			Urinalysis	81000	X
OPV	90712		Location Size Simp/Comp			Urine Culture	87088	
Pneumovax	90732		Laryngoscopy	31505		Drawing Fee	36415	
TB Skin Test	86580		Oximetry	94760		Specimen Collection	99000	
TD	90718		Punch Biopsy			**Other:**		
Unlisted Immun	90749		Rhythm Strip	93040				
Tetanus Toxoid	90703		Treadmill	93015				
Vaccine/Toxoid Admin <8 Yr Old w/ Counseling	90465		Trigger Point or Tendon Sheath Inj.	20550				
Vaccine/Toxoid Administration for Adult	90471		Tympanometry	92567				

Diagnosis/ICD-10: **N91.2, Z32.00**

I acknowledge receipt of medical services and authorize the release of any medical information necessary to process this claim for healthcare payment only. I do authorize payment to the provider.

Patient Signature _Gracie Lloyd_

Total Estimated Charges: _____

Payment Amount: _____

Next Appointment: _____

Figure 7

Capital City Medical
Fee Schedule

New Patient OV		Punch Biopsy various codes	$80
Problem Focused 99201	$45	Nebulizer various codes	$45
Expanded Problem Focused 99202	$65	Cast Application various codes	$85
Detailed 99203	$85	Laryngoscopy 31505	$255
Comprehensive 99204	$105	Audiometry 92552	$85
Comprehensive/High Complex 99205	$115	Tympanometry 92567	$85
Well Exam infant (less than 1 year) 99381	$45	Ear Irrigation 69210	$25
Well Exam 1–4 yrs. 99382	$50	Diaphragm Fitting 57170	$30
Well Exam 5–11 yrs. 99383	$55	IV Therapy (up to one hour) 90760	$65
Well Exam 12–17 yrs. 99384	$65	Each additional hour 90761	$50
Well Exam 18–39 yrs. 99385	$85	Oximetry 94760	$10
Well Exam 40–64 yrs. 99386	$105	ECG 93000	$75
Established Patient OV		Holter Monitor various codes	$170
Post Op Follow Up Visit 99024	$0	Rhythm Strip 93040	$60
Minimum 99211	$35	Treadmill 93015	$375
Problem Focused 99212	$45	Cocci Skin Test 86490	$20
Expanded Problem Focused 99213	$55	X-ray, spine, chest, bone—any area various codes	$275
Detailed 99214	$65	Avulsion Nail 11730	$200
Comprehensive/High Complex 99215	$75	**Laboratory**	
Well exam infant (less than 1 year) 99391	$35	Amylase 82150	$40
Well Exam 1–4 yrs. 99392	$40	B12 82607	$30
Well Exam 5–11 yrs. 99393	$45	CBC & Diff 85025	$95
Well Exam 12–17 yrs. 99394	$55	Comp Metabolic Panel 80053	$75
Well Exam 18–39 yrs. 99395	$65	Chlamydia Screen 87110	$70
Well Exam 40–64 yrs. 99396	$75	Cholestrerol 82465	$75
Obstetrics		Digoxin 80162	$40
Total OB Care 59400	$1700	Electrolytes 80051	$70
Injections		Estrogen, Total 82672	$50
Administration 90772	$10	Ferritin 82728	$40
Allergy 95115	$35	Folate 82746	$30
DPT 90701	$50	GC Screen 87070	$60
Drug various codes	$35	Glucose 82947	$35
Influenza 90658	$25	Glycosylated HGB A1C 83036	$45
MMR 90707	$50	HCT 85014	$30
OPV 90712	$40	HDL 83718	$35
Pneumovax 90732	$35	HGB 85018	$30
TB Skin Test 86580	$15	Hep BSAG 83740	$40
TD 90718	$40	Hepatitis panel, acute 80074	$95
Tetanus Toxoid 90703	$40	HIV 86703	$100
Vaccine/Toxoid Administration for Younger Than 8 Years Old w/ counseling 90465	$10	Iron & TIBC 83550	$45
		Kidney Profile 80069	$95
Vaccine/Toxoid Administration for Adult 90471	$10	Lead 83665	$55
Arthrocentesis/Aspiration/Injection		Lipase 83690	$40
Small Joint 20600	$50	Lipid Panel 80061	$95
Interm Joint 20605	$60	Liver Profile 80076	$95
Major Joint 20610	$70	Mono Test 86308	$30
Trigger Point/Tendon Sheath Inj. 20550	$90	Pap Smear 88155	$90
Other Invasive/Noninvasive Procedures		Pap Collection/Supervision 88142	$95
Catheterization 51701	$55	Pregnancy Test 84703	$90
Circumcision 54150	$150	Obstetric Panel 80055	$85
Colposcopy 57452	$225	Pro Time 85610	$50
Colposcopy w/Biopsy 57454	$250	PSA 84153	$50
Cryosurgery Premalignant Lesion various codes	$160	RPR 86592	$55
Endometrial Biopsy 58100	$190	Sed. Rate 85651	$50
Excision Lesion Malignant various codes	$145	Stool Culture 87045	$80
Excision Lesion Benign various codes	$125	Stool O & P 87177	$105
Curettement Lesion		Strep Screen 87880	$35
Single 11055	$70	Theophylline 80198	$40
2–4 11056	$80	Thyroid Uptake 84479	$75
>4 11057	$90	TSH 84443	$50
Excision Skin Tags (1–15) 11200	$55	Urinalysis 81000	$35
Each Additional 10 11201	$30	Urine Culture 87088	$80
I & D Abscess Single/Simple 10060	$75	Drawing Fee 36415	$15
Multiple/Complex 10061	$95	Specimen Collection 99000	$10
I & D Pilonidal Cyst Simple 10080	$105		
I & D Pilonidal Cyst Complex 10081	$130		
Laceration Repair various codes	$60		

HEALTH INSURANCE CLAIM FORM

APPROVED BY NATIONAL UNIFORM CLAIM COMMITTEE (NUCC) 02/12

1. MEDICARE MEDICAID TRICARE CHAMPVA GROUP HEALTH PLAN FECA BLK LUNG OTHER	1a. INSURED'S I.D. NUMBER (For Program in Item 1)
[X] (Medicare#) [ ] (Medicaid#) [ ] (ID#/DoD#) [ ] (Member ID#) [ ] (ID#) [ ] (ID#) [ ] (ID#)	

2. PATIENT'S NAME (Last Name, First Name, Middle Initial)	3. PATIENT'S BIRTH DATE MM DD YY SEX M [ ] F [ ]	4. INSURED'S NAME (Last Name, First Name, Middle Initial)

5. PATIENT'S ADDRESS (No., Street)	6. PATIENT RELATIONSHIP TO INSURED Self [ ] Spouse [ ] Child [ ] Other [ ]	7. INSURED'S ADDRESS (No., Street)

CITY STATE	8. RESERVED FOR NUCC USE	CITY STATE

ZIP CODE TELEPHONE (Include Area Code) ( )		ZIP CODE TELEPHONE (Include Area Code) ( )

9. OTHER INSURED'S NAME (Last Name, First Name, Middle Initial)	10. IS PATIENT'S CONDITION RELATED TO:	11. INSURED'S POLICY GROUP OR FECA NUMBER
a. OTHER INSURED'S POLICY OR GROUP NUMBER	a. EMPLOYMENT? (Current or Previous) [ ] YES [ ] NO	a. INSURED'S DATE OF BIRTH MM DD YY SEX M [ ] F [ ]
b. RESERVED FOR NUCC USE	b. AUTO ACCIDENT? PLACE (State) [ ] YES [ ] NO	b. OTHER CLAIM ID (Designated by NUCC)
c. RESERVED FOR NUCC USE	c. OTHER ACCIDENT? [ ] YES [ ] NO	c. INSURANCE PLAN NAME OR PROGRAM NAME
d. INSURANCE PLAN NAME OR PROGRAM NAME	10d. CLAIM CODES (Designated by NUCC)	d. IS THERE ANOTHER HEALTH BENEFIT PLAN? [ ] YES [ ] NO If yes, complete items 9, 9a, and 9d.

READ BACK OF FORM BEFORE COMPLETING & SIGNING THIS FORM.

12. PATIENT'S OR AUTHORIZED PERSON'S SIGNATURE I authorize the release of any medical or other information necessary to process this claim. I also request payment of government benefits either to myself or to the party who accepts assignment below. SIGNED _____ DATE _____	13. INSURED'S OR AUTHORIZED PERSON'S SIGNATURE I authorize payment of medical benefits to the undersigned physician or supplier for services described below. SIGNED _____

14. DATE OF CURRENT ILLNESS, INJURY, or PREGNANCY (LMP) MM DD YY QUAL	15. OTHER DATE QUAL MM DD YY	16. DATES PATIENT UNABLE TO WORK IN CURRENT OCCUPATION MM DD YY FROM TO MM DD YY
17. NAME OF REFERRING PROVIDER OR OTHER SOURCE	17a. ___ 17b. NPI ___	18. HOSPITALIZATION DATES RELATED TO CURRENT SERVICES MM DD YY FROM TO MM DD YY
19. ADDITIONAL CLAIM INFORMATION (Designated by NUCC)		20. OUTSIDE LAB? [ ] YES [ ] NO $ CHARGES

21. DIAGNOSIS OR NATURE OF ILLNESS OR INJURY Relate A-L to service line below (24E) ICD Ind.	22. RESUBMISSION CODE ORIGINAL REF. NO.
A. ___ B. ___ C. ___ D. ___ E. ___ F. ___ G. ___ H. ___ I. ___ J. ___ K. ___ L. ___	23. PRIOR AUTHORIZATION NUMBER

24. A. DATE(S) OF SERVICE From To MM DD YY MM DD YY	B. PLACE OF SERVICE	C. EMG	D. PROCEDURES, SERVICES, OR SUPPLIES (Explain Unusual Circumstances) CPT/HCPCS MODIFIER	E. DIAGNOSIS POINTER	F. $ CHARGES	G. DAYS OR UNITS	H. EPSDT Family Plan	I. ID. QUAL	J. RENDERING PROVIDER ID. #
1									NPI
2									NPI
3									NPI
4									NPI
5									NPI
6									NPI

25. FEDERAL TAX I.D. NUMBER [ ] SSN [ ] EIN	26. PATIENT'S ACCOUNT NO.	27. ACCEPT ASSIGNMENT? (For govt. claims, see back) [ ] YES [ ] NO	28. TOTAL CHARGE $	29. AMOUNT PAID $	30. Rsvd. for NUCC Use
31. SIGNATURE OF PHYSICIAN OR SUPPLIER INCLUDING DEGREES OR CREDENTIALS (I certify that the statements on the reverse apply to this bill and are made a part thereof.) SIGNED _____ DATE _____	32. SERVICE FACILITY LOCATION INFORMATION a. NPI b.		33. BILLING PROVIDER INFO & PH # ( ) a. NPI b.		

NUCC Instruction Manual available at: www.nucc.org **PLEASE PRINT OR TYPE** APPROVED OMB-0938-1197 FORM 1500 (02-12)

Clear Form

CARRIER — PATIENT AND INSURED INFORMATION — PHYSICIAN OR SUPPLIER INFORMATION

Figure 8

TEST 12: COMPLETE A WORKERS' COMPENSATION CLAIM

Directions: Using the source documents provided for patient Devon Ulrich and the Capital City Medical fee schedule (Figure 9), accurately complete a CMS-1500 claim form for a Workers' Compensation claim. Use the blank CMS-1500 claim form provided (Figure 10).

Complete the case on the basis of the following criteria:

- All patients have release of information and assignment of benefit signatures on file, as a condition for Workers' Compensation. Items 12 and 13 should not be completed.

- By law, all providers are participating and accept assignment. Item 27 should not be marked.

- The group practice is the billing entity.

- The national transition to NPI numbers is complete, and legacy PINs of individual payers are no longer used. If legacy PINS are still being used by your state's Workers' Compensation program, your instructor may provide legacy PINs in addition to the NPI.

- 2017 ICD-10-CM/PCS and CPT codes are used.

- Use eight-digit dates for birthdates. Use six-digit dates for all other dates.

- All street names should be entered with standard postal abbreviations, even if they are spelled out on the source documents.

- Enter ICD-10 codes in the order in which they appear on the encounter form.

- When entering CPT codes, enter the E/M code first. Enter remaining CPT codes in descending price order.

- Enter the Workers' Compensation assigned claim number in Item 1a. (Requirements will vary by state.)

© 2018 Pearson Education, Inc.

TEST 12

Capital City Medical—123 Unknown Boulevard, Capital City, NY 12345-2222 (555) 555-1234	Patient Information Form
Phil Wells, MD, Mannie Mends, MD, Bette R. Soone, MD	Tax ID: 75-0246810
	Group NPI: 1513171216

Patient Information:

Name: (Last, First) <u>Ulrich, Devon</u> ☒ Male ☐ Female Birth Date: <u>10/07/1971</u>

Address: <u>42 Stone St, Township, NY 12345</u> Phone: (555) <u>555-7159</u>

Social Security Number: <u>619-42-8736</u> Full-Time Student: ☐ Yes ☒ No

Marital Status: ☐ Single ☒ Married ☐ Divorced ☐ Other

Employment:

Employer: <u>Curb Appeal Landscaping, Inc.</u> Phone: (555) <u>555-1291</u>

Address: <u>600 Jefferson Base, Capital City NY 12345</u>

Condition Related to: ☐ Auto Accident ☒ Employment ☐ Other Accident

Date of Accident: <u>09/06/20XX</u> State: <u>NY</u>

Emergency Contact: _____ **Phone: ( )** _____

Primary Insurance: <u>Capital Workers' Compensation Insurance Co.</u> Phone: ( ) _____

Address: <u>40, Hurt Rd, Capital City, NY 12345</u>

Insurance Policyholder's Name: <u>Curb Appeal Landscaping Inc.</u> ☐ M ☐ F DOB: _____

Address: _____

Phone: _____ Relationship to Insured: ☐ Self ☐ Spouse ☐ Child ☒ Other

Employer: <u>Same as above</u> Phone: ( ) _____

Employer's Address: _____

Policy/ID No: <u>WCDU1115</u> Group No: _____ Percent Covered: ___% Copay Amt: $_____

Secondary Insurance: _____ Phone: ( ) _____

Address: _____

Insurance Policyholder's Name: _____ ☐ M ☐ F DOB: _____

Address: _____

Phone: _____ Relationship to Insured: ☐ Self ☐ Spouse ☐ Child ☐ Other

Employer: _____ Phone: ( ) _____

Employer's Address: _____

Policy/ID No: _____ Group No: _____ Percent Covered: ___% Copay Amt: $_____

Reason for Visit: <u>While working today I got excessively tired.</u>

Known Allergies: _____

Referred by: _____

© 2018 Pearson Education, Inc.

09/06/20XX
Assignment of Benefits: Y
Signature on File: Y
Referring Physician: N

S: New patient, Devon Ulrich, presents in the office today complaining of excessive tiredness. He was landscaping a client's yard today at work when he suddenly felt "weirdly exhausted."

O: HEENT: Normocephalic, atraumatic. Eyes clear. Nose clear. Throat: No masses. Chest clear. BP: 110/86, P: 74, R: 12, T: 97.6°. Abdomen is soft, nontender. No masses. Bowel sounds normal. Pt. shows signs of heat fatigue. Lytes normal values.

A: 1. Heat exhaustion due to weather— T67.5XXA, Z39.8XXA

P: 1. Plenty of rest.
   2. Plenty of vitamin-rich liquids such as vitamin water.
   3. Call office if no improvement or if dizziness, fainting, N&V occur.
   4. Return in 3 days.
   5. Off work until next appointment.
   6. Please bill his workers' compensation. His info is as follows:
      Capital Workers' Compensation Insurance Co.
      40 Hurt Rd.
      Capital City, NY 12345
      Claim #WCDU1115
   7. Phil Wells, MD state license #—MD-123456-L

Phil Wells, MD
Family Practice
NPI: 1234567890

© 2018 Pearson Education, Inc.

TEST 12

Patient Name Devon Ulrich

Capital City Medical
123 Unknown Boulevard, Capital City, NY 12345-2222

Date of Service
09-06-20XX

New Patient			Arthrocentesis/Aspiration/Injection			Laboratory		
Problem Focused	99201		Small Joint		20600	Amylase	82150	
Expanded Problem, Focused	99202		Interm Joint		20605	B12	82607	X
Detailed	99203		Major Joint		20610	CBC & Diff	85025	
Comprehensive	99204	X	**Other Invasive/Noninvasive**			Comp Metabolic Panel	80053	
Comprehensive/High Complex	99205		Audiometry		92552	Chlamydia Screen	87110	
Well Exam Infant (up to 12 mos.)	99381		Cast Application			Cholesterol	82465	
Well Exam 1–4 yrs.	99382		Location Long Short			Digoxin	80162	
Well Exam 5–11 yrs.	99383		Catheterization		51701	Electrolytes	80051	X
Well Exam 12–17 yrs.	99384		Circumcision		54150	Ferritin	82728	
Well Exam 18–39 yrs.	99385		Colposcopy		57452	Folate	82746	
Well Exam 40–64 yrs.	99386		Colposcopy w/Biopsy		57454	GC Screen	87070	
			Cryosurgery Premalignant Lesion			Glucose	82947	
			Location (s):			Glucose 1 HR	82950	
						Glycosylated HGB A1C	83036	
Established Patient			Cryosurgery Warts			HCT	85014	
Post-Op Follow Up Visit	99024		Location (s):			HDL	83718	
Minimum	99211		Curettement Lesion			Hep BSAG	87340	
Problem Focused	99212		Single		11055	Hepatitis panel, acute	80074	
Expanded Problem Focused	99213		2–4		11056	HGB	85018	
Detailed	99214		>4		11057	HIV	86703	
Comprehensive/High Complex	99215		Diaphragm Fitting		57170	Iron & TIBC	83550	
Well Exam Infant (up to 12 mos.)	99391		Ear Irrigation		69210	Kidney Profile	80069	
Well exam 1–4 yrs.	99392		ECG		93000	Lead	83655	
Well Exam 5–11 yrs.	99393		Endometrial Biopsy		58100	Liver Profile	80076	
Well Exam 12–17 yrs.	99394		Exc. Lesion Malignant			Mono Test	86308	
Well Exam 18–39 yrs.	99395		Benign			Pap Smear	88155	
Well Exam 40–64 yrs.	99396		Location			Pregnancy Test	84703	
Obstetrics			Exc. Skin Tags (1–15)		11200	Obstetric Panel	80055	
Total OB Care	59400		Each Additional 10		11201	Pro Time	85610	
Injections			Fracture Treatment			PSA	84153	
Administration Sub. / IM	90772		Loc			RPR	86592	
Drug			w/Reduc	w/o Reduc		Sed. Rate	85651	
Dosage			I & D Abscess Single/Simple		10060	Stool Culture	87045	
Allergy	95115		Multiple or Comp		10061	Stool O & P	87177	
Cocci Skin Test	86490		I & D Pilonidal Cyst Simple		10080	Strep Screen	87880	
DPT	90701		Pilonidal Cyst Complex		10081	Theophylline	80198	
Hemophilus	90646		IV Therapy—To One Hour		90760	Thyroid Uptake	84479	
Influenza	90658		Each Additional Hour		90761	TSH	84443	
MMR	90707		Laceration Repair			Urinalysis	81000	
OPV	90712		Location Size Simp/Comp			Urine Culture	87088	
Pneumovax	90732		Laryngoscopy		31505	Drawing Fee	36415	X
TB Skin Test	86580		Oximetry		94760	Specimen Collection	99000	
TD	90718		Punch Biopsy			**Other:**		
Unlisted Immun	90749		Rhythm Strip		93040			
Tetanus Toxoid	90703		Treadmill		93015			
Vaccine/Toxoid Admin <8 Yr Old w/ Counseling	90465		Trigger Point or Tendon Sheath Inj.		20550			
Vaccine/Toxoid Administration for Adult	90471		Tympanometry		92567			

Diagnosis/ICD-10: **T67.5XXA, Z39.8XXA**

I acknowledge receipt of medical services and authorize the release of any medical information necessary to process this claim for healthcare payment only. I do authorize payment to the provider.

Patient Signature _Devon Ulrich_

Total Estimated Charges: _____

Payment Amount: _____

Next Appointment: _____

Figure 9

Capital City Medical
Fee Schedule

New Patient OV		Punch Biopsy various codes	$80
Problem Focused 99201	$45	Nebulizer various codes	$45
Expanded Problem Focused 99202	$65	Cast Application various codes	$85
Detailed 99203	$85	Laryngoscopy 31505	$255
Comprehensive 99204	$105	Audiometry 92552	$85
Comprehensive/High Complex 99205	$115	Tympanometry 92567	$85
Well Exam infant (less than 1 year) 99381	$45	Ear Irrigation 69210	$25
Well Exam 1–4 yrs. 99382	$50	Diaphragm Fitting 57170	$30
Well Exam 5–11 yrs. 99383	$55	IV Therapy (up to one hour) 90760	$65
Well Exam 12–17 yrs. 99384	$65	Each additional hour 90761	$50
Well Exam 18–39 yrs. 99385	$85	Oximetry 94760	$10
Well Exam 40–64 yrs. 99386	$105	ECG 93000	$75
Established Patient OV		Holter Monitor various codes	$170
Post Op Follow Up Visit 99024	$0	Rhythm Strip 93040	$60
Minimum 99211	$35	Treadmill 93015	$375
Problem Focused 99212	$45	Cocci Skin Test 86490	$20
Expanded Problem Focused 99213	$55	X-ray, spine, chest, bone—any area various codes	$275
Detailed 99214	$65	Avulsion Nail 11730	$200
Comprehensive/High Complex 99215	$75	**Laboratory**	
Well exam infant (less than 1 year) 99391	$35	Amylase 82150	$40
Well Exam 1–4 yrs. 99392	$40	B12 82607	$30
Well Exam 5–11 yrs. 99393	$45	CBC & Diff 85025	$95
Well Exam 12–17 yrs. 99394	$55	Comp Metabolic Panel 80053	$75
Well Exam 18–39 yrs. 99395	$65	Chlamydia Screen 87110	$70
Well Exam 40–64 yrs. 99396	$75	Cholestrerol 82465	$75
Obstetrics		Digoxin 80162	$40
Total OB Care 59400	$1700	Electrolytes 80051	$70
Injections		Estrogen, Total 82672	$50
Administration 90772	$10	Ferritin 82728	$40
Allergy 95115	$35	Folate 82746	$30
DPT 90701	$50	GC Screen 87070	$60
Drug various codes	$35	Glucose 82947	$35
Influenza 90658	$25	Glycosylated HGB A1C 83036	$45
MMR 90707	$50	HCT 85014	$30
OPV 90712	$40	HDL 83718	$35
Pneumovax 90732	$35	HGB 85018	$30
TB Skin Test 86580	$15	Hep BSAG 83740	$40
TD 90718	$40	Hepatitis panel, acute 80074	$95
Tetanus Toxoid 90703	$40	HIV 86703	$100
Vaccine/Toxoid Administration for Younger Than 8 Years Old w/ counseling 90465	$10	Iron & TIBC 83550	$45
		Kidney Profile 80069	$95
Vaccine/Toxoid Administration for Adult 90471	$10	Lead 83665	$55
Arthrocentesis/Aspiration/Injection		Lipase 83690	$40
Small Joint 20600	$50	Lipid Panel 80061	$95
Interm Joint 20605	$60	Liver Profile 80076	$95
Major Joint 20610	$70	Mono Test 86308	$30
Trigger Point/Tendon Sheath Inj. 20550	$90	Pap Smear 88155	$90
Other Invasive/Noninvasive Procedures		Pap Collection/Supervision 88142	$95
Catheterization 51701	$55	Pregnancy Test 84703	$90
Circumcision 54150	$150	Obstetric Panel 80055	$85
Colposcopy 57452	$225	Pro Time 85610	$50
Colposcopy w/Biopsy 57454	$250	PSA 84153	$50
Cryosurgery Premalignant Lesion various codes	$160	RPR 86592	$55
Endometrial Biopsy 58100	$190	Sed. Rate 85651	$50
Excision Lesion Malignant various codes	$145	Stool Culture 87045	$80
Excision Lesion Benign various codes	$125	Stool O & P 87177	$105
Curettement Lesion		Strep Screen 87880	$35
Single 11055	$70	Theophylline 80198	$40
2–4 11056	$80	Thyroid Uptake 84479	$75
>4 11057	$90	TSH 84443	$50
Excision Skin Tags (1–15) 11200	$55	Urinalysis 81000	$35
Each Additional 10 11201	$30	Urine Culture 87088	$80
I & D Abscess Single/Simple 10060	$75	Drawing Fee 36415	$15
Multiple/Complex 10061	$95	Specimen Collection 99000	$10
I & D Pilonidal Cyst Simple 10080	$105		
I & D Pilonidal Cyst Complex 10081	$130		
Laceration Repair various codes	$60		

HEALTH INSURANCE CLAIM FORM

APPROVED BY NATIONAL UNIFORM CLAIM COMMITTEE (NUCC) 02/12

| | PICA | | | | | | PICA | |

1. MEDICARE **MEDICAID** **TRICARE** **CHAMPVA** **GROUP HEALTH PLAN** **FECA BLK LUNG** **OTHER** **1a. INSURED'S I.D. NUMBER** (For Program in Item 1)

[X] (Medicare#) [ ] (Medicaid#) [ ] (ID#/DoD#) [ ] (Member ID#) [ ] (ID#) [ ] (ID#) [ ] (ID#)

2. PATIENT'S NAME (Last Name, First Name, Middle Initial)

3. PATIENT'S BIRTH DATE MM | DD | YY   **SEX** M [ ] F [ ]

4. INSURED'S NAME (Last Name, First Name, Middle Initial)

5. PATIENT'S ADDRESS (No., Street)

6. PATIENT RELATIONSHIP TO INSURED Self [ ] Spouse [ ] Child [ ] Other [ ]

7. INSURED'S ADDRESS (No., Street)

CITY **STATE**

8. RESERVED FOR NUCC USE

CITY **STATE**

ZIP CODE **TELEPHONE** (Include Area Code) ( )

ZIP CODE **TELEPHONE** (Include Area Code) ( )

9. OTHER INSURED'S NAME (Last Name, First Name, Middle Initial)

10. IS PATIENT'S CONDITION RELATED TO:

11. INSURED'S POLICY GROUP OR FECA NUMBER

a. OTHER INSURED'S POLICY OR GROUP NUMBER

a. EMPLOYMENT? (Current or Previous) [ ] YES [ ] NO

a. INSURED'S DATE OF BIRTH MM | DD | YY   **SEX** M [ ] F [ ]

b. RESERVED FOR NUCC USE

b. AUTO ACCIDENT? PLACE (State) [ ] YES [ ] NO

b. OTHER CLAIM ID (Designated by NUCC)

c. RESERVED FOR NUCC USE

c. OTHER ACCIDENT? [ ] YES [ ] NO

c. INSURANCE PLAN NAME OR PROGRAM NAME

d. INSURANCE PLAN NAME OR PROGRAM NAME

10d. CLAIM CODES (Designated by NUCC)

d. IS THERE ANOTHER HEALTH BENEFIT PLAN? [ ] YES [ ] NO *If yes,* complete items 9, 9a, and 9d.

READ BACK OF FORM BEFORE COMPLETING & SIGNING THIS FORM.

12. PATIENT'S OR AUTHORIZED PERSON'S SIGNATURE I authorize the release of any medical or other information necessary to process this claim. I also request payment of government benefits either to myself or to the party who accepts assignment below.

SIGNED _____ DATE _____

13. INSURED'S OR AUTHORIZED PERSON'S SIGNATURE I authorize payment of medical benefits to the undersigned physician or supplier for services described below.

SIGNED _____

14. DATE OF CURRENT ILLNESS, INJURY, or PREGNANCY (LMP) MM | DD | YY   QUAL.

15. OTHER DATE QUAL. MM | DD | YY

16. DATES PATIENT UNABLE TO WORK IN CURRENT OCCUPATION FROM MM | DD | YY TO MM | DD | YY

17. NAME OF REFERRING PROVIDER OR OTHER SOURCE 17a. 17b. NPI

18. HOSPITALIZATION DATES RELATED TO CURRENT SERVICES FROM MM | DD | YY TO MM | DD | YY

19. ADDITIONAL CLAIM INFORMATION (Designated by NUCC)

20. OUTSIDE LAB? [ ] YES [ ] NO $ CHARGES

21. DIAGNOSIS OR NATURE OF ILLNESS OR INJURY Relate A-L to service line below (24E)   ICD Ind.

A. | B. | C. | D.
E. | F. | G. | H.
I. | J. | K. | L.

22. RESUBMISSION CODE ORIGINAL REF. NO.

23. PRIOR AUTHORIZATION NUMBER

24. A. DATE(S) OF SERVICE From MM DD YY To MM DD YY	B. PLACE OF SERVICE	C. EMG	D. PROCEDURES, SERVICES, OR SUPPLIES (Explain Unusual Circumstances) CPT/HCPCS | MODIFIER	E. DIAGNOSIS POINTER	F. $ CHARGES	G. DAYS OR UNITS	H. EPSDT Family Plan	I. ID. QUAL	J. RENDERING PROVIDER ID. #
1									NPI
2									NPI
3									NPI
4									NPI
5									NPI
6									NPI

25. FEDERAL TAX I.D. NUMBER SSN EIN [ ] [ ]

26. PATIENT'S ACCOUNT NO.

27. ACCEPT ASSIGNMENT? (For govt claims, see back) [ ] YES [ ] NO

28. TOTAL CHARGE $

29. AMOUNT PAID $

30. Rsvd. for NUCC Use

31. SIGNATURE OF PHYSICIAN OR SUPPLIER INCLUDING DEGREES OR CREDENTIALS (I certify that the statements on the reverse apply to this bill and are made a part thereof.)

SIGNED _____ DATE _____

32. SERVICE FACILITY LOCATION INFORMATION a. NPI b.

33. BILLING PROVIDER INFO & PH # ( ) a. NPI b.

NUCC Instruction Manual available at: www.nucc.org   **PLEASE PRINT OR TYPE**   APPROVED OMB-0938-1197 FORM 1500 (02-12)

Clear Form

Figure 10

TEST 13: COMPLETE A CMS-1500
CLAIM FORM FOR COMMERCIAL INSURANCE

Directions: Using the source documents provided for patient Duncan Shelton and the Capital City Medical fee schedule (Figure 11), accurately complete a CMS-1500 claim form for commercial insurance carriers. Use the blank CMS-1500 claim form provided (Figure 12).

Complete the case on the basis of the following criteria:

- All patients have release of information and assignment of benefit signatures on file.

- All providers are participating and accept assignment, by contractual agreement. Item 27 is not marked.

- The group practice is the billing entity.

- The national transition to NPI numbers is complete, and legacy PINs of individual payers are no longer used. If legacy PINs are still being used by selected payers in your region, your instructor may provide legacy PINS in addition to the NPI.

- 2017 ICD-10-CM/PCS and CPT codes are used.

- Use eight-digit dates for birthdates. Use six-digit dates for all other dates.

- All street names should be entered with standard postal abbreviations, even if they are spelled out on the source documents.

- Enter ICD-10 codes in the order in which they appear on the encounter form.

- When entering CPT codes, enter the E/M code first. Enter remaining codes in descending price order.

© 2018 Pearson Education, Inc.

TEST 13

Capital City Medical—123 Unknown Boulevard, Capital City, NY 12345-2222 (555) 555-1234

Phil Wells, MD, Mannie Mends, MD, Bette R. Soone, MD

Patient Information Form

Tax ID: 75-0246810

Group NPI: 1513171216

Patient Information:

Name: (Last, First) Shelton, Duncan ☒ Male ☐ Female Birth Date: 02/11/1962

Address: 321 Skyline Dr, Capital City, NY 12345 Phone: (555) 555-8970

Social Security Number: 608-77-3458 Full-Time Student: ☐ Yes ☒ No

Marital Status: ☐ Single ☒ Married ☐ Divorced ☐ Other

Employment:

Employer: Capital City Hardware Phone: (555) 555-6342

Address: 600 Jefferson Base, Capital City NY 12345

Condition Related to: ☐ Auto Accident ☐ Employment ☐ Other Accident

Date of Accident: _____ State: _____

Emergency Contact: _____ **Phone: ( )** _____

Primary Insurance: Blue Cross Blue Shield Phone: ( ) _____

Address: 379 Blue Plaza, Capital City, NY 12345

Insurance Policyholder's Name: Shelton, Candy ☐ M ☒ F DOB: 12/19/1964

Address: Same

Phone: _____ Relationship to Insured: ☐ Self ☒ Spouse ☐ Child ☐ Other

Employer: Channel 8 News Phone: ( ) _____

Employer's Address: Channel 8 Center, News Drive, Capital City, NY 12345

Policy/ID No: YYJ34121269 Group No: 352257 Percent Covered: ___% Copay Amt: $ 20.00

Secondary Insurance: _____ Phone: ( ) _____

Address: _____

Insurance Policyholder's Name: _____ ☐ M ☐ F DOB: _____

Address: _____

Phone: _____ Relationship to Insured: ☐ Self ☐ Spouse ☐ Child ☐ Other

Employer: _____ Phone: ( ) _____

Employer's Address: _____

Policy/ID No: _____ Group No: _____ Percent Covered: ___% Copay Amt: $_____

Reason for Visit: I am here for a follow up on my test results for testicular pain

Known Allergies: _____

Referred by: _____

02/16/20XX
Assignment of Benefits: Y
Signature on File: Y
Referring Physician: N

S: Duncan Shelton is here to find out the results of his recent ultrasound of his testicles.
O: Pt. still complains of testicular pain ranging at 9. On exam, the testicles are still very swollen. He denies any new complaints. The ultrasound does reveal twisted veins in the testicles.
A: 1. Testicular torsion— N44.00
P: 1. Pt. to see Mannie Mends, MD, for surgical consult ASAP.
　　2. Continue Percocet one p.o. q. 6h. p.r.n.

_____

Phil Wells, MD
Family Practice
NPI: 1234567890

© 2018 Pearson Education, Inc.

TEST 13

Patient Name Duncan Shelton

Capital City Medical
123 Unknown Boulevard, Capital City, NY 12345-2222

Date of Service
02-16-20XX

New Patient			Arthrocentesis/Aspiration/Injection		Laboratory	
Problem Focused	99201		Arthrocentesis/Aspiration/Injection		Amylase	82150
Expanded Problem, Focused	99202		Small Joint	20600	B12	82607
Detailed	99203		Interm Joint	20605	CBC & Diff	85025
Comprehensive	99204		Major Joint	20610	Comp Metabolic Panel	80053
Comprehensive/High Complex	99205		**Other Invasive/Noninvasive**		Chlamydia Screen	87110
Well Exam Infant (up to 12 mos.)	99381		Audiometry	92552	Cholesterol	82465
Well Exam 1–4 yrs.	99382		Cast Application		Digoxin	80162
Well Exam 5–11 yrs.	99383		Location Long Short		Electrolytes	80051
Well Exam 12–17 yrs.	99384		Catheterization	51701	Ferritin	82728
Well Exam 18–39 yrs.	99385		Circumcision	54150	Folate	82746
Well Exam 40–64 yrs.	99386		Colposcopy	57452	GC Screen	87070
			Colposcopy w/Biopsy	57454	Glucose	82947
			Cryosurgery Premalignant Lesion		Glucose 1 HR	82950
			Location (s):		Glycosylated HGB A1C	83036
Established Patient			Cryosurgery Warts		HCT	85014
Post-Op Follow Up Visit	99024		Location (s):		HDL	83718
Minimum	99211		Curettement Lesion		Hep BSAG	87340
Problem Focused	99212		Single	11055	Hepatitis panel, acute	80074
Expanded Problem Focused	99213	X	2–4	11056	HGB	85018
Detailed	99214		>4	11057	HIV	86703
Comprehensive/High Complex	99215		Diaphragm Fitting	57170	Iron & TIBC	83550
Well Exam Infant (up to 12 mos.)	99391		Ear Irrigation	69210	Kidney Profile	80069
Well exam 1–4 yrs.	99392		ECG	93000	Lead	83655
Well Exam 5–11 yrs.	99393		Endometrial Biopsy	58100	Liver Profile	80076
Well Exam 12–17 yrs.	99394		Exc. Lesion Malignant		Mono Test	86308
Well Exam 18–39 yrs.	99395		Benign		Pap Smear	88155
Well Exam 40–64 yrs.	99396		Location		Pregnancy Test	84703
Obstetrics			Exc. Skin Tags (1–15)	11200	Obstetric Panel	80055
Total OB Care	59400		Each Additional 10	11201	Pro Time	85610
Injections			Fracture Treatment		PSA	84153
Administration Sub. / IM	90772		Loc		RPR	86592
Drug			w/Reduc w/o Reduc		Sed. Rate	85651
Dosage			I & D Abscess Single/Simple	10060	Stool Culture	87045
Allergy	95115		Multiple or Comp	10061	Stool O & P	87177
Cocci Skin Test	86490		I & D Pilonidal Cyst Simple	10080	Strep Screen	87880
DPT	90701		Pilonidal Cyst Complex	10081	Theophylline	80198
Hemophilus	90646		IV Therapy—To One Hour	90760	Thyroid Uptake	84479
Influenza	90658		Each Additional Hour	90761	TSH	84443
MMR	90707		Laceration Repair		Urinalysis	81000
OPV	90712		Location Size Simp/Comp		Urine Culture	87088
Pneumovax	90732		Laryngoscopy	31505	Drawing Fee	36415
TB Skin Test	86580		Oximetry	94760	Specimen Collection	99000
TD	90718		Punch Biopsy		**Other:**	
Unlisted Immun	90749		Rhythm Strip	93040		
Tetanus Toxoid	90703		Treadmill	93015		
Vaccine/Toxoid Admin <8 Yr Old w/ Counseling	90465		Trigger Point or Tendon Sheath Inj.	20550		
Vaccine/Toxoid Administration for Adult	90471		Tympanometry	92567		

Diagnosis/ICD-10: **N44.00**

I acknowledge receipt of medical services and authorize the release of any medical information necessary to process this claim for healthcare payment only. I do authorize payment to the provider.

Total Estimated Charges: _____

Payment Amount: _____

Patient Signature _Duncan Shelton_

Next Appointment: _____

Figure 11

Capital City Medical
Fee Schedule

New Patient OV			Punch Biopsy various codes	$80
Problem Focused 99201	$45		Nebulizer various codes	$45
Expanded Problem Focused 99202	$65		Cast Application various codes	$85
Detailed 99203	$85		Laryngoscopy 31505	$255
Comprehensive 99204	$105		Audiometry 92552	$85
Comprehensive/High Complex 99205	$115		Tympanometry 92567	$85
Well Exam infant (less than 1 year) 99381	$45		Ear Irrigation 69210	$25
Well Exam 1–4 yrs. 99382	$50		Diaphragm Fitting 57170	$30
Well Exam 5–11 yrs. 99383	$55		IV Therapy (up to one hour) 90760	$65
Well Exam 12–17 yrs. 99384	$65		Each additional hour 90761	$50
Well Exam 18–39 yrs. 99385	$85		Oximetry 94760	$10
Well Exam 40–64 yrs. 99386	$105		ECG 93000	$75
Established Patient OV			Holter Monitor various codes	$170
Post Op Follow Up Visit 99024	$0		Rhythm Strip 93040	$60
Minimum 99211	$35		Treadmill 93015	$375
Problem Focused 99212	$45		Cocci Skin Test 86490	$20
Expanded Problem Focused 99213	$55		X-ray, spine, chest, bone—any area various codes	$275
Detailed 99214	$65		Avulsion Nail 11730	$200
Comprehensive/High Complex 99215	$75		**Laboratory**	
Well exam infant (less than 1 year) 99391	$35		Amylase 82150	$40
Well Exam 1–4 yrs. 99392	$40		B12 82607	$30
Well Exam 5–11 yrs. 99393	$45		CBC & Diff 85025	$95
Well Exam 12–17 yrs. 99394	$55		Comp Metabolic Panel 80053	$75
Well Exam 18–39 yrs. 99395	$65		Chlamydia Screen 87110	$70
Well Exam 40–64 yrs. 99396	$75		Cholestrerol 82465	$75
Obstetrics			Digoxin 80162	$40
Total OB Care 59400	$1700		Electrolytes 80051	$70
Injections			Estrogen, Total 82672	$50
Administration 90772	$10		Ferritin 82728	$40
Allergy 95115	$35		Folate 82746	$30
DPT 90701	$50		GC Screen 87070	$60
Drug various codes	$35		Glucose 82947	$35
Influenza 90658	$25		Glycosylated HGB A1C 83036	$45
MMR 90707	$50		HCT 85014	$30
OPV 90712	$40		HDL 83718	$35
Pneumovax 90732	$35		HGB 85018	$30
TB Skin Test 86580	$15		Hep BSAG 83740	$40
TD 90718	$40		Hepatitis panel, acute 80074	$95
Tetanus Toxoid 90703	$40		HIV 86703	$100
Vaccine/Toxoid Administration for Younger			Iron & TIBC 83550	$45
Than 8 Years Old w/ counseling 90465	$10		Kidney Profile 80069	$95
Vaccine/Toxoid Administration for Adult 90471	$10		Lead 83665	$55
Arthrocentesis/Aspiration/Injection			Lipase 83690	$40
Small Joint 20600	$50		Lipid Panel 80061	$95
Interm Joint 20605	$60		Liver Profile 80076	$95
Major Joint 20610	$70		Mono Test 86308	$30
Trigger Point/Tendon Sheath Inj. 20550	$90		Pap Smear 88155	$90
Other Invasive/Noninvasive Procedures			Pap Collection/Supervision 88142	$95
Catheterization 51701	$55		Pregnancy Test 84703	$90
Circumcision 54150	$150		Obstetric Panel 80055	$85
Colposcopy 57452	$225		Pro Time 85610	$50
Colposcopy w/Biopsy 57454	$250		PSA 84153	$50
Cryosurgery Premalignant Lesion various codes	$160		RPR 86592	$55
Endometrial Biopsy 58100	$190		Sed. Rate 85651	$50
Excision Lesion Malignant various codes	$145		Stool Culture 87045	$80
Excision Lesion Benign various codes	$125		Stool O & P 87177	$105
Curettement Lesion			Strep Screen 87880	$35
Single 11055	$70		Theophylline 80198	$40
2–4 11056	$80		Thyroid Uptake 84479	$75
>4 11057	$90		TSH 84443	$50
Excision Skin Tags (1–15) 11200	$55		Urinalysis 81000	$35
Each Additional 10 11201	$30		Urine Culture 87088	$80
I & D Abscess Single/Simple 10060	$75		Drawing Fee 36415	$15
Multiple/Complex 10061	$95		Specimen Collection 99000	$10
I & D Pilonidal Cyst Simple 10080	$105			
I & D Pilonidal Cyst Complex 10081	$130			
Laceration Repair various codes	$60			

HEALTH INSURANCE CLAIM FORM

APPROVED BY NATIONAL UNIFORM CLAIM COMMITTEE (NUCC) 02/12

☐☐☐ PICA

PICA ☐☐☐

1. MEDICARE	MEDICAID	TRICARE	CHAMPVA	GROUP HEALTH PLAN	FECA BLK LUNG	OTHER	1a. INSURED'S I.D. NUMBER	(For Program in Item 1)
☒ (Medicare#)	☐ (Medicaid#)	☐ (ID#/DoD#)	☐ (Member ID#)	☐ (ID#)	☐ (ID#)	☐ (ID#)		

2. PATIENT'S NAME (Last Name, First Name, Middle Initial)

3. PATIENT'S BIRTH DATE MM | DD | YY   SEX M ☐ F ☐

4. INSURED'S NAME (Last Name, First Name, Middle Initial)

5. PATIENT'S ADDRESS (No., Street)

6. PATIENT RELATIONSHIP TO INSURED Self ☐ Spouse ☐ Child ☐ Other ☐

7. INSURED'S ADDRESS (No., Street)

CITY | STATE

8. RESERVED FOR NUCC USE

CITY | STATE

ZIP CODE | TELEPHONE (Include Area Code) (   )

ZIP CODE | TELEPHONE (Include Area Code) (   )

9. OTHER INSURED'S NAME (Last Name, First Name, Middle Initial)

10. IS PATIENT'S CONDITION RELATED TO:

11. INSURED'S POLICY GROUP OR FECA NUMBER

a. OTHER INSURED'S POLICY OR GROUP NUMBER

a. EMPLOYMENT? (Current or Previous) ☐ YES ☐ NO

a. INSURED'S DATE OF BIRTH MM | DD | YY   SEX M ☐ F ☐

b. RESERVED FOR NUCC USE

b. AUTO ACCIDENT? PLACE (State) ☐ YES ☐ NO

b. OTHER CLAIM ID (Designated by NUCC)

c. RESERVED FOR NUCC USE

c. OTHER ACCIDENT? ☐ YES ☐ NO

c. INSURANCE PLAN NAME OR PROGRAM NAME

d. INSURANCE PLAN NAME OR PROGRAM NAME

10d. CLAIM CODES (Designated by NUCC)

d. IS THERE ANOTHER HEALTH BENEFIT PLAN? ☐ YES ☐ NO If yes, complete items 9, 9a, and 9d.

READ BACK OF FORM BEFORE COMPLETING & SIGNING THIS FORM.
12. PATIENT'S OR AUTHORIZED PERSON'S SIGNATURE I authorize the release of any medical or other information necessary to process this claim. I also request payment of government benefits either to myself or to the party who accepts assignment below.

SIGNED _____ DATE _____

13. INSURED'S OR AUTHORIZED PERSON'S SIGNATURE I authorize payment of medical benefits to the undersigned physician or supplier for services described below.

SIGNED _____

14. DATE OF CURRENT ILLNESS, INJURY, or PREGNANCY (LMP) MM | DD | YY QUAL

15. OTHER DATE QUAL | MM | DD | YY

16. DATES PATIENT UNABLE TO WORK IN CURRENT OCCUPATION FROM MM | DD | YY   TO MM | DD | YY

17. NAME OF REFERRING PROVIDER OR OTHER SOURCE

17a.
17b. NPI

18. HOSPITALIZATION DATES RELATED TO CURRENT SERVICES FROM MM | DD | YY   TO MM | DD | YY

19. ADDITIONAL CLAIM INFORMATION (Designated by NUCC)

20. OUTSIDE LAB? ☐ YES ☐ NO $ CHARGES

21. DIAGNOSIS OR NATURE OF ILLNESS OR INJURY Relate A-L to service line below (24E)   ICD Ind. |

A. | B. | C. | D. |
E. | F. | G. | H. |
I. | J. | K. | L. |

22. RESUBMISSION CODE | ORIGINAL REF. NO.

23. PRIOR AUTHORIZATION NUMBER

24. A. DATE(S) OF SERVICE						B. PLACE OF SERVICE	C. EMG	D. PROCEDURES, SERVICES, OR SUPPLIES (Explain Unusual Circumstances) CPT/HCPCS	MODIFIER	E. DIAGNOSIS POINTER	F. $ CHARGES	G. DAYS OR UNITS	H. EPSDT Family Plan	I. ID. QUAL	J. RENDERING PROVIDER ID. #
From MM	DD	YY	To MM	DD	YY										
1															NPI
2															NPI
3															NPI
4															NPI
5															NPI
6															NPI

25. FEDERAL TAX I.D. NUMBER ☐ SSN ☐ EIN

26. PATIENT'S ACCOUNT NO.

27. ACCEPT ASSIGNMENT? (For govt. claims, see back) ☐ YES ☐ NO

28. TOTAL CHARGE $

29. AMOUNT PAID $

30. Rsvd. for NUCC Use

31. SIGNATURE OF PHYSICIAN OR SUPPLIER INCLUDING DEGREES OR CREDENTIALS (I certify that the statements on the reverse apply to this bill and are made a part thereof.)

SIGNED _____ DATE _____

32. SERVICE FACILITY LOCATION INFORMATION

a. NPI   b.

33. BILLING PROVIDER INFO & PH # (   )

a. NPI   b.

NUCC Instruction Manual available at: www.nucc.org

PLEASE PRINT OR TYPE

APPROVED OMB-0938-1197 FORM 1500 (02-12)

Clear Form

Figure 12

◼

Directions: Using the source documents provided for patient Clair Carter, accurately complete a UB-04 claim form. Use the blank UB-04 form provided (Figure 13).

TEST 14

Capital City General Hospital
1000 Cherry Street
Capital City, NY 12345-2222
(555) 555-1000

Patient Information:	Clair Carter
	1409 Gunner Road, Capital City, NY 12345
	555-555-1791
DOB:	10-19-1974
Sex:	Female
SSN:	222-88-2010
Status:	Single **Student:** No
Employer:	Plastics Unlimited
	5792 Kiln Way, Capital City, NY 12345
	555-555-5792
Responsible Party:	Clair Carter
Insurance Information:	Aetna
	1625 Healthcare Bldg., Capital City, NY 12345
ID #:	423381 **Group #:** 7619
Insured's Name:	Same **Relationship to Patient:** Self
Insured's DOB:	**Insured's Sex:** F
Insured's Address:	
Insured's Employer:	
Authorization:	68235498432 **Approved # of Days:** 4
Attending Physician:	Phil Wells, MD
Federal Tax ID #:	75-0246810
Group NPI:	1234567890

Reason for visit: Heroin overdose.

© 2018 Pearson Education, Inc.

TEST 14

HPI: This is a Caucasian female admitted through the emergency department on May 13, 20XX, at 1:30 a.m. for a heroin overdose. Pt. was found unresponsive in her apartment by boyfriend. Pt. has been abusing heroin for about 2 months, per the boyfriend. There is evidence of track marks on both upper and lower extremities. The freshest mark is on the right lower extremity. Pt. has no evidence of organ failure at this time. Pt. was discharged to rehab clinic on May 17, 20XX, at 11:00 a.m.

Patient Control #:		900521	**Type of Admission:**	1
MR #:		1846533422	**Source of Admission:**	7
Hospital NPI:		1212121212	**Discharge Status:**	05
Hospital Tax ID:		75-7575757	**Type of Bill Code:**	111

Fees:

Revenue Codes	Units	Total Charges	Dates of Service
110 Room/Board/Semi	4	$ 400.00/day	05/13/20XX–05/17/20XX
250 Pharmacy	5	$1250.00	05/13/20XX–05/17/20XX
260 IV Therapy	4	$1000.00	05/13/20XX–05/16/20XX
270 Med/Surg Supplies	4	$ 400.00	05/13/20XX–05/16/20XX
300 Laboratory	3	$ 300.00	05/14/20XX–05/17/20XX
001 TOTAL		$3450.00	

Principal DX:	T40.1X1A, F11.10
Admitting DX:	T40.1X1A

Figure 13

© 2018 Pearson Education, Inc.

NOTES

Notes

NOTES

NOTES

NOTES

Notes

NOTES

NOTES

NOTES

NOTES

NOTES

NOTES

NOTES

NOTES

NOTES

NOTES